Submersion Journalism

Submersion Journalism

REPORTING IN THE RADICAL FIRST PERSON
FROM *HARPER'S MAGAZINE*

EDITED BY BILL WASIK
INTRODUCTION BY ROGER D. HODGE

THE NEW PRESS

NEW YORK
LONDON

Requests for permission to reproduce selections from this book should be mailed to:
Permissions Department, The New Press, 38 Greene Street, New York, NY 10013.

All pieces in this collection were originally published in *Harper's Magazine*.

Published in the United States by The New Press, New York, 2008
Distributed by W. W. Norton & Company, Inc., New York

LIBRARY OF CONGRESS CATALOGING-IN-PUBLICATION DATA

Submersion journalism : reporting in the radical first person from Harper's magazine /
edited by Bill Wasik; introduction by Roger D. Hodge.
p. cm.
Includes bibliographical references.
ISBN 978-1-59558-393-2 (hc)
1. Journalism—United States.   I. Wasik, Bill.   II. Harper's magazine.
PN4726.S83   2008
071'.3—dc22
2008020427

The New Press was established in 1990 as a not-for-profit alternative to the large,
commercial publishing houses currently dominating the book publishing industry.
The New Press operates in the public interest rather than for private gain, and is
committed to publishing, in innovative ways, works of educational, cultural,
and community value that are often deemed insufficiently profitable.

www.thenewpress.com

Composition by NK Graphics, a Black Dot Company
This book was set in Minion

Printed in the United States of America

2   4   6   8   10   9   7   5   3   1

Contents

Introduction

ROGER D. HODGE

EDITOR, *HARPER'S MAGAZINE*

The 2000s—perhaps we should call them the Naughts, since they will be remembered chiefly for their wants—were a decade in which the American Republic finally succumbed to a kind of auto-immune disorder; in which the social and political systems normally responsible for maintaining the healthy functioning of the body politic instead turned against it with particular savagery, as if our very Constitution were an invasive foreign organism. The causes of the disorder are obscure. As with other such diseases, this one masks itself with opportunistic infections, hides under assumed names, and thus has often escaped accurate diagnosis. The humdrum corruption of political machinery, the passivity of screen-addled citizens, ignorant pedagogues, job-gobbling immigrants, malevolent divines, greedy corporate grandees, the timidity of bourgeois journalists, the sinister conniving of neoconservative and liberal intellectuals, and homosexuals living in holy matrimony have all been adduced as causes of the national decline. Proximity cannot be denied, yet none of these putative causes appears to be sufficient to the magnitude of the disorder. What can be said with some certainty, however, is that we are now exiles in a strange land; America is no longer America.

In one domain of our national life after another, the old American ideals and liberties have been replaced by their opposites. Torture, once an ambiguous attribute of tyranny, has become official government policy. The Department of Justice has been transformed into the corrupt instrument of a partisan agenda. Habeas corpus is but a fond memory, as is the Fourth Amendment, with its fellows soon to follow. No one who possesses more than a passing acquaintance with American history can deny that in one form or another elements of the present disorder have been latent in our social genome for many generations, but something about the toxic environment of the Naughts has caused an outbreak of unprecedented scope.

The disease manifested itself almost everywhere at once, but the superficial effects were most spectacular in our national mirror: the media, which absorbed and digested the once proud opposition of the press and made of it a mere legitimizer of horrors. The self-refuting absurdity of the Bush presidency, with its pretensions to manufacture an imperial reality, parallels the rise of the aggressively oxymoronic genre of "reality television," with all its unintentional ironies. Among so-called news programming, Fox's *Fair and Balanced: We Report, You Decide* is of a piece with Anderson Cooper's *Keepin' 'Em Honest* and, to give an extreme and perhaps gratuitous example, *The CBS Evening News with Katie Couric*. More perniciously, the self-importance with which the quality newspapers fawned on George W. Bush and his retainers in the decisive years after September 11, particularly in the months leading up to the invasion of Iraq, bears comparison to the bitter satires of G.K. Chesterton and Evelyn Waugh.

The disorder from which we suffer—known among its close observers as Self-Satirizing Syndrome, or SSS—is a cruel one. Not only have we been made to witness the betrayal of almost every promise made by our Founding Fathers, and seen their direst prophesies confirmed, we must also suffer the indignity of seeing our constitutional ideal turned into a shabby mockery of itself. Somehow, by a trick of dialectical cunning, the United States of America has vaulted over the tragic phase of history in favor of a relentless pursuit of historical farce.

Even without the benefit of a proper diagnosis, a handful of critical newspapers, magazines, and book publishers have instinctively attempted to resist the infection (as have a growing number of visual artists and filmmakers), but the striving of a few can accomplish only so much against the onslaught of the disorder's most toxic expressions: opinion, and its close chemical relative publicity. Aggressive, ill-informed, irrational, and largely unsupported opinion predominates in our age of infectious autosatire (on millions of blogs, yes, but also on television and radio talk shows, in op-ed columns, news analysis, and "expert" commentary) and threatens, in a corollary of Gresham's law, to drive out all other modes of articulate human expression. And by far the greatest number of opinions expressed by any given SSS host concern the doings of celebrities and other by-products of the publicity stream (though the liberal media and the menace of foreigners provide good infectious substrates as well). The relative merits of Denzel Washington's or Russell Crowe's latest performances are discussed and analyzed with the same insipid vocabulary applied to the fund-raising prowess and speaking abilities of Rudy Giuliani and Hillary Clinton. Likewise their personal and professional challenges, their setbacks and petty triumphs. It seems that the week's highest-grossing picture is not so different from the quarter's highest-grossing candidate.

The television host convinced that Iran will somehow succeed in launching World War III, the Christian firm in his belief that Jesus wants him to be rich, the president who sees into the soul of a Russian dictator, the public radio essayist who just loves ketchup, the vice president who argues that his dear leader possesses the inherent authority to suspend laws at will—all of these individuals, we say, have a right to their opinions, no matter how meaningless or delusional or divorced from traditional canons of American governance. Apparently it's bad taste to point out that a prominent public figure is either lying or insane. And given the right publicity campaign, with a consistent message from the White House staffers and congressional aides who feed the news cycle, any narrative, no matter how fraudulent, can begin to command the front pages. ("Just look at the improved situation in Iraq!")

Short of withdrawing to an ashram in the Appalachian Mountains or to a bunker in West Texas, there is little the responsible American citizen can do to avoid contamination except turn off the television and the radio, cancel newspaper subscriptions, shun the movie theater, and meditate each day on the mantras of H.L. Mencken, Mark Twain, and Ambrose Bierce. But for those of us who must, whether out of perversity or an outmoded sense of civic duty, maintain close contact with the diseased organs of our society, there is another option. We can choose to embark on a gradual vaccination program in the form of a monthly antidote to the never-ending cycle of obscene news and the pandemic of poorly expressed, ill-reasoned, well-publicized opinion. I'm speaking, naturally, of *Harper's Magazine*.

Harper's Magazine has always sought to place a strong bulwark of wit between the reader and history's perpetual invitation to despair. Today that protective coating has become a medical necessity. In times such as these, healthy citizenship requires the insertion of a human proxy into the stream of historical happenstance. What we need is an experimental subject, an "I" sufficiently armed with narrative powers both literary and historical, gifts of irony and indirection, and the soothing balms of description and implication, to go forth and find stories that might counteract the unhappy effects of our disorder. In the pages that follow you will find fifteen such literary proxies who, at great personal risk, have braved the perils of the Bush Era and returned to tell their tales. Many of them ventured undercover; all of them worked without the supervision of a guardian publicist. What distinguishes most of the dispatches collected here is what might be called the radical first person: in each case the individual consciousness of the writer is paramount. The reader thereby becomes privy to the writer's experience and receives direct confirmation of its truth value. What results is not mere consumable opinion, the mystical commodity of mediated capitalism, but the raw material of a considered judgment, whether aesthetic, political, or ethical. In that judgment lies the cure for our affliction.

Part One

Politics

A paradox of political reporting today is that "access" as often as not yields less than nothing. *Less*, because after spending a day, say, with a campaign or a candidate, a cabinet official or a congressperson, through a succession of stage-managed meetings and gladhands and, finally, a one-on-one with the man or woman him- or herself, who sprinkles false candidness over (if one is lucky) free food—after such a day the journalist often is less capable of writing clear-eyed about that subject, indeed is less worthy to be trusted with the task, than he or she was the day before. Seen in this light, the contempt for the press shown by the Bush administration, in eschewing even the debased sort of access described above in favor of friendly sit-downs with Fox News flunkies, has been almost an act of mercy. Voters do not need more sanctioned profiles, meticulously stripped of substance. What they need is reporting that takes as a given the tall barriers against political truth telling and finds ways to circumvent them.

By necessity, a certain amount of this reporting will be undercover, and our anthology begins with three articles of this type, in which a minor deception by the reporter creates major rewards for the reader. "Bird-Dogging the Bush Vote" is Wells Tower's tale of volunteering for the Bush/Cheney reelection campaign in Orlando, Florida. For "Their Men in Washington," Ken Silverstein posed as a potential client to ensnare shady lobbyists who buff the images of overseas dictators. In "Jesus Plus Nothing," Jeff Sharlet played along as a believer in order to penetrate the Fellowship Foundation, the most powerful religious group in Washington. All three reporters emerged with stories immeasurably truer, richer, and fairer than those to be had with all the access in the world.

Bird-Dogging the Bush Vote

Undercover with Florida's Republican Shock Troops

WELLS TOWER

It is late September, and I'm alone in a room with a young woman who is saying, over and over again, "This promises to be a *very* close election, and President Bush needs your vote to work for a safer world and a more hopeful America."

Her name is Amanda, and she is one of the regular phone-bank volunteers here at the Bush-Cheney campaign branch in Winter Park, Florida, just north of downtown Orlando. She is lean and pretty in a hard-scrubbed way, a certain industrious rawness around her eyes and pale knuckles, and she delivers the calling script with a winning ease. "Hel-*lo*," she says in her pert, sidelong phone manner. "I'm calling on behalf of President Bush. You did? That's awesome. Right on, you rock."

I try to mimic Amanda's brisk yet personable calling style, but this is only my second day on the phones, and I cannot yet recite the campaign's earnest phrases as though they were my own. I'm still morose and wooden with the script, and tonight a couple of people interrupt my spieling to ask me, "Are you a machine?"

I am, at the moment, one of the thousands of constituent devices that make up the most aggressive and state-of-the-art piece of campaign machinery the G.O.P. has ever brought to bear on a presidential race. I'm here because several weeks ago, as I and a few dozen million other Americans were fretting over how we might possibly ward off another four years of George W. Bush, I decided to come to Florida and undertake a vigil for election-theft tactics from inside the Bush campaign's grassroots ranks. This was back when many of us were holding fast to the sentimental conviction that the laws of moral and political gravity still obtained in these United States, and that the electorate would surely buck the burden of a president whose frauds and bunglings were so familiar to the national discourse that they had become a species of exhausted proverb. If Bush was going to win another election, our thinking ran, he would certainly have to steal it.

Orlando seemed like ripe terrain for an electoral malfeasance hunt. It was the critical city on the contested Interstate 4 corridor, the jagged sash of highway connecting Tampa to Daytona Beach, crucial to a win in Florida and, therefore, to the whole shebang. Grim doings were already at hand. In June members of the Florida State Police had begun their own campaign, paying house calls to black voters and querying them about their voting habits while portentously tapping their fingers on their holstered pistols. Surely, there'd be plenty of mischief to stumble onto.

Amanda leans back in her chair, and its unsupple spring makes a sound like a tree limb breaking. Mortified, she quickly cups her pale hand over the receiver to shield the registered voter on the other end from the sounds of the headquarters' unluxury. These premises are dutiful and spare: industrial low-nap carpet, acoustical-tile ceiling, a motley assemblage of used furniture, standard civilian-grade telephones (no headsets or predictive dialing technology), walls haphazardly adorned with bits of paper and unframed snapshots of the President and memos and interoffice documents and strategy literature ("every contact and lead obtained through the networking process," reads a sheet on courting Christian organizations, "must be maximized and bird dogged"). On most days the offices are crowded with enthusiastic young men and women and congenial staffers who ply you with compliments and snack foods to keep your spirits high. Other than Amanda, essential personnel at the Winter Park "Victory" headquarters, as it is also known, include a trio of volunteer coordinators, all personable guys who share a pleasant, noncoercive managerial style and a convivial excess of their ideal bodyweight. Amanda hangs up, jots a note in the margin on her calling sheet, and places another call.

She gets a prospective absentee voter on the line and reminds him that if he later decides to vote at the polls he'll need to have his absentee ballot with him, otherwise he won't be allowed to vote. "So be sure to bring it," she says, canting her mouth slyly. "But of course if you're a Democrat, that doesn't apply."

John Kerry is making a campaign stop in Orlando, and I ask Jason Teaman, one of the volunteer coordinators, whether the campaign's sending over any protesters to make things hot for the Dems. Jason is a man with an un-Floridian lactescent complexion who's taking some time off from his real estate career to volunteer for the Bush campaign. He looks me over for an instant before he answers. Hectoring the Democrats, his silence gives me to understand, is not an officially sanctioned activity of Victory '04 but is rather a sort of gray-ops tactic not to be discussed with someone who's just stepped in off the street. But then he tells me, yes, "We're gonna have some people there."

The Kerry rally is taking place on the west side of town at the TD Waterhouse Centre, a squat sports arena of concrete and black glass bookended by a pair of massive concrete cylinders that resemble nothing so much as giant rolls of quilted bathroom tissue. The early evening sky is gray and ragged, shedding an aerosolized dankness upon the thousands of Kerry supporters gathered on the TD Waterhouse front walk. I hurry past men and women in Lands' End garb, and death-metal hoboes with tattooed necks and big black grommets in their earlobes, and preteen pamphleteers beetling to and fro, a man in priest's raiment, and 10,000 or so others, all of whom look excited to be out here on this clammy evening, and who seem to be sharing in something enviable and exalted, some moment of the heart. It would be very nice, I think, to share in it myself, but I brush through all of the comradely hubbub, scanning the crowd for the Bush-Cheney consternation squad.

I find them on a distant reach of sidewalk, at the southern edge of the arena. The group numbers about eighteen. They've got someone in a furry dolphin suit ("Flipper"), someone dressed as a beach thong, or a "flip-flop," as it were, and a few people wearing cardboard masks of John Kerry caricatured as a sort of toothy demon horse. They are mostly young Republicans from the University of Central Florida. The head of the UCF detachment is Chris, a lively, well-favored hotshot with bright eyes, golden curls, and an I Ching coin lashed to his neck on an Asiatic lanyard. Chris shakes my hand and flashes a brilliant crescent of teeth.

I take a Bush-Cheney placard and lurk over to a spot behind the rest of the group. The young Republicans wave their signs with great intensity, raising a chorus of faintly nautical, sails-in-high-wind-type flapping sounds. I cannot bring myself to do any full-bore brandishing, so I hold my sign in front of my face and do an abashed little wagging move with it, a kind of sign-waver's equivalent of sullenly lip-synching one's way through the national anthem at a baseball game. After a few minutes one of the UCF girls tells me that my sign is upside down.

The small Republican contingent provokes a substantial outrage. Horns are honked at them in malice; they are given the finger by people young and old and across an array of gestural dialects; they are taunted, harangued, and occasionally asked by passersby to defend their support of the President. An elfin young man comes over and swans around before the group, trying to coax them into an argument with declarations about the gay life. "Hey, I'm gay, I'm a homosexual," he says. He points to a Kerry/Edwards sticker over the zipper of his jeans. "See this sticker? You know what's under there? My penis, my homosexual penis. I'm gay, and my penis is a homosexual penis, and you can't handle that, can you?"

An older man, who announces angrily that he fought in Vietnam, asks the group, If they're so big on Bush and his war in Iraq, how many of them are enlisted? The UCF Republicans are fit and hale and would make fine conscripts, but no one speaks up.

The heckling tapers off, and the team tries to pass the time by yelling "flip-flop" and "four more years." These are, by any standard, uncaptivating chants, and before long the Republicans grow restive. So the group's ranking members hold a brief caucus and then announce a plan to parade through the throng of liberals. Chris instructs everyone to smile, to keep moving, and not to engage the enemy. Then he does a head-'em-up-move-'em-out motion with his hand, and starts toward the crowd.

A thunderous caterwauling goes up at our approach. The Kerry supporters are screaming from the sidewalks and from up on the steps of the TD Waterhouse Centre. As I walk, I cower behind my sign, but people swat it down with angry hands: "Boo!" "Go home." "Fuck you." A teenager with a shaved head blocks my way, shuffling backward like a boxer. "Hey, asshole, what's your fucking problem?" he says, sending forth a warm cloud of saliva motes. "Look at me, you fucking jerk!"

A few of the Republican brigade pause to indulge in screaming matches with seething bystanders. They're clearly enjoying the raving theatrics of the

Kerry crowd as well as their own status as perverse celebrities here. When they finally regroup at a safe remove, a self-sacrificial glow is pouring off of every brow. "Did you see how *angry* those liberals were?" asks one girl. "They were so *angry. They were crazy! They were totally insane!*" She is so alive with the abuse she is quaking with it, beatified, as though she's about to detonate into a million tiny asterisks of consecrated light.

Chris is in his own righteous transport, his Adam's apple sliding up and down, which in turn sets the I Ching token trembling in the hollow of his throat. "Did you see that?" he asks me. "That liberal? He tried to hit my sign, he charged me with his umbrella and tried to tear it up, and I went like, YOU WANT ME TO HIT YOU? Like that: YOU WANT ME TO *HIT* YOU?" And here he goes into a pantomime of the liberal's craven cringing.

The police are less pleased with the ruckus the Republicans have caused, so they exile them to an outer stretch of sidewalk on the far side of the parking lot. The banishment does not bother Chris, who is coasting happily across the asphalt, still riding high from the showdown. I am striding along beside him, and with the clamor at our backs and the drizzle putting me in mind of the spittle just now sprayed into my face, I have to agree with Chris that this is invigorating stuff, being despised by perfect strangers. The rush of combat endorphins, the shocking absurdity of being screamed at and spit on by people who don't even know my name, the buoyant feeling of being part of the team that somehow *matters* enough to be hated this way—I find myself helplessly slipping into a pretty good mood.

We take a position at the mouth of the parking lot and rest a moment. The dolphin shudders and removes its head. Inside, there is a small parboiled teenager, his sweat-moistened hair plastered across his forehead. "Cooling fan broke," he says miserably.

After a time, we are chagrined to see a delegation from the International Union of Painters and Allied Trades (IUPAT) striding our way. They are wide men with arms like cypress trunks, and we shuffle off the sidewalk to give them adequate berth. The union men outvoice us with a song that goes, "We are the union, the mighty, mighty union." We don't lay off with our chanting, but we are a little more subdued about it in the presence of these bruisers. The only remotely tough person on our team is a middle-aged guy with a huge sloping mound of a head and a flattop shorn closely to reveal a pink and seborrheic scalp. He soon begins shouting that his wife is from El Salvador, and he bets that those IUPAT men, many of whom appear to be of Latin extraction, wish that they could sleep with her—a puzzling taunt that makes everybody on both sides uncomfortable.

Besides this guy and the UCF students, we have a couple of telecom professionals, big saliva-lacquered cigars jutting from their lips, and also another tech-sector employee named David, who has a dewy tousling of brown hair and a nose like a miniature shark's fin. David shakes my hand, and almost immediately he asks me, "Did you know that 90 percent of abortions are had by liberals? I don't know why we're against it." When the union men chant "No More Bushit," David says to me, "No more Bush? What, are they gay? We *love* Bush over here." He nods at the UCF girls, all avatars of lo-rise fashions, midriffs tanned rotisserie gold, and he shoots me a Mephisphopheleon look.

We cannot compete with the IUPAT men, and we're also scared of them, so we cross the street. Safely protected by the busy boulevard, we mimic their union song: "You are looooosers!" One of the telecom guys yells, "Paint my house." Someone else screams, "I make $100,000 a year."

Then the clouds recongeal. The rain begins in earnest. The dolphin takes cover beneath a nearby tree, the UCF girls scamper off. I break away from the group. As I walk to my truck, one of the union men steps into my path. "Are you rich?" he asks me. I say no. Then how, he wants to know, could I possibly support a president who "doesn't give a fuck about poor people"?

I stand before him in silence, chewing a gland in my lip. Then I attempt a timid declaration about Bush's commitment to national security, drawing on the only time in my life when my foremost feelings toward our President were not suspicion and contempt; namely, when I was standing on a sidewalk in lower Manhattan on September 11, 2001, watching people jumping out of the north tower of the World Trade Center, and for a few hours afterward when I was back in my apartment, trying not to imagine what concatenation of incinerated things made up the sweet, chalky odor seeping in through my closed windows, and taking comfort in the sound of fighter jets shrieking overhead, and also in the certainty that George Bush was going to make a lot of people pay grievously for this day.* It's a sentiment I have never admitted to having had before this moment, and it appalls me to find myself saying these things now. Still, I'm startled by how irresistibly powerful, how despica-

---

*I was pretty well over my fleeting faith in the Bush Administration by the evening of September 12, when I realized the license this ruin would afford our President, summed up by an eerie orthographical blunder I saw spray-painted on a bedsheet hanging in Union Square: LET US PREY.

bly good it feels to stand here sanctifying my praise of the President in the lives lost that morning. "I was there," I say, and to my own horror I can feel a painful brine building behind my eyes. "I saw people dying."

The union man clenches his fist, and I see the cords in his forearm swell and flatten. "Well, it was your man who brought that shit to the table," he says in a voice full of fury and disgust.

Not far from my hotel is a tall brown range of mulch dunes. Hurricanes Frances and Charley passed through here only a few weeks ago, and the dunes are made of chipper-shredded live oaks and loblolly pines that the winds brought down. Nearly everyone staying in the hotel is an itinerant chipper-shredder operator from New York, and the parking lot, which is crowded with their apparatuses, looks like the motor pool for a horticultural jihad. The hotel itself is roughly half in ruins. The roof is bandaged with an electric-blue tarp where shingles have gone missing, and one of the wrecked halls is inhabited by a quivering translucent tube resembling a giant grub. The tube conveys a desiccating breeze from the Dumpster-size dehumidifier in the parking lot below. My room is suffused with a scent of scalded moss.

I lie down on the stiff coverlet of my bed and try to sleep. From the wall behind my head comes a sound like steel tumbleweeds drifting through the pipes. I'm also dealing with some lingering self-abhorrence from my participation at the Kerry rally, and a nonspecific dyspepsia about my little project here, which leaves me feeling tetchy and wakeful. So I go downstairs to the hotel bar, which is called the Celebrity Lounge.

I sit down next to a man with a shaggy, balding head and a beard like a mat of Florida mondo grass. He has soil on his T-shirt and exudes a certain tropical degeneracy. His name, he says, is Jay. "Are you one of the tree people?" he asks.

Next to Jay is a man with a hard red face, a golf shirt, and a tidy pancake of straw-colored hair. As soon as I sit down, the man in the golf shirt goes into a laughing fit about something, barking out an effortful, peristaltic laugh: "Uh! Uh! Uh! Uh! Uh! Uh! Uh!" Every time he says "Uh!" he clouts me on the arm. The laughing man's name is Barry. Like Jason Teaman and roughly 80 percent of the people I meet down here, Barry is in real estate. Jay does landscaping work for him from time to time.

"He's got about a hundred and fifty kinds of plants on his property," Jay says of his sometime boss. "And over by the orange tree he's got a little brass colored-boy. It's got one hand reaching up, so it looks like he's trying to pick an orange."

Barry would like to put more brass colored-boys on his lawn, but one brass colored-boy, he tells me ruefully, is all local propriety will allow. "I just wonder when the hell we're gonna get all this bullshit behind us and call it even," he says. "Anyway, the blacks aren't even minorities anymore. They're done. I'm like, 'You had your chance, you fuckers, now it's the Mexicans and the Chinese and these other motherfuckers who are gonna take over.' We need to take this country back. We need to turn this motherfucker around. The French stopped letting Muslims come into their goddamned country. We need to do the same thing. Strapping bombs to their five-year-old kids and everything. No scruples. They're a bunch of fucking weirdoes. But the way we treat 'em, I swear to God, before long you're gonna have affirmative action for terrorists. We need to turn this country around. Lock the doors and start kicking ass."

The television is showing a recent stump speech by George W. Bush. Jay, who's not planning to vote in November ("the election has nothing to do with me"), takes the remote from the bar and flips to a rerun of *Sanford and Son*. "Uh! Uh! Redd Foxx," Barry says. "That's one funny-ass black dude."

Jay notes the sickly gray shimmer on Redd Foxx's face. "You can tell he's been eating pork chops," Jay says. "Eating pork makes your face shiny like that."

Hurricane Jeanne, now stalking the Atlantic coast, has been upgraded to a Category Three weather event. The sky is full of dark hollows and gullies and big amber wounds that leak sunlight.

A skeleton crew at Victory '04 this morning; only Jason Teaman and another young guy on hand. I'm here to pull a door-to-door canvassing shift, which I may have to do alone because all the other volunteers, I'm guessing, have stayed home to board up their windows. But twenty minutes later, a fellow canvasser turns up, a short ruddy man named Dennis wearing a striped shirt and black tasseled loafers. Dennis makes his living scheduling advertisements for a local radio station—a fine job, he tells me, except that it requires him to schedule the occasional John Kerry spot. He particularly hates Hillary Clinton, and he suspects that the Democratic Party is deliberately making a botch of the Kerry campaign as part of a "big plot to make way for Hillary" in 2008. Dennis does admire the right-wing talk-radio pundit Sean Hannity: "He lets us know so we don't have to."

We park in a neighborhood of low-lying cinder-block and concrete ranch houses. This neighborhood took a grievous beating from the storms, and the sidewalks are heaved and gabled from the roots of toppled trees. A crew with a chainsaw and a truck with a cherry picker are frantically trying to amputate weak limbs from the live oaks shading the streets. Little gray lizards skedaddle from our path.

We knock on the door of the first home we come to. An elderly man answers. "Good *morning*, sir," Dennis says. He is a terrifically chipper canvasser. "Are you planning on supporting the President?"

The man digs his tongue around in his mouth until he finds a spot that, judging from his expression, tastes especially bad, and says, "Kerry. I hate the sound of his voice."

"We're with you, sir," Dennis says. "What we'd like is for Mr. Kerry to wake up on Election Day and already be behind by a few thousand votes." Dennis forks over a handful of campaign materials. The man thanks us and sends us on our way.

A little later we knock at somebody's rear gate. A wild-haired woman in an artist's smock answers. She clutches the leash of a large dog, which is barking murderously. "I don't like Bush, and neither does my dog," she says. She glances at Dennis in his tasseled loafers and deeply pleated slacks, and at me in my brown oxfords and button-down shirt with the marshy semicircles spreading from my armpits, and it is clear from her look that we strike her as a pair of perfect assholes. She shuts the gate with a clatter. We trudge off. I feel a vain temptation to double back to the woman's place and offer her an apology or a confession, as though she'd the least bit care. But I don't, and the rejection puts me in a vile mood. Our frequent successes—when people throw their doors wide and pump our hands and make grateful offerings of bottled water—make me feel far worse. Dennis maintains an eager pace, legging it briskly from house to house, but for my part, no matter who answers the door, it's pretty much guaranteed to be a big dispiriting drag.

We finish up the shift. I bid Dennis farewell, and I drive off very quickly with the winds bullying my truck all over the road.

The tree people have left the hotel in advance of Hurricane Jeanne. I find Jay sitting by the swimming pool adjacent to the Celebrity Lounge, drinking a draft beer with a maraschino cherry effervescing in the bottom of the glass. The swimming pool reflects a moon the color of old buttermilk. He gazes up at the shabby shreds of cloud sneaking through the sky and says, "That's what you call spin-off. The hurricane's a couple hundred miles away, but that's a bunch of trash clouds it's throwing our way."

Jay talks for a little while about the plants around the pool—palms and bromeliads and mondo grass—and about how much money that guy Barry has. He talks about these rich people for whom he grows tomatoes and peppers and avocados, "but they never eat them. They just like to see them growing in their yard." He explains that Colonial Boulevard, the four-laner running past this hotel, is a kind of class divide in this part of town. On the other side of it are rich people, he says. On this side, a little closer back toward the downtown, are the whores and the drug dealers, and then to the south it's regular poor black people. Around here, it's just sort of nothing, a bunch of exhausted old malls and husks of hotels without much going on.

Jay tells me that Alaska's fishing industry is "no good anymore now that the Chinks took it over." Then he talks about sea urchins, and how the Chinks are into those too, and did I know that a bunch of famous thoroughbred studs have recently gone missing? Million-dollar bloodlines that Japanese investors purchased—they mysteriously disappeared. "What happened was these rich Japanese guys ate them," Jay says. "They ate the horses, man, because they thought it'd give them special power."

Soon we're joined by Aaron, a friend of Jay's in his early twenties, who has the junky, sun-kissed gorgeousness you see in some of Florida's younger coastal folk: a healthy thatch of blond hair, unnaturally large blue eyes, a broken front tooth. Aaron appears to be pretty well zooted on some very potent amphetamine, and his eyes swivel violently in their sockets, and he talks at a superhuman rate, like the verbal fine print at the end of car commercials. He tells a story about how earlier tonight he was hanging out with a girl in Tampa who managed to arrange a ride back to Orlando with some stranger, evidently for the purpose of prostituting herself. "But then I pretended I was all worried about her, so the guy had to give me a ride too."

Then Aaron starts asking me about myself, and a lot of other questions, like whether I know any women who'd be willing to sleep with him. And then he looks at me like he's getting ready to tell a joke where the punch line is him stabbing me in the eye, so I go back to my room and go to sleep.

Ten days before Election Day I am back in Orlando. I ride over to a strip mall on the east side of town where the G.O.P. headquarters has metastasized into three separate storefronts. The pleasant young woman running the phone bank seats me at a table next to a plate of the strongest-smelling brownies I have ever encountered. It's crowded in here today. Almost none of my fellow telecanvassers fits an established stereotype of a Bush supporter. There are three teenage sisters with glasses and ankle-length denim skirts and long hair and plain faces—homeschool students, as it turns out—who are very sweet and friendly, in a faintly Branch Davidian sort of way. There's also a thirty-something guy named Kenny, who wears long green shorts, socks pulled up high, and trendy skateboarder shoes but who reads the calling script with a feeble, antique voice. When Kenny comes over to get a brownie, he drops a tissue over the stack, lifts the tissue, turns it over, and then peers warily at his bounty, like he's picked up a dog turd. The only real red-American grotesque is a girl who looks about nine and is already conspicuously wearing a bra and makeup. The most intimidating person in the room is a baby who looks like the actor Treat Williams and radiates a spooky numinousness.

The walls are decked with the usual snapshots and signage, including a big photo of Bush with a few black schoolchildren gathered around him. One of the children is opening his mouth pinkly and widely, as though the President has just told him to get ready because he's about to feed him something large.

I spend an afternoon combing the papers for cheap accommodations where they let you pay by the week, and the only thing I can come up with is a boardinghouse for Christian men, out in Apopka, a semi-rural suburb northwest of Orlando. Apopka used to be a land of citrus farms, greenhouses, and ferneries, and was once known as the Indoor Foliage Capital of the World, though now it's basically waiting to be enveloped by Orlando's ravening sprawl. Downtown Apopka is essentially a single intersection with new chain stores and neglected storefronts tenanted by down-market or transient businesses—a pawnshop, for instance, and a Bush/Cheney campaign office.

The boardinghouse is north of downtown, past some strip malls and what appears to be a mound of flaming dirt. The proprietress, Miss Linda Burnett, is standing on the concrete slab just off the garage when I pull up. She greets me warmly. "Isn't this a blessed day?" she asks, and I agree that it is—sky the color of pool water, a clean breeze drifting across the yard and holding the mosquitoes at bay. In the ample backyard there's a fine old oak as handsome as the Tree of Life, and next to the lid for the septic tank a lemon tree bearing elephantiatic fruit like huge green wasp galls.

The house is clean and unstately, comfortable in a 1960s lower-middle-class sort of way. The walls are made of grooved laminate paneling, the low ceilings are plastered with rough stucco. For $125 a week, I get a snug little room with a single bed, a desk, and a spacious bathroom with a black tile floor. The well draws water from a fouled aquifer, and the faucets deliver a mineral broth with such a concentrated copper whang that the bathroom smells like an open wound.

Miss Linda is younger and somehow more contemporary-looking than I had imagined when I was speaking to her on the phone. She is sixty-two, though she could pass for fifty. Her features are creased and rilled, but she has clear blue eyes and a lovely face that conveys much of a former vitality.

In the kitchen, Miss Linda explains the house rules. No swearing, no drinking, no bare feet around the house, shirts must be worn, clean up after yourself. She explains that a few of the men have been here for months or years, but many have briefer tenures. "We had problems with some of the men and had to ask them to leave. You hate to do it," she says, "but sometimes the Lord wants people to be here and sometimes He knows it's time for them to move on." By way of illustration she tells me about an argument she had with one of her tenants. "He was Jewish— And I love the Jewish people; I hope I'm Jewish somewhere back in my heritage. He was laughing at me, and he started praising Allah. I said, 'That's the last time you'll ever do that around here. You're out!'"

Linda tells me later that the advent of the Rapture is "quickening," and she is eager for it to happen soon. "I hope the Lord comes during my time. I'd hate to leave it for my grandchildren; I think they're an ill-prepared generation." But in the meantime she will serve the Lord in her own fashion. She would like to turn her house into a transitional home and occupational training center for single mothers, if the county will allow it. She is also planning to move to Africa, because years ago she made a holy vow to go work among the unfortunates in Ethiopia. She knows that the mission may wind up killing her, but she says she would rather die in His service than break a promise to God.

"So you're in town working on a presidential campaign," she says, which I had mentioned over the phone. "Which one, if you don't mind my asking?"

"The Bush/Cheney."

And suddenly the old muscles of her face start firing and her whole countenance swells and blooms. "Oh *good*," she says. "I pray for him to win. He is a godly man."

Miss Linda tells me that she grew up in "a good Republican family" in Tennessee, but that she "got away from the farm and fell away from our Lord." She spent some time in New York, modeling and in the theater. Then she found work with a major investment firm and moved to Geneva. In Switzerland, she says, she worked in international finance and some other cloak-and-dagger business, which she mentions only vaguely. "I saw a lot of stuff I didn't want to see. Evil things. I had guns pointed at my head, bullets flying at me. When I was involved in international finance, I saw some things that were so evil that it staggered me, and I think our sweet, sweet George Bush sees those same things."

She pours me a cup of coffee, brewed to the opacity of used motor oil. She explains that there is almost always a pot of coffee on, compliments of the house.

"I thought it was so exciting," she says of her continental years. "I thought I was so smart. But it was a dark time. It was so dark I thought all the light had gone out of me. Then the Lord started teaching me. He reduced me to working in a kitchen for a while. Pride and arrogance. Pride and arrogance."

She rolls her eyes ceilingward and gives a woozy laugh. Then she sets her jaw and says in a wondrous tone, "George Bush has known darkness, too, but look at what the Lord had in mind for him: to become president of the United States."

The following morning, at the breakfast counter, Miss Linda asks me how I liked my first night in the house. I tell her I slept well, that the place was silent as a tomb. "Everybody's real considerate," I say. "They all seem like good people."

"They *are* good people," she says. "But I'll tell you something funny. The other day I was going by this little bitty church. They had one of these signs out front, you know. And you know what it said? It said, 'Hell is full of good people.'" And then she starts to laugh.

Bush/Cheney–Apopka is no Bush/Cheney–Winter Park. No Abercrombie & Fitch youthsters from the University of Central Florida, and no Amanda saying, "Awesome" or, "You rock" in the most perfect possible way. It is a dreary suite of empty rooms on Apopka's desolate main drag, with lino floors and fluorescent light and a general atmosphere of a decommissioned teen center or an abandoned junk-bond brokerage.

The wall décor includes bumper stickers reading JOHN KERRY—GIVE TERRORISM A CHANCE and KERRY-FONDA, as well as some hand-lettered motivational signage:

Dear Republicans,
    I want to thank you for being too busy and self-absorbed to lift a finger to help get your President elected. Teresa and I appreciate your support.
    Warm regards,
    John Kerry

The core staff at Victory-Apopka is Ron and Patty Redlich, a married couple in their middle years. Patty is a stout, solicitous woman with a scalpful of stiff blonde plumage; she is in residential real estate. Ron is tan and large with carefully combed hair and a certain unwhimsical postwar paterfamiliar air. He is in commercial real estate.

Ron and I tuck into our calling lists, reciting the standard get-out-the-vote boilerplate, which I've pretty well memorized by now. Presently, a classy middle-aged woman in a sharp red suit strolls in. She wants advice on how to vote on a few upcoming ballot measures. One would cap attorney's fees in medical malpractice suits. Another would require minors to produce signed parental-consent forms in order to get abortions. Ron Redlich advises her to vote "Yes" on both of these and on another that would quash construction of a public high-speed rail system.

Then the woman confesses that she actually had an ulterior motive for stopping by today. She is a field agent for something called Longaberger baskets, and she wants to know whether we would like to buy one of these baskets (which is just an empty basket the size of a halved bowling ball that contains no jars of jam or cheese assortments or anything) for $82. "They are a *collector* item," she explains. "They go up in value." Ron does not buy one, but he takes the woman's proffered flyer and posts it on the wall beside the latest batch of polls.

Next, a woman storms into the office, her limbs and torso working in a blustery, officious stride. She says she is the pastor of a local church, and she starts laying into Ron about the paucity of sign wavers down at the public library, which is where the early voting is going on in Apopka. "They had the Women for Kerry down there. I'm surprised people haven't thrown things on them, but they haven't."

Ron mentions that it's sure to be a close one next Tuesday, and the woman gives a horrified little shriek. "I just can't believe it. We just have some blinded, blinded people in this country. I'm just concerned that if we lose, our country is going to be run by evil."

Today's news items: a Sarasota man tried to run over former Florida Secretary of State Katherine Harris, and another man in Palm Beach County threatened to stab his girlfriend in the throat with a screwdriver if she cast her vote for John Kerry.

In front of the Apopka public library, a torpid, lollygagging line of early voters crowds the sidewalk. There are women in synthetic fiber pantsuits with keen frontal creases; old people in shorts that reveal strangely lovely indigo traceries of veins on the backs of their knees; infant twins in a dual-chamber stroller, broiling under the high, white sun; a couple of rancher types with cowboy boots and UV-cured faces (the only people out here who don't seem miserable in the awful heat); women in hats bearing bright salads of artificial flora.

Inside, the line winds through the reference section, past an island of librarians' consoles, and down to the voting booths. The line's making such sluggish progress that a few of the less physically hardy voters have to go on little sitting breaks. A man sitting close to where I'm writing is carrying such a phenomenal quantity of surplus flesh on his upper body that most of it has slid floorward and rings his waist in a discrete skirt, leaving his chest and shoulders comparatively lean-looking. He talks with a friend about how standing on line has aggravated a few of his medical troubles. "I've still got open sores on my foot. I've had one for three years. It's where the bone's rubbing through, so they've gone and cut the bone off."

Nearby, a woman who could pass for either sixteen or thirty-five dandles a little girl on her lap. The woman has a soft, imploded-looking mouth and is probably toothless, though I can't tell for sure. She's dressed in pajama bottoms and a sleeveless top revealing a pair of large, unshapely arms. She speaks to the child in a gurgling baby talk so unintelligible that she herself seems prelingual. But from what I can make out she's saying that if the little girl doesn't behave she's going to tattle to her mom and dad, even though the little girl is just silently perched on the soft dome of the woman's knee, feeding herself some Smarties. Then, with no apparent provocation, the woman starts shaking the child by the shoulders and slapping her face. The little girl raises a breathless mewling, and the woman immediately presses the child to her dé-colletage, coos to her, and lips her tears away in an abstracted parody of mother-love. Then the little girl brightens and starts laughing and poking the woman on the chin, saying in a playful, lilting voice, "I'm 'a whip *you*!"

The woman goes back to nuzzling the little girl, but a few seconds later her gibberings turn angry again, and she's smacking the child with curt little blows. A lady in a sleek black suit stands a few yards away, looking appalled. "My God," she says. "What are you doing?" But the assault is already subsiding. The caressings resume, and once more all is well.

I return to the library a few days later. A pair of pollwatchers for the Kerry side sit in the shade of a molting ficus tree, watching voters feed the ballot vault. They have witnessed no conspicuous malfeasance, they say in a faintly disappointed way. They seem bored out of their wits.

And that must be the sentry from the Bush campaign sitting over there: youngish, with a big blunt instrument of chin, hair the color of peat moss, and an expensive-looking blouse striped in brave Venetian hues. She is in high dudgeon. Someone has just accosted her in front of the library, she explains into her cell phone, because she had Bush materials displayed on her car.

Her harasser, in fact, is still outside wandering the parking lot. He is a sun-stricken old man, a Kerry-Edwards button pinned over his sternum and a sheaf of campaign literature in his fist. His name is Murray Weinreb. He says that he is eighty-two years old, that he's the CEO of a company with 1,400 employees, that he owns four houses, and that he has had both a heart condition and two kinds of cancers. He tells me that one cannot imagine how singularly unpleasant it is to suffer from two kinds of cancers unless one has experienced it firsthand. Similarly, one cannot convey in words the horror of getting attacked for one's political beliefs, which he claims is what the woman in the expensive blouse and a colleague of hers did to him, not the other way around.

The trouble started, he says, when the woman parked her car in the fire lane in front of the library's main entrance and accoutred it with flags and G.O.P. campaign signs, breaking the ordinance that requires campaigners to maintain a distance of fifty feet from the polling site. He protested, and an argument ensued. A man rushed to the woman's aid, which he did by calling Murray a motherfucker and threatening to "sock" him. "He said, 'We don't want your kind in this country,' whoever 'my kind' is. 'You people are gonna go to hell, because you're for abortion, and because you're for gays.'"

Now little pinheads of perspiration are swelling on Murray's brow. He clutches the campaign pamphlets with angry might, and they quiver in his grasp. Then he tells me that yesterday he was strafed by a van full of Republican volunteers, who also told him that casting a vote for Kerry would earn him a spot in hell. When he woke up this morning, he found that vandals had gone after his yard signs and his mailbox with cans of spray paint. "Those were my neighbors, acting like Nazis!

"If Bush wins—" he says, shaking his head. "This country is already on its way to becoming a dictatorship. It's getting to be a terrible, terrible, terrible situation. I was in the Army in World War II. I slit people's throats myself. I was ready to die then, and I'm ready to die now."

Thursday before Election Day. A sinewy retiree named Larry Scotchie and I are en route to a canvassing detail. We're riding in Larry's car, which is a little gold Saturn bearing a state-issued, anti-abortion license plate—CHOOSE LIFE emblazoned in red just above the tag numbers. Larry is a former rocket engineer and was one of the many designers of the Patriot missile, which he speaks of fondly. He tells me about the technical difficulties of devising missile-defense systems; namely, the space-based model he worked on toward the end of his career. The Saturn surges through a curve on Interstate 4, and a pair of medallions on Larry's rearview mirror collide with a gentle knocking sound. One bears the face of Minnie Mouse; the other, the Pope.

Forty minutes later we arrive at a suburban tract, which is a slightly cruddier version of the last neighborhood I canvassed: cinder-block, trailer-stature houses painted merry, tropical colors. The scarcity of streetlights worries Larry, because this doesn't seem like the safest neighborhood and the gloom is already upon us.

Larry assigns me a handful of addresses and strides into the dusk.

The first house on my list has a hectic weed-swale of a lawn and an open front door out of which a strong scent of cat urine is wafting on the autumn wind. Inside, an old woman in her nightgown sits watching television, surrounded by stacks of old newspaper, failing cardboard boxes, and paper bags. "Hello, ma'am," I say. "I'm just going door-to-door for the Bush campaign, and—"

"I don't want anything to do with him," she barks abruptly, and I slink off, chastened.

I reconnoiter with Larry. "How'd you do?"

"Kerry," I say.

He notes it on his clipboard with a doleful clucking sound.

Next I visit a house overwhelmed with plastic yard fauna: squirrels, bunnies, frogs, and turtles encircled by a fence of plastic tulips. I knock. A dog goes into a high, womanly shrieking, and then I hear an actual woman shrieking back at it, and then a petite lady with gray teeth trimmed in glinting silver opens the door. Another strong dose of animal scent, and also potpourri. "Boosh," she says in Spanish-accented English. "I like Boosh."

For the next three hours, I audition dozens of reprises of this basic sentiment, with a few awkward exceptions: a man who answers the door shirtless, his face violet with sorrow or rage, who simply says, "I can't talk now"; an older couple who waves me away because they're busy watching news coverage of a family of six found dead in an apartment across town; a disembodied male voice telling me he was planning on voting for Bush until people like me started bugging him all the time, and would I please go to hell; a woman who comes to the door and informs me that her father is slowly dying in the back room and that now is not a good time.

Larry knocks at one house and an elderly white man with an American flag on his shirt and no front teeth comes to the door. "Hello, you must be Mister Diaz Ortero," Larry says in a trilling, grandfatherly way.

The man gazes back at Larry in cranky bafflement and explains that the Orteros have not lived here for some time. "But I'm not a Bush man," he says. "No way, baby."

Larry says, "Well, remember to vote. November third."

Walking back to the car, Larry chuckles. "Maybe that 'November third' will stick in his mind."

Later he hands me a crumpled baton of anti-Bush campaign literature. He says, "A little souvenir. It fell out of a door."

At a saloon in a strip mall in Apopka I lean against the bar and peruse Larry's gift. It is a glossy flyer enjoining its reader to be concerned over the billion-plus tax dollars we've spent on health care and education in Iraq, when 45 million Americans are without health insurance themselves and education costs in this country are on the rise. I flip the sheet. Health-care premiums in Florida up 59 percent; 168,000 students in Florida unable to afford a college education due to cuts in financial aid; $1.3 billion to rebuild clinics and schools in Iraq, which we spent much, much vaster sums to ruin. The flyer traffics in facts and arguments, which in their essential nature as facts, as arguments, carry about as much weight in the matterless void in which this election has been unfolding as a sprig of Florida crabgrass drifting through outer space. What's important in this electoral climate is the cozy belly-feeling that our President is a good man, a righteous man, whose war is a righteous war if for no other reason than that he's the one waging it. This document, with its strong, stern numbers, doesn't make a flyspeck's difference in the eye of such conviction. And Larry's interception of it is the closest I'll get to spotting an electoral misdeed this fall.

Someone is shouting my name, so I put the flyer in my pocket, and here is Richard, who is a roofer from Texas and an ex-convict reborn in Christ. He and his son, Bubba, are my fellow tenants at the Christian home, come to Florida in search of hurricane work. They're both drunk as lords.

Richard, who is in his fifties, confesses to me that he's a little bit in love with Miss Linda, and that last night he almost tried to kiss her, and he holds up a pair of clenched fists to show the intensity of his longing. He says that he did a five-year prison bid in Texas for DWI and that alcohol has ruined his life. He tells me that he has put himself in the Lord's hands, that he sort of hates his son, and that as of today, for reasons unknown to him, a sudden blindness has clouded one of his eyes.

He rocks back on his heels and peers foggily around the bar. He can't spot Bubba, who he supposes "might have caught himself a double-breasted split-tail."

Actually, Bubba is standing by the bar, leaning over a guy who's telling him, "My *problem* is you won't get the fuck out of my face."

A woman sitting on a nearby stool has an I VOTED sticker on her shirt. I ask her how things looked down at the polls today. "I don't know," she says solemnly. "There were a lot of blacks and a lot of liberals."

Then her boyfriend, a man with arms like a sack of oranges, asks me if Bubba and Richard are friends of mine, and I say no.

It is the Saturday before Election Day and the President is coming to town. Tickets are difficult to come by, but my canvassing labors have earned me a pair of them: one for myself and one I'm giving to Miss Linda, who said she'd be delighted to go. When it's time to leave, she comes out and meets me in her kitchen. She's wearing a simple white dress, tall wedgelike shoes, and a little bit of makeup and perfume, and she looks me straight in the face and hoists her eyebrows a little as she smiles, as if to say, "Isn't this something," because both of us know she looks like a million bucks. We get in my truck and take the back roads toward the turnpike, and the sunset glows hazard-orange on the ponds and pools and swamps of Apopka.

The rally is happening west of town at Tinker Field, which is a baseball diamond in the shadow of the football stadium where the Citrus Bowl is held each year. More than 17,000 people have turned out, and as we inch into the bottleneck at the security portals, Miss Linda and I squeeze ever more intimately against our neighbors, who are 100 percent white people, though a high proportion have deep cordovan suntans, which creates an illusion of ethnic variety. The only African Americans in my field of vision are across the street holding Kerry signs. Miss Linda frowns in their direction. "Are they really doing that?"

A woman next to us makes a grumpy honking noise in the back of her throat. "Don't they know there are a lot more of us than there are of them?"

We undergo a thorough frisking and then follow the herd onto Tinker Field. Families have staked off little encampments with picnic blankets and other tarpage and look highly pissed when Linda and I pause near their territory. We find a spot of unoccupied turf near the swell of the pitcher's mound, a hundred yards or so from the stage, behind which hangs a mammoth vinyl backdrop, a full-bleed reproduction of a computer-generated flag in mid-ripple, and the words AMERICA: SAFER, STRONGER, BETTER in the steely, industrial typeface you see riveted to the tailgates of late-model pickup trucks. The sun has sunk behind the banner and is throwing twin spars of pink light into the sky.

There is a tri-prong sacramental medley in praise of church and nation—the prayer, the Pledge of Allegiance, the national anthem—which instills a tremendous heart-swollen solemnity in the crowd. During the pledge, a nearby woman holds her child's face to her own, stares somberly into its eyes, and enunciates every word in a careful, private voice.

We hear from George Bush's little brother Marvin, and professional wrestler Shawn Michaels (real name Michael Hickenbottom), whose spiel is not so much a speech as a pharyngeal bombardment in the tradition of the WWF pre-fight shouting match. "If your babies were left all alone in the night," he roars, "who would you rather have sitting on your front porch? John Kerry with his surfboard or George Bush with his shotgun?" Michaels is one of several of this evening's speakers whose preferred oratorical posture is a few notches below purple fury. And people respond to Michaels's rhetorical throttling with nervous, electrified grins, the sort of strained baring of teeth movie astronauts use to signify a sudden onset of multiple G's.

I nip off to the portajohn to jot a few things in my notebook. When I get back, Miss Linda gives me a guarded smile, as though she isn't quite sure what I've been up to.

Up on the stage we're visited by Scott O'Grady, a fighter pilot shot down over Kosovo, who, we're told, survived for a time on a diet of leaves and insects, and also by Orange County Sheriff Kevin Beary, who dishes out an apoplectic keelhauling in a campaign-ravaged voice that sounds like a damaged kazoo. Then we enjoy a few tunes from the country music star Mark Wills, whose work, from what I can discern, is a celebration of the petit-bourgeois condominium redneck. He tells us that his music has made him a good bit of money, much of which he's been able to hold on to, thanks to W's tax breaks, and everyone applauds the solvency of the Mark Wills estate. He plays a song called "And the Crowd Goes Wild," an up-tempo paean to the concept of mass mania, which is supposed to be W's cue to come out onstage. But for unexplained reasons the President fails to appear.

A lengthy wait ensues. We are crammed in too tightly to sit. We shift from one foot to another as the lactic acid pools in our knees and spines. Miss Linda has slipped out of her wedges and stands in the grass on bare soles. My own discomfort is compounded by a woman to my left who keeps moaning, "Ooooh, where *is* he? I want to see my president," in the shrill, petulant tone a child uses to announce that its bladder is full.

At last her president arrives, flanked by former HUD Secretary Mel Martinez, who's running for Senate, and Laura Bush, her face a lunar Kabuki white. Miss Linda raises her golden arm above the crowd and waves. While Martinez makes a few remarks, the President stands to the right of the lectern. His stance is tentative and ungainly: chest thrust faintly forward, arms held out to the sides, hands dangling in a weird limp-fingered way, as though they've just been dipped to the wrist in something sticky and he's waiting for them to dry.

Bush begins his address by thanking the grassroots activists, and Miss Linda flashes me a proud, maternal look. The rest of his speech, his standard stump, is punishingly long. After it wraps up, and all 17,000 of us stumble toward the gate in an exhausted press, we are dismayed to learn that we won't be let out until the President has safely exited the premises. Miss Linda and I stand in the groaning crush, breathing air that is roughly 98.6 degrees and smells of sweat, cologne, and human mouths. A woman behind me is wailing. The wait drags on. An older man and woman lean on each other and shut their eyes. Someone promises to vomit.

The gates are loosed at last, but our part of the crowd doesn't move. Evidently, they're first letting out the people who were lucky or important enough to have merited bleacher seats before releasing the steerage class, who've been less comfortably consigned to the field. "Can you believe this?" cries the wailing woman. "We've been on our feet for three hours, and they let the people who've been sitting all night get out first?"

Finally, Miss Linda and I struggle free of the crowd. She looks a little drawn, but her big pearlescent smile is marvelous to behold. "I'm so proud of him," she says of the President. "I can still see him, standing up there in his blue shirt. And you know, when I was waving, I think he waved back at me." She recites a little of Bush's speech, not really articulating any sentences or phrases, just sort of humming the music of his words.

Then she turns to me. "When you went off to use the restroom, I promised myself I was going to ask you something."

"Okay," I say.

"If you were in the Secret Service, would you be allowed to tell me?"

By November 1, I have telephoned and trod the doorsteps of so many registered Republicans that I am seized with the grandiose anxiety that George W. Bush is going to win Florida by precisely the number of votes I myself have solicited. So I drive over to the Orlando Kerry campaign headquarters, just off Colonial Boulevard, to do some redemptory volunteering, but the place is crammed with people, and a woman there tells me they've got all the help they need. "Don't worry, Kerry's going to win," she assures me frankly, and I want to believe her. Then I call a guy I know who's registering voters out in Ohio. He tells me that he's heard some inside information that Kerry's victory is pretty much in the bag. I drive back to Apopka and get a good night's sleep.

Election Day. I wake up well rested, and, curiously, full of good portents about today. I've done as much campaigning for the President as I care to, but I'm thinking that one more day of canvassing might be a small price to pay for the

uncharitable thrill of observing the volunteer corps reexamine their convictions when America hands Bush his hat. Also, my election-fraud sleuthing has
turned up approximately zilch thus far, and if I'm going to witness anything
illicit, it'll have to happen in the coming hours.

I show up at the Orlando Bush-Cheney campaign offices a few minutes
after 10:00 A.M. A rented fleet of gleaming, bulbous minivans for shuttling
canvassers and making absentee-ballot runs is parked out front. The office has
been open since dawn. The phone bank is going great guns, resounding with
a fugue of script chatter.

I am loitering around out front, waiting to be assigned a canvassing unit.
Jessica, a woman with a blunt, hearty build and a sort of Bettie Page–ish as-
pect, is briefing me on the walking, even though I pretty well know the drill.
Today, we're trying to flush out the last few reluctant voters.

A crew from *World News Tonight* arrives. Jason Teaman comes by and
tells Jessica to have me stick around, because the TV people are going to tape
a little footage and he believes that I'd be "good for the media." I'm not sure
why this is, exactly. Hanging around the Bush people provokes in me a sort of
affective compression that I suppose comes off as a certain air of quiet capa-
bility, or maybe fat-witted sycophantism or something. It could also be that I
share the same unhealthy British Isles pallor common to a high proportion of
RNC types and therefore seem like an archetypal team member. In any case,
my confirmed status as a broadcast-quality G.O.P. drone fills me with both
shame and a cheap sort of pride. While Jessica briefs me, the TV people scrum
in around us. Somebody angles a camera into my face as I get my marching
orders. Someone else, without apology or explanation, starts wanding a big
fluffy coon's tail of a microphone over my crotch area.

My canvassing partners this morning are Jonathan—a young olive-
skinned guy wearing weathered cargo shorts, a Third World beaded necklace
bearing a plain wooden cross and punctuated with shark vertebrae, and a wild
black beard in the Nazarene style—and Linda—a friendly woman whose
business as a wedding planner is presently in a post-hurricane trough and
who has some spare time on her hands.

Neither Jonathan nor Linda has canvassed before, which makes me the
senior member of the team. We get into Jonathan's car, a white Jeep Chero-
kee. Although the headquarters is just about on the shoulder of I-4, Jonathan needs directions to the interstate, which, coupled with his Third World/
Nazarene look, makes me a little suspicious that he might be an undercover

reporter from an out-of-town college newspaper. My suspicions are pretty well confirmed when he immediately starts interrogating Linda and me about our reasons for voting for Bush.

I tell him national security, but I find myself unable to elaborate and instead go on to say that I'm not sure I understand why the President keeps telling us how delightfully it's all going in Iraq when the beheading and suicide-bombing rates are only gathering steam, and the possibility of a stable democracy seems a more fantastical prospect with each new day.

Linda nods equably and admits that she wasn't actually all that sure she'd vote for Bush at first. But she found Kerry too "flip-floppy." Furthermore, she says, Bush shares her awareness of the approaching Biblical apocalypse, which is a comfort to her. "He is a God-fearing man. He understands that we are in the End of Times."

Linda asks us what gains for the Christian faith we'd like to see Bush pursue in a second term.

"I'm sorry," Jonathan says, "I hate religion. What good has Christianity ever done in politics?"

Linda makes a few noises about Reagan, who, she acknowledges, wasn't as "out there" as Bush in the religiosity department but who did a great job nonetheless. Jonathan, unsatisfied, presses her to come up with a single political figure whose Christian faith has really done anybody any good. Linda goes quiet and then warily concedes that no one really comes to mind.

Jonathan tells us that he's been to a few Democrat rallies and has enjoyed speeches from the likes of Leonardo DiCaprio, Meg Ryan, and Robert Kennedy Jr., heightening Linda's already substantial unease. "I probably would've voted for Kerry, but there's two things, only two reasons why I voted for Bush," he says. "It's abortion, and there's gay marriage. Those things are very detrimental to our society."

"Those are liberal things," Linda says, visibly relieved. Emboldened, she goes on to share her belief that a Bush loss might prompt God to inflict His wrath upon the nation. "I just fear that if Kerry gets into office, and we get away from our core values, what God might do."

"Yes, indeed," says Jonathan, who, as it turns out, is the son and grandson of pastors, both with flocks of thousands. By way of demonstration, Jonathan disgorges several minutes' worth of Bible verse at a rapid clip, to which neither Linda nor I can come up with a comfortable rejoinder, so we ride out past the mulch dunes in silence.

.   .   .

Back at headquarters, late afternoon, the phone bank is staffed to capacity, and I have to wait around awhile for a cell phone to free up. Someone finally hands me one, and I shoulder in among a group of phone-weary people, some of whom say "shit" when a call doesn't work out and then immediately apologize for having said "shit." I spend about forty-five minutes calling people who all have the last name Hamilton. The majority of the Hamiltons already have been canvassed to a bloody pulp and tell me so in straight terms.

The coordinators are harried and impolite. Every so often a short Asian woman who's jogging around in a sort of tantrum of efficacy snatches my phone list and thrusts another into my hands. Minutes before 7:00 P.M., when the polls close, the coordinators tell us thanks for everything, now please get out of here.

All volunteers are invited to a party at the downtown Marriott to watch the poll results come in. We've gotten word that Bush's numbers are looking strong in Florida, and my colleagues' good moods are already giving me the sick heaves. But a Kerry victory, I tell myself, isn't yet out of the question, and, anyway, besides my cronies from the Bush campaign, I don't know another living soul in Orlando to watch the returns with. I go to the party just before eight.

Ladies and gentlemen in casual finery are queued up at the cash bar. Inside the second-floor ballroom, people with Styrofoam boater hats and bottles of beer plastered with damp cocktail napkins are gathered in claques around several TVs tuned to FOX News. It's tough to find a spot with a clear view of the screens, but the frequent bursts of cheering keep me pretty well apprised of how things are going: a few scattered roars and gleeful bellows as the anticipated states flash red and news of local victories starts rolling in. When the ballot measure requiring parental notification for abortion passes, a group of guys in their twenties high-five each other. By ten or so, the shrieking is more or less constant, ringing in terraced crescendos. I'm standing next to a guy with a mole that stands out on his brow a half-centimeter or so and is knurled on the sides like a barrel clasp. "You think Kerry's shitting his pants yet?" he asks his friend.

"I hope he fucking shoots himself," the other guy replies.

I run into David, the outspoken protester from the Kerry rally, standing next to a pawky, whey-faced fellow. David is pop-eyed with elation. Immediately after shaking my hand, he revisits the joke he told me at our first meeting, about how he's recently turned a corner on the abortion issue, because "90 percent of abortions are had by liberals." He does a little statistical figuring. "So that's fifty million liberals who'll never get to vote."

"That's so twisted, and I LOVE IT!" shouts his friend.

Ron and Patty Redlich walk by and give me a courtly nod. Linda, my canvassing partner from today, spots me and calls my name excitedly, and I pretend I'm on the phone. Chris, the University of Central Florida young Republican with the I Ching coin necklace, hunches in front of a television, and in the few seconds I watch him his face registers about nine different kinds of effulgent, forceful joy.

All sorts of people are here: men wearing stiff oxford shirts and huge watches; younger versions of these same men in polo shirts; a few prosperous-looking heavyset guys, big labial deltas of flesh straining below their waistbands; hourly-wage-earning types in jeans and T-shirts; a Latino man with jailhouse tattoos and Sheetrock joint compound on his pants; a woman in a tight dress whose body looks twenty years old but who has the face of an exhumed crow; a giant guy sporting a vest heavy with Vietnam War–related patches, including one with a picture of a Huey helicopter and the word HUEY embroidered didactically below it, as though it is very important that he not forget what a Huey is; Goth rockers; a young man whose neck is garlanded with a toilet seat ("Flush the Johns"); a George Bush impersonator; and a couple who start Frenching right in the middle of the floor because the victory has made them horny.

I was planning on sticking around through the end of the evening, but it's tough keeping up appearances under the influence of what's turning out to be one of the most concussive despairs I have suffered in my life. The cheering bangs in the pulp of my teeth. The sorrow is queering my equilibrium. It is as though the air, so thickly freighted with the fanfare and the chanting, has turned impassably viscous and is making it hard to walk or stand up. I lean on a wall and call a friend in New York. He answers uncertainly, his voice clotted with grief. "Well, they haven't called Ohio yet, maybe . . ." He trails off, and I hold the phone up to catch the sounds of the room. Together, we listen to the quickening explosions of laughter and applause, and my friend says, "We're fucked."

.   .   .

Morning, November 3. Richard is in Miss Linda's yard as I'm packing my truck to leave. His eyes are moist and raw. He tells me he has wrecked his life with alcohol, and that his son is skipping town, and that he's got a detached retina and blood and water are pooling in his eye, which calls for an injection straight into his eyeball, and that he is very far from home. "Man," he says in a creaking whisper, "I'm in a tornado."

He asks me about the election. Then he squints at me with his bad eye and sees that I don't look so fine myself. "You okay?" he asks.

I go back inside to tell Miss Linda good-bye. She is standing by the sink, slicing a papaya.

"Don't you worry about Richard," she says. "The Lord's dealing with him right now." She cleaves off a firm, vermilion crescent for me to eat on my trip. "But I want to talk to you about the election. I prayed hard for the Lord's mercy, for the Lord to give us four more years of President Bush. And He did— He worked through people like you." She fixes me with a smile as bright and huge as the dawn. "I'm so proud of you," she says. "You helped make history."

March 2005

Their Men in Washington

Undercover with D.C.'s Lobbyists for Hire

KEN SILVERSTEIN

In March 2007, when the U.S. State Department announced its new global survey of human rights, Secretary of State Condoleezza Rice declared that the report demonstrated America's commitment to civil liberties, the rule of law, and a free press. "We are recommitting ourselves to stand with those courageous men and women who struggle for their freedom and their rights," she said. "And we are recommitting ourselves to call every government to account that still treats the basic rights of its citizens as options rather than, in President Bush's words, the non-negotiable demands of human dignity."

Flipping through the report, however, one cannot help but notice how many of the countries that flout "the non-negotiable demands of human dignity" seem to have negotiated themselves significant support from the U.S. government, whether military assistance (Egypt, Colombia), development aid (Azerbaijan, Nigeria), expanded trade opportunities (Angola, Cameroon), or official Washington visits for their leaders (Equatorial Guinea, Kazakhstan). The granting of favorable concessions to dictatorial regimes is a practice hardly limited to the current administration: Bill Clinton came into office having said that China's access to American markets should be tied to improved human rights—specifically its willingness to "recognize the legitimacy of those kids that were carrying the Statue of Liberty" at Tiananmen Square—but left having helped Beijing attain its long-cherished goal of Permanent Most Favored Nation trade status. Jimmy Carter put the promotion of human rights at the heart of his foreign policy, yet he cut deals for South American generals and Persian Gulf monarchs in much the same fashion as his successor, Ronald Reagan.

How is it that regimes widely acknowledged to be the world's most oppressive nevertheless continually win favors in Washington? In part, it is because they often have something highly desired by the United States that can be leveraged to their advantage, be it natural resources, vast markets for trade and investment, or general geostrategic importance. But even the best-endowed regimes need help navigating the shoals of Washington, and it is their great fortune that, for the right price, countless lobbyists are willing to steer even the foulest of ships.

American lobbyists have worked for dictators since at least the 1930s, when the Nazi government used a proxy firm called the German Dye Trust to retain the public-relations specialist Ivy Lee. Exposure of Lee's deal led Congress to pass the Foreign Agents Registration Act of 1938 (FARA), which required foreign lobbyists to register their contracts with the Justice Department. The idea seemed to be that with disclosure, lobbyists would be too embarrassed to take on immoral or corrupt clients, but this assumption predictably proved to be naive. Edward J. von Kloberg III, now deceased, for years made quite a comfortable living by representing men such as Saddam Hussein of Iraq (whose government's gassing of its Kurdish population he sought to justify) and Mobutu Sese Seko of Zaire (for whose notoriously crooked regime he helped win American foreign aid). Two other von Kloberg contracts—for Nicolae Ceauşescu of Romania and Samuel Doe of Liberia—were terminated, quite literally, when each was murdered by his own citizens. In the 1990s, after Burma's military government arrested the future Nobel Peace Prize winner Aung San Suu Kyi and cracked down on the pro-democracy movement she led, the firm of Jefferson Waterman International signed on to freshen up the Burmese image.

Although there are distinct limits to what they can achieve, lobbyists are the crucial conduit through which pariah regimes advance their interests in Washington. "It's like the secret handshake that gets you into the lodge," as one former lobbyist told me. Occasionally, firms will achieve spectacular successes for a client: one particularly remarkable piece of lobbyist image management, for example, occurred in the mid-1980s, when the firm of Black, Manafort, Stone & Kelly helped refashion Jonas Savimbi, a murderous, demented Angolan rebel leader backed by the apartheid regime in South Africa, as a valiant anticommunist "freedom fighter." Savimbi visited Washington on numerous occasions, where the lobby shop had him ferried about by limousine to meetings with top political leaders, conservative groups, and TV networks. Black, Manafort checked repeated threats by members of Congress to cut off aid to Savimbi's rebel group, which was burning and raping its way through Angola with the help of American taxpayers.

Generally, though, lobbyists' victories are more discreet. In 2004 six former members of Congress served as "election observers" in Cameroon and offered an upbeat assessment of President Paul Biya's overwhelming reelection victory, which a local Roman Catholic cardinal described as "surrounded by fraud." It turned out that the firm of Patton Boggs, which worked for the Cameroonian government, had arranged the trip of allegedly independent observers, whose expenses were paid by the Biya regime. Between 1999 and 2000, the Carmen Group received more than $1 million from the government of Kazakhstan to help "establish President [Nursultan] Nazarbayev as one of the foremost emerging leaders of the New World." The lobby shop sent four writers—syndicated columnist Georgie Anne Geyer, *Providence Journal* associate editor Philip Terzian, R. Emmett Tyrrell Jr. of *The American Spectator*, and Scott Hogenson of the Conservative News Service—on all-expenses-paid trips to Kazakhstan, and upon their return all wrote stories, ranging from critical but sympathetic to slavishly fawning, which the Carmen Group circulated on Capitol Hill.[1]

The U.S. General Accounting Office estimated in 1990 that less than half of foreign lobbyists who should register under FARA actually do so, and there is no evidence that matters have improved. In theory, violators can be heavily fined and even sent to prison, but almost no one has been prosecuted for ignoring the act, so there are few risks for noncompliance. Those firms that do register generally reveal little information beyond the names of their clients, the fees they pay, and limited information about whom they contact. Because

---

[1]The most notable entry in the latter category came from Tyrrell. Despite traveling to Kazakhstan soon after a presidential balloting that was widely condemned as rigged, he wrote that the country "has at least four highly competitive political parties . . . the freedoms of our Bill of Rights, and commendable tolerance."

disclosure requirements are so lax, it is nearly impossible to monitor the activities of foreign lobbyists. What little knowledge we do have of lobbyist-orchestrated diplomacy—including most of the projects discussed above—has been gleaned not from FARA filings but from serendipitous revelations or investigative reporting.

Which leaves Americans to wonder: Exactly what sorts of promises do these firms make to foreign governments? What kind of scrutiny, if any, do they apply to potential clients? How do they orchestrate support for their clients? And how much of their work is visible to Congress and the public, and hence subject to oversight? To shed light on these questions, I decided to approach some top Washington lobbying firms myself, as a potential client, to see whether they would be willing to burnish the public image of a particularly reprehensible regime.

The first step was to select a suitably distasteful would-be client. Given that my first pick, North Korea, seemed too reviled to be credible, I settled on the only slightly less Stalinist regime of Turkmenistan. Until his sudden death last December, President-for-Life Saparmurat Niyazov built a personality cult that outdid that of any modern leader except possibly Kim Jong Il. High school students were required to study *The Ruhnama*, Niyazov's book of personal and spiritual wisdom, described on its official website as being "on par with the Bible and the Koran." The self-declared "Turkmenbashi," or "Leader of all Ethnic Turkmens," Niyazov had his image plastered on billboards and buildings across the country, as well as on the national currency, salt packets, and vodka bottles. He named after himself not only a town but an entire month of the year (the one we unenlightened non-Turkmen still call January). Any opposition to the Turkmen government is considered to be treason, and thousands of political dissidents have been imprisoned. In 2004 a man seeking permission to hold a peaceful demonstration was sent to a psychiatric hospital for two years.

Following Niyazov's demise, Minister of Health Kurbanguly Berdy-mukhamedov, the Turkmenbashi's personal dentist, became acting president.[2] He had been responsible, according to the BBC, for implementing

---

[2]Berdymukhamedov was relatively unknown when he was declared acting president. Some have speculated that he is the Turkmenbashi's illegitimate son, which would explain his unexpected ascendancy.

Niyazov's 2004 reform of the health service, "which many observers have blamed for its near collapse." Berdymukhamedov was confirmed as president in an election held in February—he ran against five other candidates, all from the ruling party, and won 89 percent of the vote—in a balloting that he described as being held "on a democratic basis that has been laid by the great [late] leader," but which just about everyone else deemed to be a sham. ("[H]is victory was always certain . . . and all official structures worked to ensure the outcome," the International Crisis Group said of Berdymukhamedov's triumph at the polls.) In an early interview after becoming president, he said that Niyazov was his role model; as for democracy, he said, "This tender substance cannot be imposed by applying ready imported models. It can be only carefully nurtured by using the wise national experience and traditions of previous generations." He has allowed two new Internet cafés to open in Ashgabat, but business has reportedly been poor, perhaps due to the soldiers posted at the doorways or to the hourly fee, which runs about $10, more than the average Turkmen's daily income.

I would have difficulty passing for Turkmen, I knew, so rather than approaching the firms as a representative of the government itself, I instead would be a consultant for "The Maldon Group," a mysterious (and fictitious) firm that claimed to have a financial stake in improving Turkmenistan's public image. We were, my story ran, a group of private investors involved in the export of natural gas from Turkmenistan to Ukrainian and other Eastern European markets. We felt it would strengthen our business position in Turkmenistan if we could convey to American policymakers and journalists just how heady were the reforms being plotted by the Berdymukhamedov government.[3]

If flacking for Turkmenistan did not in itself trouble the lobbying firms, my description of The Maldon Group was designed to raise a number of bright red flags. Turkmenistan has vast reserves of natural gas, from which it

---

[3]It is not uncommon for lobbying on behalf of foreign governments to be contracted through private firms. Sometimes the firms are apparently acting in their own business interests: for example, a Washington-area construction and real estate company called American Worldwide in 2001 hired Patton Boggs to improve relations between the United States and Angola, where the firm had been pursuing business deals. In other cases, the firms are just cutouts for the regimes in question: when Jefferson Waterman worked for Burma, it was actually paid—in the manner of the German Dye Trust—by a firm called Myanmar Resource Development, which was fronting the country's generals. But it is unclear whether U.S. lobbying firms know, or care about, the difference.

earns about $2 billion per year in export revenues, but the whole business has been marked by flagrant corruption—as can be ascertained very quickly by anyone who cares to perform a Google search. A 2006 study by London-based Global Witness reported that Niyazov kept billions of dollars in gas revenues under his effective control in overseas accounts. "Perhaps the murkiest and most complex aspect of the Turkmen-Ukraine gas trade," the report went on to say,

> is the role of the intermediary companies that have inserted themselves for more than a decade between Turkmenistan, Russia, Ukraine and Europe. These companies have often come out of nowhere, parlaying tiny amounts of start-up capital into billion-dollar deals. Their ultimate beneficial ownership has been hidden behind complex networks of trusts, holding companies and nominee directors and there is almost no public information about where their profits go.

Before approaching the lobbying firms, I made a few minimal preparations. I printed up some Maldon Group business cards, giving myself the name "Kenneth Case" and giving the firm an address at a large office building in London, on Cavendish Square. I purchased a cell phone with a London number. I had a website created for The Maldon Group—just a home page with contact information—and an email account for myself. Then, in mid-February, soon after Berdymukhamedov's ascent, I began contacting various lobbying firms by email, introducing my firm and explaining that we were eager to improve relations between the "newly-elected government of Turkmenistan" and the United States. We required the services of a firm, I said, that could quickly enact a "strategic communications" plan to help us. I hoped that the firms might be willing to meet with me at the end of the month, during a trip I had planned to Washington.

At around three on a pleasantly warm February afternoon, Barry Schumacher, a senior vice president at APCO Associates, ushered me into a conference room at the firm's downtown Washington office, near the intersection of 12th and H Streets N.W. Accompanying me was "Ricardo," a Spanish-born Maldon Group consultant (in actuality, a friend I had recruited to come along, since it seemed unlikely that a firm like mine would send a single associate to meet with potential lobbying firms). APCO was the first firm I had contacted, because it was such a natural candidate to represent Turkmeni-stan: it has experience working not just on behalf of authoritarian regimes in general—the dictatorship of General Sani Abacha in Nigeria, for example, which employed the firm in 1995, the same year it hanged nine democracy activists—but for Caspian regimes in particular, having done P.R. work for the oil-rich kleptocracy of Azerbaijan.

APCO, Schumacher had written eagerly to me by email, had "worked on image, policy, foreign investment and reputation issues for a host of govern-ments." He touted the firm's "key professionals," among them former mem-bers of Congress and former administration officials. In a follow-up note, he did ask if I might provide a bit more information about The Maldon Group, since, for obvious reasons, he hadn't been able to discover anything about it. "We prefer to be discreet due to the sensitivity of our business," I replied. Schumacher understood; he even volunteered that APCO would be "more than willing to sign a confidentiality agreement." I assured him that if we were to proceed to the stage of contract negotiations, The Maldon Group would "certainly be able to satisfy any reasonable concerns" about our ability to pay, but until then, I wrote, "we're not prepared to share much more than what I've already told you at the level of preliminary conversations." To which Schumacher promptly replied, "I understand, and this is not unusual for us."

Now, as Ricardo and I entered the meeting room, three of Schumacher's colleagues rose from their seats around a conference table to greet us. There was Elizabeth Jones, a former assistant secretary of state for Europe and Eura-sia until 2005 and an ex-ambassador to Kazakhstan; Robert Downen, a pro-fessorial type in a shirt and tie who had previously served as a senior aide to Senator Robert Dole and was a fellow at the Center for Strategic & Interna-tional Studies; and, in a pinstriped suit, Jennifer Millerwise Dyck, a former spokeswoman for the CIA (where, I later read in her biography I received that day, she "initiated the agency's first coordinated corporate branding and ad-vertising strategy") and for Vice President Dick Cheney.

The conference room, located just past the reception desk, was bland and sparsely decorated. A coffeepot and a black plastic tray of cookies lay on a coun-tertop just across from where I sat. After offering us refreshments, Schumacher commenced with a PowerPoint slide show, which he projected onto a wall. One of the first slides was called "Soft Soundings," and it ran through what Schu-macher described as a "vox populi of policymakers" on the subject of Turk-menistan, gleaned from interviews conducted by him and his colleagues in preparing for the meeting with The Maldon Group. Now is "Turkmenistan's most important moment since independence," read one quote, attributed to an unnamed foundation fellow. "No one is looking for perfection on democracy and human rights reforms," read a second sounding, this one from an administration official. I wagged my head, encouraged by this welcome news.

"This really is an opportunity to define the new government of Turkmenistan," Schumacher said, and at this point Jones took over. After speaking with her former colleagues at the State Department, she said, she had concluded that the Bush Administration was hoping to improve relations with the Berdymukhamedov government. Her contacts at State weren't expecting "miracles" in terms of political reform; even a few small steps, like the new Internet cafés, would provide some "good hooks" APCO could use to promote the regime.

"People like Beth can call up these policymakers," Schumacher said with a shake of the head, as if he himself were in awe of Jones's access. "Getting information like that with a couple of phone calls is priceless." Schumacher said he had made calls of his own and had learned from a staff director at "a key committee" that hearings on the topic of energy security were coming up. "Turkmenistan has a role to play here and [that] helps us talk about it in a positive way," he said. "It's another hook."

In addition to the core team around the table, Schumacher stressed, APCO had on hand a number of other heavies who could be called upon to assist the Turkmenistan campaign. These included former Senator Don Riegle, who, Schumacher said, was tight with Senate Majority Leader Harry Reid; and former Congressman Don Bonker, who had close ties with Tom Lantos, the new Democratic chairman of the House Foreign Affairs Committee. But what about the Republican side? I asked with concern. Schumacher assured me that the firm had access to people in both parties, "not because we've contributed money" (though APCO employees, I subsequently discovered, had contributed more than $100,000 during the last three election cycles) but because of the high esteem in which the firm's stable of former officials was generally held. And, he added with a grin, Dyck had such strong ties to the G.O.P. that she alone was "worth six" of APCO's Democratic lobbyists.

"What can I say?" Dyck crowed, throwing her arms out.

Turning to media strategy, Schumacher presented APCO's broad review of the coverage. The bad news: almost all mentions of Turkmenistan were negative. On the upside, there wasn't very much coverage to speak of. Now was the time to strike. Wasn't he worried, I asked, that the Turkmen regime would be held to impossibly high human-rights standards? Schumacher sought to put my mind at ease. With any P.R. campaign there were bound to be "isolated incidents that look bad, and it's up to the communications company to figure out a way to be honest about them, to react and to put them in proper perspective, to make sure they don't derail the campaign." On the other hand, he allowed that something "really terrible"—the words dangled in the air—would be hard to overcome.

There was also the nagging question of public disclosure. Yes, Schumacher said, APCO would have to register and The Maldon Group would need to provide some additional information at that time, but there was no need to lose sleep about that. "We live up to the spirit and letter of the law, but we would provide minimal information," he said. "[We'd] say we're working for The Maldon Group on behalf of the government and would file semi-annual reports. And that's it."

But what if we get calls from journalists? I asked.

"If they call you," Jones said with a big smile, "refer them to us."

Later in the presentation, a slide revealed the proposed budget for APCO's Turkmenistan operation: $40,000 per month, plus expenses (estimated at about 10 percent of fees), and more for any travel outside of Washington. Paid advertising and special events would cost extra, and Schumacher proposed that we set up a new website for the Turkmen embassy in Washington, which would cost The Maldon Group another $35,000.[4] In total, getting out our message about a new and improved Turkmenistan would require about $600,000 over the first year.

What would we get for our money? APCO's strategy was laid out on a slide entitled "Elements of a Communications Program," of which there were four. The first was "policy maker outreach," and thanks to its political contacts, APCO would have no problem here. "Anyone who tells you they can get a congressman to do what you want ought not to be believed, but we can get in the door and make the case," Schumacher said.

---

[4]This, admittedly, would be money well spent. The "Latest News" on the embassy's current website dates to September 18, 2000, and includes one item about a phone conversation between the Turkmenbashi and the president of Uzbekistan and another that reads, "On virgin lands cotton is harvested with machines."

APCO would easily be able to arrange meetings between Turkmen officials and key members of Congress, and might be able to organize a fact-finding trip to the country as well. Given the recent scandal surrounding the lobbyist Jack Abramoff, it would be difficult and even unwise for The Maldon Group to sponsor a congressional trip directly, Schumacher said, but there would surely be official delegations traveling to the region, and "we have the contacts to urge them to stop there."

Downen stepped in here, suggesting it was premature to rule out the possibility of organizing a private junket to Turkmenistan for a crew from Congress. True, The Maldon Group shouldn't organize it directly, but he'd had personal experience with academic groups sponsoring trips. "Maybe Turkmenistan has a think tank or university," he offered. "Under the old rules, any bona fide academic institution could sponsor [travel]. Under the new rules I'm not sure, but I can check."[5]

The second element of the strategy was a "media campaign." In a slide entitled "Core Media Relations Activities," APCO promised to "create news items and news outflow," organize media events, and identify and work with "key reporters." As this was her field of expertise, Dyck presented this slide. The media would be receptive to stories about Turkmenistan with the change of government, she said, plus "energy security is an additional hook. We can also bring things like Internet cafés to their attention."

In addition to influencing news reports, Downen added, the firm could drum up positive op-eds in newspapers. "We can utilize some of the think-tank experts who would say, 'On the one hand this and the other hand that,' and we place it as a guest editorial." Indeed, Schumacher said, APCO had someone on staff who "does nothing but that" and had succeeded in placing thousands of opinion pieces.

Discussion about the strategy's third item—building "coalition support," which meant developing seemingly independent and therefore more credible allies to offer favorable views about Turkmenistan—was brief. As a slide on the topic put it, we would need to start small, given that the "closed

---

[5]Indeed, such a trip can be arranged under the rules passed by Congress earlier this year. These rules say that lobbying firms cannot pay for or arrange for congressional travel—with three exceptions: one-day trips, travel paid for by nonprofit groups, and travel paid for by universities. So The Maldon Group's very own congressional delegation to Turkmenistan would essentially be ready for boarding as soon as APCO found a Turkmen university willing to officially sponsor it.

nature of country has inhibited investment and exchanges." For now, the best coalition partners would be current and potential corporate investors in Turkmenistan, as well as "think tank experts and academics."

How could we use think tanks and academics? I wondered. "I'm glad you asked," Schumacher said with a chuckle. He flipped to the next slide, which discussed the fourth element of the campaign: "events." One possibility, Downen said, would be to hold a forum on U.S.-Turkmen relations, preferably built around a visit to the United States by a Turkmen official. Possible hosts would include the Heritage Foundation, the Center for Strategic & International Studies, and the Council on Foreign Relations. "Last week I contacted a number of colleagues at think tanks," Downen went on. "Some real experts could easily be engaged to sponsor or host a public forum or panel that would bring in congressional staff and journalists." The only cost would be refreshments and room rental—Schumacher joked that APCO would bake the cookies to save The Maldon Group a little money—and could yield a tremendous payoff. "If we can get a paper published or a speech at a conference, we can get a friendly member of Congress to insert that in the *Congressional Record* and get that printed and send it out," Schumacher said. "So you take one event and get it multiplied."

Another option, he explained, would be to pay *Roll Call* and *The Economist* to host a Turkmenistan event. It would be costlier than the think-tank route, perhaps around $25,000, but in compensation we would have tighter control over the proceedings, plus gain "the imprimatur of a respected third party." In order that the event not seem like paid advertising, the title for the event should be "bigger than your theme," Schumacher explained, even as it would be put together in a way "that you get your message across."

So we wouldn't call it "Turkmenistan Day"? I asked.

No, Schumacher replied. "Energy Security" would be a better theme.

"Or 'Caspian Basin Pipelines,'" Jones added.

"That's how you do it," Schumacher said. The Maldon Group wouldn't have its own speaker on the dais, but APCO would line up a few people—possibilities included an administration official or an executive from an American firm involved in Turkmenistan—to speak for us. While promising reform was important, we would probably want to focus on matters like energy and regional security. "In a world where the administration wants some realism, there may be ways to get positive messages out," Schumacher said. A concluding slide laid out the broad benefits that The Maldon Group could expect to see for our $600,000. These included raising Turkmenistan's profile "as a nation important to the United States," building a "broader base of support" for the country, and improving media coverage. After a series of firm handshakes, I promised I would be back in touch as soon as I had consulted with my superiors in London.

The following morning, Ricardo and I headed to the offices of Cassidy & Associates, perhaps the most prominent of all the Washington lobby shops. It was founded thirty-two years ago by Gerald Cassidy, a former staffer for George McGovern, and for much of its existence was known as a strongly Democratic firm. Cassidy pioneered the practice of lobbying for earmarks—the polite term for pork—but also represents Fortune 500 corporations as well as foreign countries and businesses. Its current clients include Teodoro Obiang, who has ruled the small African nation of Equatorial Guinea since 1979, when he executed his uncle. Between 1998 and 2006, Cassidy was paid more than $235 million in lobbying fees, more than any other firm in Washington.

Cassidy's headquarters are just a block away from APCO's but are far more elegant. The firm occupies the entire fourth floor of its building, so that one enters the offices upon exiting the elevator. A receptionist walked Ricardo and me into a large conference room with a beautiful wood table polished to a bright sheen. There were about twenty seats around the table, and eight settings had been laid out with a glass, each set atop a paper coaster embossed with the firm's name. The table held an assortment of canned soft drinks, a pitcher of ice water with lemon slices, a cup of sharpened pencils, and a pile of yellow legal pads.

A phalanx of six Cassidy officials soon entered the conference room, all dressed in elegant business attire of varying shades of black, gray, and navy blue. There was Chuck Dolan, a former senior P.R. consultant for the Kerry-Edwards campaign; Gordon Speed, the firm's pudgy, baby-faced director of business development; tall, thin Gerald Warburg, a former Hill staffer and company vice president; Christy Moran, who during the meeting told me she had previously worked for Saudi Arabia and helped boost its image with an "allies program" that sent visitors to the country; and David Bartlett, another P.R. specialist whose firm biography said he had helped corporate CEOs "face the nation's toughest journalists."

The sixth member of the Cassidy team, and its clear leader, was firm vice chairman Gregg Hartley, who with his crew cut and serious manner initially reminded me of a drill sergeant, but soon he loosened up and proved to possess a certain folksy appeal. Until 2003 he had been a top aide to then House Majority Whip Roy Blunt, and he maintains close ties to top Republicans in Congress. When Hartley quit his Hill job and decided to become a lobbyist, a "bidding war for his services ensued," the *Washington Post* later reported. "Cassidy . . . won it with an offer of just under $1 million a year," plus a "substantial percentage" of the lobbying fees Hartley generated. Hartley's hiring marked a key moment in Cassidy & Associates' transformation during the past decade into a lobbying enterprise that is increasingly identified with the Republican Party.

As was the case with APCO, Cassidy had immediately offered to meet with me. In an initial phone conversation with Speed, Hartley, and Dolan, the three had asked only a few softball questions about The Maldon Group (and, like APCO, offered to sign a confidentiality agreement) before they began their sales pitch. Hartley pointed out that Cassidy's work for Equatorial Guinea was "a very similar sort of representation to what you're talking about" with Turkmenistan. The Obiang regime had received a bit of bad publicity—he mentioned here a banking scandal involving the government—and Cassidy's first job had been "to identify inaccurate or biased stories and try to correct them."[6] Hartley also boasted about Cassidy's political contacts, saying, "We strongly believe in a bipartisan [approach] and mirroring the power structure. . . . You have to find champions on both sides."

Hartley returned to that theme during the meeting at Cassidy's office. His firm, he said after passing Ricardo and me copies of a corporate brochure,[7] had "strong personal relationships" with policymakers, and not just to a committee chairman here and there, as was the case with some of its competitors. Cas-

---

[6] I found this amusing, because he almost certainly was thinking of me: in 2003, while working at the *Los Angeles Times*, I had broken the story of the hundreds of millions of dollars of Equatorial Guinea's oil revenues that were deposited at Riggs Bank in Washington, under Obiang's effective control. A Senate investigation not only confirmed what I had reported but uncovered even more dirt, such as the fact that Obiang and family members had stashed millions of dollars in offshore accounts.

[7] The brochure said that Cassidy offered "A Tradition of Ethics and Integrity that goes to the core of our beliefs" and made the claim, a brazenly cynical one even by the standards of Washington, that Gerald Cassidy had founded the firm "to ensure that Americans have access and the ability to exercise their First Amendment right to petition their government."

sidy had ties across the board—at the staff level, the committee level, the Republican and Democratic leadership, and the administration.

"We know you're talking to other firms," Hartley said pointedly. "You're going to have a hard time matching . . . [the] types of successes" his firm had racked up. For example, thanks to Cassidy's aggressive media strategy and trips it had organized to Equatorial Guinea for congressional staffers, things were now looking up for the government there. The proof: three years ago, Hartley said, *Parade Magazine* had ranked Obiang as "the world's sixth worst dictator," grimacing as he stated that last word. "He's still not a great guy," he went on, "but he's not in the top ten anymore, and we can take some credit for helping them figure out how to work down that list. Is he going to win the U.N. humanitarian award next year? No, he's not, but we're making progress."[8]

Now Warburg took over the meeting. He talked with some passion about two "remarkable lobbying campaigns" that the firm had been involved with, both of which had succeeded in getting the U.S. government to move "against its express will." The first was eliminating a longtime trade embargo against Vietnam, which the firm had achieved over the opposition of the families of POWs and MIAs. The key to success was assembling an outside pressure group called the Multinational Business Development Coalition, which was made up of major American corporations seeking business in Vietnam. "The U.S. had no relations," Warburg said. "We changed that policy, ended the embargo, and opened Vietnam up to U.S. economic exchange."

The second campaign, Warburg said, involved winning permission in 1995 for President Lee Teng-hui of Taiwan to make a private visit to the United States "over the express opposition of the executive branch." At the time, Taiwan's embassy wasn't even allowed to lobby in Washington without permission from the State Department. Evading that obstacle was simple: since the government couldn't retain Cassidy, a Taiwanese think tank fronting for it did. President Bill Clinton had said he wouldn't allow Lee to come to the United States, so Cassidy, Warburg recounted, began a campaign to lobby Congress. After both chambers passed resolutions in support of a visit by Lee, the White House caved. "The president of the United States reversed policy,"

---

[8]When I checked later, the progress seemed pretty modest. Obiang is indeed out of *Parade*'s top ten list for 2007; now he's number eleven. In a brief summary, *Parade* noted that in 2003, "state radio announced that Obiang 'is in permanent contact with The Almighty' and that he 'can decide to kill without anyone calling him to account and without going to Hell.'"

said Warburg. The campaign had been so brilliant, in fact, that graduate students had written theses on it.

Warburg also mentioned his past work for Merhav, an Israeli firm with major interests in Turkmenistan, for which Cassidy had obtained Export-Import Bank financing for a trans-Caspian pipeline. Unlike the case with other lobbying firms The Maldon Group might hire, "We really know Turkmenistan. It wouldn't be on-the-job training for us."

When Warburg had represented Merhav, he met a number of Turkmen officials. "Unfortunately, the previous government had a history of shuffling ministers," he said. "I won't pursue the metaphor." To which Hartley added, "We won't ask where all of them were shuffled!" There was general merriment, which seemed inappropriate, given that sixteen ministers were jailed or sent into internal exile last year, one of whom is believed to have died in prison.

Hartley announced that he and his colleagues had a few questions about The Maldon Group. I would be as helpful as I could, I replied, but discretion was our firm's lifeblood; while it pained me "to look like I'm being evasive," there wasn't much I could say.

"We're going to ask questions, and you may have to throw the wall up," Hartley said. "Don't mention names if you can't mention names."

The questions were quite easy to handle: I did little more than toss out the same scraps of information I had given them before. We were a small group of British, Middle Eastern, and Eastern European investors; we had a close relationship to the government, but there were no Turkmen officials involved in The Maldon Group. I reiterated my concerns about public-disclosure requirements, and Hartley assured me I could rest easy. "We have to disclose who we represent, but there doesn't have to be great detail," he said. "The way we would handle this, there'd be very little about you and virtually none about your investors."

When it was time for the hard sell, Warburg began by giving me a piece of intelligence he had picked up—something, he said, for me to share "with your friends and investors back in England." The previous week, he claimed, there had been a meeting on Turkmenistan at the highest level of the U.S. government. "We'd like to make sure you're on the agenda for the next such meeting," he said pointedly. "We'd like to be involved in prepping the individuals before such a meeting, and we'd like to be involved in interpreting the outcome to your investors, and through you to the government in a way that really empowers you in that market." Hartley, too, sought to emphasize how interested Cassidy was in winning the contract. "This is the sort of thing we do extremely well," he said at one point. "It's the kind of stuff that gets our juices flowing."

Of course, there was the question of money, specifically how much of it The Maldon Group would need to hire Cassidy. For Turkmenistan, Hartley said, there could be no quick, easy solutions; hence, he proposed a three-year effort at from $1.2 million to $1.5 million annually—and that could run higher, he warned, if a do-gooder organization like a human-rights group targeted the regime, necessitating intensified spin control by the firm's lobbyists. "You've looked at our bios," he said. "Look at our track record and what we've charged for other representations . . . and you'll see you're not being gouged."

While insisting that I didn't write the checks, I said the figure seemed reasonable to me.

"Others will do it for less, but you won't get people with our experience, our knowledge of Turkmenistan, our ties to [the] State [Department], National Security Council, and some parts of the intelligence community," Warburg said.

Cassidy saw its strategy as having two central prongs, one targeting policymakers and the other targeting the media. Among the questions I'd asked had been whether it was advisable to arrange a trip to Turkmenistan for members of Congress. Hartley said that it was, but it would be critical to pick "the right members of Congress," which he defined as those with "a leaning that will be instrumental in us making progress on our representation." As at APCO, the Cassidy team said that the post-Abramoff climate would make it harder to arrange a private trip for members of Congress—"but not impossible," in Hartley's words. In the meantime, a less visible trip for Hill staffers could be more easily accomplished.

Bringing Turkmen officials to Washington was also a must, though we needed to be realistic. If The Maldon Group said it wanted Berdymukhamedov to address a joint session of Congress, Cassidy would tell you that's not possible, Warburg said. On the other hand, might Cassidy be able to arrange "a coffee in the Senate Foreign Relations hearing room of the U.S. Capitol where the foreign minister is warmly received?" Yes, it very well might.

Also, The Maldon Group should not underestimate the value of arranging a trip to Turkmenistan for journalists and think-tank analysts, which was something Dolan said he had done for the Valdai International Discussion Club, a group funded by Russian interests that offers all-expenses-paid trips to Russia. Amid the general pampering, the Western academics and reporters who attend are granted audiences with senior Russian political figures. During the meeting, Dolan simply described it as a way to give people "firsthand information" and mentioned that past attendees had included Ariel Cohen of the Heritage Foundation, Marshall Goldman of Harvard, and Jim Hoagland of the *Washington Post*.[9] A similar program might work for Turkmenistan, he suggested.

Two weeks after the meeting, Cassidy laid out more of its strategic thinking in a twelve-page proposal that it sent to me by email. The firm's lobbyists would educate senior government officials and opinion makers "on positive developments taking place in Turkmenistan," and would sell the country on the basis of its "strategic importance in Central Asia" and the "critical role" it could play in American energy security. Cassidy's preliminary research already had determined that there was "accelerated interest" in Turkmenistan "at the highest levels of the U.S. government." This was a great opportunity, since it would make it easier to reach out to government officials as well as the media, but it also presented a challenge, as "greater attention can bring greater scrutiny."

Of course, "attention" and "scrutiny" are essentially synonymous; the only reason that more of it posed a challenge to Cassidy's proposed lobbying campaign was that in the case of Turkmenistan, the truth was almost never good. Cassidy had, in fact, already uncovered troubling news: "We have become aware," the proposal said ominously, "of U.S. determination to aggressively push an agenda of human rights and democratic reforms in exchange for greater engagement with Ashgabat." (This supposed discovery was surely

---

[9]After returning from his Valdai trip last year, Hoagland wrote a critical but not entirely unflattering piece about Vladimir Putin, whom he and other junketeers had met "at his sprawling dacha in suburban Moscow." The Russian president had taken questions from the group "between servings of octopus carpaccio, baked sea bass and figs with yogurt sorbet, all prepared by his Italian chef and washed down by an unassuming pinot grigio." Other Valdai Club members have been even more cooperative. Soon after returning from his Valdai-sponsored excursion, Cohen co-authored an essay that called on Congress to approve Permanent Normal Trade Relations with Russia, saying that successful approval of such legislation would be "an important step in strengthening the U.S.-Russia economic relationship." Unlike Hoagland, he didn't mention anything about who sponsored his vacation.

a scare tactic. The Bush Administration has openly prioritized trade and business promotion, not human rights, with other major Caspian energy producers. According to a well-placed source, State Department officials have made it very clear that the Bush Administration's major policy goal in Turkmenistan is opening the country to investment by U.S. energy firms.) To deal with the threat of scrutiny, Cassidy would seek to drive "the story being told about Turkmenistan by the media, rather than merely reacting to it. By engaging with correspondents, we will coordinate a global message about political, social and economic progress."

As part of this initiative, the firm would plant pro-Turkmenistan op-eds from friendly authors it recruited. Cassidy would also put together "a list of potential vulnerabilities, such as humanitarian issues, social conditions and otherwise. . . . With these issues in mind, we will conduct 'worst-case' scenario planning and response development by anticipating crises, preparing spokespeople, [and] drafting statements." In other words, Cassidy would have an emergency-response network in place should, for example, opposition members happen to be mowed down by government guns. "We will be your eyes and ears in Washington, D.C.," the proposal said.

In the weeks after my meetings, both APCO and Cassidy contacted me, eager to carry out the Turkmen campaign. I replied with notes of regret, explaining that The Maldon Group was unsure about how to proceed but that for the time being, at least, their services would not be required. Still, it was hard not to daydream about what might have been accomplished for the "newly elected government of Turkmenistan" if I'd actually had the few million dollars to spare. In May, I attended "Angola Day," an all-day conference that had been organized on behalf of the regime of President José Eduardo Dos Santos, which, while not equaling the Turkmen rulers in flair, is nevertheless one of the most crooked and predatory in the world. Angola Day's sponsors included the Woodrow Wilson International Center for Scholars, which hosted the event at its downtown headquarters, the Angolan government, and the U.S.-Angola Chamber of Commerce, which receives financial support from American oil companies.

It was impossible to say whether a lobbying firm was directly involved in orchestrating the event. But other than its unfortunate title—had APCO been running the show, it would have been something like "Africa and American Energy Security: Partners in Prosperity"—Angola Day was straight out of the playbooks laid out for Turkmenistan: it had the imprimatur of a respected third party (the Wilson Center), a coalition of corporate allies, and a smattering of pliant academics and officials who seemed more than willing to pen a friendly op-ed if need be. The keynote speaker was Joaquim David, Angola's elegantly tailored industry minister, and as I watched him deliver his address, it was hard not to think of a Turkmen official on that same dais, giving voice to the same empty slogans and catchwords, speaking (as David did) of his government's commitment to sustainable development, environmental protection, and social justice—despite the fact that Dos Santos has done absolutely nothing to demonstrate these commitments. I was especially wistful during the coffee break, when I could see the real business of the conference being conducted. Here was Witney Schneidman, a former State Department official and member of the U.S.-Angola Chamber, approaching every Angolan official he saw with an unctuous ear-to-ear grin on his face; Hank Cohen, a former assistant secretary of state and former lobbyist for Angola, chatting up the diamond magnate Maurice Tempelsman; a Chevron executive and an official from the U.S. Agency for International Development, greeting each other like long-lost friends.

It was a vision of just how regimes like Angola and Azerbaijan, Nigeria and Equatorial Guinea, the serial abrogators of "human dignity," can make and keep their wealthy American friends. Someday soon, perhaps, the same will happen for Turkmenistan—God and lobbyists willing.

July 2007

Jesus Plus Nothing

Undercover Among America's Secret Theocrats

JEFF SHARLET

And a man's foes shall be they of his own household.
—Matthew 10:36

This is how they pray: a dozen clear-eyed, smooth-skinned "brothers" gathered together in a huddle, arms crossing arms over shoulders like the weave of a cable, leaning in on one another and swaying like the long grass up the hill from the house they share. The house is a handsome, gray, two-story colonial that smells of new carpet and Pine-Sol and aftershave; the men who live there call it Ivanwald. At the end of a tree-lined cul-de-sac, quiet but for the buzz of lawn mowers and kids playing foxes-and-hounds in the park across the road, Ivanwald sits as one house among many, clustered together like mushrooms, all devoted, like these men, to the service of Jesus Christ. The men tend every tulip in the cul-de-sac, trim every magnolia, seal every driveway smooth and black as boot leather. And they pray, assembled at the dining table or on their lawn or in the hallway or in the bunk room or on the basketball court, each man's head bowed in humility and swollen with pride (secretly, he thinks) at being counted among such a fine corps for Christ, among men to whom he will open his heart and whom he will remember when he returns to the world not born-again but remade, no longer an individual but part of the Lord's revolution, his will transformed into a weapon for what the young men call "spiritual war."

"Jeff, will you lead us in prayer?"

Surely, brother. It is April 2002, and I have lived with these men for weeks now, not as a Christian—a term they deride as too narrow for the world they are building in Christ's honor—but as a "believer." I have shared the brothers' meals and their work and their games. I have been numbered among them and have been given a part in their ministry. I have wrestled with them and showered with them and listened to their stories: I know which man resents his father's fortune and which man succumbed to the flesh of a woman not once but twice and which man dances so well he is afraid of being taken for a fag. I know what it means to be a "brother," which is to say that I know what it means to be a soldier in the army of God.

"Heavenly Father," I begin. Then, "O Lord," but I worry that this doesn't sound intimate enough. I settle on, "Dear Jesus." "Dear Jesus, just, please, Jesus, let us fight for Your name."

Ivanwald, which sits at the end of Twenty-fourth Street North in Arlington, Virginia, is known only to its residents and to the members and friends of the organization that sponsor it, a group of believers who refer to themselves as "the Family." The Family is, in its own words, an "invisible" association, though its membership has always consisted mostly of public men. Senators Don Nickles (R., Okla.), Charles Grassley (R., Iowa), Pete Domenici (R., N.Mex.), John Ensign (R., Nev.), James Inhofe (R., Okla.), Bill Nelson (D., Fla.), and Conrad Burns (R., Mont.) are referred to as "members," as are Representatives Jim DeMint (R., S.C.), Frank Wolf (R., Va.), Joseph Pitts (R., Pa.), Zach Wamp (R., Tenn.), and Bart Stupak (D., Mich.). Regular prayer groups have met in the Pentagon and at the Department of Defense, and the Family has traditionally fostered strong ties with businessmen in the oil and aerospace industries. The Family maintains a closely guarded database of its associates, but it issues no cards, collects no official dues. Members are asked not to speak about the group or its activities.

The organization has operated under many guises, some active, some defunct: National Committee for Christian Leadership, International Christian Leadership, the National Leadership Council, Fellowship House, the Fellowship Foundation, the National Fellowship Council, the International Foundation. These groups are intended to draw attention away from the Family, and to prevent it from becoming, in the words of one of the Family's leaders, "a target for misunderstanding."[1] The Family's only publicized gathering is the National Prayer Breakfast, which it established in 1953 and which, with congressional sponsorship, it continues to organize every February in Washington, D.C. Each year 3,000 dignitaries, representing scores of nations, pay $425 each to attend. Steadfastly ecumenical, too bland most years to merit much press, the breakfast is regarded by the Family as merely a tool in a larger purpose: to recruit the powerful attendees into smaller, more frequent prayer meetings, where they can "meet Jesus man to man."

In the process of introducing powerful men to Jesus, the Family has managed to effect a number of behind-the-scenes acts of diplomacy. In 1978 it secretly helped the Carter Administration organize a worldwide call to prayer with Menachem Begin and Anwar Sadat, and more recently, in 2001, it brought together the warring leaders of Congo and Rwanda for a clandestine meeting, leading to the two sides' eventual peace accord last July. Such benign acts appear to be the exception to the rule. During the 1960s the Family forged relationships between the U.S. government and some of the most anticommunist (and dictatorial) elements within Africa's postcolonial leadership. The Brazilian dictator General Costa e Silva, with Family support, was overseeing regular fellowship groups for Latin American leaders, while, in Indonesia, General Suharto (whose tally of several hundred thousand "Communists" killed marks him as one of the century's most murderous dictators) was presiding over a group of fifty Indonesian legislators. During the Reagan Administration the Family helped build friendships between the U.S. government and men such as Salvadoran general Carlos Eugenios Vides Casanova, convicted by a Florida jury of the torture of

---

[1]The *Los Angeles Times* reported in September that the Fellowship Foundation alone has an annual budget of $10 million, but that represents only a fraction of the Family's finances. Each of the Family's organizations raises funds independently. Ivanwald, for example, is financed at least in part by an entity called the Wilberforce Foundation. Other projects are financed by individual "friends": wealthy businessmen, foreign governments, church congregations, or mainstream foundations that may be unaware of the scope of the Family's activities. At Ivanwald, when I asked to what organization a donation check might be made, I was told there was none; money was raised on a "man-to-man" basis. Major Family donors named by the *Times* include Michael Timmis, a Detroit lawyer and Republican fund-raiser; Paul Temple, a private investor from Maryland; and Jerome A. Lewis, former CEO of the Petro-Lewis Corporation.

thousands, and Honduran general Gustavo Alvarez Martinez, himself an evangelical minister, who was linked to both the CIA and death squads before his own demise. "We work with power where we can," the Family's leader, Doug Coe, says, "build new power where we can't."

At the 1990 National Prayer Breakfast, George H.W. Bush praised Doug Coe for what he described as "quiet diplomacy, I wouldn't say secret diplomacy," as an "ambassador of faith." Coe has visited nearly every world capital, often with congressmen at his side, "making friends" and inviting them back to the Family's unofficial headquarters, a mansion (just down the road from Ivanwald) that the Family bought in 1978 with $1.5 million donated by, among others, Tom Phillips, then the C.E.O. of arms manufacturer Raytheon, and Ken Olsen, the founder and president of Digital Equipment Corporation. A waterfall has been carved into the mansion's broad lawn, from which a bronze bald eagle watches over the Potomac River. The mansion is white and pillared and surrounded by magnolias, and by red trees that do not so much tower above it as whisper. The mansion is named for these trees; it is called The Cedars, and Family members speak of it as a person. "The Cedars has a heart for the poor," they like to say. By "poor" they mean not the thousands of literal poor living barely a mile away but rather the poor *in spirit*, for theirs is the kingdom: the senators, generals, and prime ministers who coast to the end of Twenty-fourth Street in Arlington in black limousines and town cars and hulking S.U.V.'s to meet one another, to meet Jesus, to pay homage to the god of The Cedars.

There they forge "relationships" beyond the din of vox populi (the Family's leaders consider democracy a manifestation of ungodly pride) and "throw away religion" in favor of the truths of the Family. Declaring God's covenant with the Jews broken, the group's core members call themselves "the new chosen."

The brothers of Ivanwald are the Family's next generation, its high priests in training. I had been recommended for membership by a banker acquaintance, a recent Ivanwald alumnus, who had mistaken my interest in Jesus for belief. Sometimes the brothers would ask me why I was there. They knew that I was "half Jewish," that I was a writer, and that I was from New York City, which most of them considered to be only slightly less wicked than Baghdad or Amsterdam. I told my brothers that I was there to meet Jesus, and I was: the new ruling Jesus, whose ways are secret.

.   .   .

At Ivanwald, men learn to be leaders by loving their leaders. "They're so busy loving us," a brother once explained to me, "but who's loving them?" We were. The brothers each paid $400 per month for room and board, but we were also the caretakers of The Cedars, cleaning its gutters, mowing its lawns, whacking weeds and blowing leaves and sanding. And we were called to serve on Tuesday mornings, when The Cedars hosted a regular prayer breakfast typically presided over by Ed Meese, the former attorney general. Each week the breakfast brought together a rotating group of ambassadors, businessmen, and American politicians. Three of Ivanwald's brothers also attended, wearing crisp shirts starched just for the occasion; one would sit at the table while the other two poured coffee.

The morning I attended, Charlene, the cook, scrambled up eggs with blue tortillas, Italian sausage, red pepper, and papaya. Three women from Potomac Point, an "Ivanwald for girls" across the road from The Cedars, came to help serve. They wore red lipstick and long skirts (makeup and "feminine" attire were required) and had, after several months of cleaning and serving in The Cedars while the brothers worked outside, become quite unimpressed by the high-powered clientele. "Girls don't sit in on the breakfasts," one of them told me, though she said that none of them minded because it was "just politics."

The breakfast began with a prayer and a sprinkle of scripture from Meese, who sat at the head of the table. Matthew 11:27: "No one knows the Son except the Father, and no one knows the Father except the Son and those to whom the Son chooses to reveal him." That morning's chosen introduced themselves. They were businessmen from Dallas and Oregon, a Chinese Christian dissident, a man who ran an aid group for Tibetan refugees (the Dalai Lama had been very positive on Jesus at their last meeting, he reported). Two ambassadors, from Benin and Rwanda, sat side by side. Rwanda's representative, Dr. Richard Sezibera, was an intense man who refused to eat his eggs or even any melon. He drank cup after cup of coffee, and his eyes were bloodshot. A man I didn't recognize, whom Charlene identified as a former senator, suggested that negotiators from Rwanda and Congo, trapped in a war that has slain more than 2 million, should stop worrying about who will get the diamonds and the oil and instead focus on who will get Jesus. "Power sharing is not going to work unless we change their hearts," he said.

Sezibera stared, incredulous. Meese chuckled and opened his mouth to speak, but Sezibera interrupted him. "It is not so simple," the Rwandan said, his voice flat and low. Meese smiled. Everyone in the Family loves rebukes, and here was Rwanda rebuking them. The former senator nodded. Meese murmured, "Yes," stroking his maroon leather Bible, and the words "Thank you, Jesus" rippled in whispers around the table as I poured Sezibera another cup of coffee.

The brothers also served at the Family's four-story, redbrick Washington town house, a former convent at 133 C Street S.E. complete with stained-glass windows. Eight congressmen—including Senator Ensign and seven representatives[2]—lived there, brothers in Christ just like us, only more powerful. We scrubbed their toilets, hoovered their carpets, polished their silver. The day I worked at C Street I ran into Doug Coe, who was tutoring Todd Tiahrt, a Republican congressman from Kansas. A friendly, plainspoken man with a bright, lazy smile, Coe has worked for the Family since 1959, soon after he graduated from college, and has led it since 1969.

Tiahrt was a short shot glass of a man, two parts flawless hair and one part teeth. He wanted to know the best way "for the Christian to win the race with the Muslim." The Muslim, he said, has too many babies, while Americans kill too many of theirs.

Doug agreed this could be a problem. But he was more concerned that the focus on labels like "Christian" might get in the way of the congressman's prayers. Religion distracts people from Jesus, Doug said, and allows them to isolate Christ's will from their work in the world.

"People separate it out," he warned Tiahrt. "'Oh, okay, I got religion, that's private.' As if Jesus doesn't know anything about building highways, or Social Security. We gotta take Jesus out of the religious wrapping."

"All right, how do we do that?" Tiahrt asked.

"A covenant," Doug answered. The congressman half-smiled, as if caught between confessing his ignorance and pretending he knew what Doug was talking about. "Like the Mafia," Doug clarified. "Look at the strength of their bonds." He made a fist and held it before Tiahrt's face. Tiahrt nodded, squinting. "See, for them it's honor," Doug said. "For us, it's Jesus."

---

[2]According to the *Los Angeles Times*, congressmen who have lived there include Rep. Mike Doyle (D., Pa.), former Rep. Ed Bryant (R., Tenn.), and former Rep. John Elias Baldacci (D., Maine). The house's eight congressman-tenants each pay $600 per month in rent for use of a town house that includes nine bathrooms and five living rooms. When the *Times* asked then-resident Rep. Bart Stupak (D., Mich.) about the property, he replied, "We sort of don't talk to the press about the house."

Coe listed other men who had changed the world through the strength of the covenants they had forged with their "brothers": "Look at Hitler," he said. "Lenin, Ho Chi Minh, bin Laden." The Family, of course, possessed a weapon those leaders lacked: the "total Jesus" of a brotherhood in Christ.

"*That's* what you get with a covenant," said Coe. "Jesus plus nothing."

To the Family, Jesus is not just a name; he is also a real man. "An awesome guy," a Family employee named Terry told the brothers over breakfast one morning. "He excelled in every activity. He was a great teacher, sure, but he was also a real guy's guy. He would have made an *excellent* athlete."

On my first day at Ivanwald, on an uneven court behind the house, I learned to play a two-ball variant of basketball called "bump" that was designed to sharpen both body and soul. In bump, players compete at free throws, each vying to sink his own before the man behind him sinks his. If he hits first then you're out, with one exception: the basket's net narrows at the chute so that the ball sometimes sticks, at which point another player can hurl his ball up from beneath, knocking the first ball out. In this event everyone cries "*Bu-u-ump*," with great joy.

Bengt began it. He was one of the house's leaders, a twenty-four-year-old North Carolinian with sad eyes and spiky eyebrows and a loud, disarming laugh that made him sound like a donkey. From inside the house, waiting for a phone call, he opened a second-floor window and called to Gannon for a ball. Gannon, the son of a Texas oilman, worked as a Senate aide[3]; he had blond hair and a chin like a plow, and he sang in a choir. He tossed one up, which Bengt caught and dispatched toward the basket. "Nice," Gannon drawled as the ball sank through.

As soon as the ball bounced off the rim, Beau was at the free-throw line, taking his shot. Beau was a good-natured Atlantan with the build of a wrestler; as a bumper he was second only to Bengt.

"It's okay if you bump into the other guys, too," Gannon told me as my turn approached. "The idea's kinda to get that tension building." Ahead of me Beau bent his knees to take another shot. The moment the ball rolled off his fingers, Wayne, also from Georgia, jumped up and hurled his own ball over

[3]Gannon worked for Senator Don Nickles, then the second-ranking Republican. The man who oversaw Ivanwald and interviewed us for admission was a lawyer named Steve South, who formerly had been Senator Nickles's chief counsel and was still a close associate.

Beau's head. As he returned to earth, his elbow descended on Beau's shoulder like a hammer. "Bump *that*," he said.

Bump was designed to bring out your hostilities. The Family believes that you can't grow in Jesus unless you "face your anger," and then abandon it. When bump worked right, each man was supposed to lose himself, forgetting even the precepts of the game. Sometimes you wanted to get the ball in, sometimes you wanted to knock it out. In, out, it didn't matter. Your ball, his, who cared? Bump wasn't horseplay, it was a physicalized theology. It was to basketball what the New Testament is to the Old: stripped down to one simple story that always ends the same. Bump, Jesus. Bump, Jesus.

I stepped to the line and, after missing, moved in for a layup. Wayne jumped to the line and shot. "Dude!" he shouted. I looked up. His ball, meant to hit mine, slammed into my forehead. *Bu-u-ump!* the boys hollered. They had bumped me with Christ.

Bengt bumped. Beau bumped. Gannon bumped. I was out of contention. Gannon joined me, then Beau. The game was down to Bengt and Wayne. When Wayne threw from behind Bengt, he hurled the ball with such force that it sent Bengt chasing his ball into the neighboring yard. "Tenacious Wayne!" Gannon roared. Wayne scooped up his own ball, leapt, and slam-dunked Bengt out. "That's yo motha!" he hollered.

Trotting back to the court, Bengt shook his head. "You the man, Wayne," he said. "Just keep it calm." Wayne was ready to burst.

"Huddle up guys," said Bengt. We formed a circle, arms wrapped around shoulders. "Okay," he said. "We're gonna pray now. Lord, I just want to thank you for bringing us out here today to have fellowship in bump and for blessing this fine day with a visit from our new friend Jeff. Lord, we thank you for bringing this brother to us from up north, because we know he can learn to bump, and just—love you, and serve you and Lord, let us all just—Lord, be together in your name. Amen."

The regimen was so precise it was relaxing: no swearing, no drinking, no sex, no self. Watch out for magazines and don't waste time on newspapers and never watch TV. Eat meat, study the Gospels, play basketball: God loves a man who can sink a three-pointer. *Pray to be broken.* O Heavenly Father. Dear Jesus. Help me be humble. Let me do Your will. Every morning began with a prayer, some days with outsiders—Wednesdays led by a former Ivanwald brother, now a businessman; Thursdays led by another executive who used

tales of high finance to illuminate our lessons from scripture, which he sup-
plemented with xeroxed midrash from *Fortune* or *Fast Company*; Fridays with
the women of Potomac Point. But most days it was just us boys, bleary-eyed,
gulping coffee and sugared cereal as Bengt and Jeff Connolly, Bengt's childhood friend and our other house leader, laid out lines of Holy Word across the
table like strategy.

The dining room had once been a deck, but the boys had walled it in and
roofed it over and unrolled a red Persian carpet, transforming the room into
a sort of monastic meeting place, with two long tables end to end, ringed by a
dozen chairs and two benches. The first day I visited Ivanwald, Bengt cleared
a space for me at the head of the table and sat to my right. Beside him, Wayne
slumped in his chair, his eyes hidden by a cowboy hat. Across from him sat
Beau, still wearing the boxers and T-shirt he'd slept in. Bengt alone looked
sharp, his hair combed, golf shirt tucked tightly into pleated chinos.

Bengt told Gannon to read our text for that morning, Psalm 139: "'O
Lord, you have searched me and you know me.'" The very first line made
Bengt smile; this was, in his view, an awesome thing for God to have done.
Bengt's manners and naive charm preceded him in every encounter. When
you told him a story he would respond, "*Goll-y!*" just to be nice. When genuinely surprised he would exclaim, "*Good ni-ight!*" Sometimes it was hard to
remember that he was a self-professed revolutionary.

He asked Gannon to keep reading, and then leaned back and listened.

"'Where can I go from your Spirit? Where can I flee from your presence?
If I go up to the heavens, you are there; if I make my bed in the depths, you are
there.'"

Bengt raised a hand. "That's great, dude. Let's talk about that." The room
fell silent as Bengt stared into his Bible, running his finger up and down the
gilded edge of the page. "Guys," he said. "What—how does that make you feel?"

"Known," said Gannon, almost in a whisper.

Bengt nodded. He was looking for something else, but he didn't know
where it was. "What does it make you think of?"

"Jesus?" said Beau.

Bengt stroked his chin. "Yeah . . . Let me read you a little more." He read
in a monotone, accelerating as he went, as if he could persuade us through a
sheer heap of words. "'For you created my inmost being; you knit me together
in my mother's womb,'" he concluded. His lips curled into a half smile. "Man!
I mean, that's intense, right? 'In my mother's womb'—God's right in there

with you." He grinned. "It's like," he said, "it's like, you *can't* run. Doesn't matter where you turn, 'cause Jesus is gonna be there, just waiting for you."

Beau's eyes cleared and Gannon nodded. "Yeah, brother," Bengt said, an eyebrow arched. "Jesus is *smart*. He's gonna get you."

Gannon shook his head. "Oh, he's already got me."

"Me, too," Beau chimed, and then each man clasped his hands into one fist and pressed it against his forehead or his chin and prayed, eyes closed and Jesus all over his skin.

We prayed to be "nothing." We were there to "soften our hearts to authority." We instituted a rule that every man must wipe the toilet bowl after he pisses, not for cleanliness but to crush his "inner rebel." Jeff C. did so by abstaining from "shady" R-rated movies, lest they provoke dreams of women. He was built like a leprechaun, with curly, dark blond hair and freckles and a brilliant smile. The Potomac Point girls brought him cookies; the wives of the Family's older men asked him to visit. One night, when the guys went on a swing-dancing date with the Potomac Pointers, more worldly women flocked to Jeff C., begging to be dipped and twirled. The feeling was not mutual. "I just don't like girls as much as guys," he told me one day while we painted a new coat of "Gettysburg Gray" onto Ivanwald. He was speaking not of sex or of romance but of brotherhood. "I like"—he paused, his brush suspended midstroke—"*competence*."

He ran nearly every day, often alone, down by the Potomac. On the basketball court anger sometimes overcame him: "*Shoot* the ball!" he would snap at Rogelio, a shy eighteen-year-old from Paraguay, one of several international brothers. But later Jeff C. would turn his lapse into a lesson, citing scripture, a verse we were to memorize or else be banished, by Jeff C. himself, to a night in the basement. Ephesians, chapter 4, verses 26–27: " 'In your anger do not sin': Do not let the sun go down while you are still angry, and do not give the devil a foothold."

Jeff C.'s pride surfaced in unexpected ways. Once, together in the kitchen after lunch, I mentioned that I'd seen the soul singer Al Green live. Jeff C. didn't answer. Instead he disappeared, reemerged with a Green CD, and set it in the boom box. He pressed PLAY, and cracked his knuckles and his neck bones. His hands balled into fists, his eyes widened, and his torso became a jumping bean as his chest popped out on the downbeat. He heard me laughing, applauding, but he didn't stop. He started singing along with the Reverend. He grabbed his crotch and wrenched his shirt up and ran his hand over his stomach. Then he froze and dropped back to his ordinary voice as if narrating.

"I used to work in this pizza parlor," he said. "It was, like, a buncha . . . I dunno, *junkies*. Heroin." He grinned. "But man, they *loved* Al Green. We had a poster of him. He was, he was . . . man! Shirtless, leather pants. *Low* leather pants." Jeff C. tugged his waistband down. "Hips cocked." He shook his head and howled. Moonwalking away, he snapped his knees together, his feet spread wide, his hands in the air, testifying.

Jeff C. figured I had a thing against Southerners. Once, he asked if I thought the South was "racist." I got it, I tried to tell him, I knew the North was just as bad, but he wouldn't listen. He told me I could call him a redneck or a hillbilly (I never called him either), but the truth was that he was "blacker" than me. He told me of his deep love for black gospel churches. Loving black people, he told me, made him a better follower of Christ. "Remember that story Cal Thomas told?" he asked. Thomas, a syndicated columnist, had recently stopped by Ivanwald for a mixer with young congressional staffers. He had regaled his audience with stories about tweaking his liberal colleagues, in particular about when he had addressed a conference of nonbelievers by asking if anyone knew where to buy a good "negro." Jeff C. thought it was hilarious but also profound. What Thomas had meant, he told me, was that absent the teachings of Jesus there was no reason for the strong not to enslave the weak.

Two weeks into my stay, David Coe, Doug's son and the presumptive heir to leadership of the Family, dropped by the house. My brothers and I assembled in the living room, where David had draped his tall frame over a burgundy leather recliner like a frat boy, one leg hanging over a padded arm.

"You guys," David said, "are here to learn how to rule the world." He was in his late forties, with dark, gray-flecked hair, an olive complexion, and teeth like a slab of white marble. We sat around him in a rough circle, on couches and chairs, as the afternoon light slanted through the wooden blinds onto walls adorned with foxhunting lithographs and a giant tapestry of the Last Supper. Rafael, a wealthy Ecuadoran who'd been a college soccer star before coming to Ivanwald, had a hard time with English, and he didn't understand what David had said. So he stared, lips parted in puzzlement. David seemed to like that. He stared back, holding Raf's gaze like it was a pretty thing he'd found on the ground. "You have very intense eyes," David said.

"Thank you," Raf mumbled.

"Hey," David said, "let's talk about the Old Testament. Who would you say are its good guys?"

"David," Beau volunteered.

"King David," David Coe said. "That's a good one. David. Hey. What would you say made King David a good guy?" He was giggling, not from nervousness but from barely containable delight.

"Faith?" Beau said. "His faith was so strong?"

"Yeah." David nodded as if he hadn't heard that before. "Hey, you know what's interesting about King David?" From the blank stares of the others I could see that they did not. Many didn't even carry a Hebrew Bible, preferring a slim volume of just the New Testament Gospels and Epistles and, from the Old, Psalms. Others had the whole book, but the gold gilt on the pages of the first two thirds remained undisturbed. "King David," David Coe went on, "liked to do really, really bad things." He chuckled. "Here's this guy who slept with another man's wife—Bathsheba, right?—and then basically murders her husband. And this guy is one of our heroes." David shook his head. "I mean, Jiminy Christmas, God likes this guy! What," he said, "is *that* all about?"

The answer, we discovered, was that King David had been "chosen." To illustrate this point David Coe turned to Beau. "Beau, let's say I hear you raped three little girls. And now here you are at Ivanwald. What would I think of you, Beau?"

Beau shrank into the cushions. "Probably that I'm pretty bad?"

"No, Beau. I wouldn't. Because I'm not here to judge you. That's not my job. I'm here for only one thing."

"Jesus?" Beau said. David smiled and winked.

He walked to the National Geographic map of the world mounted on the wall. "You guys know about Genghis Khan?" he asked. "Genghis was a man with a vision. He conquered"—David stood on the couch under the map, tracing, with his hand, half the northern hemisphere—"nearly everything. He devastated nearly everything. His enemies? He beheaded them." David swiped a finger across his throat. "Dop, dop, dop, dop."

David explained that when Genghis entered a defeated city he would call in the local headman and have him stuffed into a crate. Over the crate would be spread a tablecloth, and on the tablecloth would be spread a wonderful meal. "And then, while the man suffocated, Genghis ate, and he didn't even hear the man's screams." David still stood on the couch, a finger in the air. "Do you know what that means?" He was thinking of Christ's parable of the wineskins. "You can't pour new into old," David said, returning to his chair. "We elect our leaders. Jesus elects his."

He reached over and squeezed the arm of a brother. "Isn't that great?" David said. "That's the way everything in life happens. If you're a person known to be around Jesus, you can go and do anything. And that's who you guys are. When you leave here, you're not only going to know the value of Jesus, you're going to know the people who rule the world. It's about vision. 'Get your vision straight, then relate.' Talk to the people who rule the world, and help *them* obey. Obey Him. If I obey Him myself, I help others do the same. You know why? Because I become a warning. *We* become a warning. We warn everybody that the future king is coming. Not just of this country or that, but of the world." Then he pointed at the map, toward the Khan's vast, reclaimable empire.

One night I asked Josh, a brother from Atlanta who was hoping to do mission work overseas, if I could look at some materials the Family had given him. "Man, I'd love to share them with you," he said, and retrieved from his bureau drawer two folders full of documents. While my brothers slept, I sat at the end of our long, oak dining table and copied them into my notebook.

In a document entitled "Our Common Agreement as a Core Group," members of the Family are instructed to form a "core group," or a "cell," which is defined as "a publicly invisible but privately identifiable group of companions." A document called "Thoughts on a Core Group" explains that "Communists use cells as their basic structure. The mafia operates like this, and the basic unit of the Marine Corps is the four man squad. Hitler, Lenin, and many others understood the power of a small core of people."

Another document, "Thoughts and Principles of the Family," sets forth political guidelines, such as

> 21. We recognize the place and responsibility of national *secular* leaders in the work of advancing His kingdom.
> 23. To the world in general we will say that we are "in Christ" rather than "Christian"—"Christian" having become a political term in most of the world and in the United States a meaningless term.
> 24. We desire to see a leadership led by God—leaders of all levels of society who direct projects as they are led by the spirit.

and self-examination questions:

> 4. Do I give only verbal assent to the policies of the family or am I a
> partner in seeking the mind of the Lord?
> 7. Do I agree with and practice the financial precepts of the family?[4]
> 13. Am I willing to work without human recognition?

When the group is ready, "Thoughts on a Core Group" explains, it can set to work:

> After being together for a while, in this closer relationship, God will give
> you more insight into your own geographical area and your sphere of
> influence—make your opportunities a matter of prayer. . . . The primary
> purpose of a core group is not to become an "action group," but an invisi-
> ble "believing group." However, activity normally grows out of agreements
> reached in faith and in prayer around the person of Jesus Christ.

Long-term goals were best summarized in a document called "Youth Corps Vision." Another Family project, Youth Corps distributes pleasant brochures featuring endorsements from political leaders—among them Tsutomu Hata, a former prime minister of Japan, former secretary of state James Baker, and Yoweri Museveni, president of Uganda—and full of enthusiastic rhetoric about helping young people to learn the principles of leadership. The word "Jesus" is unmentioned in the brochure.

But "Youth Corps Vision," which is intended only for members of the Family ("it's kinda secret," Josh cautioned me), is more direct.

> The Vision is to mobilize thousands of young people world wide—
> committed to principle precepts, and person of Jesus Christ. . . .
>   A group of highly dedicated *individuals who are united together* hav-
> ing a total commitment to use their lives to daily seek to mature into
> people who talk like Jesus, act like Jesus, think like Jesus. This group will
> have the responsibility to:

[4]The Family's "financial precepts" apparently amount to the practice of soliciting funds only privately, and often indirectly. This may also refer to what some members call "biblical capitalism," the belief that God's economics are laissez-faire.

—see that the commitment and action is maintained to the overall vision;

—see that the finest and best invisible organization is developed and maintained at all levels of the work;

—even though the structure is hidden, see that the family atmosphere is maintained, so that all people can feel a part of the family.

Another document—"Regional Reports, January 3, 2002"—lists some of the nations where Youth Corps programs are already in operation: Russia, Ukraine, Romania, India, Pakistan, Uganda, Nepal, Bhutan, Ecuador, Honduras, Peru. Youth Corps is, in many respects, a more aggressive version of Young Life, a better-known network of Christian youth groups that entice teenagers with parties and sports, and only later work Jesus into the equation. Most of my American brothers at Ivanwald had been among Young Life's elite, and many had returned to Young Life during their college summers to work as counselors. Youth Corps, whose programs are often centered around Ivanwald-style houses, prepares the best of its recruits for positions of power in business and government abroad. The goal: "Two hundred national and international world leaders bound together relationally by a mutual love for God and the family."

Between 1984 and 1992 the Fellowship Foundation consigned 592 boxes—decades of the Family's letters, sermons, minutes, Christmas cards, travel itineraries, and lists of members—to an archive at the Billy Graham Center of Wheaton College in Illinois. Until I visited last fall, the archive had gone largely unexamined.

The Family was founded in April 1935 by Abraham Vereide, a Norwegian immigrant who made his living as a traveling preacher. One night, while lying in bed fretting about socialists, Wobblies, and a Swedish Communist who, he was sure, planned to bring Seattle under the control of Moscow, Vereide received a visitation: a voice, and a light in the dark, bright and blinding. The next day he met a friend, a wealthy businessman and former major, and the two men agreed upon a spiritual plan. They enlisted nineteen business executives in a weekly breakfast meeting and together they prayed, convinced that Jesus alone could redeem Seattle and crush the radical unions. They wanted to give Jesus a vessel, and so they asked God to raise up a leader. One of their number, a city councilman named Arthur Langlie, stood and said, "I am ready to let God use me." Langlie was made first mayor and later governor, backed in both campaigns by money and muscle from his prayer-breakfast friends, whose number had rapidly multiplied.[5] Vereide and his new brothers spread out across the Northwest in chauffeured vehicles (a $20,000 Dusenburg carried brothers on one mission, he boasted). "Men," wrote Vereide, "thus quickened." Prayer breakfast groups were formed in dozens of cities, from San Francisco to Philadelphia. There were already enough men ministering to the down-and-out, Vereide had decided; his mission field would be men with the means to seize the world for God. Vereide called his potential flock of the rich and powerful, those in need only of the "real" Jesus, the "up-and-out."

Vereide arrived in Washington, D.C., on September 6, 1941, as the guest of a man referred to only as "Colonel Brindley." "Here I am finally," he wrote to his wife, Mattie, who remained in Seattle. "In a day or two—many will know that I am in town and by God's grace it will hum." Within weeks he had held his first D.C. prayer meeting, attended by more than a hundred congressmen. By 1943, now living in a suite at Colonel Brindley's University Club, Vereide was an insider. "My what a full and busy day!" he wrote to Mattie on January 22.

> The Vice President brought me to the Capitol and counseled with me regarding the programs and plans, and then introduced me to Senator [Ralph Owen] Brewster, who in turn to Senator [Harold Hitz] Burton— then planned further the program [of a prayer breakfast] and enlisted their cooperation. Then to the Supreme Court for visits with some of them . . . then back to the Senate, House. . . . The hand of the Lord is upon me. He is leading.

By the end of the war, nearly a third of U.S. senators had attended one of his weekly prayer meetings.

In 1944, Vereide had foreseen what he called "the new world order." "Upon the termination of the war there will be many men available to carry

[5]As Vereide recounted in a 1961 biography, *Modern Viking,* one union boss joined the group, proclaiming that the prayer movement would make unions obsolete. He said, "'I got down on my knees and asked God to forgive me . . . for I have been a disturbing factor and a thorn in Your flesh.'" A "rugged capitalist who had been the chairman of the employers' committee in the big strike" put his left hand on the labor leader's shoulder and said, "'Jimmy, on this basis we go on together.'"

on," Vereide wrote in a letter to his wife. "Now the ground-work must be laid and our leadership brought to face God in humility, prayer and obedience." He began organizing prayer meetings for delegates to the United Nations, at which he would instruct them in God's plan for rebuilding from the wreckage of the war. Donald Stone, a high-ranking administrator of the Marshall Plan, joined the directorship of Vereide's organization. In an undated letter, he wrote Vereide that he would "soon begin a tour around the world for the [Marshall Plan], combining with this a spiritual mission." In 1946, Vereide, too, toured the world, traveling with letters of introduction from a half dozen senators and representatives, and from Paul G. Hoffman, the director of the Marshall Plan. He traveled also with a mandate from General John Hildring, assistant secretary of state, to oversee the creation of a list of good Germans of "the predictable type" (many of whom, Vereide believed, were being held for having "the faintest connection" with the Nazi regime), who could be released from prison "to be used, according to their ability in the tremendous task of reconstruction." Vereide met with Jewish survivors and listened to their stories, but he nevertheless considered ex-Nazis well suited for the demands of "strong" government, so long as they were willing to worship Christ as they had Hitler.

In 1955, Senator Frank Carlson, a close adviser to Eisenhower and an even closer associate of Vereide's, convened a meeting at which he declared the Family's mission to be a "worldwide spiritual offensive," in which common cause would be made with anyone opposed to the Soviet Union. That same year, the Family financed an anticommunist propaganda film, *Militant Liberty*, for use by the Defense Department in influencing opinion abroad. By the Kennedy era, the spiritual offensive had fronts on every continent but Antarctica (which Family missionaries would not visit until the 1980s). In 1961, Emperor Haile Selassie of Ethiopia deeded the Family a prime parcel in downtown Addis Ababa to serve as an African headquarters, and by then the Family also had powerful friends in South Africa, Nigeria, and Kenya. Back home, Senator Strom Thurmond prepared several reports for Vereide concerning the Senate's deliberations. Former president Eisenhower, Doug Coe would later claim at a private meeting of politicians, once pledged secret operatives to aid the Family's operations. Even in Franco's Spain, Vereide once boasted at a prayer breakfast in 1965, "there are secret cells such as the American Embassy [and] the Standard Oil office [that allow us] to move practically anywhere."

By the late sixties, Vereide's speeches to local prayer breakfast groups had become minor news events, and Family members' travels on behalf of Christ had attracted growing press attention. Vereide began to worry that the movement he had spent his life building might become just another political party. In 1966, a few years before he was "promoted" to heaven at age eighty-four, Vereide wrote a letter declaring it time to "submerge the institutional image of [the Family]." No longer would the Family recruit its powerful members in public, nor recruit so many. "There has always been one man," wrote Vereide, "or a small core who have caught the vision for their country and become aware of what a 'leadership led by God' could mean spiritually to the nation and to the world. . . . It is these men, banded together, who can accomplish the vision God gave me years ago."

Two weeks into my stay, Bengt announced to the brothers that he was applying to graduate school. He had chosen a university close enough to commute from the house, with a classics program he hoped would complement (maybe even renew, he told me privately) his relationship with Christ. After dinner every night he would disappear into the little office beside his upstairs bunk room to compose his statement of purpose on the house's one working computer.

Knowing I was a writer, he eventually gave me the essay to read. We sat down in Ivanwald's "office," a room barely big enough for the two of us. We crossed our legs in opposite directions so as not to knock knees.

My formal education has been a progression from confusion and despair to hope, the essay began. Its story hewed to the familiar fundamentalist routine of lost and found: every man and woman a sinner, fallen but nonetheless redeemed. And yet Bengt's sins were not of the flesh but of the mind. In college he had abandoned his boyhood ambition of becoming a doctor to study philosophy: Nietzsche, Kierkegaard, Hegel. Raised in the faith, his ideas about God crumbled before the disciplined rage of the philosophers. "I cut and ran," he told me. To Africa, where by day he worked on ships and in clinics, and by night read Dostoevsky and the Bible, its darkest and most seductive passages: Lamentations, Job, the Song of Songs. These authors were alike, his essay observed: *They wrote about [suffering] like a companion.*

I looked up. "A double," I said, remembering Dostoevsky's alter egos.

Bengt nodded. "You know how you can stare at something for a long time and not see it the way it really is? That's what scripture had been to me." Through Dostoevsky he began to see the Old Testament for what it is: relentless in its horror, its God a fire, a whirlwind, a "bear, lying in wait," "a lion in se-cret places." Even worse is its Man: a rapist, a murderer, a wretched thief, a fool.

"But," said Bengt, "that's not how it ends."

Bengt meant Jesus. I thought of the end of *The Brothers Karamazov*: the saintly Alyosha, leading a pack of boys away from a funeral to feast on pan-cakes, everyone clapping hands and proclaiming eternal brotherhood. In Africa, Bengt had seen people who were diseased, starving, trapped by war, but who seemed nonetheless to experience joy. Bengt recalled listening to a group of starving men play the drums. "Doubt," he said, "is just a prelude to joy."

I had heard this before from mainstream Christians, but I suspected Bengt meant it differently. A line in Dostoevsky's *The Possessed* reminded me of him: when the conservative nationalist Shatov asks Stavrogin, the cold-hearted radical, "Wasn't it you who said that even if it was proved to you mathemati-cally that the Truth was outside Christ, you would prefer to remain with Christ outside the Truth?" Stavrogin, who refuses to be cornered, denies it.

"Exactly," Bengt said. In Africa he had seen the trappings of Christianity fall away. All that remained was Christ. "You can't argue with absolute power."

I put the essay down. Bengt nudged it back into my hands. "I want to know what you think of my ending."

As I have read more about Jesus, it ran, *I have also been intrigued by his style of interaction with other people*. He was fascinated in particular by an en-counter in the Gospel of John, chapter 1, verses 35–39, in which Jesus asks two men why they are following him. In turn, the men ask where Jesus is staying, to which he replies, "Come and see." *I am not sure how Jesus asks the question*, Bengt had concluded, *but from the response, it seems like he is asking, "What do you desire?"*

"That's what it's about," Bengt said. "Desire." He shifted in his chair. "Think about it: 'What do you desire?'"

"God?"

"Yes."

"That's the answer?" I asked.

"He's the question," Bengt retorted, half-smiling, satisfied with his inver-sion by which doubt became the essence of a dogma. God was just what Bengt desired Him to be, even as Bengt was, in the face of God, "nothing." Not for aesthetics alone, I realized, did Bengt and the Family reject the label "Chris-tian." Their faith and their practice seemed closer to a perverted sort of Bud-dhism, their God outside "the truth," their Christ everywhere and nowhere at once, His commands phrased as questions, His will as simple to divine as one's own desires. And what the Family desired, from Abraham Vereide to Doug Coe to Bengt, was power, worldly power, with which Christ's kingdom can be built, cell by cell.

Not long after our conversation, Bengt put a bucket beside the toilet in the downstairs bunk room. From now on, he announced, all personal items left in the living room would go into the bucket. "If you're missing anything, guys," Bengt said over dinner, "look in the bucket."

I looked in the bucket. Here's what I found: One pair of flip-flops. One pocket-sized edition of the sayings of Jesus. One Frisbee. One copy of *Executive Orders*, by Tom Clancy, hardcover. One brown-leather Bible, well worn, beautifully printed on onion skin, given to Bengt Carlson by Palmer Carlson. One pair of dirty underwear.

When I picked up the Bible the pages flipped open to the Gospel of John, and my eyes fell on a single underlined phrase, chapter 15, verse 3: "You are already clean."

Whenever a sufficiently large crop of God's soldiers was bunked up at Ivanwald, Doug Coe made a point of stopping by for dinner. Doug was, in spirit, Christ's closest disciple, the master bumper; the brothers viewed his visit as far more important than that of any senator or prime minister. The night he joined us he wore a crisply pressed golf shirt and dark slacks, and his skin was well tanned. He brought a guest with him, an Albanian politician whose pale face and ill-fitting gray suit made Doug seem all the more radiant. In his early seventies, Doug could have passed for fifty: his hair was dark, his cheeks taut. His smile was like a lantern.

"Where," Doug asked Rogelio, "are you from, in Paraguay?"

"Asunción," he said.

Doug smiled. "I've visited there many times." He chewed for a while. "Asunción. A Latin leader was assassinated there twenty years ago. A Nicaraguan. Does anybody know who it was?"

I waited for someone to speak, but no one did. "Somoza," I said. The dictator overthrown by the Sandinistas.

"Somoza," Doug said, his eyes sweeping back to me. "An interesting man."

Doug stared. I stared back. "I liked to visit him," Doug said. "A very bad man, behind his machine guns." He smiled like he was going to laugh, but instead he moved his fork to his mouth. "And yet," he said, a bite poised at the tip of his tongue, "he had a heart for the poor." Doug stared. I stared back.

"Do you ever think about prayer?" he asked. But the question wasn't for me. It wasn't for anyone. Doug was preparing a parable.

There was a man he knew, he said, who didn't really believe in prayer. So Doug made him a bet. If this man would choose something and pray for it for forty-five days, every day, he wagered God would make it so. It didn't matter whether the man believed. It wouldn't have mattered whether he was a Christian. All that mattered was the fact of prayer. Every day. Forty-five days. He couldn't lose, Doug told the man. If Jesus didn't answer his prayers, Doug would pay him $500.

"What should I pray for?" the man asked.

"What do you think God would like you to pray for?" Doug asked him.

"I don't know," said the man. "How about Africa?"

"Good," said Doug. "Pick a country."

"Uganda," the man said, because it was the only one he could remember.

"Fine," Doug told him. "Every day, for forty-five days, pray for Uganda. God please help Uganda. God please help Uganda."

On the thirty-second day, Doug told us, this man met a woman from Uganda. She worked with orphans. Come visit, she told the man, and so he did, that very weekend. And when he came home, he raised a million dollars in donated medicine for the orphans. "So you see," Doug told him, "God answered your prayers. You owe me $500."

There was more. After the man had returned to the United States, the president of Uganda called the man at his home and said, "I am making a new government. Will you help me make some decisions?"

"So," Doug told us, "my friend said to the president, 'Why don't you come and pray with me in America? I have a good group of friends—senators, congressmen—who I like to pray with, and they'd like to pray with you.' And that president came to The Cedars, and he met Jesus. And his name is Yoweri Museveni, and he is now the president of all the presidents in Africa. And he is a good friend of the Family."

"That's awesome," Beau said.

"Yes," Doug said, "it's good to have friends. Do you know what a difference a friend can make? A friend you can agree with?" He smiled. "Two or three agree, and they pray? They can do anything. Agree. Agreement. What's that mean?" Doug looked at me. "You're a writer. What does that mean?"

I remembered Paul's letter to the Philippians, which we had begun to memorize. *Fulfill ye my joy, that ye be likeminded.*

"Unity," I said. "Agreement means unity."

Doug didn't smile. "Yes," he said. "*Total* unity. Two, or three, become one. Do you know," he asked, "that there's another word for that?"

No one spoke.

"It's called a covenant. Two, or three, agree? They can do anything. A covenant is . . . powerful. Can you think of anyone who made a covenant with his friends?"

We all knew the answer to this, having heard his name invoked numerous times in this context. Andrew from Australia, sitting beside Doug, cleared his throat: "Hitler."

"Yes," Doug said. "Yes, Hitler made a covenant. The Mafia makes a covenant. It is such a very powerful thing. Two, or three, agree." He took another bite from his plate, planted his fork on its tines. "Well, guys," he said, "I gotta go."

As Doug Coe left, my brothers' hearts were beating hard: for the poor, for a covenant. "Awesome," Bengt said. We stood to clear our dishes.

On one of my last nights at Ivanwald, the neighborhood boys asked my brothers and me to play. There were roughly six boys, ranging in age from maybe seven to eleven, all junior members of the Family. They wanted to play flashlight tag. It was balmy, and the streetlight glittered against the blacktop, and hiding places beckoned from behind trees and in bushes. One of the boys began counting, and my brothers, big and small, scattered. I lay flat on a hillside. From there I could track movement in the shadows and smell the mint leaves planted in the garden. A figure approached and I sprang up and ran, down the sidewalk and up through the garden, over a wall that my pursuer, a small boy, had trouble climbing. But once he was over he kept charging, and just as I was about to vanish into the trees his flashlight caught me. "Jeff I see you you're It!" the boy cried. I stopped and turned, and he kept the beam on me. Blinded, I could hear only the slap of his sneakers as he ran across the driveway toward me. "Okay, dude," he whispered, and turned off the flashlight. I recognized him as little Stevie, whose drawing of a machine gun we had posted in our bunk room. He handed the flashlight to me, spun around, started to run, then stopped and looked over his shoulder. "You're It now," he whispered, and disappeared into the dark.

March 2003

Part Two

Violence

Bombshells, takedowns, hatchet jobs, hit pieces—journalism is often analogized to acts of violence, and perhaps with good reason. Like war, reportage at times demands infiltration, at times surprise attack, and imagines its betrayal and brutality absolved through the justice of its ultimate ends. But the same aggressive spirit that invigorates the gathering of news can also cripple the telling of it, especially when one's story is itself set amid danger—a battlefield, a boxing ring, a crime scene, a cliff face. An insipid swagger can come creeping in. Good journalism may be the moral equivalent of war, but too much of our journalism *about* war, and about violence more generally, is the aesthetic equivalent of masturbation: maximum masculinity put to minimum effect.

This chapter brings together two pieces that represent two different ways of looking at guns, both notable for their unwillingness to brandish these guns in service of a writerly machismo. In Charles Bowden's masterful "Teachings of Don Fernando," the guns are kept entirely out of sight, but what propels the tale—about a career drug informer for the DEA, the dealers he puts away, the agents he aids, and the journalist Bowden himself—is precisely the fear, shared by all these men, about when guns will be aimed at them and by whom. By contrast, Steve Featherstone, in "The Line Is Hot," comes out firing literally from the very first paragraph, shooting his way through a complete history of the machine gun while attending a gathering of rapid-fire enthusiasts in Knob Creek, Kentucky. Yet the focus remains on the devastation wrought by the weapons, past and present; the story of the machine gun in history reads as tragedy, and in Featherstone's own hands as farce.

Teachings of Don Fernando

A Life and Death in the Narcotics Trade

CHARLES BOWDEN

The man in the coffin wears a gray western suit and white cowboy shirt, and his large hands clutch a rosary. I look hard at the hands, and I can see them as they were three years ago, hoisting a rock for a wall he was building—then pausing as a jolt in his chest marked the revolt of his body. He did not tolerate revolt. He was that thing most unnerving for us: a finished man, complete and at ease with his private universe. A fine Stetson rests on the box, and just over his head gleams a color photograph of him astride his horse. Off to the side on a table, he looks up as a young man in a suit, as an older man getting married, and as an old man dancing with his wife. About four hundred people file past to pay their respects. Most are wearing freshly pressed jeans, clean shirts, and cowboy hats. The parking lot is full of pickups. A newspaper death notice sums it up neatly: "Terrazas, Fernando, 83, miner."

Vases of mums, azaleas, and red roses dot the front of the sanctuary while a mariachi band plays off to the side. I sit next to a young woman who knew Fernando. When she was in college, he would suddenly show up at her door with fresh fruit for her father. He was always courtly, she recalls. But she found out about his real life only last night.

After the rosary and mass, in the soft light of February that washes over the desert, the men stand outside, smoking and talking. A guy in his late for-ties ambles over to one cluster of men wearing suits. He is a former Customs agent and spent a part of his career undercover buying dope on the border. He knew Fernando for over fifteen years. They spent time in each other's houses, drinking coffee and talking about life and horses, the usual patter of rural Ari-zona. He knew Fernando as a miner, a gentleman, a guy who always asked the same question: "You need anything?" But he recognizes this cluster of suits as D.E.A. and so he figures he'll say hello. One agent is up from Guadalajara, evacuated because a cartel has put out a contract on him. Another ran D.E.A. intelligence. He hears them talking of big scores, of multiton busts, of back pages. And on each of these pages looms Fernando.

He suddenly realizes that the man he'd known for years he did not know at all. But then maybe ten people of the four hundred at the funeral mass knew the truth about Fernando Terrazas's life. Hundreds of people in prisons have dreamed for years of seeing him in a coffin and tried for years to put him there. He was that man, the double, trusted but always unknown.

I can hear him making me an offer at this moment. His voice courtly, his face calm, his body singing of ease, I will trust him completely. And he will de-stroy me.

I have learned a simple lesson: You can trust no one. But in the end, you must trust someone. And when you are betrayed, and you will be betrayed, the ruin will come from the person you trusted. Fernando always warned me that when a man is saying one thing he is thinking another, and that I must also hear this other thought.

Fernando came into my life because of my hunger to know informants. He lived a few hours from my house, and so from 1999 until his death in February I'd drop in on him from time to time. I was attracted to the solo nature of the work, to the fact that informants floated free of both the law and the drug merchants. The drug industry had become my prison, in a way: I had set out to do a simple magazine story, which became a book, and the book devoured seven years of my life. For a time, I was obsessed with one figure, Amado Carrillo Fuentes, head of the Juárez cartel. I'd had to trust people, knowing that only the people I trusted could betray me. Fernando was an independent who lived in a realm of self-created freedom. Unlike most informants, he was successful and survived for decades, a black hole moving through the drug galaxy and disappearing loads and people into his vortex, all the while remaining undetected.

I have never had a candid conversation with a D.E.A. agent when a third party, even another agent, was present. Never. Distrust is a growth industry in our culture, as the tiny microphones and cameras multiply and the strange hands paw through cyberspace, reading our lives. For decades, Fernando would leave his blue-collar job in the mines at least once a month and disappear into the drug world. He hurled hundreds if not thousands into the gulag of our prisons, and his deals without question sent countless others to secret graves along the border. And yet he remained unknown, his name always missing from the newspaper stories about his deals. The drug merchants he ruined were seldom if ever sure Fernando was the traitor who blew up the transaction. He lived the history of our future.

It's May of 1999. The fresh green of spring licks the sierras, and I've been on the road for over a week with Julian Cardona, a Mexican friend. We've plunged down the eastern slope of the Sierra Madre, a green roll of hills, oak, pine, and *narcotraficantes*. More than thirty times we are stopped by armed men, some in uniform, some not, and always they ask: Why are you here? Where are you going? Just north of the city of Durango, around midnight, in the rain, the army pulls us over and searches. We are at the turnoff to a town against the mountains that is functionally a gated community for drug merchants. I remember sitting in a Texas prison with a convict as he circled the place on the map and said, "Go there. You won't believe it, they've got shops like on Rodeo Drive."

A contract on Fernando's life has come from this area, and as I drive people are probing Phoenix trying to pick up the old man's scent. About an hour north of Zacatecas, the federal police pull us over at a checkpoint. They tear my truck apart. A crowd gathers, and Julian drifts away, and I am alone.

A fat *federale* with a .45 thumps me in the chest and asks, "You mad at me?" He does this again and again as the minutes tick past. I think: They want the truck, they will plant something if I turn my back.

I know if I react, I will lose. I know if they have access to a computer, I will lose. There is a list, I've been told, and my name is on that list. Julian is standing at the back of the crowd now, and still he is drifting away. All the while big semis pull over for the check and are automatically waved through to the border with a laugh between the cops and the drivers.

Finally, after half an hour or so, they let us go.

Ten minutes down the road, Julian says, "They will call ahead. We are in trouble."

About this time, a retired D.E.A. agent named Phil Jordan calls my home looking for me. He's a friend, but I have not told him about my trip. When he hears where I am, he explodes to the person who's answered the phone: "Doesn't he know he can't do that anymore? Doesn't he know how fucking dangerous it is? It's not safe for him down there. That's over."

What I think as I drive the eight hundred miles of highway north to the line is this: Julian. He is my friend.

But that's how you go down. That is the velvet wrapped around the betrayal when it comes for you.

I take comfort from the fear in Julian's face. And then I stare through the windshield and wonder if the fear is feigned.

He comes out of the house for that first visit in July of 1999 and I feel the iron of his hand as we shake. He's eighty, but his big frame still intimidates. He's tall and moves like a horseman, body erect, gut tight. The face is warm, inviting, and yet closed. Meeting his eyes is like staring into a mask. Seven doctors keep track of his body, a thing busted up from a lifetime of horses, mines, and heavy equipment. His bones bear the mark of a Caterpillar tractor that rolled over onto him. We sit on the porch, his wife of fifty years serving cold drinks, his grandchildren underfoot. He has raised two sons and three daughters, and they have given him nine grandchildren and now a great-grandchild. He built the house with his own hands.

"I'm a lying son of a bitch," Fernando says, and beams.

He leans toward me and asks, "You are not going to use my name, are you? Or tell where I live?"

"No. No one will know where you live."

As the afternoon crawls along, clouds begin to spew off the peaks and hint at rain in the valley. Fernando tries to teach me the work.

He would meet a stranger in a town where he himself was unknown. Fernando would talk, then he would listen, and bit by bit an atmosphere of trust would fill the air. Sometimes this trust would take time. Once, a perfect stranger told Fernando to get into the driver's seat of a car, and then the man climbed into the passenger seat and thrust a gun into Fernando's ribs and said, "I'm going to find out if you're for fucking real." Fernando had no gun. He is of the belief that guns cause trouble.

He tells me, "Assholes never kill you. Anybody who shows you a gun won't kill you, because he is a coward." As he felt the cold metal of the pistol against his side, Fernando decided. He got out of the car and sat on the ground.

He told the stranger, "Shoot me and I'll keep my fucking money and you keep your fucking shit."

Fernando notes, "I got pretty damn cold blood."

"What happened?" I ask.

He looks at me with mild surprise.

"He did the deal."

The late Amado Carrillo Fuentes, head of what was then the biggest drug combine in the world, had a simple rule: to root out all the Fernandos of the world. If a load was lost, everyone connected with the load was killed to ensure that the traitor died. He also often ordered "a dose of milk," some quicklime to be tossed on the corpse to hasten its decomposition.

Fernando speaks English with the formality and cadence of a man whose first language was Spanish. He hands me a heap of clippings and I read, over and over: HEROIN DEALERS TO JAIL.

"All you gotta be," he calmly explains, "is be quiet. Don't tell. It's not the business of anyone else. My children didn't know. My wife knew, I had no secrets from my wife. To do this kind of job you have to be a liar and don't forget what you say. It's easy, it's easy: Don't tell.

"The only way you can do the big cases is: I'm the dumb one. I don't know anything about drugs. I buy, you sell, we make money. That's it. Never be smarter than the other guy, even if you're just selling a pickup. When you talk, don't tell them anything you don't know or anything they don't need to know. Don't open your mouth if you're not supposed to. Be nice, buy drinks, go out to eat. Never lose control."

It begins in the early days of the Great Society, in 1964, and feels as casual as having a cold beer after a hard day in the mines. In his mid-forties, Fernando thinks he'd like to own a bar. At a joint in rural Arizona he sees someone plant a bag of marijuana in the car of the man who owns the place. He and the owner are friends, so Fernando tells him what he has seen. Later, they pitch the bag into the river. Fernando goes to the state police and offers to inform on drug guys if the cops will help him get a liquor license. They turn him down, as do federal agents.

But he becomes a phone number in a file, and a year later the feds call him up. There is an old man peddling heroin near Phoenix whom they can never nail. After making a deal, the buyer must walk alone eight miles into the desert to a tree where the product is waiting. The old man stays clear of the stuff. Fernando talks and talks with the old man, draws him in until finally he is offered a partnership. The trap is set. The old man goes away for what is the rest of his life.

Fernando discovers he is a natural and that he loves the work.

A man tells me to check the back room at the restaurant. And he tells me about the parties at the mansion. This is in 1992, before the drug business seriously entered my life, a time when I still trusted without thought. The guy, who owned the restaurant and the mansion, did big real estate deals and got big loans without a blink. He was rumored to hire whores and have coke parties in the back room. They were secretly videotaped. The same for the parties at his house. I'm deep into a book on Charles Keating, the poster boy for the savings-and-loan crisis of the eighties. The tip has nothing to do with Keating himself but does connect with people involved in his deals. Soon I find a man who had been to such a party.

In the midst of this research, I get a call. A woman I visited six hundred miles away has been hounded by guys pounding at her door late at night, demanding to know about me. So have her neighbors.

I start moving, buy a gun, use pay phones, travel to unknown addresses.

But first I warn the guy who told me of the parties. Then I tell a lawyer looking into the financial case. The lawyer blows me off. A few weeks later the F.B.I. intercepts a contract coming out of Miami aimed at the lawyer's children.

I never found out who was doing it, though I'm certain Keating himself was not involved. Nor could I figure out where I had slipped up, or if I had simply been betrayed. You always have to trust someone.

I became very close to the man who first told me about the coke parties and whores. Then we drifted apart. I was busy, things to do. One Father's Day, about two years later, he sat alone and put a round through his skull. The bone and flesh must have taken a toll on the bullet because when it hit the window, its force was spent, and it fell to the floor like a pebble.

I thought, I should have called. I thought I had betrayed something I could not quite name. I put that suicide behind me but still I would think about it, a memory floating like lace, so delicate in still air, a memory with a savage rent in it where I had clumsily torn it with my hand. He had trusted me, told me things I'm sure he never told his wife. I had won his trust slowly but surely. I had made my sale. But I'd been busy. He was part of a story I had finished, and now I'd moved on to new stuff. I'm a writer. I listen, I win trust, I pour coffee and cook dinners. I lean close until I disappear inside their hearts and fears and dreams. And then I tell. It was a small thing, a sliver really of the world in which Fernando lived and thrived. To this day I picture that bullet spilling off the glass and falling to the floor. I remember the man telling me the lessons of his youth, how in the summer of his fifteenth year he broke horses in Kentucky and created the bankroll that got him out into the greater world. I know that I lack what it takes to close the deal, to really do people. But I wear a feeling of betrayal.

"If you really want to buy something," Fernando advises, "you need good jewelry." He goes to the back room and returns with a small cloth bag. He shows me his $1,800 gold bracelet, the gold watch swaddled in what look like diamonds, $400 cowboy boots, the finely stitched cowboy shirts, gold rings with rubies, a $350 Stetson. His wife forbids him to wear these things where they live. She thinks they make him look like a criminal.

I handle the heavy bracelet while he watches to make sure I understand the importance of its weight. A small pile of rings grows as he empties his sack. One by one he holds them up to the light with his big hand. He fingers the fabrics of his drug wardrobe and outlines the cut and quality. The closet in his home is lined with boots of the very finest leather. A man without pride cannot do the deal.

And then he plunges again into the life. He tells me about entering a cantina in San Luis, Sonora, across the border. At the time, this little town of dust was a major crossing point for drugs. The stranger is beside him and Fernando says, "I need something good."

The man delivers a sampler of kilos so they can be tested for quality. In the beginning Fernando did kilo deals, but soon he sought greater weight and deals had to be in tons. The samples prove to be low-grade.

Fernando returns to the cantina and snaps at the man, "You give me shit. You embarrass me before my people."

Apologies fill the air. The real shipment is high-grade. The stranger wants to win over this new soul in his life named Fernando. The man goes down. In almost three decades Fernando never fails, not once.

.   .   .

In the mid-sixties, Fernando teams up with Phil Jordan, a Mexican American out of El Paso, who became a federal agent in 1965. Jordan is in his early twenties and fresh off a university basketball career. He treats Fernando as an equal. This is rare in the work, since most Cooperating Individuals, C.I.s (typically, flipped felons nabbed doing drug deals), are disdained as snitches. Fernando is an independent operator, and when anyone treats him like a doper or a lesser being he bridles. He has more street smarts than most of the agents, and so, in his reserved way, he holds them in contempt as clumsy instruments he must use for his special work. Jordan is a product of the barrio and knows how to treat a man with proper respect. Fernando becomes his mentor, and their work makes Jordan's career. They make three to four hundred cases over the years. Their families socialize. The woman at Fernando's funeral who has just learned what Fernando really did, she is Phil Jordan's daughter and has known Fernando since childhood.

In the early seventies, Fernando returns to San Luis. He crosses the border and within four hours makes a deal in a cantina. His probing has brought him inside a cell that will become the school for almost all the major cartel leaders of the eighties and nineties. Pedro Aviles Perez heads the organization, and his young underlings include Rafael Caro Quintero, who will later torture and slaughter D.E.A. agent Enrique "Kiki" Camarena; Amado Carrillo Fuentes, who will become the biggest drug merchant on earth; Amado's uncle Don Neto Carrillo and Felix Gallardo, both of whom will help to create the Guadalajara cartel; and many other drug dealers who in a few years will be handling hundreds of millions and then billions of dollars' worth of dope.

Some of Aviles's lieutenants are lured to the United States in 1973 and taken down right next door, as it happens, to a fund-raiser for Senator Barry Goldwater. A joint raid with Mexicans in Sonora bags ten tons of marijuana. One of the raiders, a young Mexican *federale*, rises in the ranks through the years. He becomes the *federale* that the U.S. agents lean on, the one who is different. Years later he kills a cartel leader and becomes a kind of hero in the F.B.I. And years after that the U.S. agencies discover he did the killing only because Amado Carrillo paid him $1 million for the hit. Carrillo had been very close to the dead man and used to freebase with him. When the dead man was cut down he was wearing a fine gold watch given to him by Carrillo. You have to trust, in the end.

Fernando leans toward me as he recounts this episode and says, "The only reason you are here is because of Phil."

He asks again if I am going to use his name, reveal his location. And then he smiles, because he already knows.

I am in his home because another man gave his word. And that is all that is necessary. If I am a traitor, the other man is responsible.

Fernando tells me with pride of his marksmanship with a .45.

"I trust Phil like a brother," he continues.

I remember the feel of the cartel's breath on my neck. I'd been looking into a murder in Juárez in August of 1995. It was officially listed as a drowning, but I had asked questions. I was naive. I remember drinking in a bar with a Mexican and asking about Amado Carrillo. The man winced, instantly crouched down, and searched the room for faces and ears. Later, I learned Carrillo drank in that bar.

On the U.S. side I'd been dealing with the D.E.A. at EPIC (El Paso Intelligence Center), and that is where I met Phil Jordan, who headed it. He gave me leads. Then one day, one of the Juárez dailies came out with a story about an American writer looking into a drowning and claiming it was murder. The story gave the city where I lived. I knew the paper was controlled by the cartel.

I called up the D.E.A. and asked why they had burned me. They denied it. Jordan's aide said, "We would never do that."

I slowly calmed down. It is so much easier to trust. It is a beckoning drug.

I kept looking, coming and going unannounced, changing where I stayed. In the fall of 1996, I found out that someone very close to Phil Jordan and his family, someone he trusted, had partied with the cartel leaders in Juárez. And knew Carrillo.

So I disappeared with a .9mm, boxes of notes, and some black coffee. Later, I learned Phil Jordan had been calling, trying to find me. Eventually, we became friends.

He told me he would never do that, put me in play.

But I'd had a taste. You think betrayal is something covered by those cheatin' songs in the country bars. You think it is the co-worker who burns you with the boss, or even that business partner who tries to sell you out. I've had all of those and more. But they are something else, they call for some weaker word. They lack the surprise of the knife going into your guts. The floor falls away, you are spinning, and you are absolutely alone. And no one can hear you, no one can help you. And the only trace of trust you have is acid on your tongue. Phil Jordan had that person close to him who was dirty.

There was that story in the Mexican newspaper that came out of nowhere and bothered to mention where I lived.

But still I came in from the cold after a few weeks. You have to trust someone. That is the rub. You have to make your deals. It is a fact of life.

"When I see a drunkard," Fernando says, "I turn away." Those who use drugs are also to be despised. Fernando lives off control. His childhood in southern Chihuahua meant almost no schooling—he made it to maybe the second grade—and endless hours of ranch work. Toiling alone at age fourteen, he planted and brought in, with the help of horses, an eighty-ton crop of pinto beans.

At fifteen, someone shot at him. He walked home to the ranch, got a rifle, walked back, and shot his assailant in the neck.

He leans forward and asks, "Could you kill someone?"

I answer, "I don't know."

He waits a minute and says, "I can."

He falls silent for a moment and adds, "I did pretty good. I'm alive."

"What protected you?" I ask.

He smiles and points toward the sky.

There is a tiny window into Fernando's soul. It's the early eighties, and Fernando is in Dallas. The D.E.A. puts him and a bodyguard up in a business hotel while they wait for the pieces to fall into place.

The bodyguard is a young cop, on the edge of his undercover career. He picks Fernando up at the airport and he's stunned at first because he thinks this old man shouldn't be doing this work. After an hour or so in the hotel room, Fernando asks the guy to get him a bottle of Jack Daniel's. He tells him he does not smoke but to get him some cigarettes also.

They sit up that night drinking the whiskey straight, the butts growing in the ashtray. And Fernando shifts into that voice he uses with me, that voice that teaches the facts of a different level of life.

Fernando explains, "I don't need to do this for the money. I don't need the money."

The cop listens. Fernando tells him that at the heart of the deal, what the other person senses is strength. That is the key, that they smell the strength in you. They want you because they want your strength. They have money and they have power, but it is not enough. That is their weakness. Nothing is enough, because they do not really know what they want. They do not really know who they are. And so they must keep doing deals, expanding, reaching out, Fernando continues, for this thing they cannot name.

But you, if you have strength, you know who you are and what you need, and so you pull them into you, and then you are in control.

Years later, the cop, now seasoned, now a man living undercover, still remembers one thing Fernando pounded into his head that night as they drank the whiskey and the man who did not drink and did not smoke lit cigarette after cigarette.

Fernando put it this way: "No matter what you do, never forget, you are always alone. No one can save you or help you. Alone."

In the late sixties one of Fernando's sons comes out into the yard and sees his father's pink Cadillac gleaming in the sunlight. The boy is about eight, and he goes around to the driver's side and finds seven bullet holes in the door. He looks at his father, who smiles, but the boy says nothing. Finally, years later when he is in college, he figures out what his father has been up to all those years. He comes to him and asks, "Did you get caught with a load? Did they turn you? Is that why you are doing this?"

Fernando looks at his boy and says, "No, son, it is not like that."

He tells his son that drugs are a cancer and they are killing their people and that his son must stay "on the right side of the law."

Nothing more is explained. The work stays in a sealed world. Because there are fresh holes waiting in the desert, gray masking tape across the mouth, bullets through the head, a splash of quicklime. And so Fernando's life goes on, unexplained even to his sons and daughters.

Once, in 1971, he followed up on an invitation to visit a drug laboratory in Chihuahua. A ton of heroin was in the offing, but the D.E.A. would not put up the money for the visit. So he and Jordan went in with no backup, no communications system, no permission from the agency, and, of course, no money. Fernando pulled the car off into the desert of Chihuahua, opened the trunk, and brought out an arsenal. He gave Jordan a .357 magnum and kept a .44 magnum for himself. He said to Jordan, "We must now practice. They will fear such guns." And Jordan complied, because he realized that he was in Fernando's house, in the culture and throb of Chihuahua.

"Phil was nervous," Fernando remembers with a smile. They were packing guns in violation of Mexican law and U.S. agency regulations. And Jordan had another good reason to be nervous, since in Mexico a D.E.A. agent is despised by every man, woman, and child as a foreign police agent operating on their soil.

They kept in touch with the agency by using Mexican pay phones. At the drug lab there were *pistoleros*, huge black dogs, and, of course, lots of dope. At such places in the sierra a man dies and no one cares or even hears the cries. The deal collapsed because it eventually meant tons of heroin, and the D.E.A. balked at fronting the necessary money.

Fernando received good chunks of money for his work, with one payment over a hundred thousand dollars, but he waited until he turned sixty-five to leave his brutal job at the mines. He did not understand life without work. He came from a world of toil and never let the D.E.A. money or the gold chains of the drug merchants he ruined touch his own rock-hard core.

Once he went to Los Angeles and took down ten tons of hashish. The agency gagged on the percentage he deserved for such a haul. Finally, they cut a check for a piddling amount, a few hundred dollars. Jordan came to Fernando's house and gave him the check. Fernando looked at it and said, "Give it back to them and tell them to shove it up their ass."

But he did not quit. He said, "I would work for Phil for nothing." And sometimes he did just that. He wasn't doing it for the money, or at least not only for the money. Nor do I think he did it because of a deep hatred of drugs. I think he did it because he could, and the rest of us cannot.

I've known Fernando for about a year, and we are sitting on the porch. A storm is growing off the mountains, and black clouds start to float over the hills around his home. His old frame comes alive as he tells me how to cut the deal. Never, he tells me, taste the product. Tell them it is a business and you don't want to mess up your mind. You have to drink, but don't drink much, just some beer and water.

I ask about the contract killers looking for him. Just a few months earlier, they had been stirring in a nearby city, sniffing the wind for him. One had called his son asking for him.

He offers this thought: "When they come, there will be only two of us. And one will be dead."

I ask him to explain. But there is no more detail: When the man comes, either he will die or Fernando will die.

·   ·   ·

He enters the El Camino Real, the old hotel in El Paso near the bridge into Juárez. It is 1989 and Fernando, seventy, has come to test himself against a legend. The Herreras operate a drug business that stretches from the Mexican state of Durango to Chicago. The organization is the family—around 3,000 blood members and several thousand more associates. They hail from a village in the Sierra Madre called Las Herreras, their own company town surrounded by their own fields lush with their own dope. Starting right after World War II, the founder, Don Jaime Herrera Nevares, set up heroin labs. No one can penetrate deeply into their organization except by marriage. And no one can cross them without facing 3,000 blood-related enemies scattered from Mexico to the American heartland. The Herreras often carry badges of various Mexican police agencies, a commonplace in the drug world. They spend money on parks, streetlights, and other Robin Hood touches to buy the complicity of the poor.

At the El Paso hotel, a father and son, one sixty-three, the other thirty-four, await Fernando. This is a coup in itself, this wooing of the Herreras to cross the line and discuss business in the United States. The D.E.A. has gotten the deal this far but can go no further without Fernando. The Herreras and Fernando go to the coffee shop, and they talk for three hours. His talks with the Herreras go on for two to three weeks, as he slowly reels in his prey. Years later, when he recounts this last deal—the big one—he relishes each little moment of their conversations.

The older Herrera is very bright and asks many questions of Fernando. "What do you do?"

"Oh, I buy things and then sell things."

"Where do you live?"

"Oh, that hardly matters. I am here to buy something good, not to talk about my house."

The older Herrera keeps trying to get Fernando off balance. "Pancho," the older Herrera will say, or "Arturo," or "Paco," or "Chuy." He keeps talking and then tossing out these different names to see if Fernando will react, to see if he can catch him off guard.

Fernando is at ease. This is the part he loves, the reeling in of the stranger. He talks of horses, thoroughbred horses, of how he loves to race his horses in Baltimore. The old man listens: the Herreras with their millions are into thoroughbred stock.

And then suddenly another name pops out. Fernando does not flinch and continues to ignore the probe. He is feeling better and better, but the older Herrera is the smartest stranger he has ever met.

They get into real matters, money. Fernando says he is looking at, say, a $2 million deal as a way of launching their relationship and testing its future. He represents some very large people, and they do not wish to do little things.

"Ah, that is no problem," the older Herrera replies. "We can get any amount of goods and deliver it. Where do you live? We will fly it to you, our planes will go right under the American radar, it is no problem."

"No, no," Fernando says, "my people prefer to handle their own shipments."

"No, Señor," the older man replies, "let us. It is easy. We have tons warehoused right here, just across the river in Juárez."

"That is very kind," Fernando says, "but we handle our own deliveries. You just get it to El Paso."

"But the money," he says, "we want you to bring the money to Juárez."

"No, Señor," Fernando says, smiling, "I am not going into Juárez with my money. That would not be the act of a wise man."

This goes on for hours, this probing, this testing.

And they agree to talk some more later.

Fernando has become the closer, the man they bring in on deals that are there, right there, but just out of reach, cases that the D.E.A. has been building but cannot finish because there the agency leaves its own scent in the air. So Fernando flies to San Francisco, Dallas, Los Angeles, wherever. He is never Mr. Big, he is the man who represents Mr. Big. And he has lots of money. He will be there for an hour, a day, a week, and then the deal goes down. He never fails, not once. And when the deal goes down, he wants out. He insists, always, on being taken immediately to the airport and returned to his family.

The Herreras try to find him. They call a dummy number he has given them, a line controlled by the D.E.A. When he comes to the second meeting at the El Camino Real hotel, they sit in the bar, a place legend says was once visited by Pancho Villa. The bar has a Tiffany-style dome above its circular black marble top. Splashes of green and blue play across the faces as the sun streams through the stained glass overhead. The room is full of soft chairs and sofas. They sit there for hours.

"Where were you?" the older Herrera asks. "We called and you were not there."

"Oh, I had some business in Las Vegas."

"How did it go?"

"Very well, Señor."

Fernando can feel him relaxing, feel it getting closer. Fernando tells jokes, many jokes, and the older Herrera never laughs, but Fernando can sense he is rising to the bait.

The older Herrera says, "Look, why don't you come to Mexico with me, we will go to Durango, to my village, Las Herreras. We have just built a public park there for the people, everyone there works for us. It will be easy. We will send a plane for you."

"No, Señor, I cannot do that. This is business, and I do not mix pleasure with business. Surely you understand."

Hours of this, hours. And then the older Herrera says, "We will do a deal. For over two million. No problem."

And they go into the fine restaurant of the hotel and eat thick steaks.

"He was ready to go. It was already made," Fernando says.

There are always surprises. That is part of the art of the deal. Sure, control—control is necessary, and being alert and careful and at ease. But no matter how much planning and thought go into the work, there will be surprises. Once, in the eighties, Fernando is at a family funeral in an isolated hamlet deep in Chihuahua when a man walks in. Years before, Fernando did a deal, and the man went down hard and spent years in prison.

He sees Fernando and comes over. Fernando turns to the man and says, "You fool, remember that deal? I told you not to come to the meeting, I could sense something, no? But you came and look what happened to you, you fool." The man is cowed, he is on the defensive. Control. That is what it takes if you are to come out of these deals alive.

The final meeting is in the hotel coffee shop. Here is the arrangement: The older Herrera sits with Fernando, and they talk. Across the street is a parking lot where the car with the kilos of heroin is to be delivered right before their eyes. Then one of Fernando's men will take the car away and test the load for quality. At the same moment, the younger Herrera will be in a nearby bar where he will be paid for the load. Fernando and the older Herrera will not get near the load.

So they sit and drink coffee and wait.

They look out the window and see a man approach the car and then drive it away. *Perfecto.* Fernando, full of coffee, tells the older Herrera that he must use the bathroom. As he leaves, the agents move in and take the man down. When Fernando comes back from the bathroom, the waiter comes over and says, "What is going on? The police came and took your friend away."

Fernando shakes his head and says, "I don't know, I hardly know the guy."

And then the police come and handcuff Fernando to give him cover. They take him to the D.E.A. office, and then he goes to the airport and home.

The Herreras get twelve to twenty years, and this time Fernando testifies. He likes the experience of testifying. Normally, a deal is structured so that no one can be certain who was the traitor. The matter is further clouded by bringing in several agents toward the end to give cover to the Fernandos of the world. But when you testify, then they know.

As he recounts the trial to me, he pauses and says with a smile, "I wanted him to know I did him."

In this case, Fernando's last big case, there is a special satisfaction. The Herreras have been stung, and this is something that never happens, and it feels good. The heroin, it turns out, is Colombian, from the Medellín cartel, and that gives even more satisfaction. But there is an extra bonus: the man brokering the heroin for the Colombians is a baron, the infamous Frog One, who escapes at the end of the film *The French Connection.* This time he does not escape.

In the thieves' market of Tepito, men come up to me and ask if I want heroin. I can feel eyes pawing my back as I walk through this fabled warren of Mexico City. I have come here tracking Amado Carrillo, the head of the Juárez cartel, for a project of mine. It is the spring of 1997. I have not let Phil Jordan know of my journey.

I stay in a hotel owned by the Juárez cartel. I look at a cartel bank when I drink at the rooftop bar. I visit with Mexican reporters who spread word that I am C.I.A. or D.E.A. I go to the restaurant where a hit was attempted on Amado Carrillo, and when I leave, after drinking and making notes, men from the restaurant follow me. I have been living this way for months, and I feel a clock ticking, and I do not believe time is on my side.

When I finally get home, I learn from a friend that he dined at the American embassy in Mexico City while I was down there looking for traces of Amado Carrillo. He sat next to the D.E.A. head of station, and when he mentioned where he lived in the States the man asked if he knew me. He said, "Tell him there is a contract on him." I will never know if this was true or if the information was ever shared with Phil Jordan. Or if he knew and for his own reasons did not tell me. But it's not what you can or cannot know; it's that you cannot ever completely trust anyone. I will know only one thing for certain, what Fernando taught that bodyguard, and me: You are always alone.

What I knew as I looked for these details was that my story on Amado Carrillo was in type, that I was only phoning in little changes, and that no matter what happened to me nothing could stop this story. I knew I had won. I had done him, I would make him famous, and in the drug industry fame leads to death. He had kept his name out of the Mexican media, he had managed to be almost entirely ignored by the U.S. media. In Juárez, a city he virtually ran, his name never appeared in print. Even the *corridos*, the folk songs of Mexican popular music that commonly celebrate major drug figures, never mentioned his name. And I think I felt exactly what Fernando felt again and again as the stranger finally said yes and gave Fernando that trust that made the stranger's doom possible.

About ninety days after my story on Carrillo ran in *GQ*, and after I appeared on the *Today* show, publicizing his power, he was dead.

Fernando tells me, you have to hug. Always hug. Embrace the stranger, pull him to you, say, Amigo, and hug him. That way you can feel if he is armed.

I like Fernando. I respect him. But I cannot be him. Not because I am better than he or even believe I am as moral as he. But because I lack something he possesses. In *The Shootist*, John Wayne's last film, a boy asks him why he is a famous gunfighter when he has just demonstrated in target practice that he is only an average shot. "Because I was willing," Wayne says, "and most men are not."

I ask Fernando if he was ever frightened.

He smiles and looks at me and is silent.

I ask him if he worries about the men who still hunt him.

He remains silent. And serene. My questions are beneath contempt. They hail from a world he left long ago, shortly after birth, somewhere in that hard childhood.

As he eats his chili and beans, the Herreras are still hunting him; he knows this, the D.E.A. has picked up their probes. No matter. He himself has fielded phone calls from hunters. Once he picked up the phone and a voice asked, "Does Fernando Terrazas live there?" and he calmly answered, "No, no one of that name lives here. I'm sorry but you have the wrong number." He keeps a .45 loaded and he practices with it. There will be two men, he knows, him and the other man. One man will die.

I ask his wife if she worried about him when he would go off to do deals. "Yes," she says. "I wondered if he would come back alive."

So I ask him once again, Why did you risk your life? And he gives the same answers: He hates drugs, he liked the money, he liked the work. But this time he keeps talking, talking about a long time ago. He came up as a teenager from Mexico, he rode the rails, worked the fields—damn hard work for little money.

Once his two sons came to him and said they did not want to go to college. He thought about it. Then he took them to California for the summer, put them in a tent, and had them work in the fields. They said the work was too hard. He said, "You better get used to it. Because if you do not go to college, you will work like this the rest of your life." They went to college. Years later, one of his sons had a chance at a bigger and better job. He told his father he did not know if he would take it. His father said, "You can go up there. If you don't like it, you can always come back down. But you have the chance to go up there." So his son went up there.

Fernando went up there, up with the big guys and their gold chains and millions, up there with the agents and their college degrees and badges. He did not come back down.

Theoretically, of course, Fernando has his Achilles' heel: he trusted me. While he was alive, he had to trust that I would hide his home and change his name. What intrigues me is that he had to trust someone. I know the feeling, the unease later when I sit there and wonder if I am being set up. I know what it is like to drive from a meeting and watch the rearview mirror because, well, because I have trusted and could be betrayed and in some instances betrayal would mean no one would ever know what happened to me. Still, knowing all this, I trust. It is a need. This need made Fernando's career. And this need has now placed his safety in my hands.

We are all, I believe, prisoners of this desire.

Phil Jordan has flown in from Dallas for Fernando's rosary and funeral. He has come for the burial of the other half of his own identity. He sees the same flock of four hundred mourners I see and knows they do not know. He has felt the blows of Fernando's world. He has a murdered brother, the subject of the book that had dragged me for seven years into the drug world. The case has never been solved. He once talked to Fernando about it, and the old man listened and said, There, there is the traitor. And he pointed to a person close to the core of Jordan's own blood. But the murder is filed away in Jordan's head at the moment and kept safe for a while from his thoughts.

He has come here to close the books on a friend and to keep things wrapped up and tidy. Fernando Terrazas was the partner that made his career, the friend who taught him rules in a world free of rules. He was the liar who was always the honorable man. I would have trusted Fernando with my life without a second's thought.

I look out at the full church, scan the faces of his children and their children. I talk to a son who is now a federal agent, the same son who as a boy found the bullet holes in Fernando's car, and I ask him if he ever saw his father have too much to drink. He thinks and says, yes, once or twice he saw him kind of light up from alcohol. I remember years ago meeting this son in a border bar. He sat with his back to the corner of the room, a black bag with his gun on the table between us. I did not mention his father and he never mentioned such a father existed. This silence is part of that world. Never trust. And yet you wind up trusting, just as the son did when he met me in the bar with his pistol and his back to the wall. The son asks me not to mention where his father lived. When I ask why, he says, "It never stops."

Phil Jordan comes over to the son and asks if he can pin a D.E.A. badge on his father's lapel. The son nods agreement. I watch Jordan delicately pin on the badge, then stand back and look almost with love into Fernando's cold face.

I want to say more. I want to say that Fernando Terrazas was a very fine man. And he was. I want to say, Never forget you are alone, always alone, that there is no backup. And you are. But I want to live somewhere else, someplace safe from the cold truths of Fernando.

Now the old man has been properly filed. Now he has been made safe for all of us. And we can feel comfortable in our worlds and our words. We can forget what we have learned.

June 2002

The Line Is Hot

A History of the Machine Gun, Shot

STEVE FEATHERSTONE

The story of the machine gun begins with the Maxim, designed in 1884. It lacks a conventional trigger: to fire, the shooter presses a flanged metal tab, which is positioned between two wooden spade grips at the back of the receiver. I wrapped my fingers around the grips, flipped the hinged safety catch, and waited for the signal.

"Shooters to my left, lock and load your weapons," crackled the loudspeaker. "Shooters to my right, move up to the firing line. Remember, everybody, have your eyes and ears on. Everybody ready? The line is . . . *hot!*"

I pressed the trigger with both thumbs, and the gun shook my shoulders like a jackhammer. It was a British-made Vickers Mark 1, manufactured in 1917 but licensed from Hiram Maxim's original design. Maxim was an American who had moved to England, where, a friend had told him, a vast market existed for a weapon that would "enable these Europeans to cut each others' throats with greater facility." Crouched behind his gun in black coattails and top hat, Maxim would slice mature trees in half to the astonishment of visiting royal delegations. What his invention might do to the front rank of a charging cavalry regiment, the highest expression of nineteenth-century tactical doctrine, was left to his visitors' imagination.

I swung the Vickers around to enfilade a car seat one hundred yards downrange. The feed block gobbled up the ammunition belt and spat empty shell casings on the ground. Long bursts of fire caused the muzzle to buck upward—a phenomenon, inherent to all automatic weapons, called "muzzle climb." I wrestled the Vickers to a horizontal position and fired again. The water jacket, a corrugated steel cylinder filled with water to cool the hot gun barrel, hissed and sputtered and billowed steam into my face.

Watching the seat fly apart, I could understand the British Army's reluctance to adopt the machine gun. To a nation that celebrated the nobility of even failed military ventures—*Into the valley of Death rode the six hundred*—the machine gun offended every rule of honorable sportsmanship. The rule book was discarded in the darker corners of the empire. At the "battle" of Omdurman, in 1898, a small contingent of British troops equipped with ten Maxim guns faced 50,000 disciples of the Mahdi army, dervishes of the Sudan fabled for their courage and daring. Wielding swords and rifles, the dervishes charged in broad daylight. Ten thousand of them were cut down before the British cavalry, hoping to share in the glory, spurred their horses forward in pointless counterattack.

At the outbreak of World War I, British military leaders still considered the machine gun best suited to slaughtering savages. Even after it became clear that the gun was equally adept at killing white Europeans, the home front was treated to patriotic tales of machine-gun crews firing their Vickerses to boil water for tea—helping to prolong the romantic fantasy that modern battles could still be won by individual resolve. One year after the British Army formed the Machine Gun Corps in 1915, nearly 20,000 British soldiers died in the first day of the Somme offensive as they marched rank-and-file toward German machine guns, bagpipes skirling and cavalry bugles ashriek.

Ammunition box empty, I peeled my shaking hands from the spade grips and released the trigger button. My thumbs were cramped and numb. I had never fired a machine gun before, but I could think of nothing else besides when I would fire the next.

Knob Creek Gun Range is on a former naval proving ground adjacent to Fort Knox, thirty miles south of Louisville, Kentucky. Twice a year it hosts "the nation's largest machine gun shoot and military gun show," a three-day exhibition of raw firepower on a scale rarely seen outside war zones. I arrived on a misty October morning and walked up a rutted dirt road past heaps of junked cars and appliances. Trucks and ATVs rumbled in every direction, towing crates of guns and ammunition. At the upper range—Knob Creek is divided into two ranges, the upper being reserved for serious machine-gun collectors—spectators stood on bleachers and pressed against a chain-link fence, hoping to catch a glimpse of their favorite guns and the lucky men who owned them. Most of the guns were American models, from the hand-cranked Gatling to its spiritual heir, the M134 Minigun, which is powered by a General Electric motor. Belt-fed weapons of every variety and vintage rested on tripods, muzzles pointed skyward. An antiaircraft battery adequate to defend a battleship anchored one end of the firing line. Its owner reclined on a seat inside the turret, adjusting one of the battery's four .50-caliber machine guns. Water-cooled guns, their polished bronze jackets gleaming in the hazy light, looked like Victorian bathroom fixtures next to the dull, anodized austerity of their present-day descendants.

The lower range was open to all. Vendors had posted signs outside tents stocked with automatic weapons chosen specifically for their mass-market appeal. For roughly a dollar per round, anyone capable of holding an AK47 without dropping it could shoot up an old Chevy or Frigidaire. Young men dressed in camouflage, some with rifles slung over their shoulders or handguns strapped to their thighs, strolled alongside suburban families who looked as if they'd gotten off the wrong highway exit for the amusement park. One middle-aged man wearing a black cowboy hat and pink shirt stepped up to a vendor's table, surveyed the guns, and asked if he could run a belt through one.

"I just been waiting for a man that had enough guts," the vendor said, opening his metal cashbox.

I waited in line to shoot the BAR (Browning Automatic Rifle), which was designed by legendary gunsmith John Browning and rushed to the front in 1918. The war had long before devolved into a bloody stalemate, owing both to the machine gun and to a fatal lack of imagination among the generals. To punch through German lines and hold them against counterattack, firepower had to become mobile. This was the principle behind both the tank—a bulletproof battering ram—and the BAR, the first automatic rifle-caliber weapon that could be fired on the run. It resembled an oversized infantry rifle with a machined steel receiver sturdier than an anvil. The BAR entered World War I too late to make much difference, but it provided the main fire support at the squad level during World War II and the Korean War. It was typically issued to the biggest or most reliable man in the squad. Merely hearing it in the heat of combat tended to boost morale. In a study of weapons usage during the Korean War, military historian S.L.A. Marshall observed that "wherever the BAR moves and fires, it gives fresh impulse to the rifle line."

The man in front of me held the BAR at his waist and emptied its twenty-round magazine in two long bursts that pushed him back on the heels of his work boots.

"Lot of recoil?" I asked as he returned to the back of the line.

"Well hell yeah!" he said. The corners of his handlebar mustache curled upward. "Why else would you want to shoot it?"

I thought it safest to shoot from a prone position, resting the BAR on its bipod. A hinged steel butt plate capped the gun's broad wooden stock. I squared my shoulder firmly against the butt plate and set my sights on the smooth white flank of a washing machine fifty yards away. The butt plate hammered my collarbone. The bipod skidded in the dirt. Empty cartridges whistled from the smoking ejection port into the woods, tearing leaves off tree branches. When the smoke cleared, I realized I hadn't hit the washing machine. I wasn't sure what I had hit. "Good shooting," the vendor said, helping me off the ground.

Ed Weitzman, a doctor from Pennsylvania, had his own tent on the upper firing range—a sort of mobile operating room for machine guns, filled with tools, spare parts, and crates of surplus Czech ammunition. Hundreds of empty shell casings littered the dirt floor, which was contaminated in places by milky blue pools of antifreeze that had bled from Ed's collection of vintage water-cooled machine guns. Ed pulled out his wallet and showed me a picture of his grandchildren. A little boy sat in firing position behind one of two Maxim guns arranged in front of a brick fireplace. A little girl stood to the side, holding an ammunition belt.

"She's supervising my grandson," he chuckled. "She's telling him what to do."

"Adorable," I said, and complimented him on the Maxim guns. I asked him about the pristine Model 1897 Gatling gun that stood in a corner of the tent on a spoke-wheeled carriage. Trying not to sound too solicitous, I speculated whether the gun had once belonged to Lt. John Parker's battery of Gatlings that raked Spanish rifle pits on San Juan Hill in 1898, clearing the way for Teddy Roosevelt's charge.

"Maybe." Ed shrugged, and adjusted his earplugs in preparation for the next shooting session. I stood behind him for a while, watching and waiting as he worked a belt through a shiny bronze Maxim that kept jamming. When it became clear that Ed was not going to invite me to shoot the Gatling, or anything else for that matter, I returned to the lower range in search of a Thompson submachine gun.

The Thompson was the first machine gun to find frequent use off the battlefield. During the 1863 draft riots in New York City, *New York Times* owner (and former *Harper's* editor) Henry Raymond successfully defended his newspaper's favorable opinion of draft exemptions for the wealthy by pointing two Gatling guns—not technically machine guns but "rapid-fire" weapons—into the street from his office windows. And four months before World War I, while U.S. Army officers minced about with sabers on the parade ground, National Guard troops machine-gunned a tent colony of striking miners in Ludlow, Colorado, killing thirteen. But for the most part, pre-Thompson machine guns were too large and too expensive to be readily adapted for personal use. The "tommy gun" was the first machine gun sold directly to civilians.

Colonel J. T. Thompson initially marketed his invention as the Trench Broom, coining the term "submachine gun" to describe what would become a new class of automatic weapon. The weapon did not reach the front in time to sweep the Hun from his trenches, but, to Thompson's dismay, there was indeed a niche market for a relatively light, reliable gun that could lay down a formidable field of fire from the running board of a getaway car. Prohibition's bloody gang wars raised Thompson's gun to pop-culture status, and gave it a new name in the process: the Chicago Typewriter. In 1928 Chicago, where owning a six-shot revolver required a permit, one could have a Thompson submachine gun, with a fifty-round drum magazine, delivered to one's door for $221. The Thompson also became de rigueur for private detectives hired to protect the interests of union-busting industrialists.

"You'll really like this," the vendor said, and stood behind me.

I lowered the Thompson to my hip and squeezed the trigger. Shells arced gracefully from the ejection port. Thirty yards away, slugs splashed in the dirt around the base of a hot-water heater. The Thompson's recoil was smooth and steady. It was a civilian Model 1927, with all the trimmings that the military would later strip away to streamline production: a muzzle compensator, which minimized climb, and polished walnut furniture. The stock was as big as a rifle's, and the scalloped fore grip fit my hand like a well-worn doorknob.

Perhaps the best description of how easily a Thompson handles comes from Paul Muni's character in the 1932 gangster movie *Scarface*: "You can carry it around like a baby." Ernest Hemingway often used a tommy gun to kill sharks from the rolling deck of his fishing boat.

I emptied the magazine in one long rip that plowed into the hot-water heater, causing it to lurch. Submachine guns fire pistol cartridges, and the Thompson chambers .45-caliber ACP ammunition, one of the biggest pistol rounds available. But they weren't powerful enough to dispatch the heater entirely. Moments later I heard the distinctive report of the BAR, and the heater toppled over into a pile of shredded pink insulation. The man with the handlebar mustache nodded and pumped his fist in the air. Onlookers clapped him on the shoulder.

"Laid that sucker down!" he shouted, and paused. "Damn, I like this!"

Germany showed more foresight than its imperial rivals with regard to the machine gun and how best to employ it. After attending a demonstration of the Maxim gun in the 1890s, Kaiser Wilhelm II had expressed his enthusiasm with Teutonic directness, stating, "That is the gun; there is no other." Germans soon were using Maxim guns to mow down rebellious tribesmen in African colonies. But Germany, unlike England, learned something from this gruesome work. During World War I, Germany was more flexible than was England or France in organizing units and tactics around the machine gun. And although the Treaty of Versailles banned German development of automatic weapons, military and industrial leaders circumvented the ban through a network of proxy companies: German engineers drew the blueprints, and Swiss firms, among others, manufactured the prototypes. Thus by 1939, Germany, which had fought the previous war with foreign machine-gun designs, possessed a wide range of homegrown automatic weapons that revolutionized machine-gun design, tactics, and production.

Lou Pacilla, who has participated in Knob Creek's shoot for twenty years, collected only vintage German weapons. It was hard not to notice Lou. He wore a black T-shirt with the words HITLERJUGEND TOUR printed on the back, its list of tour dates beginning with NORREY, FRANCE, 1944. A gold *Totenkopf*, the leering skull symbol of the Waffen SS, dangled on a thick gold chain around his neck. It matched the gold *Totenkopf* ring on his right hand, except for the twinkling red stones mounted in the ring's eye sockets. The ammunition box of his MG42 featured a hand-painted *Totenkopf*, and a *Totenkopf* was etched on the receiver of his ZB26 machine gun, although that appeared to have been the work of actual Nazis.

"Looking at a pretty woman is like looking at these old antique guns. I mean, beauty is beauty, and ugly is ugly," Lou said, shaking a can of WD-40. He sprayed some on a hot gun barrel. The oil vaporized into a stinking white mist. "Every guy that's at this show comes and shows me them Russian guns. I said, 'You know why you guys collect that Russian shit?'—I used to tell them Jap collectors the same thing—'Because it's cheap! And it's ugly!'"

A sign tacked to a support beam above his position read THE ORIGINAL WILD BUNCH. Lou led the bunch, if only because he owned all the guns. He showed me his collection, and I helped him swab gun barrels. I handed him tools and rags.

"He's one of the Wild Bunch already," Lou said to one of his colleagues as I helped him carry a crate of ammunition. "See how I draft them in?"

To his credit, Lou's sympathies with German fascism, like his appreciation of German machine guns, seemed purely aesthetic. Anticipating the start of the next shooting session, he danced a happy jig on the firing line and pulled back the charging handle on his MP38 submachine gun. Orange-shirted security guards roamed the line, loaded pistols holstered to their hips. Fire discipline was a serious matter at Knob Creek. No one was allowed to load weapons or shoot until the announcer gave the signal.

"Do not shoot into that rockface," the announcer warned. "Do not shoot over the hill. We have neighbors over the hill. Okay, shooters—"

—A burst of gunfire.

"Cease fire! Cease fire!"

"Who did that?!"

Lou bowed his head and raised his hand. A wisp of white smoke trickled from the muzzle of his MP38.

"It was them Nazis!"

Laughter echoed down the line, and then the shooting began. Lou scooped up an ammunition belt and waved me over to his MG42, considered to be the finest, most vicious machine gun ever made. In the decades between the two world wars, the proliferation of new machine guns—submachine guns, heavy machine guns, light and medium machine guns—had resulted in a hodgepodge of competing calibers and redundant roles. Every country had its own idea of how the next war would be fought. Germany, however, designed weapons, from dive-bombers to tanks, to suit the singular tactical theory of blitzkrieg. From this concept evolved the MG34, the first general-purpose machine gun. In the defensive role, it had the sustained-fire capabilities of a heavy machine gun, yet it was light enough to be carried forward with attacking infantry. One gun, one cartridge, one training regimen. But there was one problem: conventional manufacturing methods could not keep up with blitzkrieg's demands. At the time, even firearms less complex than the MG34 were cut from solid blocks of steel. Each of their many complicated parts required milling, drilling, and grinding at the hands of a skilled machinist.

The MG42 was the first machine gun built almost entirely out of stamped and welded sheet metal, just like toasters or Volkswagens. It was cheaper, more reliable, and easier to manufacture than the MG34. Its ferocious rate of fire—1,200 rounds per minute, nearly twice the rate of any other belt-fed weapon on the battlefield—earned it the nickname "Hitler's Buzzsaw." Allied soldiers compared its terrifying report to a piece of heavy canvas being ripped in half; "like a tin roof ripping off," preferred Lou. Many countries, including Germany, still equip their soldiers with MG42s that have been modified only in nomenclature.

Lou's MG42 was fixed on a modern Leopard tank mount. A spring-loaded lever similar to a motorcycle clutch worked the trigger. I flexed my fingers and squeezed. The MG42 smoked and crackled and spilled empty casings over my boots. The ammunition belt evaporated before I could register what had happened. Lou flipped up the feed tray, loaded a new belt, and snapped the tray shut.

"Get your sight picture," he shouted, "and just kill 'em!"

I felt as if I'd grabbed the end of a live wire. The initial jolt locked my elbows and fused my feet to the dirt. I resisted the urge to pull away. I didn't think. I didn't even move.

"They're coming at you, Steve! Kill 'em!"

The world telescoped to a point floating off the tip of the MG42's jittering muzzle. Time seemed to flicker. A target presented itself—a blackened car, a white refrigerator—and I sliced into it with a zippering roar. I wanted it to go on forever. Three seconds after the circuit opened, the last cartridge passed through the chamber. The MG42 became inert.

"Shooters clear your weapons," the announcer said. "Security up and down the firing line, make sure these weapons are clear."

A twilight haze of smoke and burnt gunpowder settled over the range.

Shafts of sunlight swept the debris field, illuminating strange tableaus: a gutted kitchen range, its sheet-metal skin twisted and teased outward like warm taffy; a fan-shaped carpet of smoldering confetti that had once been a stack of telephone books; five-gallon steel propane tanks so honeycombed with bullet holes that gusts of wind would later roll them across the range like tumbleweeds. Two hundred yards downrange, a figure in a shiny silver suit spurted a ragged jet of flame at a boat. *Whoosh!* The boat vanished in an orange fireball. Greasy black smoke boiled up high above the ridgeline.

"Flamethrowers," Lou said, sneering. "Now why do they let them do this?" He pulled out an American-flag handkerchief and wiped his shooting glasses with it. "All part of the show, I guess."

Were the act of killing as simple as pulling a trigger, all soldiers would carry the same gun, which also would be mounted on tanks and helicopters. Our allies, and our enemies, would equip their armies with it, and one defense contractor would get rich selling it. No such superweapon exists, of course, because killing involves many unpredictable variables. But the modern assault rifle comes closest to the one-gun ideal.

In 1944, Adolf Hitler is said to have invented the term "assault rifle" to describe the latest superweapon developed by Nazi engineers, the StG44, or *SturmGewehr*, 1944. The StG44 was lighter and easier to control under fire than were automatic rifles or belt-fed machine guns, and it had greater range, killing power, and accuracy than did submachine guns. With few encouraging reports emerging from the eastern front, the excellent performance of the MP43, the StG44's predecessor, came as welcome news. Little was changed other than the name, which reflected Hitler's dream of eternal conquest, of never-ending assault. Only half a million were manufactured before the Russians rolled into Berlin less than a year later.

I spied an MP43 at the sign-in table for the Jungle Walk course, poking out from behind a box of glazed doughnuts. At first I wasn't sure what kind of gun it was, but something about it seemed oddly familiar. The steeply raked pistol grip, counterbalanced by the curved magazine. The tall, triangular foresight. It had the iconic profile of an AK47, but it lacked certain refinements. I licked my thumb, rubbed the model number stamped into the gun's receiver below the gas tube, and there it was: MP43. I couldn't believe my luck.

The MP43 belonged to Bob Hurley, one of Knob Creek's many volunteer range officers. Bob was talking to a Dutch documentary filmmaker, a thin, bespectacled young man named Max, who seemed to have learned English from watching American game shows. Max put his arm around Bob's narrow shoulders.

"Thank you, Bob. Fantastic television." Max winked at Bob, and then added a thumbs-up. "You were born for television." After the film crew packed up and left, Bob remained perplexed by his moment in the limelight. He had taken the crew down the Jungle Walk trail, he said, and had shown them the targets set up in the underbrush. Max had kept asking questions. Did Bob have specific names for the targets, like Ho Chi Minh or bin Laden? Did he hate them? Did he want to shoot Ho Chi Minh and bin Laden in the face with an Uzi?

"I don't know what that means." Bob shrugged. "Do you know what that means? They're just pieces of steel."

Bob ran the Jungle Walk course with George Patterson. Bob and George were old Army buddies from Vietnam, and only the Army could have made friends of these men. George's pressed fatigues and spit-polished boots left some doubt as to whether he had actually been discharged. Bob, by contrast, wore khaki shorts with white gym socks pulled up to his knobby knees and seemed unlikely to survive a ride to boot camp, let alone combat. Despite Max's professional opinion, Bob was not made for television. I asked him if I could fire his MP43.

"You never heard anything so loud in your life," George piped in. "Sounds like two guys hitting an anvil. Like two junked cars fighting it out inside there."

Bob looked stricken. The MP43 chambered a special shortened, or "Kurz," version of the standard Mauser rifle round, and he didn't have any. With any luck, he said, I might find vintage Kurz cartridges for sale in the pole barn on the upper range.

In the barn I wandered the crowded aisles, shouting, "Kurz? Got any Kurz ammo?" None of the gun dealers I spoke to understood a word of German. They did, however, recognize the swastika and Wehrmacht eagle printed on the empty cardboard ammunition box that Bob had given me. They squinted at the curled paper label and murmured, "Eight-millimeter Kurz, very hard to come by," after which they would point me to another dealer. I had begun to despair until I noticed a Ziploc bag of bullets locked behind a display case that also contained a Nazi Iron Cross.

"Is that eight-millimeter Kurz?"

"Son, this stuff here is the real deal," the dealer said, unlocking the case so I could take a closer look. The copper jackets were tarnished and dull, and corrosion bloomed green around the primers. The dealer told me not to worry about it. The bullets would work.

Bob and I took the Ziploc bag of old Nazi bullets and the MP43 into the woods, stopping in a clearing on the bank of a sluggish brown creek. Mosquitoes swarmed in the undergrowth. I slid the clip into the gun's magazine guide and popped it in with the base of my palm.

"Charge it," Bob said.

I pulled back the bolt and sighted down the barrel. The gun's walnut stock felt warm and smooth against my cheek. Across the creek five steel disks painted fluorescent orange hung from a pole. I took a deep breath, aimed, and pulled the trigger. The gun jerked. A blast of what felt like hot sand needled my face, blinding me. Bob gripped my shoulder. "Oh my God," he shouted. "Are you okay? Can you see?" Grit scraped under my right eyelid. Black soot powdered my arms, and bits of burnt powder stuck in my teeth. I spat into my hand.

"Jesus, when's the last time you cleaned this thing?"

"I take very good care of my guns," Bob said.

I switched to shoot from my right shoulder. In a series of short bursts, I emptied the magazine. Bullets smacked into the damp earth, sending up spouts of dirt and leaves. George Patterson was right. The MP43 was loud and obnoxious. It sounded like a snare drum lined with tin foil. But there was something else going on with the gun—a weird kind of feedback. I could feel it in my fingertips. Maybe it was the return spring sizzling inside the stock, or the heavy bolt pounding beneath the thin skin of the receiver. Whatever it was, the MP43 hummed like a living thing.

It was almost dark when we came out of the woods, slapping at mosquitoes. Walking up the dirt road to the upper range, we passed a trash barrel stuffed with burning cardboard. Someone must also have dumped live ammunition into it: the barrel exploded in a shower of sparks. I shielded my face and skittered across the road.

"Incoming!" Bob shouted. "Charlie in the wire!" Flakes of burning cardboard fluttered down around us.

Studies undertaken after World War II confirmed what the Nazis already knew when they designed the MP43. Most combat took place within a 300-meter killing zone, well within the maximum effective range of standard-issue infantry rifles such as the German Mauser and the U.S. Garand. The rifle's fire-power was largely wasted. Some studies also indicated that only a small frac-tion of U.S. soldiers fired their rifles in combat, with machine gunners accounting for the majority of effective fire. The rifle's days were numbered; it would soon be replaced in every corner of the globe by the assault rifle.

The reasons for this shift were not just tactical in nature but political as well. Before World War II, automatic weapons were exclusively on the side of imperialism, a lopsided balance of power summarized in Hilaire Belloc's tidy couplet, *"Whatever happens, we have got/The Maxim Gun, and they have not."* But the story in the latter half of the twentieth century was quite the opposite. With the onset of the Cold War, and of the attendant "hot" wars of liberation in decaying colonial regimes from Africa to Asia to South America, the great powers eagerly supplied their clients with guns, mainly assault rifles. Small, often indigenous forces equipped with little more than machine guns and guerrilla tactics could now win battles, and even wars, against nations armed with the most sophisticated technologies of destruction available. The latest incarnation of the Mahdi army, led by Shiite cleric Moktada al-Sadr in Iraq, is less than one fifth the size of the dervish army butchered at Omdurman, and yet these modern Mahdists have won concessions from a military force infi-nitely more lethal than ten Maxim guns.

Of the contemporary assault rifles, I tried the M16 first. In the early six-ties, when the rifle (then called the AR15) was issued to American security forces in South Vietnam, soldiers were skeptical: its forged aluminum receiver, black plastic furniture, and tight tolerances between seams suggested a gun cast in a toy factory. Nothing about it—particularly not its small .223-caliber cartridge, a "varmint" round designed for picking off gophers—resembled the big, shoulder-bruising automatic rifles that soldiers had trained on, such as the BAR and the M14.

I leaned forward on the balls of my feet and fired a three-round burst at a Winnebago. The report was sharp and cracking, but I overestimated the recoil; it was much lighter than any of the other weapons I had fired that day. I lost my balance. The vendor tugged the back of my shirt to keep me from stepping over the line. I found my footing and cleared the magazine. The only part of the M16 that seemed to move when I pulled the trigger was the ejection port dust-cover. It flipped open, spent casings poured out, and then it flipped shut.

"This M16 ain't gonna cut it," said George Steele, recalling his feelings af-ter first being ambushed in Vietnam. Soon afterward, he swapped his M16 for a belt-fed M60 machine gun. Now, thirty-three years after Vietnam, Steele had driven from Tennessee to Knob Creek in an effort to remember how it felt to sling "the pig," as the M60 was called, over his shoulder. Unfortunately, none of the vendors had one for rent, and George stood at the edge of the crowd marveling at all the weapons and noise, his arms folded over his chest.

I was waiting to shoot the AK47, and so I asked him what he thought of it.

"Man, we would find them damn things buried in the ground," George said. "They'd wrap them in plastic, bury them in creeks and things. We'd pull them babies out and—let's roll! Just empty the water out of them. They'd fire good, boy. Whole lot better than the M16, far as I was concerned."

After the overengineered efficiency of the M16, I was eager to shoot the AK47. To my disappointment, however, the weapon advertised was not a classic AK47 but rather a modernized version of the gun called the AKMS. Gone was the swept-back wooden shoulder stock; in its place, a minimalist steel frame folded beneath the receiver. The pistol grip was made of plastic. Because of its larger cartridge and loose build quality, I expected a pounding recoil, but the AKMS delivered only a modest, rhythmic kick. Neither the M16 nor the AKMS was very accurate beyond two hundred yards, where the Winnebago rested on its rusted rims. My shots spattered in all directions against the hillside. It seemed as if the very essence of the machine gun, of a century's worth of blood, had been refined out of these weapons. And indeed, although assault rifles will continue to play a crucial role in armed conflict, this is how the story of the machine gun ends—not with a bang but with a chaste sequence of pops.

In the developing world, the assault rifle has transcended the battlefield altogether, shifting from an unacknowledged tool of imperial subjugation to an accoutrement of resistance. The totemic silhouette of the AK47, of which more than 50 million have been manufactured since 1947, adorns the flags of Mozambique and Hezbollah; the only prop allowed in most of Osama bin Laden's studiously arranged videotaped messages has been a Kalashnikov.

At the same time, tactics and weapons devised to circumvent the machine gun, such as aerial bombardment and tanks, have a far greater impact on the battlefields of today. Indeed, even the idea of a battlefield—a defined place where combatants meet to destroy each other—is now considered obsolete. The West's enemies, we are told, are everywhere and nowhere at once. Military planners refer to this situation as "asymmetric warfare," which is another way of admitting they have no idea what to do about it.

Our own military's answer has been an increasing reliance on specialization and new technologies that promise to single out malefactors with a minimum of casualties. Unmanned spy drones scour vast regions, day and night. Cruise missiles are programmed with the precise coordinates of distant bases. Elite Special Forces units rappel from helicopters under the cover of darkness. The U.S. Army catchphrase "An Army of One" emphasizes this theme of bloodless precision, of achieving clear objectives with minimal cost. In such a context of sleek techno-war, the machine gun seems a hopeless antique.

Thousands of spectators crowded the upper range for the night shoot, packing the bleachers and jostling for spots at the fence behind the firing line. I pushed through the throng and sat on an empty ammunition crate. A teenage boy with curly blond hair and blue eyes stood at a nearby shooting bench. He acknowledged me with a curt tip of his baseball cap and removed from his case a bolt-action .50-caliber Barrett "anti-matériel" rifle, the type favored by U.S. sniper teams in Iraq. Out on the range, flashlights bobbed in the darkness as the Knob Creek staff attached pyrotechnic charges to barrels of diesel fuel marked with green glow sticks.

"All you shooters remember this," the loudspeaker crackled. "Do not shoot the flares—the flares are *not* the targets. The glow sticks, that's where the charges are."

I had been warned not to miss the night shoot. One man told me it looked like the bombing of Baghdad. I assumed he meant the precision-guided campaign that preceded the invasion of Iraq, because the explosions that kicked off the night shoot seemed similarly choreographed for "shock and awe." In two minutes a dozen detonations rippled across the range. The ground trembled. Molten orange fireballs shot hundreds of feet into the air on churning columns of fire. Vehicles were hurled end over end. Tornadoes of flame whipped up by convection currents danced amid the debris, igniting everything they touched.

The explosions subsided. Tracer rounds, bullets embedded with a magnesium compound, streaked red and yellow and green through the night. Some skipped off the tops of vehicles and shot straight into the sky. Others bounced over the ground and caromed crazily through the trees. The Minigun's electric motor moaned, its spinning barrels ringed by a halo of sparks, at the center of which a torrent of tracers poured forth in a pulsing river of red light that forked into the earth and caused it to boil. For a moment the range was obscured in a pall of dust and smoke. The spectators cheered wildly.

After exhausting their tracer ammunition, the shooters switched to conventional jacketed rounds. Gun barrels glowed red like iron rods drawn from a forge. There was something desperate and joyless about the shooting now. It was all senseless noise and smoke. Shells piled up in mounds as men emptied magazine after magazine, belt after belt, like factory workers tending to some infernal machine, their grim faces illuminated by muzzle blast.

The blond boy with the Barrett sniper rifle lay on his stomach, baseball cap on backward, searching the darkness for a target. He fingered the trigger—*boom!* The blast moved the hair on my head. As the kid reloaded, I tapped him on the shoulder and asked what he was shooting at.

He looked up at me, his face as blank as a doll's. His glassy blue eyes caught the reflection of fires burning downrange. "You know," he said. "Anything I can see."

December 2005

Part Three

Illness

When writing on the subject of sickness, reporters themselves are susceptible to a variety of journalistic maladies. To profile the recovering, or actively ill, or (God help us) actually deceased individual is to teeter on the brink of "human interest" reporting—a phrase used solely, of course, to denote reporting of zero interest to intelligent humans. A second, and related, affliction is an undue deference to the medical profession, doctors having somehow escaped the reflexive suspicion of authority learned (and then, all too often, unlearned) by the press during the past half century. Health stories tend to ply clichéd tropes of victimhood and survivorship (the plucky patient), or genius and derring-do (the valiant doctor), all the while eliding the economic and social forces that determine who gets sick—or gets called sick—in America today.

Such traps pose no less danger when the story concerns the reporter's own health. Our next two pieces are uncommonly vigorous specimens, whose authors, meditating on their own arduous trips through the medical-industrial complex, succeed in pushing past the merely personal to draw out impersonally scrupulous indictments. "Welcome to Cancerland" is Barbara Ehrenreich's own story of surviving breast cancer, from mammogram to chemotherapy to remission, and at every turn she resists easy appeals to the reader's sympathy. She focuses her rage instead at the infantilizing pink-ribbon cult of "survivorhood" and shows how that cult distracts us from more serious concerns, such as the environmental pollution that has been linked to higher cancer rates. In "Manufacturing Depression," Gary Greenberg, a practicing psychotherapist, subjects himself to a pharmaceutical trial on depression, using the experience to reflect on who wins and who loses when an enormous industry has a vested interest in construing sadness as illness.

Welcome to Cancerland

A Mammogram Leads to a Cult of Pink Kitsch

BARBARA EHRENREICH

I was thinking of it as one of those drive-by mammograms, one stop in a series of mundane missions including post office, supermarket, and gym, but I began to lose my nerve in the changing room, and not only because of the kinky necessity of baring my breasts and affixing tiny X-ray opaque stars to the tip of each nipple. I had been in this place only four months earlier, but that visit was just part of the routine cancer surveillance all good citizens of HMOs or health plans are expected to submit to once they reach the age of fifty, and I hadn't really been paying attention then. The results of that earlier session had aroused some "concern" on the part of the radiologist and her confederate, the gynecologist, so I am back now in the role of a suspect, eager to clear my name, alert to medical missteps and unfair allegations. But the changing room, really just a closet off the stark windowless space that houses the mammogram machine, contains something far worse, I notice for the first time now—an assumption about who I am, where I am going, and what I will need when I get there. Almost all of the eye-level space has been filled with photocopied bits of cuteness and sentimentality: pink ribbons, a cartoon about a woman with iatrogenically flattened breasts, an "Ode to a Mammogram," a list of the "Top Ten Things Only Women Understand" ("Fat Clothes" and "Eyelash Curlers" among them), and, inescapably, right next to the door, the poem "I Said a Prayer for You Today," illustrated with pink roses.

It goes on and on, this mother of all mammograms, cutting into gym time, dinnertime, and lifetime generally. Sometimes the machine doesn't work, and I get squished into position to no purpose at all. More often, the X ray is successful but apparently alarming to the invisible radiologist, off in some remote office, who calls the shots and never has the courtesy to show her face with an apology or an explanation. I try pleading with the technician: I have no known risk factors, no breast cancer in the family, had my babies relatively young and nursed them both. I eat right, drink sparingly, work out, and doesn't that count for something? But she just gets this tight little professional smile on her face, either out of guilt for the torture she's inflicting or because she already knows something that I am going to be sorry to find out for myself. For an hour and a half the procedure is repeated: the squishing, the snapshot, the technician bustling off to consult the radiologist and returning with a demand for new angles and more definitive images. In the intervals while she's off with the doctor I read the *New York Times* right down to the personally irrelevant sections like theater and real estate, eschewing the stack of women's magazines provided for me, much as I ordinarily enjoy a quick read about sweat-proof eyeliners and "fabulous sex tonight," because I have picked up this warning vibe in the changing room, which, in my increasingly anxious state, translates into: femininity is death. Finally there is nothing left to read but one of the free local weekly newspapers, where I find, buried deep in the classifieds, something even more unsettling than the growing prospect of major disease—a classified ad for a "breast cancer teddy bear" with a pink ribbon stitched to its chest.

Yes, atheists pray in their foxholes—in this case, with a yearning new to me and sharp as lust, for a clean and honorable death by shark bite, lightning strike, sniper fire, car crash. Let me be hacked to death by a madman, is my silent supplication—anything but suffocation by the pink sticky sentiment embodied in that bear and oozing from the walls of the changing room.

My official induction into breast cancer comes about ten days later with the biopsy, which, for reasons I cannot ferret out of the surgeon, has to be a surgical one, performed on an outpatient basis but under general anesthesia, from which I awake to find him standing perpendicular to me, at the far end of the gurney, down near my feet, stating gravely, "Unfortunately, there is a cancer." It takes me all the rest of that drug-addled day to decide that the most heinous thing about that sentence is not the presence of cancer but the absence of me—for I, Barbara, do not enter into it even as a location, a geographical reference point. Where I once was—not a commanding presence perhaps but nonetheless a standard assemblage of flesh and words and gesture—"there is a cancer." I have been replaced by it, is the surgeon's implication. This is what I am now, medically speaking.

In my last act of dignified self-assertion, I request to see the pathology slides myself. This is not difficult to arrange in our small-town hospital, where the pathologist turns out to be a friend of a friend, and my rusty Ph.D. in cell biology (Rockefeller University, 1968) probably helps. He's a jolly fellow, the pathologist, who calls me "hon" and sits me down at one end of the dual-head microscope while he mans the other and moves a pointer through the field. These are the cancer cells, he says, showing up blue because of their overactive DNA. Most of them are arranged in staid semicircular arrays, like suburban houses squeezed into a cul-de-sac, but I also see what I know enough to know I do not want to see: the characteristic "Indian files" of cells on the march. The "enemy," I am supposed to think—an image to save up for future exercises in "visualization" of their violent deaths at the hands of the body's killer cells, the lymphocytes and macrophages. But I am impressed, against all rational self-interest, by the energy of these cellular conga lines, their determination to move on out from the backwater of the breast to colonize lymph nodes, bone marrow, lungs, and brain. These are, after all, the fanatics of Barbaraness, the rebel cells that have realized that the genome they carry, the genetic essence of me, has no further chance of normal reproduction in the postmenopausal body we share, so why not just start multiplying like bunnies and hope for a chance to break out?

It has happened, after all; some genomes have achieved immortality through cancer. When I was a graduate student, I once asked about the strain of tissue-culture cells labeled "HeLa" in the heavy-doored room maintained at body temperature. "HeLa," it turns out, refers to one Henrietta Lacks, whose tumor was the progenitor of all HeLa cells. She died; they live, and will go on living until someone gets tired of them or forgets to change their tissue-culture medium and leaves them to starve. Maybe this is what my rebel cells have in mind, and I try beaming them a solemn warning: The chances of your surviving me in tissue culture are nil. Keep up this selfish rampage and you go down, every last one of you, along with the entire Barbara enterprise. But what kind of a role model am I, or are multicellular human organisms gener-ally, for putting the common good above mad anarchistic individual ambition? There is a reason, it occurs to me, why cancer is our metaphor for so many runaway social processes, like corruption and "moral decay": we are no less out of control ourselves.

After the visit to the pathologist, my biological curiosity drops to a lifetime nadir. I know women who followed up their diagnoses with weeks or months of self-study, mastering their options, interviewing doctor after doctor, assessing the damage to be expected from the available treatments. But I can tell from a few hours of investigation that the career of a breast-cancer patient has been pretty well mapped out in advance for me: You may get to negotiate the choice between lumpectomy and mastectomy, but lumpectomy is commonly followed by weeks of radiation, and in either case if the lymph nodes turn out, upon dissection, to be invaded—or "involved," as it's less threateningly put—you're doomed to chemotherapy, meaning baldness, nausea, mouth sores, immunosuppression, and possible anemia. These interventions do not constitute a "cure" or anything close, which is why the death rate from breast cancer has changed very little since the 1930s, when mastectomy was the only treatment available. Chemotherapy, which became a routine part of breast-cancer treatment in the eighties, does not confer anywhere near as decisive an advantage as patients are often led to believe, especially in post-menopausal women like myself—a two or three percentage point difference in ten-year survival rates,[1] according to America's best-known breast-cancer surgeon, Dr. Susan Love.

I know these bleak facts, or sort of know them, but in the fog of anesthesia that hangs over those first few weeks, I seem to lose my capacity for self-defense. The pressure is on, from doctors and loved ones, to do something right away—kill it, get it out now. The endless exams, the bone scan to check for metastases, the high-tech heart test to see if I'm strong enough to withstand chemotherapy—all these blur the line between selfhood and thing-hood anyway, organic and inorganic, me and it. As my cancer career unfolds, I will, the helpful pamphlets explain, become a composite of the living and the dead—an implant to replace the breast, a wig to replace the hair. And then what will I mean when I use the word "I"? I fall into a state of unreasoning passive aggressivity: They diagnosed this, so it's their baby. They found it, let them fix it.

---

[1] In the United States, one in eight women will be diagnosed with breast cancer at some point. The chances of her surviving for five years are 86.8 percent. For a black woman this falls to 72 percent; and for a woman of any race whose cancer has spread to the lymph nodes, to 77.7 percent.

I could take my chances with "alternative" treatments, of course, like punk novelist Kathy Acker, who succumbed to breast cancer in 1997 after a course of alternative therapies in Mexico, or actress and ThighMaster promoter Suzanne Somers, who made tabloid headlines last spring by injecting herself with mistletoe brew. Or I could choose to do nothing at all beyond mentally exhorting my immune system to exterminate the traitorous cellular faction. But I have never admired the "natural" or believed in the "wisdom of the body." Death is as "natural" as anything gets, and the body has always seemed to me like a retarded Siamese twin dragging along behind me, an hysteric really, dangerously overreacting, in my case, to everyday allergens and minute ingestions of sugar. I will put my faith in science, even if this means that the dumb old body is about to be transmogrified into an evil clown—puking, trembling, swelling, surrendering significant parts, and oozing postsurgical fluids. The surgeon—a more genial and forthcoming one this time—can fit me in; the oncologist will see me. Welcome to Cancerland.

Fortunately, no one has to go through this alone. Thirty years ago, before Betty Ford, Rose Kushner, Betty Rollin, and other pioneer patients spoke out, breast cancer was a dread secret, endured in silence and euphemized in obituaries as a "long illness." Something about the conjuncture of "breast," signifying sexuality and nurturance, and that other word, suggesting the claws of a devouring crustacean, spooked almost everyone. Today however, it's the biggest disease on the cultural map, bigger than AIDS, cystic fibrosis, or spinal injury, bigger even than those more prolific killers of women—heart disease, lung cancer, and stroke. There are roughly hundreds of websites devoted to it, not to mention newsletters, support groups, a whole genre of first-person breast-cancer books; even a glossy, upper-middle-brow, monthly magazine, *Mamm*. There are four major national breast-cancer organizations, of which the mightiest, in financial terms, is the Susan G. Komen Foundation, headed by breast-cancer veteran and Bush's nominee for ambassador to Hungary Nancy Brinker. Komen organizes the annual Race for the Cure©, which attracts about a million people—mostly survivors, friends, and family members. Its website provides a microcosm of the new breast-cancer culture, offering news of the races, message boards for accounts of individuals' struggles with the disease, and a "marketplace" of breast-cancer-related products to buy.

More so than in the case of any other disease, breast-cancer organizations and events feed on a generous flow of corporate support. Nancy Brinker relates how her early attempts to attract corporate interest in promoting breast cancer "awareness" were met with rebuff. A bra manufacturer, importuned to affix a mammogram-reminder tag to his product, more or less wrinkled his nose. Now breast cancer has blossomed from wallflower to the most popular girl at the corporate charity prom. While AIDS goes begging and low-rent diseases like tuberculosis have no friends at all, breast cancer has been able to count on Revlon, Avon, Ford, Tiffany, Pier 1, Estée Lauder, Ralph Lauren, Lee Jeans, Saks Fifth Avenue, JC Penney, Boston Market, Wilson athletic gear—and I apologize to those I've omitted. You can "shop for the cure" during the week when Saks donates 2 percent of sales to a breast-cancer fund; "wear denim for the cure" during Lee National Denim Day, when for a $5 donation you get to wear blue jeans to work. You can even "invest for the cure," in the Kinetics Assets Management's new no-load Medical Fund, which specializes entirely in businesses involved in cancer research.

If you can't run, bike, or climb a mountain for the cure—all of which endeavors are routine beneficiaries of corporate sponsorship—you can always purchase one of the many products with a breast-cancer theme. There are 2.2 million American women in various stages of their breast-cancer careers, who, along with anxious relatives, make up a significant market for all things breast-cancer-related. Bears, for example: I have identified four distinct lines, or species, of these creatures, including "Carol," the Remembrance Bear; "Hope," the Breast Cancer Research Bear, which wears a pink turban as if to conceal chemotherapy-induced baldness; the "Susan Bear," named for Nancy Brinker's deceased sister, Susan; and the new Nick & Nora Wish Upon a Star Bear, available, along with the Susan Bear, at the Komen Foundation website's "marketplace."

And bears are only the tip, so to speak, of the cornucopia of pink-ribbon-themed breast-cancer products. You can dress in pink-beribboned sweatshirts, denim shirts, pajamas, lingerie, aprons, loungewear, shoelaces, and socks; accessorize with pink rhinestone brooches, angel pins, scarves, caps, earrings, and bracelets; brighten up your home with breast-cancer candles, stained-glass pink-ribbon candleholders, coffee mugs, pendants, wind chimes, and night-lights; pay your bills with special BreastChecks or a separate line of Checks for the Cure. "Awareness" beats secrecy and stigma of course, but I can't help noticing that the existential space in which a friend has earnestly advised me to "confront [my] mortality" bears a striking resemblance to the mall.

This is not, I should point out, a case of cynical merchants exploiting the sick. Some of the breast-cancer tchotchkes and accessories are made by breast-cancer survivors themselves, such as "Janice," creator of the "Daisy Awareness Necklace," among other things, and in most cases a portion of the sales goes to breast-cancer research. Virginia Davis of Aurora, Colorado, was inspired to create the "Remembrance Bear" by a friend's double mastectomy and sees her work as more of a "crusade" than a business. This year she expects to ship 10,000 of these teddies, which are manufactured in China, and send part of the money to the Race for the Cure. If the bears are infantilizing—as I try ever so tactfully to suggest is how they may, in rare cases, be perceived—so far no one has complained. "I just get love letters," she tells me, "from people who say, 'God bless you for thinking of us.'"

The ultrafeminine theme of the breast-cancer "marketplace"—the prominence, for example, of cosmetics and jewelry—could be understood as a response to the treatments' disastrous effects on one's looks. But the infantilizing trope is a little harder to account for, and teddy bears are not its only manifestation. A tote bag distributed to breast cancer patients by the Libby Ross Foundation (through places such as the Columbia Presbyterian Medical Center) contains, among other items, a tube of Estée Lauder Perfumed Body Crème, a hot-pink satin pillowcase, an audiotape "Meditation to Help You with Chemotherapy," a small tin of peppermint pastilles, a set of three small inexpensive rhinestone bracelets, a pink-striped "journal and sketch book," and—somewhat jarringly—a small box of crayons. Marla Willner, one of the founders of the Libby Ross Foundation, told me that the crayons "go with the journal—for people to express different moods, different thoughts . . ." though she admitted she has never tried to write with crayons herself. Possibly the idea is that regression to a state of childlike dependency puts one in the best frame of mind with which to endure the prolonged and toxic treatments. Or it may be that, in some versions of the prevailing gender ideology, femininity is by its nature incompatible with full adulthood—a state of arrested development. Certainly men diagnosed with prostate cancer do not receive gifts of Matchbox cars.

But I, no less than the bear huggers, need whatever help I can get, and start wading out into the Web in search of practical tips on hair loss, lumpectomy versus mastectomy, how to select a chemotherapy regimen, what to wear after surgery and eat when the scent of food sucks. There is, I soon find, far more than I can usefully absorb, for thousands of the afflicted have posted their stories, beginning with the lump or bad mammogram, proceeding through the agony of the treatments; pausing to mention the sustaining forces of family, humor, and religion; and ending, in almost all cases, with warm words of encouragement for the neophyte. Some of these are no more than a paragraph long—brief waves from sister sufferers; others offer almost hour-by-hour logs of breast-deprived, chemotherapized lives:

> Tuesday, August 15, 2000: Well, I survived my 4th chemo. Very, very dizzy today. Very nauseated, but no barfing! It's a first. . . . I break out in a cold sweat and my heart pounds if I stay up longer than 5 minutes.
>
> Friday, August 18, 2000: . . . By dinner time, I was full out nauseated. I took some meds and ate a rice and vegetable bowl from Trader Joe's. It smelled and tasted awful to me, but I ate it anyway. . . . Rick brought home some Kern's nectars and I'm drinking that. Seems to have settled my stomach a little bit.

I can't seem to get enough of these tales, reading on with panicky fascination about everything that can go wrong—septicemia, ruptured implants, startling recurrences a few years after the completion of treatments, "mets" (metastases) to vital organs, and—what scares me most in the short term—"chemo-brain," or the cognitive deterioration that sometimes accompanies chemotherapy. I compare myself with everyone, selfishly impatient with those whose conditions are less menacing, shivering over those who have reached Stage IV ("There is no Stage V," as the main character in *Wit*, who has ovarian cancer, explains), constantly assessing my chances.

Feminism helped make the spreading breast-cancer sisterhood possible, and this realization gives me a faint feeling of belonging. Thirty years ago, when the disease went hidden behind euphemism and prostheses, medicine was a solid patriarchy, women's bodies its passive objects of labor. The Women's Health Movement, in which I was an activist in the seventies and eighties, legitimized self-help and mutual support and encouraged women to network directly, sharing their stories, questioning the doctors, banding together. It is hard now to recall how revolutionary these activities once seemed, and probably few participants in breast-cancer chat rooms and message boards realize that when post-mastectomy patients first proposed meeting in support groups in the mid-1970s, the American Cancer Society responded with a firm and fatherly "no." Now no one leaves the hospital without a brochure directing her to local support groups and, at least in my case, a follow-up call from a social worker to see whether I am safely ensconced in one. This cheers me briefly, until I realize that if support groups have won the stamp of medical approval this may be because they are no longer perceived as seditious.

In fact, aside from the dilute sisterhood of the cyber (and actual) support groups, there is nothing very feminist—in an ideological or activist sense—about the mainstream of breast-cancer culture today. Let me pause to qualify: You can, if you look hard enough, find plenty of genuine, self-identified feminists within the vast pink sea of the breast-cancer crusade, women who are militantly determined to "beat the epidemic" and insistent on more user-friendly approaches to treatment. It was feminist health activists who led the campaign, in the seventies and eighties, against the most savage form of breast-cancer surgery—the Halsted radical mastectomy, which removed chest muscle and lymph nodes as well as breast tissue and left women permanently disabled. It was the Women's Health Movement that put a halt to the surgical practice, common in the seventies, of proceeding directly from biopsy to mastectomy without ever rousing the patient from anesthesia. More recently, feminist advocacy groups such as the San Francisco–based Breast Cancer Action and the Cambridge-based Women's Community Cancer Project helped blow the whistle on "high-dose chemotherapy," in which the bone marrow was removed prior to otherwise lethal doses of chemotherapy and later replaced—to no good effect, as it turned out.

Like everyone else in the breast-cancer world, the feminists want a cure, but they even more ardently demand to know the cause or causes of the disease without which we will never have any means of prevention. "Bad" genes of the inherited variety are thought to account for fewer than 10 percent of breast cancers, and only 30 percent of women diagnosed with breast cancer have any known risk factor (such as delaying childbearing or the late onset of menopause) at all. Bad lifestyle choices like a fatty diet have, after brief popularity with the medical profession, been largely ruled out. Hence suspicion should focus on environmental carcinogens, the feminists argue, such as plastics, pesticides (DDT and PCBs, for example, though banned in this country, are still used in many Third World sources of the produce we eat), and the industrial runoff in our ground water. No carcinogen has been linked definitely to human breast cancer yet, but many have been found to cause the disease in mice, and the inexorable increase of the disease in industrialized nations—

about one percent a year between the 1950s and the 1990s—further hints at environmental factors, as does the fact that women migrants to industrialized countries quickly develop the same breast-cancer rates as those who are native born. Their emphasis on possible ecological factors, which is not shared by groups such as Komen and the American Cancer Society, puts the feminist breast-cancer activists in league with other, frequently rambunctious, social movements—environmental and anticorporate.

But today theirs are discordant voices in a general chorus of sentimentality and good cheer; after all, breast cancer would hardly be the darling of corporate America if its complexion changed from pink to green. It is the very blandness of breast cancer, at least in mainstream perceptions, that makes it an attractive object of corporate charity and a way for companies to brand themselves friends of the middle-aged female market. With breast cancer, "there was no concern that you might actually turn off your audience because of the life style or sexual connotations that AIDS has," Amy Langer, director of the National Alliance of Breast Cancer Organizations, told the *New York Times* in 1996. "That gives corporations a certain freedom and a certain relief in supporting the cause." Or as Cindy Pearson, director of the National Women's Health Network, the organizational progeny of the Women's Health Movement, puts it more caustically: "Breast cancer provides a way of doing something for women, without being feminist."

In the mainstream of breast-cancer culture, one finds very little anger, no mention of possible environmental causes, few complaints about the fact that, in all but the more advanced, metastasized cases, it is the "treatments," not the disease, that cause illness and pain. The stance toward existing treatments is occasionally critical—in *Mamm*, for example—but more commonly grateful; the overall tone, almost universally upbeat. The Breast Friends website, for example, features a series of inspirational quotes: "Don't Cry Over Anything that Can't Cry Over You," "I Can't Stop the Birds of Sorrow from Circling my Head, But I Can Stop Them from Building a Nest in My Hair," "When Life Hands Out Lemons, Squeeze Out a Smile," "Don't wait for your ship to come in . . . Swim out to meet it," and much more of that ilk. Even in the relatively sophisticated *Mamm*, a columnist bemoans not cancer or chemotherapy but the end of chemotherapy, and humorously proposes to deal with her separation anxiety by pitching a tent outside her oncologist's office. So pervasive is the perkiness of the breast-cancer world that unhappiness requires a kind of apology, as when "Lucy," whose "long term prognosis is not good," starts her personal narrative on breastcancertalk.org by telling us that her story "is not the usual one, full of sweetness and hope, but true nevertheless."

There is, I discover, no single noun to describe a woman with breast cancer. As in the AIDS movement, upon which breast-cancer activism is partly modeled, the words "patient" and "victim," with their aura of self-pity and passivity, have been ruled un-P.C. Instead, we get verbs: Those who are in the midst of their treatments are described as "battling" or "fighting," sometimes intensified with "bravely" or "fiercely"—language suggestive of Katharine Hepburn with her face to the wind. Once the treatments are over, one achieves the status of "survivor," which is how the women in my local support group identify themselves, A.A.-style, as we convene to share war stories and rejoice in our "survivorhood": "Hi, I'm Kathy and I'm a three-year survivor." For those who cease to be survivors and join the more than 40,000 American women who succumb to breast cancer each year—again, no noun applies. They are said to have "lost their battle" and may be memorialized by photographs carried at races for the cure—our lost, brave sisters, our fallen soldiers. But in the overwhelmingly Darwinian culture that has grown up around breast cancer, martyrs count for little; it is the "survivors" who merit constant honor and acclaim. They, after all, offer living proof that expensive and painful treatments may in some cases actually work.

Scared and medically weakened women can hardly be expected to transform their support groups into bands of activists and rush out into the streets, but the equanimity of breast-cancer culture goes beyond mere absence of anger to what looks, all too often, like a positive embrace of the disease. As "Mary" reports, on the Bosom Buds message board:

> I really believe I am a much more sensitive and thoughtful person now. It might sound funny but I was a real worrier before. Now I don't want to waste my energy on worrying. I enjoy life so much more now and in a lot of aspects I am much happier now.

Or this from "Andee":

> This was the hardest year of my life but also in many ways the most rewarding. I got rid of the baggage, made peace with my family, met many amazing people, learned to take very good care of my body so it will take care of me, and reprioritized my life.

Cindy Cherry, quoted in the *Washington Post*, goes further:

If I had to do it over, would I want breast cancer? Absolutely. I'm not the same person I was, and I'm glad I'm not. Money doesn't matter anymore. I've met the most phenomenal people in my life through this. Your friends and family are what matter now.

The First Year of the Rest of Your Life, a collection of brief narratives with a foreword by Nancy Brinker and a share of the royalties going to the Komen Foundation, is filled with such testimonies to the redemptive powers of the disease: "I can honestly say I am happier now than I have ever been in my life—even before the breast cancer." "For me, breast cancer has provided a good kick in the rear to get me started rethinking my life. . . ." "I have come out stronger, with a new sense of priorities . . ." Never a complaint about lost time, shattered sexual confidence, or the long-term weakening of the arms caused by lymph-node dissection and radiation. What does not destroy you, to paraphrase Nietzsche, makes you a spunkier, more evolved, sort of person.

The effect of this relentless brightsiding is to transform breast cancer into a rite of passage—not an injustice or a tragedy to rail against, but a normal marker in the life cycle, like menopause or graying hair. Everything in mainstream breast-cancer culture serves, no doubt inadvertently, to tame and normalize the disease: the diagnosis may be disastrous, but there are those cunning pink rhinestone angel pins to buy and races to train for. Even the heavy traffic in personal narratives and practical tips, which I found so useful, bears an implicit acceptance of the disease and the current barbarous approaches to its treatment: you can get so busy comparing attractive head scarves that you forget to question a form of treatment that temporarily renders you both bald and immuno-incompetent. Understood as a rite of passage, breast cancer resembles the initiation rites so exhaustively studied by Mircea Eliade: First there is the selection of the initiates—by age in the tribal situation, by mammogram or palpation here. Then come the requisite ordeals—scarification or circumcision within traditional cultures, surgery and chemotherapy for the cancer patient. Finally, the initiate emerges into a new and higher status—an adult and a warrior—or in the case of breast cancer, a "survivor."

And in our implacably optimistic breast-cancer culture, the disease offers more than the intangible benefits of spiritual upward mobility. You can defy the inevitable disfigurements and come out, on the survivor side, actually prettier, sexier, more femme. In the lore of the disease—shared with me by oncology nurses as well as by survivors—chemotherapy smoothes and tightens the skin, helps you lose weight; and, when your hair comes back, it will be fuller, softer, easier to control, and perhaps a surprising new color. These may be myths, but for those willing to get with the prevailing program, opportunities for self-improvement abound. The American Cancer Society offers the "Look Good . . . Feel Better" program, "dedicated to teaching women cancer patients beauty techniques to help restore their appearance and self-image during cancer treatment." Thirty thousand women participate a year, each copping a free makeover and bag of makeup donated by the Cosmetic, Toiletry, and Fragrance Association, the trade association of the cosmetics industry. As for that lost breast: after reconstruction, why not bring the other one up to speed? Of the more than 50,000 mastectomy patients who opt for reconstruction each year, 17 percent go on, often at the urging of their plastic surgeons, to get additional surgery so that the remaining breast will "match" the more erect and perhaps larger new structure on the other side.

Not everyone goes for cosmetic deceptions, and the question of wigs versus baldness, reconstruction versus undisguised scar, defines one of the few real disagreements in breast-cancer culture. On the more avant-garde, upper-middle-class side, *Mamm* magazine—which features literary critic Eve Kosofsky Sedgwick as a columnist—tends to favor the "natural" look. Here, mastectomy scars can be "sexy" and baldness something to celebrate. The January 2001 cover story features women who "looked upon their baldness not just as a loss, but also as an opportunity: to indulge their playful sides . . . to come in contact, in new ways, with their truest selves." One decorates her scalp with temporary tattoos of peace signs, panthers, and frogs; another expresses herself with a shocking purple wig; a third reports that unadorned baldness makes her feel "sensual, powerful, able to recreate myself with every new day." But no hard feelings toward those who choose to hide their condition under wigs or scarves; it's just a matter, *Mamm* tells us, of "different aesthetics." Some go for pink ribbons; others will prefer the Ralph Lauren Pink Pony breast-cancer motif. But everyone agrees that breast cancer is a chance for creative self-transformation—a makeover opportunity, in fact.

Now, cheerfulness, up to and including delusion and false hope, has a recognized place in medicine. There is plenty of evidence that depressed and socially isolated people are more prone to succumb to diseases, cancer included, and a diagnosis of cancer is probably capable of precipitating serious depression all by itself. To be told by authoritative figures that you have a deadly disease, for which no real cure exists, is to enter a liminal state fraught with perils that go well beyond the disease itself. Consider the phenomenon of "voodoo death"—described by ethnographers among, for example, Australian aborigines—in which a person who has been condemned by a suitably potent curse obligingly shuts down and dies within a day or two. Cancer diagnoses could, and in some cases probably do, have the same kind of fatally dispiriting effect. So, it could be argued, the collectively pumped-up optimism of breast-cancer culture may be just what the doctor ordered. Shop for the Cure, dress in pink-ribbon regalia, organize a run or hike—whatever gets you through the night.

But in the seamless world of breast-cancer culture, where one website links to another—from personal narratives and grassroots endeavors to the glitzy level of corporate sponsors and celebrity spokespeople—cheerfulness is more or less mandatory, dissent a kind of treason. Within this tightly knit world, attitudes are subtly adjusted, doubters gently brought back to the fold. In *The First Year of the Rest of Your Life*, for example, each personal narrative is followed by a study question or tip designed to counter the slightest hint of negativity—and they are very slight hints indeed, since the collection includes no harridans, whiners, or feminist militants:

> Have you given yourself permission to acknowledge you have some anxiety or "blues" and to ask for help for your emotional well-being?
>
> Is there an area in your life of unresolved internal conflict? Is there an area where you think you might want to do some "healthy mourning"?
>
> Try keeping a list of the things you find "good about today."

As an experiment, I post a statement on the Komen.org message board, under the subject line "angry," briefly listing my own heartfelt complaints about debilitating treatments, recalcitrant insurance companies, environmental carcinogens, and, most daringly, "sappy pink ribbons." I receive a few words of encouragement in my fight with the insurance company, which has taken the position that my biopsy was a kind of optional indulgence, but mostly a chorus of rebukes. "Suzy" writes to say, "I really dislike saying you have a bad attitude towards all of this, but you do, and it's not going to help you in the least." "Mary" is a bit more tolerant, writing, "Barb, at this time in your life, it's so important to put all your energies toward a peaceful, if not happy, existence. Cancer is a rotten thing to have happen and there are no answers for any of us as to why. But to live your life, whether you have one more year or 51, in anger and bitterness is such a waste . . . I hope you can find some peace. You deserve it. We all do. God bless you and keep you in His loving care. Your sister, Mary."

"Kitty," however, thinks I've gone around the bend: "You need to run, not walk, to some counseling. . . . Please, get yourself some help and I ask everyone on this site to pray for you so you can enjoy life to the fullest."

I do get some reinforcement from "Gerri," who has been through all the treatments and now finds herself in terminal condition: "I am also angry. All the money that is raised, all the smiling faces of survivors who make it sound like it is o.k. to have breast cancer. IT IS NOT O.K.!" But Gerri's message, like the others on the message board, is posted under the mocking heading "What does it mean to be a breast-cancer survivor?"

"Culture" is too weak a word to describe all this. What has grown up around breast cancer in just the last fifteen years more nearly resembles a cult—or, given that it numbers more than two million women, their families, and friends—perhaps we should say a full-fledged religion. The products—teddy bears, pink-ribbon brooches, and so forth—serve as amulets and talismans, comforting the sufferer and providing visible evidence of faith. The personal narratives serve as testimonials and follow the same general arc as the confessional autobiographies required of seventeenth-century Puritans: first there is a crisis, often involving a sudden apprehension of mortality (the diagnosis or, in the old Puritan case, a stern word from on high); then comes a prolonged ordeal (the treatment or, in the religious case, internal struggle with the Devil); and finally, the blessed certainty of salvation, or its breast-cancer equivalent, survivorhood. And like most recognized religions, breast cancer has its great epideictic events, its pilgrimages and mass gatherings where the faithful convene and draw strength from their numbers. These are the annual races for a cure, attracting a total of about a million people at more than eighty sites—70,000 of them at the largest event, in Washington, D.C., which in recent years has been attended by Dan and Marilyn Quayle and Al and Tipper Gore. Everything comes together at the races: celebrities and corporate sponsors are showcased; products are hawked; talents, like those of the "Swinging, Singing Survivors" from Syracuse, New York, are displayed. It is at the races, too, that the elect confirm their special status. As one participant wrote in the *Washington Post*:

> I have taken my "battle scarred" breasts to the Mall, donned the pink shirt, visor, pink shoelaces, etc. and walked proudly among my fellow veterans of the breast cancer war. In 1995, at the age of 44, I was diagnosed and treated for Stage II breast cancer. The experience continues to redefine my life.

Feminist breast-cancer activists, who in the early nineties were organizing their own mass outdoor events—demonstrations, not races—to demand increased federal funding for research, tend to keep their distance from these huge, corporate-sponsored, pink gatherings. Ellen Leopold, for example—a member of the Women's Community Cancer Project in Cambridge and author of *A Darker Ribbon: Breast Cancer, Women, and Their Doctors in the Twentieth Century*—has criticized the races as an inefficient way of raising money. She points out that the Avon Breast Cancer Crusade, which sponsors three-day, sixty-mile walks, spends more than a third of the money raised on overhead and advertising, and Komen may similarly fritter away up to 25 percent of its gross. At least one corporate-charity insider agrees. "It would be much easier and more productive," says Rob Wilson, an organizer of charitable races for corporate clients, "if people, instead of running or riding, would write out a check to the charity."

To true believers, such criticisms miss the point, which is always, ultimately, "awareness." Whatever you do to publicize the disease—wear a pink ribbon, buy a teddy, attend a race—reminds other women to come forward for their mammograms. Hence, too, they would argue, the cult of the "survivor": If women neglect their annual screenings, it must be because they are afraid that a diagnosis amounts to a death sentence. Beaming survivors, proudly displaying their athletic prowess, are the best possible advertisement for routine screening mammograms, early detection, and the ensuing round of treatments. Yes, miscellaneous businesses—from tiny distributors of breast-cancer wind chimes and note cards to major corporations seeking a woman-friendly image—benefit in the process, not to mention the breast-cancer industry itself, the estimated $12–$16 billion-a-year business in surgery, "breast health centers," chemotherapy "infusion suites," radiation treatment centers, mammograms, and drugs ranging from anti-emetics (to help you survive the nausea of chemotherapy) to tamoxifen (the hormonal treatment for women with estrogen-sensitive tumors). But what's to complain about? Seen through pink-tinted lenses, the entire breast-cancer enterprise—from grassroots support groups and websites to the corporate providers of therapies and sponsors of races—looks like a beautiful example of synergy at work: cult activities, paraphernalia, and testimonies encourage women to undergo the diagnostic procedures, and since a fraction of these diagnoses will be positive, this means more members for the cult as well as more customers for the corporations, both those that provide medical products and services and those that offer charitable sponsorships.

But this view of a life-giving synergy is only as sound as the science of current detection and treatment modalities, and, tragically, that science is fraught with doubt, dissension, and what sometimes looks very much like denial. Routine screening mammograms, for example, are the major goal of "awareness," as when Rosie O'Donnell exhorts us to go out and "get squished." But not all breast-cancer experts are as enthusiastic. At best the evidence for the salutary effects of routine mammograms—as opposed to breast self-examination—is equivocal, with many respectable large-scale studies showing a vanishingly small impact on overall breast-cancer mortality. For one thing, there are an estimated two to four false positives for every cancer detected, leading thousands of healthy women to go through unnecessary biopsies and anxiety. And even if mammograms were 100 percent accurate, the admirable goal of "early" detection is more elusive than the current breast-cancer dogma admits. A small tumor, detectable only by mammogram, is not necessarily young and innocuous; if it has not spread to the lymph nodes, which is the only form of spreading detected in the common surgical procedure of lymph-node dissection, it may have already moved on to colonize other organs via the bloodstream. David Plotkin, director of the Memorial Cancer Research Foundation of Southern California, concludes that the benefits of routine mammography "are not well established; if they do exist, they are not as great as many women hope." Alan Spievack, a surgeon recently retired from the Harvard Medical School, goes further, concluding from his analysis of dozens of studies that routine screening mammography is, in the words of famous British surgeon Dr. Michael Baum, "one of the greatest deceptions perpetrated on the women of the Western world."

Even if foolproof methods for early detection existed, they would, at the present time, serve only as portals to treatments offering dubious protection and considerable collateral damage. Some women diagnosed with breast cancer will live long enough to die of something else, and some of these lucky ones will indeed owe their longevity to a combination of surgery, chemotherapy, radiation, and/or anti-estrogen drugs such as tamoxifen. Others, though, would have lived untreated or with surgical excision alone, either because their cancers were slow-growing or because their bodies' own defenses were successful. Still others will die of the disease no matter what heroic, cell-destroying therapies are applied. The trouble is, we do not have the means to distinguish between these three groups. So for many of the thousands of women who are diagnosed each year, Plotkin notes, "the sole effect of early detection has been to stretch out the time in which the woman bears the knowledge of her condition." These women do not live longer than they might have without any medical intervention, but more of the time they do live is overshadowed with the threat of death and wasted in debilitating treatments.

To the extent that current methods of detection and treatment fail or fall short, America's breast-cancer cult can be judged as an outbreak of mass delusion, celebrating survivorhood by downplaying mortality and promoting obedience to medical protocols known to have limited efficacy. And although we may imagine ourselves to be well past the era of patriarchal medicine, obedience is the message behind the infantilizing theme in breast-cancer culture, as represented by the teddy bears, the crayons, and the prevailing pinkness. You are encouraged to regress to a little-girl state, to suspend critical judgment, and to accept whatever measures the doctors, as parent surrogates, choose to impose.

Worse, by ignoring or underemphasizing the vexing issue of environmental causes, the breast-cancer cult turns women into dupes of what could be called the Cancer Industrial Complex: the multinational corporate enterprise that with the one hand doles out carcinogens and disease and, with the other, offers expensive, semi-toxic pharmaceutical treatments. Breast Cancer Awareness Month, for example, is sponsored by AstraZeneca (the manufacturer of tamoxifen), which, until a corporate reorganization in 2000, was a leading producer of pesticides, including acetochlor, classified by the EPA as a "probable human carcinogen." This particularly nasty conjuncture of interests led the environmentally oriented Cancer Prevention Coalition (CPC) to condemn Breast Cancer Awareness Month as "a public relations invention by a major polluter which puts women in the position of being unwitting allies of the very people who make them sick." Although AstraZeneca no longer manufactures pesticides, CPC has continued to criticize the breast-cancer crusade—and the American Cancer Society—for its unquestioning faith in screening mammograms and careful avoidance of environmental issues. In a June 12, 2001, press release, CPC chairman Samuel S. Epstein, M.D., and the well-known physician activist Quentin Young castigated the American Cancer Society for its "long-standing track record of indifference and even hostility to cancer prevention. . . . Recent examples include issuing a joint statement with the Chlorine Institute justifying the continued global use of persistent organochlorine pesticides, and also supporting the industry in trivializing dietary pesticide residues as avoidable risks of childhood cancer. ACS policies are further exemplified by allocating under 0.1 percent of its $700 million annual budget to environmental and occupational causes of cancer."

In the harshest judgment, the breast-cancer cult serves as an accomplice in global poisoning—normalizing cancer, prettying it up, even presenting it, perversely, as a positive and enviable experience.

When, my three months of chemotherapy completed, the oncology nurse calls to congratulate me on my "excellent blood work results," I modestly demur. I didn't do anything, I tell her, anything but endure—marking the days off on the calendar, living on Protein Revolution canned vanilla health shakes, escaping into novels and work. Courtesy restrains me from mentioning the fact that the tumor markers she's tested for have little prognostic value, that there's no way to know how many rebel cells survived chemotherapy and may be carving out new colonies right now. She insists I should be proud; I'm a survivor now and entitled to recognition at the Relay for Life being held that very evening in town.

So I show up at the middle-school track where the relay's going on just in time for the Survivors' March: about 100 people, including a few men, since the funds raised will go to cancer research in general, are marching around the track eight to twelve abreast while a loudspeaker announces their names and survival times and a thin line of observers, mostly people staffing the raffle and food booths, applauds. It could be almost any kind of festivity, except for the distinctive stacks of cellophane-wrapped pink Hope Bears for sale in some of the booths. I cannot help but like the funky small-town *Gemütlichkeit* of the event, especially when the audio system strikes up that universal anthem of solidarity, "We Are Family," and a few people of various ages start twisting to the music on the jerry-rigged stage. But the money raised is going far away, to the American Cancer Society, which will not be asking us for our advice on how to spend it.

I approach a woman I know from other settings, one of our local intellectuals, as it happens, decked out here in a pink-and-yellow survivor T-shirt and with an American Cancer Society "survivor medal" suspended on a purple ribbon around her neck. "When do you date your survivorship from?" I ask her, since the announced time, five and a half years, seems longer than I recall. "From diagnosis or the completion of your treatments?" The question seems to annoy or confuse her, so I do not press on to what I really want to ask: At what point, in a downwardly sloping breast-cancer career, does one put aside one's survivor regalia and admit to being in fact a die-er? For the dead are with us even here, though in much diminished form. A series of paper bags, each about the right size for a junior burger and fries, lines the track. On them are the names of the dead, and inside each is a candle that will be lit later, after dark, when the actual relay race begins.

My friend introduces me to a knot of other women in survivor gear, breast-cancer victims all, I learn, though of course I would not use the V-word here. "Does anyone else have trouble with the term 'survivor'?" I ask, and, surprisingly, two or three speak up. It could be "unlucky," one tells me; it "tempts fate," says another, shuddering slightly. After all, the cancer can recur at any time, either in the breast or in some more strategic site. No one brings up my own objection to the term, though: that the mindless triumphalism of "survivorhood" denigrates the dead and the dying. Did we who live "fight" harder than those who've died? Can we claim to be "braver," better, people than the dead? And why is there no room in this cult for some gracious acceptance of death, when the time comes, which it surely will, through cancer or some other misfortune?

No, this is not my sisterhood. For me at least, breast cancer will never be a source of identity or pride. As my dying correspondent Gerri wrote: "IT IS NOT O.K.!" What it is, along with cancer generally or any slow and painful way of dying, is an abomination, and, to the extent that it's man-made, also a crime. This is the one great truth that I bring out of the breast-cancer experience, which did not, I can now report, make me prettier or stronger, more feminine or spiritual—only more deeply angry. What sustained me through the "treatments" is a purifying rage, a resolve, framed in the sleepless nights of chemotherapy, to see the last polluter, along with, say, the last smug health-insurance operative, strangled with the last pink ribbon. Cancer or no cancer, I will not live that long of course. But I know this much right now for sure: I will not go into that last good night with a teddy bear tucked under my arm.

November 2001

Manufacturing Depression

Notes on the Economy of Melancholy

GARY GREENBERG

Doctor George Papakostas has some bad news for me. For the last half hour, he's been guiding me through a catalogue of my discontent—the stalled writing projects and the weedy garden, the dwindling bank accounts and the difficulties of parenthood, the wife I see mostly in the moments before sleep or on our separate ways out the door, the typical plaint and worry and disappointment of a middle-aged, middle-class American life, which you wouldn't bore your friends with, which you wouldn't bore yourself with if you could avoid it and if this sweet man with his solicitous tone hadn't asked. He's been circling numbers and ticking boxes, occasionally writing a word or two in the fat three-ring binder on his desk, and now he has stopped the interview to flip the pages and add up some numbers. His brown eyes go soft behind his glasses. He looks apologetic, nearly embarrassed.

"I'm sorry, Greg," he says. "I don't think you're going to qualify for the study. You just don't meet the criteria for Minor Depression."

Even if my confessor had gotten my name right, I would still be a little humiliated. I had come to his office at the Depression Clinical and Research Program of the Massachusetts General Hospital, insisting that I would *qualify*. I had told him that I figured anyone paying sufficient attention was bound to show the two symptoms out of the nine listed in the *Diagnostic and Statis-tical Manual* (*DSM-IV*) of the American Psychiatric Association—sadness, diminished pleasure, weight loss or gain, trouble sleeping, fatigue or malaise, guilt, diminished concentration, and recurrent thoughts of death—that are required for the diagnosis.[1] To explain my certainty and my interest in his study, I had told Papakostas that these days my native pessimism was feasting on a surfeit of bad news—my country taken over by thugs, the calamity of capitalism more apparent every day, environmental cataclysm edging from the wings to center stage, the brute facts of life brought home by the illnesses and deaths of people I love and by my own creeping decrepitude. I told him that I had more or less resigned myself to my dourness, that it struck me as reasonable, realistic even, and no more or less mutable than my short stature, my constitutional laziness, my thinning hair, my modest musical talents, the quirks of my personality that drive away some people and attract others. I told him that, as a therapist, I lean toward talk therapies for psychic distress, but I am not at all opposed to better living through chemistry. If the drugs offered by his clinical trial—Celexa, Forest Laboratories' blockbuster antidepressant, and Saint-John's-wort, an herb with a reputation as a tonic for melancholy—did what they promised, I might like that, and if I did not, at least I'd know what I was turning down. And, finally, I had told him that I was going to write about whatever happened, which meant that either way, I wouldn't come away empty-handed.

Unless I didn't meet the criteria.

But before I can get too upset, Papakostas has more news. "What you have is Major Depression." He looks over the notebook again. "It's mild, but it's not minor. Nope. Definitely major depressive disorder, atypical features, chronic." Which means, he seems pleased to tell me, that I meet the criteria for at least four other studies that Mass General is running. I can take Celexa or Mirapex or Lexapro or something called s-adenosyl-l-methionine. I can climb into an MRI, get hooked up to an EEG, take home a device to monitor my pulse and breathing. I can get paid as much as $360 for my trouble. I can

---

[1] Minor Depression is a provisional diagnosis, listed at the back of the *DSM-IV*, where it awaits further study. Research that uses this diagnosis thus has a twofold aim: to provide another FDA-approved indication for a particular drug and to give Minor Depression medicine's most lucrative imprimatur—the five-digit code that allows doctors to bill insurance companies for treatment.

go back to the waiting area, read over the consent forms that spell out in great detail—down to the final disposition of the two tablespoons of blood that they will take—what will happen to me, what is expected of me, what my rights are, how I can bail out if I want to, and then I can make my decision.

I'm a quick shopper, and when Papakostas returns, I have already signed the papers for research study 1-RO1-MH74085-01A1, agreeing to return to Mass General next week and then every other week for the next two months, so that they can evaluate the alleged antidepressant properties of omega-3 fatty acids—in other words, fish oil.[2]

Which is why Julie and Caitlin—tall and attractive and polished bright, like all the research assistants here—are soon hovering over me in a tiny exam room that contains a metal table and a scale and a phlebotomist's chair, tweezing tentatively through the thatch on my chest and worrying out loud that they are hurting me. They finally clear the spots for the EKG electrodes and run the scan. They take my pulse and blood pressure, weigh and measure me, and draw my blood into a vial. Fair-skinned Caitlin is blushing a little as she hands me the brown paper bag with a cup for my urine specimen. I can see how cowed these young women are by this forced intimacy, and I try to tell them they needn't be so shy. But they know I have just been declared mentally ill, and I wonder if reassurance from the likes of me just makes things worse.

But I haven't come here to minister to them or, for that matter, to maintain my dignity. In this nondescript office building beside the towers and pavilions of Massachusetts General Hospital in Boston, these dedicated people do the research that determines whether drugs work—which is to say, whether drugs will come to market as government-sanctioned cures. In the process, they turn complaint into symptom, symptom into illness, and illness into diagnosis, the secret knowledge of what really ails us, what we must do to cure it, and who we will be when we get better. This is the heart of the magic factory, the place where medicine is infused with the miracles of science, and I've come to see how it's done.

---

[2]According to the World Health Organization, the countries with the highest consumption of fish have the lowest rates of depression. And it happens that omega-3s make cell membranes, such as the receptors in your brain that absorb serotonin and other neurotransmitters, more permeable. To a psychiatrist already convinced that depression is the result of deficiencies in serotonin transmission, the significance of this correlation outweighs any of the other possible explanations for why someone in fish-deprived France might be more prone to depression than someone in Korea or Japan.

.   .   .

I never used the term "magic factory"—you wouldn't want to seem paranoid in a place like this—but I told Papakostas about my suspicions of the drug industry and even referred him to what I had already written about it. If he caught a whiff of bad faith here, if he thought me a bluestocking on an evidence-gathering excursion to the porn shop, or if he worried that I would lie to him just to get a story (he knew I was a therapist, that I was intimately acquainted with that checklist of symptoms), he was too good-natured to say so.[3] But then again, he is a doctor and has to believe that if depression is the medical illness that the antidepressant industry is built on—if it is, as the drug company ads say and as doctors tell their depressed patients, a chemical problem with a chemical solution—then my intentions shouldn't matter. Diseases don't care whether you believe in them. What matters is the evidence, how much insulin is in the blood or how much sugar is in the urine and all the other ways nature has of telling you something is wrong.

But there is no lab to send my bodily fluids to in order to assay my level of depression. Instead, there are tests like the Hamilton Depression Rating Scale. The HAM-D was invented in the late 1950s by a British doctor, Max Hamilton. He was trying to find a way to measure the effects of the antidepressants that the drug companies were just bringing to market. To figure out what to test for, he observed his depressed patients and distilled their common characteristics into seventeen items, such as insomnia and guilt. Patients could get as many as four points per item, and a total of eighteen of the fifty-two possible points is now considered the threshold for depression. Ten of the seventeen items were about neurovegetative signs like sleep and appetite, the kind most likely to respond to antidepressants—something Hamilton knew because he'd worked with the drugs. Not surprisingly, this drug-friendly test quickly became a favorite of drug companies. In fact, it remains the gatekeeper to the antidepressant industry, used by the Food and Drug Administration to evaluate candidate drugs.

Because the people from whom Hamilton derived the items were determined already to be sick, the HAM-D cannot be used to *diagnose* depression. So psychiatrists have developed the Structured Clinical Interview for *DSM-IV* (SCID), which is tied to the *DSM-IV*'s catalogue of the 270 afflictions that

---

[3]Or too hard up for subjects. The investigators expect that it will take five years to enroll the three hundred subjects needed to complete the study.

cause people sufficient "psychic distress" to be considered diagnosable mental illnesses (the second edition of the *DSM*, published in 1968, lists a mere 168 diagnoses). The *DSM-IV*'s fifty-one possible mood disorders take up 74 of its 886 pages, which list criteria and specifiers that a clinician assembles into such diagnoses as Major Depressive Disorder with Melancholic Features, Chronic with Seasonal Pattern.

There is no magic to the SCID. To determine whether you meet the *DSM-IV* criterion of "depressed mood most of the day, every day," it asks, "In the last month, has there been a period of time when you were feeling depressed or down most of the day nearly every day?" To find out whether you have a "diminished ability to think or concentrate," it asks, "Did you have trouble thinking or concentrating?" And so on with the lists of symptoms, until, based on your answers, you get shunted, like coins in a sorter, from one chute to another, and you drop into the drawer with all the other pennies.

I never saw the scoring from my SCID, so I'm not sure how I ended up with my diagnosis. (I was relieved, however, that it would not be entered into my medical dossier, where it might wreak havoc on future attempts to get life or health insurance or to run for president.) I do know that I told Papakostas the truth, at least to the extent that I could figure out how to answer his questions about my psychic life. And I also know that in the course of a quarter century as a practicing therapist, I have met people who are hammered flat, unable to get out of bed or find solace in any quarter, who are nearly insensate to anything other than their abject misery, who can think of little other than dying—who, in short, meet the criteria for Major Depression in my own private *DSM*. There have been a handful of them, maybe ten or twenty out of the seven hundred or so patients I've seen. Whatever my score on the SCID, it was hard to believe that Papakostas really thought I had Major Depression. I wasn't tearful with him, and although I whined about the things that the SCID invited me to whine about, I was alert and smiling, joking, more effusive—perhaps out of nervousness—than I normally am.

I didn't say this to Papakostas, didn't protest that my aches and complaints were not really Major Depression. Just as well: Item 17 ("Insight") on the HAM-D awards two points to anyone who "denies being ill at all."

Julie greets me when I arrive the next week. I'm eavesdropping on the receptionist, who is reassuring someone on the phone that many of the doctors at the Depression Clinical and Research Program teach at Harvard. I get my medicine today, assuming that my EKG checked out, that my blood and urine were clean of illicit drugs and indication of disease. Julie hands me a clipboard with three questionnaires and a pen. The Quick Inventory of Depressive Symptomotology (Self-Report)—the QIDS-SR—comprises sixteen multiple-choice questions. Here is number 11:

> View of Myself
> 0.   I see myself as equally worthwhile and deserving as other people
> 1.   I am more self-blaming than usual
> 2.   I largely believe that I cause problems for others
> 3.   I think almost constantly about major and minor defects in myself

The Q-LES-Q-SF, the Quality of Life Enjoyment and Satisfaction Questionnaire (Short Form), wants me to circle the numbers from 1 (Very Poor) to 5 (Very Good) that describe how satisfied I've been during the past week with sixteen aspects of my life, from my economic status to my sex drive, interest, and/or performance. And on the Ryff Well-Being Scale, I can express—by filling in the little bubbles, like on the SAT—one of six degrees of agreement with fifty-four statements about my attitude toward life, such as, "For me, life has been a continuous process of learning, changing, and growth," or, "My daily activities often seem trivial and unimportant."[4]

The tests in the women's magazines dotting the waiting-room tables aren't much different from these, save for one thing: social scientists have stamped their approval on the official questionnaires after subjecting them to various statistical challenges and worrying over such considerations as the fact that people will answer according to how they want to look to the tester. But aside from a passing frisson over telling Julie, however elliptically, about my *very good* sexual performance, I am not thinking about impressing her. I am thinking about how little I seem to know of myself. I didn't know, for instance, that wondering if "life is empty" or "if it's worth living," which I do at least once a week, is, as the QIDS insists, a Thought of Suicide or Death. I think I march to my own drummer just as much as the next guy, but when the

---

[4]The way that researchers decide whether these tests can accurately indicate depression is by correlating responses on them to responses on tests already known to measure depression—a good idea, unless there is no anchor at the end of the chain, in which case you may well have created a self-validating semiotic monster.

Well-Being Scale asks me to rate how difficult it is "for me to voice my own opinions on controversial matters," I think of how often I disagree with myself over what my opinion is, how the closer I get to fifty the less sure I feel of anything, even of the answer to this question, and I cannot find a place to bubble in that uncertainty. I wonder what it means that I hesitate so long over these questions, whether I should circle the QIDS item that says, "My thinking is slowed down."

I haven't finished with the Well-Being Scale when Papakostas comes to fetch me. I tell him I'm confused about a consent form Julie just handed me; she explained that the one Papakostas and I signed last week was "outdated." But, I tell him, this new form seems to be for a different study, one that requires me to take two different pills at the same time. He looks perplexed, excuses himself, and returns with Julie. Together they explain that the study I signed up for last week was full, so they reassigned me. He looks mortified. Julie, who told me she was fresh out of Amherst, looks worried. They're explaining, apologizing, reassuring, as if they were waiters in a restaurant who have just delivered the wrong meal to a valued customer.

But we all know what has happened here. They have broken the code, the Nuremberg Code, the one that says that they cannot conduct experimentation on a human unless the human in question knows exactly what he's getting himself into, of which it is their responsibility to inform me. Not only that—and this is bad enough, since the U.S. government is paying for this research,[5] and the funding is contingent on scrupulous attention to such matters—but for a moment they have laid bare the thing that all this scrupulous attention to my autonomy is supposed to obscure: that they are using me, that my Well-Being, my Life Satisfaction, my blood, my piss will all get rendered into raw data for these doctors and their sponsors. They have moved me around like a pork belly, and for a split second the bald fact of the commerce we are conducting is right in front of our faces.

I reassure them that I am satisfied with their disclosures, that I just wanted to make sure we were all on the same page. Julie leaves the room with a last apology, and Papakostas hands me my copy of the form, countersigned by him. He opens the binder again and asks me how my week was. Papakostas has a way of making the HAM-D into a reasonable facsimile of an actual conversation. So when he asks me for an example of what I feel self-critical about

---

[5]About $2.5 million over five years.

(Item 2), I open the spigot a little, telling him I worry that my insistence on working at my therapy practice part-time, my giving up a plum teaching job, my indulgence in writing and other less savory vices, my seemingly endless desire for free time—that these reflect a hedonism and irresponsibility that have led me to squander my gifts. Papakostas waits a beat, then nods and says, "In the past week, Greg, have you had any thoughts that life is not worth living?" It's time for Item 3.

Papakostas is so unfailingly kind—and I want him to *care*, I want him to tell me that I am not really feckless—that I cannot be mad at him for sticking to the script, let alone correct him about my name. He's not doing it because he's a bad man, or a disingenuous one, or a shill for the drug companies. On the contrary. He does it because he wants to help me, because he thinks I am suffering, and because he is a doctor and this is what he knows how to do: to find the targets and send in the bullets, then to ask the questions and circle the numbers and decide if those bullets really are doing their job. We're not here to talk about *me*, at least not about the homunculus we call a *self*. We're trying instead to figure out what's going on in my head—in the gray, primordial ooze where thought and feeling, according to the latest psychiatric fashion, arise.

Back on the street, blinking in the noonday sun, I peek into the brown paper bag they have given me. The "study medicine" comes in a pair of plastic bottles stuffed with two weeks' worth of glistening amber gel caps. They look just like regular prescription drugs but for the sticker that says, DRUG LIMITED BY FEDERAL LAW TO INVESTIGATIONAL USE. That seems a little dramatic for something I can get at any health-food store or by eating however much salmon it would take to provide two grams of omega-3s per day. But under the agreement we've made—that they are doctors, that I am sick, that I must turn myself over to them so they can cure me—the medicine must be treated with the reverence due a communion wafer.

Not that anyone at Mass General would say so. In fact, they've designed this study to minimize the possibility that something as unscientific as faith or credulity or the mystifications of power could be at work here. The trial is a so-called three-armed study. I have been randomly assigned to one of three groups. One group gets placebos in both bottles. Another group gets eicosapentanoic acid and a placebo, and the third group gets docosahexaenoic acid and a placebo. Only the anonymous pharmacist laboring in the bowels of

Mass General, armed with a random number generator and sworn to secrecy, knows which group I'm in. The study will then be able to show which of the two omega-3s has more effect, and whether either one is more powerful than a placebo.

This method is known as the "double-blind, placebo-controlled design," and it provides a way to deal with something that the drug industry would rather forget: that in any given clinical trial, especially one for a psychiatric drug, people are very likely to respond to the fact that they are being given a pill—any pill, even one containing nothing but sugar. Which is why the FDA requires all candidate drugs to be tested against placebos—to try to separate the medicine from the magic, to see what the drug does when no one is looking. But, like a pain-in-the-ass brother-in-law, the placebo effect keeps showing up, curing people at a rate alarming to both regulators and industry executives. In fact, in more than half the clinical trials used to approve the six leading antidepressants, the drugs failed to outperform the placebos, and when it came time to decide on Celexa, an FDA bureaucrat wondered on paper whether the results were too weak to be clinically significant, only to be reminded that all the other antidepressants had been approved on equally weak evidence.[6]

Despite the fact that the placebo effect is the indirect subject of virtually every clinical trial, no one really understands how it works. Science, designed to break things down to their particulars, cannot detect something so ineffable, so diffused throughout the encounter between physician and patient. Until there is money to be made in sugar pills—at which point the drug companies are sure to investigate them thoroughly[7]—about the best we can say is that the placebo effect has something to do with the convergence between the doctor's authority and the patient's desire to be well. But this relative ignorance

[6]The advantage of antidepressants over placebos in those trials was an average of two points on the HAM-D, a result that could be achieved if the patient ate and slept better. The average improvement in antidepressant clinical trials is just over ten points, which means, according to Irving Kirsch, a University of Connecticut psychologist, that nearly 80 percent of the drug effect is actually a placebo effect.

[7]In 2002, researchers observing the EEGs of patients in an antidepressant-versus-placebo trial stumbled on a pattern of brain activity common to those subjects who respond to placebos. Drug companies were very interested in this discovery, not because it allowed them to study the placebo effect but because it might allow them to identify those placebo responders and bounce them out of a trial before it starts.

doesn't stop doctors, wittingly or not, from using their power as a healing device. For instance, they can reshape you in a way that makes you a good fit for the drugs. That's what these questionnaires, with their peculiar way of inventorying personhood, do; they alert you to what it is in yourself that is diseased—casting your introspection as "excessive self-criticism," your suspicions of your own base motives as "low self-esteem," your wish to nap in the afternoon as "excessive daytime sleepiness," your rooting hunger late at night as "increased appetite"—and they prepare you for the cure by letting you know how you will feel better.

Just before I got my pills, Papakostas asked me how long it had been since I had felt good for any appreciable time. Good? I asked him.

"Symptom-free," he said, as if we had agreed that my feelings were symptoms.

"For how long?"

"Thirty days. Or more. At least a month."

I wanted to tell him that I was a writer, that I counted myself lucky to feel good from the beginning of a sentence to the period. I wanted to ask him if he had ever heard of betrayal, of disappointment, of mortality. Instead, I laughed—derisively, I suppose (was this the "irritability" of Item 10?)—and said I had no idea what a month of feeling good would feel like.

Of course, this only confirmed his diagnosis.

But *thirty days* is ringing in my ears as I head back to my car. I make a sudden decision: to duck into a restaurant, to order a glass of water with my meal, to start the trial not tomorrow morning but right now. I cannot resist the wish, the temptation, to lay down my pessimism at this altar, to put myself in the hands of these doctors, to take their investigational drug and let them cure me of myself. I gulp down my six golden pills.

Drugs do work. By themselves, I mean, even without the benefit of the placebo effect. Just ask the tuberculosis patients at Sea View Hospital in New York who, in 1952, took a derivative of hydrazine, a chemical that Germany used in the waning days of World War II to power its V-2s. The drug, called Marsilid, worked not only on their lungs but also on their heads; enough of them reported feeling euphoric—there was even a rumor they were dancing in the wards—that doctors started prescribing it for their melancholic patients.

In a society famously ambivalent about pleasure and the use of intoxicants to achieve it, however, it isn't enough to take drugs to feel better. It's preferable, especially for a drug company, if you have an actual illness to treat. When it was discovered that Marsilid prevented the brain from manufacturing an enzyme that broke down serotonin, an intriguing chemical that had just been found in the brain, scientists had their disease. Depression, the new theory went, was not a psychological or existential condition but a brain disease caused by a "serotonin deficiency" or some other "chemical imbalance." Drug companies spread this gospel aggressively. In the early 1960s, for example, Merck bought 50,000 copies of *Recognizing the Depressed Person*, a book by a doctor who had pioneered the serotonin theory and the use of drugs to treat it, in order to distribute the book to doctors who might not yet have heard that depression was the disease for which the new drugs were the cure.

But the evidence for the serotonin theory was circumstantial to begin with, and it has remained so for the last half century. Although scientists have mapped the jungle of nerve fiber through which serotonin makes its way from brain stem to synapse, analyzing the biochemistry of that journey and inventing drugs that inhibit or encourage it along the way, they have never proved that a serotonin deficiency actually exists in depressed people or, for that matter, figured out how much serotonin we ought to have in our brains in the first place. Nor have they explained certain inconvenient facts: that reserpine, for instance, a drug that *decreases* serotonin concentrations, also has antidepressant effects, or that so many people fail to respond to antidepressants—which, if antidepressants were really arrows aimed at a molecular bad guy, simply shouldn't be the case.[8] In the face of these dismal results, many scientists have begun to move on to theories about neurogenesis and cellular damage and other brain events of which serotonin may be only a marker, the finger pointing to the mood.

None of this stops doctors from continuing to manipulate serotonin in order to relieve depression. The omega-3s I'm taking are thought to render neurons more supple, allowing them to make the most efficient use of whatever serotonin is available. So far, however, the pills don't seem to be having an effect. Indeed, as I end my second week, I notice only one change. When I wake up early in the morning, when I crave my afternoon nap, when I find myself frustrated by my shortcomings or deflated by the seeming impossibil-

---

[8]Neither have they shown that in identifying the brain chemistry of a given mood or experience they have found the *cause* rather than the *correlates*; that is, they could have found the ways the brain provides, but doesn't originate, that mood or experience.

ity of getting done what I want to get done, when I read the newspaper and, like Ivan Karamazov with his catalogue of atrocity, want to return my ticket, when I feel sorry for all of us, I wonder if indeed I've been suffering from an illness all along.

But I am still thinking about those thirty days, preoccupied with the idea that there are others right now in the midst of that month of resilience to setback and hardship who are not simply luckier (or, as I think in my self-flattering moments, *shallower*) but *healthier* than I, that they have dodged a bullet that has caught me; that I can don some armor and make up for what nature has, so these doctors say, denied me.

The third visit, the first one after I started the drugs, is shorter, more perfunctory than the first two. Papakostas moves briskly from one question to the next and looks at his watch if we digress. But the protocol calls for him to ask whether I have any questions. So I tell him I wasn't sure I had understood him in our last meeting. How long was it that he thought I should be feeling good?

"For at least a month," he says

I ask him why he wanted to know.

"People, when they're depressed, they get a sort of recall bias," he says. "They tend to feel that their past is *all* depressed."

Which would suggest, I want to point out, that depression is more like an ideology than an illness, more false consciousness than disease.

This isn't the first impertinence I've stifled today. Earlier he asked, "Are you content with the amount of happiness that you get doing things that you like or being with people that you like?"

"I'm not big on contentment," I said. *Is anyone?* I wondered. Is anyone ever convinced that his or her pursuit of happiness has reached its goal? And what would happen to the consumer economy if we began to believe that any amount of happiness is enough? "I'm sorry to seem dense," I explained, "but it's not how I usually think about things."

Papakostas was reassuring. "You know, this question condenses a lot of areas of life into just a number. It doesn't work well," he said. "Some questions we just don't like."

Well, if these are dumb questions, I wanted to shout, *then why are you asking them?* Why are we pretending that these answers mean anything? Indeed, if I'm just the middleman here, the guy you've got to go through to get to the molecular essence of my troubles, then why ask me any questions at all?

Later, when he asked how many days there were in the last week that I had napped for more than thirty minutes, and I told him four, he said, "See, some of the questions are really nice in terms of being objective," before putting me down for two points on that item.

"I suppose it would be easier if there were biochemical markers," I offered. "Otherwise, you're just stuck with language."

"Hey, we're psychiatrists," Papakostas said. "Language is good."

Now I was really confused. Hadn't we just spent the last half hour circumventing language's approximations? If language is good, then why wasn't *he* taping this visit, taking down my words instead of translating them into the tests' pale simulacrum of language? For the same reason, I suppose, that he doesn't seem to think that consciousness itself, in all its insuperable indeterminacy, matters very much, as I discover when we meet two weeks later. I ask Papakostas about a promising new experimental treatment for depression, one that uses an anesthetic drug called ketamine. A government psychiatrist was trying to bring ketamine in from the cold, from the psychiatric underground where LSD and psilocybin are used for transformative purposes[9] and where ketamine has a reputation for delivering a powerful and salutary (if terrifying) experience of being disembodied and dislocated—not unlike a near-death encounter. To Papakostas—who is not familiar with this unofficial research, discredited since the excesses of the sixties grew like an adipose layer over the therapeutic promise of psychedelic drugs—I'm explaining the idea that a single whack upside the head, one glimpse into the cosmos and all its glory and indifference, can set you straight for a long time. I am getting to the part about how inconvenient the economics of a one-time-only drug are for an industry addicted to One-A-Days, when he interrupts me.

"Sort of like ECT," he says, using the new and improved name for electroshock therapy. "The way it's supposed to reset your neurotransmitters. But we know that theory doesn't work, because ECT patients relapse."

"But isn't there a difference between ECT and ketamine?"

---

[9] As it happens, these are also drugs that affect serotonin. The concept of "serotonin deficiency" was invented in 1954 by two Rockefeller University scientists. In a short notice in the back of *Science*, they noted that LSD, whose profound effects on consciousness were well known, contained within itself a copy of the serotonin molecule, and that serotonin had recently been discovered in the brain. They speculated that a lack of serotonin, whose role in neurotransmission was still not accepted, must have something to do with mental illness.

"Well, of course ketamine works mostly on glutamate pathways . . ."

"No. I mean that you're conscious when you take ketamine and unconscious when you get ECT."

The distinction seems lost on Papakostas, or maybe he just doesn't have time for a discussion on the nature of consciousness. Either way, you cannot help but admire the purity of his devotion to the material, the way he has pared down psychic life to its bare bones. His is a spare and unrelenting pursuit, and his single-mindedness right now seems nearly ascetic.

Papakostas may be circumscribing my subjectivity in order to make it work for the drugs, but he's also renouncing his own subjectivity, putting aside whatever curiosity he might have about the shape of the self, the objects of consciousness, the raw nature of our encounter, in order to make good his claim to possess the instruments of science. Armed with them, he can take my emotional measure and report my depression with the dispassion and confidence of an astronomer reporting the distance to a star. The truth thus derived, decontaminated of aspiration and expectation, is better, truer somehow, than the one we know through our credulous senses and fickle sensibilities. Maybe that's why I don't argue with him when he adds up my numbers and tells me that in the world behind the world, the one in which I am officially depressed, the survey says I'm getting better.

Which is news to me. I hadn't been keeping track of my HAM-Ds and Q-LES-Qs, but apparently my numbers were trending steadily toward health. I'm discomfited, disturbed, maybe even a little depressed at this, at my apparent inability to know my own inner state—not to mention the possibility that I will have to relinquish my own idea of happiness and settle for "symptom-free" living instead.

I arrive at my next visit resolved to get the dazzle out of my eyes and to make my psychiatrist take account of the seams I think I'm seeing in the Matrix. But as I'm finishing up with the tests on my clipboard, a petite woman with short hair and large eyes comes into the waiting room. She's not quite looking at me as she introduces herself quickly, beckons me to follow her, and, before I can tell her that there must be some mistake, that I am Dr. Papakostas's patient, she turns her back and briskly leads the way into the warren of offices beyond the waiting room.

Papakostas must be away on vacation, I think. It is August, after all. But when we pass his office, there he is at his desk, leaning into his computer screen. He doesn't see me. I imagine that he has tired of my questions or that his colleagues have caught wind of our extracurricular discussions, all that *language*, decided it's time to remind me who is asking the questions around here, and pulled him off the case. Whatever the explanation, it is hard not to take this personally—which, of course, is exactly how a depressed person, whose disease makes him "rejection-sensitive," would take it.

In fact, I can't seem to escape the gravitational field of my diagnosis today. When I tell the new psychiatrist I didn't catch her name, she repeats it carefully and slowly, as if to account for my "psychic retardation." When I explain why I am going to record our session (she asked, something Papakostas never did), she says, "Oh . . . in-ter-est-ing," filling the spaces between syllables with professional smarm. I suspect that she's running the numbers in her head and wondering whether this will be the "difficult" interview that's worth three points on Item 8.

If the purpose of the switch was to make things more businesslike, then Christina Dording was the perfect choice. She is cold and unflappable, her lines well rehearsed, her inflected concern perfectly pitched. When she asks me if I think my depression is a punishment for something that I've done (Item 2), and I try joking—"It's an entertaining thought, but I haven't had that one"—she seems not to notice. When I confess that I'm baffled, even after all this time, by the HAM-D's questions—"This past week, have you been feeling excessively self-critical?"—that require me to parse words like "excessively" and "normally" and "especially" (something that Papakostas has dealt with affably by letting me ramble on until I say something that allows him to circle a number), she answers with such crisp condescension—"If there's a comparator implied, it's always to when you're not depressed"—that I wonder whether *I'm* the one asking silly questions. Maybe I'm the only person who wonders whether "excessive" means more than I think others do or more than I think I ought to. Maybe her answer isn't as circular as it sounds, maybe it means more than saying it's a problem when it's a problem and not when it's not, maybe it isn't yet another denial of the basic assumption here—that they are the experts about my mental health, that depression isn't something I'm equipped to detect in myself, because if I was, I'd be in the other study, the one for the Minor Depression I thought I had in the first place. Or maybe all these maybes, and my resulting inability just to blurt out a yes or a no, are just another example of my "excessive self-criticism."

Dr. Dording and I are not off to a good start. Which makes it a little easier to interrupt the interview to ask her whether she really thinks self-criticism is pathological.

"Pathological?" she asks, as if such a thing had never occurred to her. "I don't know if I'd call it pathological."

"Symptomatic, then," I offer.

"Well, it's certainly not optimal."

"Optimal," I say, deploying the therapist's repeat-and-pause tactic, hoping she'll tell me exactly how much self-criticism is optimal, and how she knows.

"*Certainly* not optimal." She does her own pause.

"But being self-critical is something that helps people succeed, isn't it?"

"Sometimes yes, sometimes no. I don't think being *excessively* self-critical is ever a great thing. No." She starts turning pages again, resumes. But I don't want to let it drop. I've come to pull back the curtain, and, the numbers aside, I want to know, colleague to colleague, just between us pros, do I really seem depressed to her? *Majorly* depressed? I ask her to tell me what she thinks the difference is between Major Depression and Dysthymia, a *DSM-IV* mood disorder that, if I have to be diagnosed, comes closest to capturing my melancholy.

"You're getting into close quarters here," she says.

In another world, one in which psychiatrists actually liked language, we might explore this slip—for she really means to say that I'm getting into fine diagnostic distinctions here—and its revelation of discomfort at my intrusion into her professional space. But she seems unaware of what she has just said as she explains: "Dysthymia is more low-level chronic. Minor Depression may or may not be long term, but it typically has less criteria than Major Depression."

And before I can ask her how any of this compares with what she actually sees, she closes the notebook and walks me out.

George Papakostas is a few paces in front of me as I round the corner of the reception desk. He's headed for the men's room. I decide to spare him strained pleasantries at adjoining urinals. But I dawdle to the elevator, and he shows up just as it arrives. We ride down and walk out of the building together. I tell him how fascinating I find this process, and how many questions I still have. I'm working toward asking him if we can extend our next meeting somehow, maybe go out for lunch or something, so that I can debrief him. But he tells me he is going to Greece to visit his ailing father, and he won't be back in time. We shake hands good-bye.

I imagine that he is relieved to be done with me. I know how this looks

to him, the patient challenging the boundaries of the professional relationship, the *What About Bob?* nightmare. Or I think I do. Maybe I don't know
anything about this. Maybe what he really sees as we stand on the threshold of
his concrete fortress is a conversation orchestrated by ion channels and neu-
ral pathways and axonal projections, two people deep in the grips of their
chemicals, one of them still clinging (because of those chemicals, no doubt)
to his old-fashioned idea that he is more than the sum of his electromolecu-
lar outputs, that a conversation like this one, not to mention recalcitrant unhappiness, might be complex and mysterious and meaningful.

I am already deflated when I arrive for my last interview. Of course, there's no
place in the HAM-D to express this, to talk about the immeasurable loss that
I think we all suffer as science turns to scientism, as bright and ambitious
people devote their lives to erasing selfhood in order to cure it of its discon-
tents. The HAM-D questions, Dording's unconvincing solicitude, the banal-
ity of this exercise, the tyranny of the brain—they all seem as unassailable,
solid, and impenetrable as the office building itself. I'm downright unpleasant
when Dording asks me if I've been feeling guilty or self-critical. "A constant
feature of my life," I say. She ignores me.

But then she does something strange. She skips the Insight item, the one
where she's supposed to ask whether I think I'm suffering from an illness and
to give me points if I don't think I am. I ask her why. "You typically don't ask,"
she replies. "It's atypical that a person is something other than a zero. Clearly
psychotic people could have a two. There are occasions when you can get a
one, like if a person thinks their lack of interest or energy doesn't have anything
to do with being depressed. But typically people who are in here are a zero."

"So you would have to be either psychotic or believe that your symptoms
are the result of some other conditions?"

"Yeah."

"As opposed to just saying, 'Well, you know, this is just how I am.'"

"That's a good question. I think that an answer like that would require
an explanation. You would need to talk a little more about an answer like
that." And I'm thinking that we should have this discussion, right now, because I am that patient, and I don't think I'm psychotic.

But that isn't going to happen. Instead, Dording is going to give me a
physical. She goes to find out if the exam room is available, returns to tell me
that it is not, that I can wait or do it on my next visit.

"Next visit?" I ask. According to the protocol, this is my last.

"You're not coming in for the follow-up?" She looks as surprised as I am, as if no one would pass up that opportunity. I ask whether it would be any different from what we've been doing. It wouldn't, she says. So I tell her I'll skip the follow-up and wait for my exam.

Julie is also gone for vacation, so Caitlin takes my vitals and draws my blood. Then Dr. Dording comes in. She taps my knees, looks in my mouth, listens to my heart and lungs. When she asks me to follow her finger with my eyes, she puts her hand on my bare knee. The touch of her fingertips is firm and cool and impersonal, my knee just a prop to hold her up.

She repeats her offer of follow-up, then elaborates on something she mentioned at the end of our interview. "Give me one second here," she had said as she flipped the pages of my binder. "Look at your scores. Nice response." Now she says, in case I didn't get it the first time, "I think you've done very well, you're *much improved*." She doesn't ask whether I agree, nor does she explain why if I'm better I would need *follow-up*, why I would need to do more than buy some fish oil at the Whole Foods next door.

If, that is, I have been taking fish oil for the last eight weeks.

I ask her if I was on placebo or drug. She's befuddled for a moment. "I don't think we unblind the study," she says. She deliberates over my paperwork. "No, not in this one. No unblinding."

I protest. "I don't get to find out?" It's as if she's never been asked, as if no one in the whole history of clinical trials had ever wanted to know which side he had been a witness for.

"No," she says. "But you had a good response."[10] She's chipper now, like she's trying to convince me that I ought to take my improvement and go home happy, another satisfied customer. And really, it doesn't matter. Because the point here is not to teach me anything about myself, or for them to learn anything from me. It's not even to prove whether or not omega-3s work. It's to strengthen the idea that this is what we are: machines fueled by neurotransmitters at the mercy of our own renegade molecules.

---

[10]All of which raises the question of how the doctors know what kind of follow-up to provide, whether to give a drug or not. Later, the lead investigator on the study, David Mischoulon, told me that they "take their best guess" about whether the subject was on drug or placebo. The reason for not disclosing my experimental condition, he explained, was so that doctors wouldn't detect a pattern in the responses and thus "break the blind." He added that I could indeed find out when the study is completed—about five years from now, he estimated.

.   .   .

Once upon a time, the scientific explanation for depression sounded something like this:

> If one listens patiently to a melancholiac's many and various self-accusations, one cannot in the end avoid the impression that often the most violent of them are hardly at all applicable to the patient himself, but that with insignificant modifications they do fit someone else, someone whom the patient loves, has loved or should love. . . . So we find the key to the clinical picture: we perceive that the self-reproaches are reproaches against a loved object which have been shifted away from it on to the patient's ego.

For a modernist like Freud, who wrote *Mourning and Melancholia* in 1917, depression was embedded in history, personal and cultural, and untangling that history, rescuing it from the oblivion of the unconscious by turning it into a coherent story, was the key to a cure. A fascinating and tragic notion—that we carry within us an other whom we can never fully know, but whom we must try to know—is headed for the dustbin of history. Freud, with his extravagant hermeneutics, his because-I-said-so epistemology, his unfalsifiable claims—not to mention the sheer inefficiency of psychoanalysis—has given way to the Dordings and Papakostases of the world, with their inventories and brain scans and pills. They have replaced Freud's unconscious, the repository of that which is too much to bear and which will only stop tormenting us to the extent that we give it language, with an unconscious populated by carbon and hydrogen and nitrogen and oxygen, the basic building blocks of the material world, essential but forever dumb.

Still, I'm not exactly pining for Freud as I leave Mass General for the last time. He got too much wrong, some of it inexcusably so. Indeed, as I drive through the lunch-hour scurry on the hospital-zone streets, the doctors in blue scrubs hurrying between buildings, wan patients wheeling IV stands down the sidewalks, ambulances and private cars delivering a legion of the sick to this city of hope shimmering in the late summer heat, I am once again struck by temptation—to believe, as I hurtle down Storrow Drive having these thoughts, passing all these other I's having their own thoughts, convinced that we are driving ourselves just as surely as we are driving our cars, that I am wrong about who I am, that we are all wrong. That scientists peering into the darkness in our skulls will eventually illuminate it entirely and show us that such thoughts and the conviction with which they are held are only accidental: spandrels of our cerebral architecture that can be rearranged with surgical precision. And just as we once were playthings for the gods or sinners poised over a fiery pit or enlightened rationalists cogitating our way to the truth of ourselves, we will become the people who needn't take ourselves too seriously, who will stop mistaking the vicissitudes of personal history for the vagaries of personal biochemistry, who will give up the ghost for the machine.

Because irresistible ideas about who we are only come along every so often, and here at Mass General they've gotten hold of a big one. They have figured out how to use the gigantic apparatus of modern medicine to restore our hope: by unburdening us of self-contradiction and uncertainty, by replacing pessimism with "optimization," by inventing us as the people who seek Life Enjoyment and Satisfaction, who will buy from the pharmacy what we need to forge ahead toward Well-Being unhindered by Depressive Symptomatology, to pursue antidepression if not happiness. Who can resist this idea that our unhappiness is a deficiency that is in us but not of us, that it is visited upon us by dumb luck, that it can be sent packing with a dab of lubricant applied to a cell membrane?

The epiphany makes me wonder whether I've been unduly churlish to Christina Dording; maybe I should take her word for it, accept that I am better now, and thank her. But remorse lasts only as long as it takes to get the results from the lab to which, out of curiosity, I sent my pills. There wasn't a drop of fish oil among them; I was on the placebo.

May 2007

Part Four

Vice

Sex, for the narrative journalist, poses much the same dilemma as does violence: namely, how to paint a mighty waterfall without standing so near as to wet one's trousers. Because nonfiction narrators often cannot help but be characters in their own work, they must choose roles very carefully, especially when the theme is a bawdy one. To portray oneself as unblemished by vice seems arid, not to mention implausible. Yet to wallow in the stuff is, well, wretched. The successful depiction of sex must split the difference, as it were: sedulous but never salacious, engaged but never engorged.

In this chapter, three writers set out across the globe to pursue different truths about sex. Kristoffer A. Garin ("A Foreign Affair") goes undercover and flies east, to Kiev in the former Soviet republic of Ukraine, as part of a tour group of American men seeking pliant Slavic brides. Jay Kirk ("My Undertaker, My Pimp") quits his job and heads west, to Nevada, where the professional undertaker Mack Moore has opened a legal bordello and invited Kirk to stay in the "Fantasy Bungalow." Finally, William T. Vollmann ("They Came Out Like Ants!") crosses the border south into Mexicali, in fevered search for the mythical tunnels—home to brothels and opium dens—that Chinese workers were said to have built there during the nineteenth century. Improbably, all three men manage to find what they seek without losing their dignity, or worse.

A Foreign Affair

On the Great Ukrainian Bride Hunt

KRISTOFFER A. GARIN

"These are *not* American women," our guide was telling us. "They do *not* care about your age, looks, or money. And you are not going to have to talk to them for half an hour and then have your *testicles* handed back to you! Let me tell you: over here, *you're* the commodity; you're the piece of meat. I've lived in St. Petersburg for two years, and I wouldn't date an American woman right now if you *paid* me!"

It was three weeks before Christmas, and I was sitting in a Ukrainian business hotel with perhaps thirty men, mostly American and mostly on the later side of middle age, listening as a muscular, impossibly loud ex–radio D.J. who answers to "Dan the Man" promised that our lives were about to change forever. We were all strangers, but I knew at least one thing about these men: each was there because he was frustrated, angry, and tired of being alone. Each had decided that his best chance at happiness was to pay nearly $4,000 to a company called A Foreign Affair, which would ferry him through Ukraine on a two-week bride hunt, "like an alpha-male wolf," as one testimonial for the tour giddily assured us, "having the sheep brought in."

We were to be provided with cleanish hotels, temperature-controlled buses, a platoon of young female translators (most in miniskirts, each available for hire as a "full-time gal Friday" to manage our presumably busy dating schedules; Dan the Man warned that under no circumstances should we employ a translator whom we'd become attracted to, as she might want us for herself and sabotage our dates), and access to a "hospitality suite" within the hotel where we would find stacks of color-coded binders containing profiles of thousands of women in and around Kiev, each of whom had specifically expressed a desire to meet American men. In the coming days we would attend a series of social events engineered to bring our little group into contact with more than 500 of these Ukrainian ladies—women, according to the tour agency's literature, "prepared to leave the only life they have ever known." This, then, was globalization's answer to the mail-order brides of the Old West.

When the group had set out from JFK Airport the day before, it had not seemed like an especially friendly bunch. The first member I met, when I said it was nice to meet him, had shot me a challenging look and countered, "How do you know? I could be an axe murderer." Fat-faced and bearded, he turned out to be a plaintiff's lawyer with a fondness for describing his clients' injuries in graphic, breathy detail (e.g., "The cops tasered a kid till they burnt the hair off his face"). Other attempts at small talk likewise fell flat until, finally, a few of the tour veterans—or "repeat offenders," as one jokingly called himself—began to dispense advice. Some had been on as many as five of these trips before; at least two had brought home fiancées in the past, though they hadn't actually married. They promised that we, too, would surely become repeat offenders once we saw what was in store. "Remember," said one silver-haired gent in a well-cut suit and polo shirt, "they've only been liberated for ten years. They're going through a social and sexual revolution like we went through in the 1970s."

By the time of our orientation, my decision to come had started to feel like pure recklessness. Not only was I nearly ten years younger than the next youngest man on the trip; just three months earlier I had married the love of my life, and I couldn't shake the sensation that my happiness and good fortune must be obvious somehow, dripping off me like exploding ink from a bank robber's sack of cash.[1] Wanting to fit into the group as I'd imagined it, I

---

[1] In order to move among these men without incurring suspicion, I had concocted an elaborate cover story that involved my having booked the trip in the aftermath of a bad breakup; between when I had paid for the nonrefundable trip and when the group was to rendezvous at JFK, my ex and I had decided to get back together. Since I was stuck with the trip, but didn't want to ruin my chances of making things work, I would treat it like any other group tour and stay away from the women. The guys thought I was pretty absurd, but they accepted the story. If anything, I became a sort of mascot/fool for the group.

had altered much of my grooming routine in the weeks before leaving. My beard was so untrimmed as to make me feel itchy and dirty; what little hair I have had grown longish, curled in unruly wings on the side of my head and the back of my neck.

Dan the Man smiled from the front of the room. He knew we were skeptical, a little scared, a little embarrassed to be here, and reasonably so. After all, what did our presence say about us? What could we possibly have in common, other than failure?

Tomorrow would be the first of our three "socials": four-hour events with free champagne, where the ratio of women to men promised to be five to one or better. But today, we were reminded, was for relaxing, for settling in and getting comfortable with our companions. "Look around," enjoined Dan the Man. "A lot of people come here thinking this is going to be some kind of loser patrol—but it's exactly the opposite. These are professional, successful guys. These are *great* guys." He suggested we each introduce ourselves, and we did.

"I'm a doctor, but I'm not a doctor anymore. Now I'm in the world of finance."

"I raise avocados."

"I'm a former soldier, a former professor, and now I'm a lawyer."

"I'm a plumbing contractor."

"I deal in finance."

"I raise llamas, but I'm really a physician, and I have two beautiful boys and I think there's nothing better you can do than raising kids."

"I live in Texas but now I'm a welder in Iraq."

"I own a construction company."

"I'm a credit-card processor; I own two corporations."

"I'm a farmer."

"I work with real estate investments."

"I write for a living—I'm a lawyer."

I did not share the fact that I was a journalist, nor did I mention the wedding band concealed on a chain around my neck. Instead I stood and said: "My name is Kris, and I'm in advertising in New York City. I'm just here to see what happens, you know?"

Dan the Man nodded contentedly. "You see? I'm telling you, the camaraderie always ends up being a big part of this—I've had guys make half-million-dollar business deals on these trips," he said. "Now, take everything you know about dating and throw it away. After a few days, *you guys are going to become like American women!* A woman you would have killed to have lunch with back in the U.S., she'll be wanting to go out with you, but you'll start noticing little faults—her ankles are too big, you don't like the shape of her earlobes. And you will throw her back, because you have so many choices."

Shyly, slyly, hopefully, the men around the table smiled; these damaged guys, so desperate to believe.

In one form or another, the so-called mail-order bride has been part of American life since colonial days. Even today, many of New Orleans' older families claim to be descended from the "casket girls" Louis XV sent from France to wed Louisiana colonists in the early eighteenth century, the term derived from the chests the women were given to carry their few belongings. And although westerns and Harlequin novels have perhaps oversold the ubiquity of mail-order marriages on the frontier—much as the role of gunfighters in those days has been oversold—such unions, whether organized by religious groups or entrepreneurs, did take place throughout the pioneer era. Bachelor farmers wrote in search of wives not only to their support networks back East but all the way to the old country. The men's magazines of the day advertised the services of marriage brokers right alongside ads for snake-oil miracle cures and such cutting-edge mechanical marvels as the chain-driven bicycle. In turn-of-the-century Chicago alone, police broke up as many as 125 fraudulent marriage agencies, seizing and burning "wagon loads" of photographs of fictitious brides.

During most of the twentieth century, however—what with manifest destiny having been achieved, and the focus of American life having shifted from mining camps and cattle ranges to cities, suburbs, and malls—the phenomenon all but died out, except for a small traffic, impossible to quantify, which seems to have focused on women from Southeast Asia. Companies like A Foreign Affair (AFA) have sprung up only since the mid-1990s, when their founders spotted vast opportunity in the contemporaneous collapse of the Soviet Union and emergence of the Internet. Whatever one chooses to call it, the bride's road from Kiev—or Moscow, or Bangkok, or Odessa, or Cartagena, Lima, Krivoi Rog, Manila, and dozens of other places where the women are desperate enough to sign up—begins online, where a lonely man can search a functional infinity of inviting profiles and then purchase the contact information of the women he likes for a few dollars apiece ("ADD TATIANA

[77631] TO MY ORDER"), or at a volume discount ("FIND MORE WOMEN FROM DNEPROPETROVSK"). From there, he can correspond with them via email or telephone, visit their country for the in-person meeting required to begin the fiancé visa process, and ultimately bring his chosen girl back to America within six to ten months. A full-service outfit like AFA can take a man from mouse click to matrimony for less than $10,000, orchestrating everything from travel and hotel arrangements to legal services to home delivery of flowers and chocolate—complete with digital photos of the woman's ecstatic reaction—while she waits for her paperwork to go through.

Steadily, the mail-order bride business has been industrializing, even as one recent poll indicated that three fourths of the American population is not aware that these so-called international marriage brokers (IMBs) can operate legally in the United States. The industry's profile, however, has been raised considerably in recent years by, among other things, a number of well-publicized murder cases: in 2000, the killing of a twenty-year-old woman from Kyrgyzstan named Anastasia King, whose husband turned out not only to have had a restraining order against him from a previous mail-order bride but to be seeking a new, third wife through an IMB; in 1995, of a Filipina named Susana Blackwell, eight months pregnant, whose husband gunned her down outside a Seattle courtroom on the last day of divorce proceedings; in 2003, of a twenty-six-year-old Ukrainian named Alla Barney, whose husband stabbed her to death in front of their young son's day-care facility.[2]

Today, it is estimated that well over 100,000 women around the world are listed on the Internet as available for marriage to Western men. (AFA alone lists nearly 30,000.) Wherever the women come from, such websites as A Special Lady, Chance for Love, and Latin Love Search tout their traditional values,

---

[2]Such tragedies make for powerful headlines and fine political oratory, and in January, with Washington State, Missouri, Texas, and Hawaii all having already passed laws aimed at protecting foreign brides, President Bush signed the International Marriage Broker Regulation Act of 2005, or IMBRA. Under the new law, which a marriage broker is challenging in court, IMBs falling under U.S. jurisdiction would be required to provide prospective brides with detailed information on any client requesting their information, including a search of federal and state sex-offender registries and a copy of the client's stated marital and criminal background. Nor would prospective brides have to rely solely on the IMBs for information; Homeland Security has always run background checks on Americans petitioning for a fiancée or spousal visa, and under the new law these results would be shared with their prospective wives, along with a pamphlet informing them of their rights, and the resources available to them, in the event of domestic violence.

their submissiveness, their willingness to put husband and family ahead of themselves. Google the seemingly innocuous search term "single women," and five out of the first ten results will be websites offering to connect Western men with would-be wives from around the world. Unlikely as it might sound, at the outset of the twenty-first century, marriage brokering is growing increasingly less fringe, not more so.

We were lodged at the Hotel Rus, a massive structure perched on a hill at the edge of Kiev's downtown, with a flashing neon sign on top and, as with nearly every establishment in Kiev, bouncer-doormen in black leather jackets. On arrival we had been told that, since the bouncers get a cut from the in-house prostitutes' earnings, they would expect a $25 bribe if we wanted to bring any women back to our rooms during the course of the week; otherwise, the hotel would charge us for an extra guest. Our first two socials were to take place in the Rus's banquet hall, which meant that in theory we wouldn't have to leave the hotel for days, other than for dates.

As the orientation session finished, I noticed one of the men slipping out of the room, a hulking fellow in his mid-thirties with broad, goofy features and the kind of deep red sunburn one wears for a lifetime. He had introduced himself during the orientation, almost inaudibly, as simply "a farmer," and now he was looking more than a little overwhelmed. I went after him and invited him for a beer at the hotel bar.

Over drinks he told me his story. He lived and worked on the family farm in the Southwest, where he had grown up and married very young, though his wife soon had enough of farm life and left him ("Guess that's what you get when you marry a Mexican call girl," he drawled with a mournful smile). Eventually, he had turned to the Internet and begun corresponding with a Ukrainian woman whose profile he had purchased from an online broker. She knew no English whatsoever, but they nevertheless wrote to each other for several months, running their letters through a translation website before sending them. It was an imperfect system, to say the least, and after a few major misunderstandings he had decided that if matters were to move forward they would have to meet. She was set to arrive at the Kiev central train station at 5:45 the following morning—at her own expense, she was taking a thirteen-hour train ride to see him. His plan had been to spend the first couple of days with her, missing the first social, and then, if the match didn't work out, to try his luck along with the rest of the group. He was excited, he said, but what he had heard at the orientation had left him shaken.

If Dan the Man had hammered one point home during his talk, it had been to not get attached to any one woman before having gone to all three socials—and, above all, to not allow ourselves to be talked out of attending the full slate of events. We owed it to ourselves, he told us. Until we met a few dozen of these women, how could we responsibly make a choice? If there was someone we really liked, he suggested that we think of the socials as a barometer: "If you go through three socials and she's still the one you're crazy about, then that really tells you something. On the other hand, if you're not still crazy about her, then that tells you something, too." He warned us that he had seen it many times: men whose confidence had been so trampled upon by American women that they could no longer comprehend that they were *worthy* of stunning, intelligent, and much younger women. As if that were not enough, skipping the events would also be taken by Ukrainian women as a sign of weakness. "They really like a guy that's a guy here," Dan had assured us. "If they talk you out of a social, they won't respect you." What we needed to do was to focus, to be disciplined. The really enterprising men would be going on six dates a day.

When Dan the Man swung by our table later that evening, my companion was apologetic as he inquired about arranging a taxi for his early-morning pickup: "I know I've done the opposite of what you said, but I can't stand her up."

Our leader sighed. "This is a long way to come for a blind date," he said, his tone hectoring. "I can't tell you how many times I've seen this before." After he drifted away, I bought us both another round.[3]

Later that night, after a few hours of note taking in my room, I made one last pass through the bar and found another of our group, a Midwesterner whose construction company built guard booths for the Army. Even though it was well past midnight on what had been a grueling day of travel, the tie under his sweater retained its crisp knot and his gray hair was immaculately parted.

"Looks like there are a few professional women out in the lobby," he said at almost the moment I sat down to join him. "Do you know how much they are? Do you think $100 would do it?" When I suggested he simply go outside and ask, he walked off into the lobby to do just that—leaving me alone in

---

[3]The farmer never did come to any of the socials; he picked up his girl at the train station as planned, they spent the week together, and within a few days they were engaged.

mid-sentence—only to return moments later. "The pretty one got in the elevator," he muttered. "The others were a little chunky. So you don't know how much for one of them, huh?"

He told me with a clinical chill in his voice about the time he had gone to Mexico on business and seen "The Donkey Show," in which a female performer fellates and then copulates with a donkey. "I didn't know a woman could take a donkey," he said. "But she did. She took it." He informed me that in Mexico the hookers had cost $40. When I asked him if he was really here in Ukraine looking for a wife, he just shrugged.[4]

At the first social the next evening, most of the men were already there when I arrived; wearing name tags, they clustered around the bar, as the women—200 of them or more—massed in a long line at the door. AFA enforces a strict policy prohibiting local women from attending more than one social during any single tour, and so each woman's registration must be checked before she is allowed in. Violators risk an out-and-out ban from future events.

Nearly forty minutes passed before the women, trickling in ones and twos past the unsmiling attendants at the door, began to outnumber our group—plenty of time for bluster and small talk. "You ready?" the men asked one another. "What kind of numbers you think you'll get?" They looked less like globalized predators than dateless eighth-grade boys at a school dance. Some carried Polaroid cameras slung over their shoulders to help them keep track of the women they would meet; many held folios full of pictures from back home—the dog, the house, the car, the local supermarket.[5] Several of the

---

[4]The next day, on a guided walking tour of downtown Kiev, I approached him and asked whether he had gotten an answer to his question. In that same toneless voice he informed me that he had eventually hired one of the hotel prostitutes for $130 an hour and before I could stop him told me in graphic detail about what they'd done and, worse, what she would not do. Then a stray dog trotted past. "Oh!" he exclaimed, turning away from me suddenly and bending to hold out his hand with a radiant, ear-to-ear smile. "Look at the little puppy! Yee-ess! *Who's* a cute little puppy?"

[5]In the summer months, expats living in Kiev have told me, the outdoor cafés in the tourist district are aflutter with older American men showing these albums to their young Ukrainian dates. One NGO worker said he remembers eavesdropping on a dentist who was actually showing his would-be bride pictures of teeth. "You overhear them all the time," he told me. "The girl's feigning interest, but, God bless her, she's giving him some attention—because a normal person like you or I would slit our wrists over such a conversation."

men stood near the entranceway, scanning the line with a more specific antic-ipation than the others; AFA had allowed us, if we liked, to anonymously in-vite women from the website so that we could check them out in person without feeling obligated to entertain them. Women thus invited are often told that they have been requested but not by whom.

Wandering back and forth I saw one of the more colorful members of our group, a fish farmer whose wife had died five years earlier and who saw no prospects in the tiny rural community where he lived. Unlike most of the men, who were dressed up in one way or another—some in business suits, others in blazers or a shirt and tie—he wore a T-shirt (red, white, and blue horizontal stripes, tucked over his vast beer belly and into his jeans) and a pair of Wranglers. He clapped me on the back and gestured toward the doors. "Nice, watching the stock come in," he said.

Ninety percent or more of the "stock" looked to be under the age of thirty-five, and more than half of them a good ten years younger than that. Most had dressed to impress, though there were a variety of styles in play, from the demure to the outrageous. Roughly half of the women, especially the older ones, came dressed in evening attire, business suits, or simply slacks and sweaters. But among the younger ladies, exposed midriffs and plunging neck-lines abounded. In the Ukrainian manner, there were miniskirts, fishnet stockings, and vertiginous high-heeled boots; ruffles, sequins, and sheer, frilly sleeves. A pair of girls, neither of whom could have been over twenty-two, were covered in glitter and wore their hair in identically cut Cleopatra bangs. Heavy makeup, especially around the eyes and cheekbones, was de rigueur. Almost all of the women had long, straight hair. I had the distinct impression that many were wearing their one nice outfit for the occasion.

As the room filled in earnest, I encountered Dan the Man, and I mar-veled to him about the sheer number of women who had come out for the event. Are things *really* so desperate for them here in Kiev? I asked.

The money, Dan told me, is only part of the problem. Even for the women who can make a good living, he claimed, it was all but impossible to find a good man. He gave me a practiced mini-seminar on the shortcomings of Ukrainian and Russian men—how they drink, philander, alternately beat and neglect their women; how even if the men were worth a damn, the popu-lation has grown so out of balance thanks to war and a short life expectancy for males that there simply aren't enough of them to go around; how men, in fact, are so scarce that more and more Ukrainian women are turning to lesbianism, so starved are they for sexual satisfaction.[6]

"Wow," I said. "Well, I guess I'm going to go walk around."

The banquet hall at the Rus holds about two dozen tables, and at each of them three, four, or more women sat and drank champagne and waited for one of us to introduce ourselves. "You have *got* to move," we had been instructed. "If you don't move, you can't get the numbers." And so the men circulated relentlessly, in keeping with the gospel of Dan the Man—writing down their favorites' contact information on individual pieces of paper rather than on notepads so that the women could not see how many others were already on the list. As I wandered around the room, the men kept trying to pull me toward tables where they were speaking with five or six women. "This is Kris," one said. "He has a very good heart." Another introduced me as "one of his best friends."

Ninety minutes in, the music grew louder and the D.J. began to stage dance contests, party games. In the first game, he and his assistant chose several long-legged, miniskirted ladies from the crowd to navigate a slalom of empty champagne glasses set up on the dance floor. Three finalists tried it blindfolded; the lucky winner received a cash prize amounting to more than two weeks' pay for those in the room with jobs. "Oh my God," one of the interpreters exclaimed, stunned. "She just got $100!" The men barely seemed to notice, but a ripple of anticipation spread through the overwhelmingly female crowd. So far out of line with the realities of Ukrainian life, the prize effectively underscored the extent to which these men held the key to another world. But the rest of the evening's prizes—for the sexiest dancer, for the lady whose man did the best job using tinsel to decorate her like a Christmas tree—seemed to consist of chocolate bars, movie tickets, and the like. The point had been made, so there was presumably no point in going overboard.

By the time the social ended at 10:00 P.M., many of the men were positively radiant—the attention had transformed them, if only temporarily. The happy ones were positively brimming. A few left then and there on "dates" to

---

[6]According to the CIA's estimates, the overall ratio of men to women in Ukraine is 86:100, as compared with 96:100 in Germany or 97:100 in the United States. But this statistic is heavily weighted toward citizens sixty-five and older; for Ukrainians fifteen to sixty-four, the ratio is a considerably healthier 92:100, a noteworthy gap, to be sure, though hardly a pretext for Sapphic revolution on a national scale.

local nightclubs, three or more girls in tow. The rest of us headed for the bar to compare notes. The taser-loving lawyer I'd spoken to at the airport showed off his Polaroids: "The twenty-five-year-old, I'm seeing tomorrow," he narrated. "She was beautiful. Beautiful! And *very* intelligent." Even as he spoke, the young woman in question passed by on her way out. Very pretty, and impossibly small alongside his bulk, she smiled at him and said good night, clearly not speaking more than a word or two of English. "See you Sunday," he replied, waggling his sausage of a finger and speaking in a weird, coquettish singsong. "You'd better be here or you'll be in trouble. I'll have the handcuffs; if you're not here, the handcuffs will be out."

Historically, IMBs have declined to provide any information about their male clients to the women with whom they seek to match them; and, in fact, this one-sidedness has been a selling point. A New York–based advocacy group called Equality Now demonstrated it in stark terms in 1999, when they sent a blanket email inquiry to dozens of IMBs, purporting to be from a physician who had assaulted two ex-wives; his email asked whether this history would be an issue. Out of sixty-six responses, only three IMBs turned him down, and only two others expressed serious reservations about taking him on as a client; a few actually praised him and commiserated regarding the occasional need for violence when it comes to keeping women in line. Among the responses:

"Having also been accused of asult by western women, who are usually the instigaters of domestic violence I can tell you: A) don't let it bother you and B) most Thais avoid confrontation, Buddhist philosophy, so they are not likely to start something that may end in violence." (www.loveasia.com)

"Thank you for your open and honest letter. I believe we all have skeletons in the closet and do not let them fall out when we meet someone. When I look into my past it also does not look too rosy. In heated arguments we all say and do things we did not mean, it does not make us a bad person. What I am trying to say is, let the ladies get to know the real you." (www.russianwives.com)

"We are an agency and our purpose is to try to help people meet each other. We never refuse any clients that come to us with the exception of incarcerated people. So the answer is yes we will do our very best to help you, as we do for everybody else, but you should try to work on these problem you have for your own benefit and the benefit of your future wife." (www.missright.com)

At the AFA orientation in Kiev, the point was made in a similar way when one of the men asked if the women at our events would have any sort of access to information on his age, financial status, or anything else in his personal history. "Oh no," said Dan the Man, shaking his head emphatically. "Absolutely not. We don't tell them anything. That's *your* job."

Again and again, my companions declared that they weren't looking for a sex tour, and that neither were they simply looking for a servant to cook for them and clean their home—that it was a real companion they sought. Each consistently made a point of saying how intelligent their dates were, even if their outing had only lasted for half an hour and had taken place without a common language between them. One, a California contractor with a seething, hostile energy and the blue-eyed, mustachioed handsomeness of a 1970s porn star, summed it up thusly: "I don't want someone that I'm going to run; I need somebody's help. I need an *opinion*. I'm not out to pound a bunch of pussy. If that's what I want, I'll go down to the whorehouse."

But what they really wanted, and what most imagined they would find in Ukraine, was a fusion of 1950s gender sensibilities with a twenty-first-century hypersexuality. Along with everything else, the men had heard that the women here were "wild," "uninhibited," that being with them was "a whole different ball game." As always, Dan the Man had done his part to stoke this fantasy, peppering his talk of traditional values and wifely devotion with just the right amount of lasciviousness. "I've heard stories from all the guys who have been married to them, and they all say the same thing: they definitely are much, much, much more passionate, much more open-minded," he told us at one point. "This guy, he's been married for six, seven years and his wife is just as crazy, they have threesomes all the time." The vision was Madonna and *puttana* rolled together, an American male desire shaped in equal parts by the Promise Keepers and Internet porn.

The glow from the first social having receded, many of the men found themselves a bit demoralized. A night on the town was one matter, but finding an actual wife was going to be more difficult than they had thought. Many of the women they had met, while friendly enough and certainly accessible for conversation, turned out to have had little or no interest in leaving Ukraine. They had come out to practice their English, or for the free champagne, or simply because they were curious. Even among the ones who had agreed to "date," many seemed to be in it for little more than a free meal at a nice restaurant they would never be able to afford otherwise. It was hard to imagine that the men would be shocked by such innocent opportunism, but they were. "I wouldn't say disappointed, but I got up with mixed feelings today," the California contractor told me. Later in the week, another would confess that when the first date he had scheduled stood him up, he returned to his room and wept.

Beer after beer, the men analyzed their dates—whether the women had ordered pricey menu items, whether they had taken the official taxis from in front of the hotel or insisted on walking down to the street to catch a gypsy cab at a better price. A grizzly New Englander, who said he lived in a log cabin and tended to predict the imminent destruction of whatever American city came up in conversation, recounted a date that had raised several red flags. "Well, I took out a money girl," he confessed. They had gone to T.G.I. Friday's, a popular date venue. Apparently her appetizer had arrived before his, and she had set in on it without waiting. We all clucked and shook our heads—selfish, we agreed; a bad sign. To compound matters, for her main course she had made what everyone in the group agreed was the distinctly unfeminine choice of ribs. "Wow," said one of the veterans. "I've *never* seen a Ukrainian girl order ribs."

The conversations ranged from future finances and former marriages to politics, the economy, and whether or not Latin is in fact the root of "almost every language." When I bought a beer for one of the men I had grown to sympathize with most, he gave me a big smile and said, "Thanks, whitey!" I stammered that I supposed I would take that as a compliment. "You're goddamn right it's a compliment," he replied with a wink, clinking his glass against mine.

Every one of the men I spoke with said they planned to restrict their future wife's involvement in their finances, and radically so. "You don't ever let them touch your money, bottom line," said one, to vigorous agreement from the rest of the table. "Set them up with their checking account that they use to pay all of the household supplies. You cover the core of the mortgages and the car and everything else. *Never* give them joint access." When I remarked that the arrangement sounded more like an employer/employee relationship than a marriage, the group went a little quiet, and I suddenly found myself being accused of cultural intolerance—this at a table where "bluegums" appeared to be a perfectly unobjectionable way of referring to African Americans.

"You're bringing all your value premises and laying them over relationships," the New Englander objected. "You're thinking about how *you* view it as, not what she's looking for." He became angry. "Have you been married and divorced before?" he continued, apoplectic now, forcefully jabbing his finger in my direction to punctuate each thought. "No? So you know *nothing*. When you've been fucked; when you let a woman take your life and everything you've worked for up to that point, and rip it out of your guts and then use the kids to keep fucking with you for ten years—then you'll have been cauterized to learn caution. And that's why I'm almost sixty and not married again."

A God-fearing plumber, who would actually be engaged by the end of the week, agreed that I had no idea what I was talking about, but tried to soften the tone by warning me about the dangers I would face if I sought love back in the United States. "When she gets over it, you're not going to know for two years," he told me. "And at the end of two years, she's going to have you so tied up, wrapped up, and packaged in such a neat little bow, that when she finally does tell you, ka-boom, you're done, she's already got the deck stacked in her favor before you even know what's going on. That's the truth. You can ask anybody that's been divorced."

Even the most likable of them approached the idea of marriage as if through a time machine. One, for example, a sweet-tempered, chubby Canadian businessman, spoke with passion and conviction about the female orgasm, and openly about loneliness; at one point he leaned over to me and whispered, "We're all hurting in one way or another, that's why we're here. We're all trying to make our lives better, we're all looking for love." He told me he wanted a genuine partner, but with the caveat that on the big issues—house buying, for example—he must be in charge, for the good of them both. "A ship cannot have two captains," he insisted. When I suggested that he and his hypothetical spouse might eliminate the need for a "captain" by simply shopping for a house they both liked, he went silent for a moment before he managed both to concede my point and to reframe it entirely: "Actually, that's an important thing you just said, because for a woman, she would take a lot of pride in her house. The kitchen area, the living-room area, the entertainment area, she's got to be compatible with that. So that's something I would gladly defer to a woman on."

Our last scheduled group event was a trip to Vinnitsa, roughly three hours from Kiev, for the tour's third and final social. The city's primary claim to fame was having been the site of an infamous Nazi construction project; thousands of prisoners were put to work building a vast underground command bunker and subsequently murdered in order to keep its plans secret.

This was not among the things Dan the Man told us about Vinnitsa, which was touted in our trip materials as a "bonus city," though it was acknowledged that the place "has had its ups and downs." What we were told was that this little industrial backwater was home to "motivated women" and was a "gem" when it came to romance tours. "Vinnitsa has much to offer for its guests," read the literature, "but nothing compares to the beauty of the women. Don't miss your chance to meet the girl of your dreams!" Around two thirds of the group had decided to make the trip; the rest stayed in Kiev for dates with women they had found in the binders or had met at the second social. Those on the bus traveled with high hopes. "I guarantee you that some of you guys will not be coming back tomorrow," Dan the Man had promised.

On the road to Vinnitsa, we began to see roadside stands, one after another, selling straw brooms, kindling wood, or a few cans of food, the vendors huddled back from the road burning pitifully small fires to keep warm. With little cheer to be found in the bleak, unbroken landscape, Dan the Man walked up and down the aisle delivering his spiel. He joked that what we really needed were "extreme romance tours," to places like Chechnya, Baghdad, Afghanistan. Of course, the joke had more than a grain of truth to it. We were visiting this place only because its population of 360,000 contained a critical mass of women desperate for new horizons. Indeed, the more miserable the place, the more capital a visiting man will have to leverage against his prospective wives; that was why we had left the United States for Kiev, and why we had left Kiev for Vinnitsa. One tour veteran had told me earlier that one of the best experiences of his life was being on the first Romance Tour into the Russian city of Novgorod, not long after the fall of the Soviet Union. "We were thirteen guys," he said, his voice tinged with awe. "And almost four hundred women showed up. You could barely make it through the room."

The social that night was held at a place called Club Pharaoh, a hole-in-the-wall that was apparently the largest nightclub in town. The level of skill and enthusiasm shown on the dance floor was astonishing—kick steps, turns, hair flips, all executed in nosebleed heels while crushed elbow to elbow into the crowd. The handful of men who had been lured out onto the dance floor were far out of their league but happy, swaying arhythmically on rooted feet as their partners danced circles around them. Unlike in Kiev, there was a noticeable group of women over forty—some of the most beautiful women of the evening, actually, in fur and mascara that they wore with surprising elegance; real catches, some of them, and embodiments of what so many of the men had said they wanted during the sessions at the hotel bar. With few exceptions, though, the men ignored them as they cycled through tables full of girls twenty, thirty years younger than they.

At one point I found myself next to Dan the Man, and I asked him, finally, if he had thought about the dark side of his industry. Had he heard about the killings? The cases of abuse? With an agility that must have come from his radio years, he immediately replied: "There's no doubt about it, we have guys who come through here once in a while and leave a wake of women behind them, damaged, destroyed, used, and abused." But then he added: "They talk about that in the media, of course—the women are being brought over from Ukraine and Russia, and they're being treated horribly. That may be true in some cases, but why don't you also do a story about the American men abusing the American women? It's just not sensational enough, because it's right there at home. So they make a big story out of this."

Soon afterward I told him that I was going to make it an early night, that I wished him well. "I just hate to have a guy come all this way and not find what he's looking for," he said, before turning away with a shrug.

For the ride back to Kiev the morning after the Vinnitsa social, the men boarded the bus in high spirits, slinging duffels into the cargo hold and trading good-humored, hungover banter like some minor-league ball club on a winning streak. Again they compared notes: about whom they had gone out with, how far into the wee hours they had stayed at the nightclub, how much vodka they had drunk while French-kissing a twenty-five-year-old named Olga.

One of the most successful of the group, an importer from the Great Lakes region, was flush with his conquests, and he talked a blue streak about the different women he had met and slept with throughout the trip. He switched between describing his "girlfriends" and talking about the years he spent trapped in a "passionless" marriage to a "soft American woman." His golf cap was turned backward, and he wore a leather jacket. "I'm moving from quantity to quality," he told me. "I'm changing my strategy. After the divorce, I just went wild; I guess I'd thought I would never find someone again. I think there's a good chance I'll marry one of the girls on this trip."

A few of the men paired off in animated, earnest conversations about life, marriage, women. "I'm not going to spend every bit of my life in America," one was saying. "Because I'm sick and tired of being blamed for everything—the white man, you're all responsible for everything. And American women are just rude, obnoxious. I won't marry another American woman. I won't do it. I'll stay single first."

A few rows back, another showed around photos of his front-runner with a moony, rapturous smile on his face. "Look at those eyes," he said again and again as he held out a computer printout of her profile, even as a quarter-inch-thick stack of competing profiles sat in his lap. "She just *melts* me." Quite a few of the men would find what they were looking for: by the time I left the group at the end of the first week (the full tour left several days of supported dating after the end of the group events), our tally of engagements would reach three—or six, if one includes the man who was engaged to three different women.

But when the urologist from Minnesota pulled out his video camera and started walking up and down the aisle, asking the men for memories from the trip, the chattiness evaporated.

"I'm here to see the world," one offered, stiffly.

"I'm just visiting beautiful Ukraine," another muttered, and everyone around him chuckled softly at the crazy notion.

June 2006

My Undertaker, My Pimp

Looking for Grace in a Desert Brothel

JAY KIRK

For a year I worked in an office where I spoke to dying people on the telephone every day. The office was that of a funeral-consumer watchdog, which meant that we kept an eye on the funeral industry and helped the imminently bereaved and imminently deceased to make affordable funeral plans. Above my desk I kept an index card with a Faulkner quotation, "Between grief and nothing I will take grief." On a particularly bad day I scratched out the last word and changed it to "nothing."

Because I am a person who has obsessively meditated on his own death since the age of five, my friends and family thought it uncanny, if not alarming, that I had taken the job. When I was six my parents were worried enough that my father, a minister, took me to funerals, thinking (reasonably) that my trouble was all in my mind and that a swift dose of reality might cure me. What my father did not understand was that no matter how assuringly he winked at me over the bowed heads, death is ultimately a problem of the imagination. The funerals only gave mine dark fodder.

As did, inevitably, the job that put me on the phone with death every day. When I found myself flirting with a terminally ill twenty-two-year-old girl, I knew it was time to "move on." On my last day, my co-workers gave me a cardboard coffin, which they had all signed, like a giant crematable birthday card. I absconded with two numbers: the girl's (I wanted to meet her in person—to sleep with a dying girl, I think—and from our conversations it seemed mutual, but it never happened, I never called, and then she died) and that of an Oregon undertaker who, after some controversy with his mortuary board, had fled the state and opened a brothel. The man's name is Mack Moore, and the brothel, in Beatty, Nevada, is called Angel's Ladies. Because this man had made what I saw as the happy leap from Thanatos to Eros, I knew that I had to seek him out. He was older than I expected—seventy-one—but when he shook my hand, in the driveway of his Las Vegas mansion, what struck me were the lustrous strawberry-blond curls that fell like a halo around his ears.

The eponymous Angel, Mack's wife, helped Mack and me pack my trunk with whorehouse provisions—laundry detergent, toilet paper, tubs of mayonnaise, hot cocoa—before we set out on the 120-mile drive to Beatty. Angel stayed behind to tidy up, since the police had returned their confiscated belongings just a week earlier and the house was still a disaster. I was soon to hear much about the night that Angel had been held hostage in her living room while the cops looked for evidence of illegal "outcalls."

The elderly pimp shuttles back and forth between his Vegas mansion and the desert brothel a few times a week. The lonesomeness of the drive is total and exhilarating: a haunting landscape of gray-green sagebrush broken here and there by a streak of Martian red, a rumpled mountain range, a demonic cactus. In almost two hours the only blips of civilization are the town of Amargosa Valley (Mack points out and curses the Cherry Patch 2 bordello, a rival), a New Age temple, and the south entrance to the Nevada Test Site.

Beatty, in Nye County, is the last town to survive from among the many that popped up during the 1904 Rhyolite gold rush. Now Rhyolite, once the fourth-largest city in Nevada, is a ghost town, and Beatty is the place where you had better stop to buy gas. The Bullfrog Mine, the major employer until central banks across Europe released large parts of their gold reserves into the market, shut down in 1998 and is now down to a skeleton crew doing mop-up; Beatty's population has dwindled severely as a result. The economy is sporadic, and stability is as fleeting as it was for the nomadic Shoshone, who summered on the oasis. Other jobs are scarce to nonexistent. Even the Nevada Test Site, despite being literally just over the hill, provides only a handful of jobs to the few willing to commute—the nearest gates are 103 miles north and

54 miles south. The Yucca Mountain Project, a planned federal graveyard for 77,000 tons of high-level radioactive decay, offers possible hope for the future, but it's less than certain, and even if it flies it won't guarantee jobs for Beatty. For now, the town survives on tourism: Death Valley hikers, truckers, gamblers, and men visiting Angel's Ladies.

The prostitutes settled this area with the miners. Only the former remain in business. The only other trace of the miners are the wild burros that roam the town like dust-shrouded ghosts. Mack says that if some people get their way and Angel's is closed, the town will suffer, badly, and it's probably true. The Beatty Chamber of Commerce is one of the brothel's greatest boosters.

Mack wears thick-soled Adidas tennis shoes with ankle socks and a powder-blue cardigan, and as he rambles on in his puttering unpunctuated way, every so often his eyes get flirty, like he's going to share something extremely funny or something deep and meaningful, but each time he tries to address the sex-death continuum, or answer my timid, oblique questions to that end, he veers into the sententious whey of condolence cards.

The first time I called he answered from his shower and let me know, over vigorous lathering, that his brothel had been suspended because of a sting coming out of a conspiracy involving the sheriff, a rival brothel owner, a former madam, and maybe even the assistant D.A.; that he was going to sue the shit out of Nye County for violating his civil rights; that he took Viagra; that he and his wife were swingers; and that when I came to visit he would put me up in the Fantasy Bungalow. Most of the drive he talked about which swinging magazines are best for meeting other swingers and how since Angel was so much younger and prettier than he she got more dates than he did, but by the way he told me this I was led to believe that it was probably the other way around, that he was the Lothario, something later confirmed unenthusiastically by the girls who make up Angel's staff. Despite his candor about his sex life, the circumstances surrounding his abrupt exit from the funeral trade remain hazy. There is ample stuff for nightmares, if you believe all the accusations: The matter of a missing corpse. Bodies buried in the wrong graves. Bodies exhumed on the sly. Bodies cremated in parties of two. Between 1992 and 1994 alone, eighteen complaints were filed against Moore with the Oregon Cemetery and Mortuary Board. But, thanks to the state's confidentiality laws, the board's investigative records are sealed, and I'm left without a full grasp of the mystery behind the man with whom I'm now zooming into the heart of nowhere.

Mack started out selling headstones to put himself through Bible college, but when Oregon cemeteries colluded to require that markers be purchased directly from them, driving out the independent monument dealers, he was nearly put out of business. Fighting mad, Mack became a spectacle, getting dragged out of more than one cemetery in handcuffs for barging in with wheelbarrow and spade to plant a rebel headstone. Fourteen years, three trials, and three appeals after he filed a lawsuit against the cemeteries in 1969, the exclusive installation requirement was ruled a violation of the Sherman Anti-Trust Act; Mack took over four of the defendants' cemeteries—financially weakened by the judgment—built more funeral homes, and began his necropolitan reign over Lane County. He promptly made new enemies of rival funeral directors, who bristled at his aggressive salesmanship—full-page color ads of caskets, coupons, raffles, cut-rate burials—ploys, they felt, more suitable for selling box springs. One Christmas he advertised a special "Holiday Memorial Service," promising a special appearance by Santa Claus, who, "in person, will tell how he remembers his wife who died of cancer."

Soon after Angel was hired as a janitor (she quickly worked her way up to hairdresser, and, according to Mack, did a lovely job with the women's hair), her youngest son was killed in a motorbike accident. Mack embalmed the boy. Not a year later, Angel's husband died. Mack did that funeral too. Mack's wife and business partner, Eva, grew suspicious of his relationship with his widowed employee, but he denied any hanky-panky: "I never got involved with any woman that I'd served as a funeral director. But it was not because I didn't have the chance." After Eva divorced Mack and they divided the properties—making them, in essence, competitors—he tacked an addition onto one of his parlors, rechristened it Celestial Funeral Home and Wedding Chapel, and invited the entire town to his and Angel's wedding. Because of her tragic losses, Mack says, Angel made an excellent funeral professional. It is the same compassion for human frailty, Mack says, that's made her such a damn good prostitute—but that's rushing ahead.

The odd rivalry with Eva came to a head, gruesomely, in late August 1993, when a man died who had prearranged for his funeral at Chapel of Memories (owned by Eva) but who had bought a cemetery plot at Springfield Memorial

Gardens (owned by Mack). His body was taken to Eva's. The man's stepson went to Mack's, understandably confused. Mack, with mattress-salesman finesse, persuaded the stepson that since his father was going to be buried at Mack's cemetery *anyway*, it might be easier, less *grief*, not to mention cheaper, because, well, Mack was prepared to give him a great deal, if he just let Mack do the burial *and* the funeral. All he'd have to do is sign the transfer and Mack would go over to Eva's and get his stepdaddy. The stepson was persuaded. Unfortunately for Mack, Eva had dumped the body in the casket, wearing nothing but diapers, covered in its own postmortem foulness. "We worked on that damn casket for hours trying to get the damn stink out," Mack says. Sometime during the mayhem, no doubt perturbed, probably thinking that his wife had done this to him on purpose—"she did dirty"—Mack took color photos of the soiled dead man and showed them to the stepson, suggesting he file a complaint against Eva. The stepson was not pleased, and the family took both Moores to court for $7 million. Eva was eventually dropped from the suit, and Mack settled for $21,000. By this point, however, the mortuary board was fed up and proposed suspending Mack's license for illegally soliciting bodies from a rival funeral home. This was, after all, not the first time.

Then Angel's eldest son, Jesse, died from drug abuse. The boy and his father had allegedly argued about who had the worse kidneys; it's not clear that the father won by dying first, since Jesse died just a week short of his thirtieth birthday. For Angel, it was a world-ending blow.

Given their troubles, leaving was an easy decision. In October 1995, Mack sold to a corporate funeral home, and by March 1996 he and Angel had moved to Vegas. Then they bought the brothel, and Angel, vanquished by grief, registered as a legal prostitute.

Mack has since found new loopholes to finger, and the Nevada Brothel Owners Association has castigated him for jeopardizing an industry that likes to keep as low a profile as the funeral trade. The director of the association, George Flint, says that Mack has "turned what is a fairly halfway respected industry into a kind of farce." Angel's Ladies was busted in the spring of 1999 after sending their blondest girl, Cindi, to a motel when a cop, posing as a trick, called for room service. (Prostitution is only legal in Nevada *inside* a licensed brothel.) It took three calls for the cop to persuade the madam, Wanda Towns, but Wanda and her husband, Clint, who works as a security guard at Angel's Ladies and who drove Cindi to the motel, were arrested and convicted with Cindi for attempting to solicit an illegal outcall. Mack argues that Cindi was just going to "dance" for the man, that it was just an "escort" date, a distinction not made by the Nye County brothel ordinance. A month later the county sheriff's office simultaneously raided the brothel and the Moores' Vegas home. Evidence showed a history of outcalls, and the county commissioners shut down the brothel for two weeks, but an appeals judge later ruled entrapment, reversed the convictions, and ordered the Moores' belongings returned. Still, a gross misdemeanor charge of conspiracy to engage in illegal prostitution looms over the Townses and Cindi, pending a possible settlement with the county. But with Mack blaming everyone for being part of a conspiracy and threatening to sue the county for violating his civil rights (holding Angel hostage, depriving Clint, who has asbestosis, of his oxygen, refusing to return important personal documents), and the county dredging up new pandering charges (trafficking girls to Vegas), the fight will likely drag on until both sides run out of steam. On the other hand, if Mack makes good on his threat to sue the county and wins, he may expand his business. There's a vacant building across from the Burro Inn and Casino that he's thinking about buying and turning into a funeral parlor.

Mack walks the line of the law as deftly as he walks the line between grief and lust. How very blurry that line is in a free-market culture that survives on the myopic propaganda of manufactured need, in which need is predicated on fear of loss, fear of not having; in which images of grief are routinely brought into focus as images of desire. Between grief and nothing, nothing sells better than grief. Except maybe pussy.

We pull around the side of the brothel, a compound of linked trailers painted antacid pink. Electric angels dance over the front porch of the double-wide. "That's Shanda," Mack says before we get out of the car. "She is a bubbling-over girl. So is Cindi. Those two girls will kill you off." Shanda, in a bowler and a pajama top unbuttoned to the navel, is ankle deep in cats; she ministers to one with an eyedropper. Thirty or forty surround her like pigeons. She drops the kitten and greets me with a chipper Texan drawl. Two litters of the feral cats were born this week; their eyes are weepy and shuttered. Shanda helps Mack and me unload my car. We can't help but toe mewling cats out of our path to the brothel.

Dinner is already on the table, waiting (Mack called from twenty miles back to let them know to set an extra plate for me). Wanda takes off an oven mitt to greet me and then runs to the kitchen for a last-minute dish. Mack sits at the head of the table; at the other end sits Clint Towns, who watches the news, an oxygen tube strapped under his nose. Cindi is a jittery blonde in a red leather jacket. Diane tells me that if I want a good story then I should ask her about the time she and her daughter got lost in the Sahara and her daughter ran out of Kool-Aid and they were saved by a mysterious being.

On the counter is a row of egg timers, each with a girl's name. Angel's has a license for five girls but employs eight, so they work in shifts. Angel, out of compassion and pity, has been known to take on men that the other girls refuse, and for less money. The dining room doubles as the madam's office, with phones, a copier, and a status board on the wall. The board says in green Magic Marker that Coco, Cajun, Dizyre, and Mia are "off property." A joke traffic sign by the door says, "Parking for L♥vers Only, All Others Will Be Towed." On the wall between the TV room and dining room is an authentic Old West wood placard:

Why Walk Around Half Dead When We Can Bury You
For Only $22.00
We Use Choice Pine Coffins (Select Pine from Mexico)
Our New Burial Coach—Finest in the Arizona Territory
TOMBSTONE UNDERTAKERS

Mack lets me know that they pray before meals. He takes my hand, and I take Shanda's, to my left. During his prayer, Mack caresses my hand with his thumb, not in a kinky way but in the same way my mother does during her blessing over Thanksgiving dinner, describing the same rosette with her thumb. Unlike most Nevada whorehouses, Angel's Ladies does not have a bar. Mack does not drink, or smoke, or gamble. He and Angel are born-again, and Angel's is the closest thing anyone is going to get to a Christian brothel. They like to say that they "live the example." Why not? The ancients lived happily for millennia with the paradox of temple prostitution. A timer goes off and we are presently joined by Nikki, wearing a peignoir, looking freshly showered. Wanda asks if her "guy" doesn't want to join us, and she murmurs that no, he does not. The other women look her over and then pass the casserole.

Because we are allegedly across the street from Area 51, I broach the subject of UFOs. Instant hit. Everyone at the table, except Mack, has had a sighting. Twice since she's been here, Wanda has seen lights above the ridge over Area 51. The second time was with a trick. He'd just buzzed and she was opening the front door. It was a brilliant yellow flare, almost gold. Clint, who worked for the government, has seen stuff, too. Diane has had the most sightings. She is writing a book, she says, called *The Hooker and the Aliens*. Mack gets irritated with the bunkum and pulls the dessert, a pan of chocolate-frosted cake, his way. He cuts two bricks and serves me one. He takes a bite and then asks, sternly, "You like yella cake?" I say that yeah, I like yella cake. "Me too," he says. Then there's a buzz and the girls scurry. Mack excuses himself.

The girls keep out of sight till called to the front parlor for the lineup. Peeking around the corner, I can't see much more than the visitor's shoes on the pink carpet. When we overhear the trick tell Mack that on his way over tonight he saw eight cop cars outside the Exchange Club, one of the three casino hotels in town, Wanda looks shaken. Mack sits on the couch, ankle crossed over his knee, wooing the man in his warm, unforced voice, telling him what a fine selection of ladies he has to choose from, how this place is different from other brothels: The others will rush you, the others are just in it for the money, the others aren't Christian, but here there's free pop and free coffee and seventy-seven acres to take a moonlight stroll or take a girl for a skinny-dip in the natural spring-fed pool. Hell, one former girl, Jennifer—"she had these great big natural titties"—ended up *marrying* a trick; that's right, dreams do come true. Hell, Mack had the honor of giving her away at the chapel in Reno, and after you've gruntled yourself with sex every which way you ever wanted, if you're hungry, why, feel free to join us for supper, there's still some on the table now.

During the lineup, Wanda clears dishes, and I flick crumbs, lulled by the mechanical sips of Clint's oxygen. Wanda joins me with a cup of tea. She wears green satin pajamas. She is not a glamorous or gaudy madam. The Townses went to the Beatty Community Church until the pastor, Reverend Jeff Taguchi—also the owner of the one-hour Photoshop and, ironically, a county commissioner on the brothel-licensing board—exhorted the couple one Sunday after their arrests to "go forth and sin no more." Wanda holds her husband's hand on the table. She is terrified that Clint, who's dying of the same thing that Shanda claims is taking the kittens, could go to jail. They're holding their breath till the trial; it's been postponed twice already. She never sent a girl on an outcall before that night, she says. They only did it because the detective lied and said he was in a wheelchair. Her son, actually both her children, are wheelchair bound. She gets up and brings me a picture: a kid with long greasy hair, in a wheelchair. Diane enters the room, naked but for a black gauzy body stocking that smooshes her nipples. She drops $600 on the table and says the guy wants two and a half hours. While Wanda "books" the cash, Diane tells me that if I want, later, she'll let me read a chapter from her book. Then Wanda sets a timer, and Diane leaves.

After a trick chooses which girl he wants from the lineup, the price negotiation is done privately in the girl's room. (Each girl's room is supposed to have a panic button.) Wanda listens in over an intercom hidden in the spice cabinet. Each woman is an independent contractor who sets her own price, generally $200–$400 an hour; 45 percent goes to the house. Each sex act is negotiated and priced separately—done piecework, à la carte. Or, as Lora Shaner, a former madam, puts it in her book, *Madam: Chronicles of a Nevada Cathouse*, "You want to play with my tits? That's an extra fifty. Suck my nipples? Seventy-five more. Nibble my toes? Forty bucks. . . ." Funeral expenses, as mandated by the Federal Trade Commission funeral rule, are similarly itemized.

Mack has given me a key to the Fantasy Bungalow, a dismal trailer set a hundred yards behind the main compound. Mack accused his last madam of burning down the first Fantasy Bungalow. Its charred remains are scattered at the bottom of the hill. The one where I get to sleep is perched on cement blocks, snuggled against a steep crag that bears a giant white *A*, like an aleph of shame. To get there I rely largely on instinct, stepping over cats tensed like fists in the dark. A few stars make an effort in the sky.

The decor of the Fantasy Bungalow is meant to be homey, as the Angel's Ladies website put it recently, for "playing house or something different!" Angel oversaw the decorating, just as she did for their Oregon funeral parlors. The curtains are quaint and the wallpaper quainter. Mirrors in the bungalow apprise me of my whereabouts at all times, including one that surely registers my expression when I open the refrigerator and find, alone on the second shelf, a jumbo-sized box of chilled latex gloves. The video library is sparse: *Hung and Hard, Bang 'Er 17 Times*, and *SEASLUTS*, Volume 2. In the back, past a beaded curtain, is my bedroom, furnished with more mirrors, and a vanity, where I leave my car keys by a Virgen de Guadalupe candle with a hornet entombed in the wax. Two lurid lamps with red bulbs clinch the mood. I try to call my wife, but I'm beyond cellular range. Mindful of a story that Shaner tells about a moll who once forced a trick to his knees at knifepoint to persuade him to accept Jesus as his personal savior, I look everywhere but find no panic button, only an unplugged Radio Shack intercom, and beneath the nightstand a five-quart stainless-steel bowl with a dozen Liquid Tight Hygienic Disposal System Safe-T-Bags. To my dismay, the smoke detector is missing its battery.

I pick up *Bang 'Er 17 Times*, left in the VCR, *in medias res*, while I fix myself a cup of Lemon Zinger from the complimentary tea sampler. The actors look lonely and bored, insincere, like the professional mourners in Greece who wail and writhe and tear out their hair for a fee; it's easy to sift out the truly bereaved from the faker, like pointing out the professional laugher in the studio audience, just as it's easy to tell that this porn actress is only miming lust. There is no precipice behind her eyes; she is too sober, she looks up at the camera, her audience, hungry only for ratings; she is a busker, a drone. Although the video is a bit proctologic for my tastes, I watch while listening to snippets of tape of Mack in the car.

> ME: You know how some authors put sex and death together in literature. Why do you think that is?
>
> MACK: Well, I think probably because death is so devastating in our emotions, and sex is so exciting in our emotions. It's two highs. Or you might call one *extreme* low and the other high. If you want to get a newspaper, see, the most things that's written in the newspaper is what gets the headlines, is death-murder or, uh, Clinton got his dick sucked by that girl.

Having finished the movie, now filled with a lonely, hollow pubescent guilt, I go outside. I stand in the blowing dark. Looking down at the brothel, I wonder which of the five whores will share their master's bed tonight while his bereaved wife sleeps alone 120 miles away. Mostly, I'm disappointed that this man, who panders to those most human conundrums, grief and lust— the very antipodes of the carnal spectrum—a man who possesses a meat-and-potatoes soul if ever there was one, finds the subject of sex and death to be just that, meat and potatoes. When I go to bed I read the grief self-help book I brought. I couldn't help but notice that the death-and-dying section is coterminous with the human-sexuality section at my Barnes & Noble. This book recommends getting a puppy.

.   .   .

In the morning, after I shower with the heart-shaped soap that I found on the back of the toilet, Shanda cooks me eggs. She is wearing her bowler, and her slippered toes peekaboo like miniature marshmallows. Diane sits at the table smoking and flipping through cookie recipes. It's going to be a slow day. Almost everyone in the industry refers to prostitutes as girls. But, as it happens, Shanda just became a grandma and Diane has two kids in college. Mack would have you think that Angel's ladies are the demimonde, but the women I've met are worn and mournful. They have the wan charm of (I imagine) the whores of ancient Rome, the *bustuariae*, sexual servants of the gods of the dead, who made their assignations in cemetery groves. Angel herself, just a few years younger than Mack, is the most weathered. I have yet to spend any time with Angel, but I have gotten to know her, a little, from the photo album in the parlor of her and Mack copulating. It is a plain album, the sort in which you would expect to find vacation photos. A number of pictures include another man having sex with Angel while Mack, pouchy and removed, looks on. In one snapshot, her contorted face looks carved out of grief, but it could be the strain of ecstasy turning her inside out. When Mack comes in with his newspaper, Shanda runs off to dress for a Halloween Fantasy Fetish Ball in Vegas. There are Halloween parties everywhere in Nevada this weekend. Mack will not participate. He is staying in to put the finishing touches on a forty-page missive of gripes, ammunition for his lawyer. Since Mack has work to do, he can't join me at the Burro Races, the highlight of Beatty Days, this weekend's celebration of Nevada's anniversary of statehood (Halloween 1864), but he encourages me to go anyway, saying he's heard that they're "sort of funny." I ask Diane if she wants to go, but Mack answers for her. Of course she can't. Someone has to be here when the fornicators ring the bell.

High noon finds a crowd around the burro pit, an arena the size of a ball field, behind the Burro Inn and Casino. Stranded in the center is a rusty oil drum. There are aisles of pickups and spectators roosting on car hoods. We are under a bleak hill painted with a giant white *B*. Back in the fifties, when Beatty was the closest town to the aboveground nuclear tests, residents gathered at this same spot behind the Burro Inn, né Atomic Club, in the early morning with lawn chairs and coolers to watch the apocalyptic fireballs light up over the hills. Fortunately, Beatty lies upwind of the Nevada Test Site, and residents have been spared the tragedy that has befallen many downwinders, though, according to the Department of Energy, which tests the town for radionuclides weekly—as often as the girls at Angel's Ladies are tested for sexually transmitted diseases—the town runs a little hot. In the semi-shade of the announcer's box, a tin-roofed platform on stilts, are three docile burros tied to the fence. The animals are cute, almost toy-sized, except for their distractingly big genitalia.

Since the species originated in North Africa, the burro adapted quickly to Nevada's desert climate and made the perfect pack animal for the nomadic prospector. The beasts were thought to be preternaturally "tuned" to precious metals. In fact, the prospector who filed the first claim in Rhyolite was allegedly led to the gold by his own pack of ungulate dowsers.

I grab a spot close to the fence, between a perambulator and a collegiate-looking guy with a camera. There must be two hundred people now, maybe more. A burro wails, just as mournful as Eeyore. There are a number of leathery-armed folk wearing visors that span the visor spectrum from monogrammed cotton to blue sparkle plastic, but more wear cowboy hats. A scruffy-looking guy dressed in suspenders and a sand-dusted crushed hat climbs up onto a tin box and hollers the rules:

All gear must be unpacked and placed neatly on the ground before starting fire or mixing batter.

No sweets or other foods are to be used to assist in leading burros.

Pancake must be cooked on both sides. Hold pancake between thumb and forefinger for judge's approval before it is offered to the burro.

Originally, before harassing wild burros was outlawed, the contestants first had to catch one, which they then led, over the course of three days, about forty miles, not without some violence upon the contestants' persons. Today, the burros are tame, and the three "prospectors" are students at Beatty High School.

The arena turns to dust the instant the announcer blasts a pistol, and the jockeys launch forward in slow motion. Five minutes into this race nobody has yet inveigled their animal to the oil drum. A rangy kid with baggy shorts and white socks hiked up to his kneecaps—his name is Jeff—gets about a foot before his burro ceases to be persuaded and stops cold. Todd, who looks like the school quarterback, leads by a nose. Dottie, with red streaks in her hair, is first to round the drum, do-si-do. Before Todd even crosses the drum's lengthening shadow, Dottie has hitched her burro near where a judge sits at one of the three equidistant stations and begun unloading the waiting gear (shovel, matches, kindling, skillet) from its scrawny back. Todd clears the barrel but loses speed on the lee side of the drum. Poor Jeff might as well be trying to persuade a dog to evolve. Just as Todd starts to pack his gear, Dottie's burro sets back out for the second loop around the drum and then back to her station, where she begins to prepare a firepit. Just a fetlock behind, Todd digs a hole the size of a pet's grave, cracks wood over his knee, and starts striking matches. He contends with wind more than Dottie, given that his judge doesn't block the wind as well as Dottie's judge, deliberately or not, hard to say. Jeff's judge sits pensively, the shovel and gear unclaimed at her feet. Dot's judge yells "flame!" but recants when the smoke ends up just being dust kicked up by the burro. Todd takes the lead tenuously; he shelters a weak flame with his hands. Dottie has fire in the hole and it's a good fire, better than Todd's.

Dottie warms the skillet while Todd still struggles, blowing. She pours batter. Oops. There's a problem. The judges huddle. Dottie forgot to oil her pan. For a second it's unclear if this means disqualification, but they let it slide. The crowd is seized with suspense as Dottie lifts the now nicely browned flapjack to the burro's muzzle. It takes a sniff. Oddly purses its lips. Then, to the shock of all, the burro bolts backward with a violent capriole. It hates pancakes. The infuriated burro storms across the pen, dragging behind it the terrified girl who is unfortunately connected to the dreaded griddlecake. Todd patiently oils his pan, pours batter, and proffers the lightly browned flapjack to his burro, who blithely opens its mouth and accepts communion.

Later that afternoon, after Mack's nap, he and I take a drive in his RAV4 out to Rhyolite. We wind upward to the ghost town, wrapped around the slagged remains of the Bullfrog Hills, past half-dismantled mills, to a sweeping view of the tailings pond, a 340-acre lake of slurry laced with cyanide that reflects the setting sun bluish-greenly. Rhyolite is nothing but ruins. Devoured facades. The wind actually whistles in a creepy minor key. Ancient street signs poke comically out of the sagebrush. Just past the once opulent bank, a three-story concrete husk, Mack turns the RAV onto a rutted path, and we bump roughly down Gold Lane, toward the trepanned mountainside. Up close it looks like the burrows of some stygian sparrowlike dirt-hill-dwelling people.

Trundling along here, I find Mack easy company. In this ghost town, speaking about cycles of boom and bust, I ask how well his business rode the New Economy, and it takes us, not as circuitously as you might wish, to the heart of Angel's grief-lust nexus. Which should have been a good thing. I had been struggling over how to approach the subject. It seemed so obvious, yet delicate, and I was momentarily elated to have an inroad into what I expected would prove to be the key to understanding this central paradox. But the subject bores him. He points out a shack where miners slept. The whores back then kept "cribs," little huts much like the ancient Roman prostitutes' *cellae*, grim mausoleums with the names of each woman etched over the entrance. By my third day with Mack, talking about funeral parlors and sex parlors, sometimes in the same breath, it's hard not to become confused, so that the tenor of my thoughts is macabre-erotic to the point that I half-consciously think of these fallen angels, in turn, as ghosts, necrophilic whores, floozily dressed zombies . . .

Eleven A.M., Sunday morning, the Beatty Community Church is packed. The church is on a hill, exposed to the raw wind that hasn't let up since yesterday. (The Fantasy Bungalow creaked like a dinghy all night.) The walls are decorated with Sunday-school handiwork, and the windows are pink-and-blue stained glass. Reverend Taguchi, a brawny Japanese American with longish hair and a goatee, mounts the pulpit. Service starts with three hymns back to back (all in F major). I sit out "Blessed Be the Name of the Lord" but, to mark time, sing along with "All Hail, King Jesus."

After "Unto Thee, O Lord," everybody gets up to greet and mingle. I am touched, if uneasy, when most come over to shake my hand, all except a strung-out-looking guy who stands in his pew, nodding forlornly. Tucked in his coat is a pit-bull puppy.

After the service the guy with the pit bull comes over while I'm waiting for Reverend Taguchi. He sits beside me in the pew and asks my name. His is Walter. For a second it doesn't look like it's going to go any further between us and then he starts to cry. Finally he manages to ask if we can go outside. He needs to talk privately. Why not? I follow Walter out to the parking lot. It is blustery. In fact, at that moment I see my first and only tumbleweed. It is a bantam, disappointing little thing that bounces across the parking lot and then wheels out of sight. Walter wants to know if I'm going to Vegas, he needs a ride. But I'm not going back to Vegas for three more days. Walter seems like an imperiled enough character that I briefly consider making a detour for him, but I've already spent an afternoon watching the burro races, a detour that led me to no conclusions except that I do not believe a burro would put up with a sport like that if he were conscious of his own mortality. I ask Walt if he worked at the gold mine, and he says that he's on "disability," he's only lived here six months, that he's from Philadelphia, which I ignore, since I live in Philadelphia and I don't feel like having anything in common at the moment. Walt starts to cry again when the dog laps his thumb; a meniscus gently swells at the rim of his left nostril. His brow quivers. He really needs to go to Vegas. There's this model, he says. This is the sad old story, I think, until he says Hobbytown USA, and I gather that it's a model airplane he's pining after.

After a potluck lunch Reverend Taguchi invites me over to his house, a block away, a peeling wind-rattled home with chimes dangling on the porch. As a county commissioner who vice-chairs the brothel-licensing board, Taguchi, despite his moral qualms, cannot say much about Mack's case, except that he thinks Beatty will survive just fine without Angel's if the brothel goes under, so we talk about whether or not Beatty will turn into a ghost town now that the mine's gone. He thinks not. I ask him again how dependent Beatty is on the revenue of Angel's, and he brushes it off. He cannot abide the suggestion that his town is in any way dependent on the sinful lucre of merchandised sex. There are plenty of other economic options, he says. Like the Yucca Mountain Project? As for the $38 million that the DOE will have given the county by the time the final site recommendation gets approved by President Bush later this year, his official position, he grins, as a commissioner, is "neutral." He's more eager to talk about the county getting money from Mercedes, BMW, Chevy, and Ford, who all do heat testing in the summertime in Death Valley. "They can actually go from below sea level to 10,000 feet in a two-hour period. The *extremes.*" When the reverend walks me out the door we find Walt on the porch. He's still looking for a ride to Hobbytown USA. By the way that Reverend Taguchi kindly sends him on his way, I get the impression that this is an ongoing thing and by refusing I'm not supposed to feel bad, but I can't help feeling like I should help Walt escape this place, maybe even take him back to Philadelphia, if that's where he's really from. Walt is the saddest thing I've seen since I got here; sadder than the burros, sadder than the bored whores flipping through cookie recipes. He is clearly bereaved—of what, I know not. But I can help him no more than the aging pimp can help me. When it comes to grief and lust we are all tumbleweeds.

I end up going to Vegas alone. Halloween morning, I meet Mack for the last time at his gated stucco mansion in northwest Vegas. He answers the door wearing a pink shirt and looking five years younger than the last time I saw him. He's just gone to his "beautician," he says. His cherubic curls look freshly gilt. Elvis croons in the background. Angel is off somewhere sorting through their returned possessions, which choke the hallway along with chaotic piles of court records, unopened mail, and boxes. Mack says that everything hasn't been returned by the cops, including some pictures of Angel's dead boys. When he goes in search of something he wants me to see, I poke around. In every nook and cranny is an Elvis doll, an Elvis telephone, or a tiny Elvis under a bell jar. I'm on my knees looking at a video in an evidence bag when Angel emerges, hovering over me.

Her face pale, her mouth drawn, she looks convalescent. She takes me for a tour of her Elvis collection, down the hallway, where pictures of her boys hang on the wall beside portraits of Elvis, to a back room, where all four walls are covered floor-to-ceiling with plates from the King's Franklin Mint collection. There is not enough cake in the world to fill all the plates.

Then for no real reason—other than that I was just nosing around their video collection—Angel starts to tell me about the night that the cops searched her house and kept her hostage in the living room. Her voice quavers, and she clutches the bagged video in her hands the way a woman about to be mugged would clutch her purse. She was alone. Mack was in Beatty. When she thought she would lose it (they wouldn't let her get her "pressure" pills), she got up and put a video in the VCR. It was a tape her son Jesse had made two months before he died. He wanted it played at the funeral, she says, "mainly to apologize to anybody that he had ever done any wrong thing to." Her eyes jump when a bird flies past the window; after a long moment, while she struggles not to cry, she says that her son told her on the tape, "If you think that you're alone, you're not. He said, It's going to be all right, Mom. It's Our Father in Heaven." I am, I think, convinced when she tells me that the cop guarding her was moved to tears, too.

Mack bustles into the room and, with a pained expression, shows me an official inventory from the police; typed at the top it reads, "Swinging File has been removed from this evidence bag and placed in evidence bag marked employee/record files. Report#: 00-0578." This list of potential lovers, Mack lets me know, has not been returned. It makes him mad enough to launch into a hot tirade about suing the bastards. This is a great loss to him. He wants that list back and he cannot quite believe that it is gone. I can see it in his eyes. It is a dire, horrible loss.

.   .   .

For the rest of the day, waiting for my midnight flight, ominously moody because I have to fly, I nap in my room at the Imperial Palace to minimize exposure to the Strip and thereby avoid the migrainous hell's bells and numismatic crepitations of the slots. When the sun goes down I meekly venture out for something to eat. Although it's Halloween, hardly anyone on the street is in costume. I see the pope hailing a cab. Then I see a hooker in a black velvet cape and a silvery metallic top. I don't know if she's a real hooker or not—it doesn't matter. I stand still until it is all thoroughly convincing. The smell of chlorine from the fountain. The unpared fingernails of the Mexican kid who hands me a flyer for an escort service. The couple that passes and the man who says to his wife: "It beats a sharp stick in the eye!" These details come to life. My life, like the night, seems never-ending.

March 2002

They Came Out Like Ants!

Searching for the Chinese Tunnels of Mexicali

WILLIAM T. VOLLMANN

It was on Good Friday night, at the threshold of that church on Avenida Reforma, in Mexicali, Mexico, with the Virgin of Guadalupe's image invisible overhead and the border wall faintly discernible, like a phosphorescent log in a dark forest, that I first met the sisters Hernández. When the loudspeaker sighed *María, la Madre de Jesús,* I thought they looked sincerely distressed, Susana in particular. The Crucifixion had just occurred again. When they mentioned Jesus, Mary, and Judas, they were speaking of people they knew intimately. Later our talk turned to Mexicali, and they began to tell me about the time of the great fire when all the Chinese who lived secretly and illegally under the ground came out "like ants," to escape the burning; and everybody was shocked at how many of them there were. Susana and Rebeca had not yet been born when that happened, but it remained as real to them as the betrayal of Christ. I couldn't decide whether to believe them. When was this great fire? They weren't sure. But they knew that Chinese—*many, many* Chinese, as they kept saying—used to hide in tunnels in Mexicali.

Chinese tunnels. Well, why shouldn't there be Chinese tunnels in Mexicali? I'd seen the Valley of the Queens in Egypt (dirt and gravel hills, sharp-edged rock shards, then caves); I'd convinced myself of the existence of

Pompeii's Anfiteatro, which is mainly a collar of grass now, with a few concentric ribs of stone beneath. Havre, Montana, still maintains its underground quarter as a source of tourist revenue: here's the bordello; there's the purple-glassed skylight; and don't forget to see the old black leather dentist drill, a foot drill, actually, which was operated by the patient! Why shouldn't there be more than sand beneath Mexicali?

José Lopez, a freelance tour guide with two blackened front teeth, told me that a year or two ago a friend of his had delivered a truckload of fresh fish from San Felipe up to a certain Chinese produce market in Mexicali. What was the address of this market? José couldn't say. It was surely somewhere in the Chinesca, the Chinatown. The merchant opened a door, and José's friend glimpsed a long dark tunnel walled with earth. What's that? he asked. You don't need to know, came the answer. José's understanding was that even now the Chinese didn't trust banks. They kept their money under the ground.

The owner of the Golden China Restaurant believed that there were four or five thousand Chinese in Mexicali. A certain Mr. Auyón, said to be a world-famous painter of horses, informed me that there were currently eight thousand Chinese, thirty-two thousand half-Chinese, and a hundred Chinese restaurants.

Most of the Chinese were legal now, but in the old days they'd come illegally from San Felipe, and then their relatives or Tong associates had concealed them in those tunnels, which, it was widely believed, still extended under "all downtown"; and there was even supposed to be a passageway to Calexico, California, though none of the storytellers had seen it, and some allowed that it might have been discovered and sealed off decades ago by the Border Patrol. I've read that during Prohibition *in the Chinese district of Mexicali, tunnels led to opium dens and brothels, and for the convenience of bootleggers, one of them burrowed under the international line to Calexico,* which might have been that tunnel, or a precursor, under the cantina around the corner from the Hotel Malibu. Mexicans bought me drinks there, and insisted that the tunnel still existed.

A tunnel under the Hotel Del Norte was discovered and closed in the 1980s; the Chinese didn't have anything to do with that one, I'm told. In the autumn of 2003, people with guns and uniforms found another tunnel that began in a mechanic's shop east of the Chinesca and came up in Calexico—in a fireplace, I was told—but it wasn't a Chinese tunnel. A whore in the Hotel Altamirano said she knew for a fact that the Chinese had been behind that tunnel, because *they always work in secret.* Frank Waters recalls in his memoir of the days when the Colorado River still flowed to the sea that in 1925 Chinese were smuggled across the border *in crates of melons, disguised as old Mexican señoras, and even carried by plane from Laguna Salada.* Perhaps they traveled by tunnel as well. From the Chinatown in Mexicali to the one in Los Angeles, both of which have since burned. *They came out like ants!*

My own mental image of the tunnels grew strangely similar to those long aboveground arcades on both sides of the border; on certain very hot summer nights when I have been under a fever's sway, with sweat bursting out on the back of my neck and running down my sides, the archways have seemed endless; their sidewalks pulse red like some science-fiction nightmare about plunging into the sun, and as I walk home out of Mexico, the drunken woman and the empty throne of the shoeshine man are but artifacts, lonely and sparse, within those immense corridors of night. I wander down below the street and up again for the border formalities, which pass like a dream, and suddenly I find myself in the continuation of those same arcades, which are quieter and cooler than their Mexican equivalents. Bereft of the sulphur-sweet stink of the feculent New River, which loops northwest as soon as it enters the United States, they extend block after block in the same late-night dream.

It seemed that everyone knew about these tunnels—everybody in Mexicali, that is. But when I crossed the border to inquire at the Pioneers Museum, two old white men who'd lived in Imperial County all their lives stared at me, not amused at all, and replied they'd never heard anything about any tunnels. Up in Brawley, Stella Mendoza, wife, mother, ex-director and continuing representative of her Imperial Irrigation District, passionate defender and lifelong resident of Mexican America, who spoke Spanish, traced back her ancestry to Sonora, and went to Mexicali "all the time," said that the tunnels were likewise news to her. But why should we Americans know anything about Chinese tunnels in Mexico?

Vampires and Cigarettes

The clandestine nature of the tunnels lent itself to supernatural evocations. About thirty years ago a rumor had settled on Mexicali that the Chinese were harboring a vampire down there. Later it came out that the creature was human but a "mutant," very hairy, two of whose lower teeth had grown like fangs right through the skin above his upper lip. He "escaped," said the woman who'd seen him, but the Chinese recaptured him, and that was the end of the story. I asked José Lopez whether he believed this tale, and he said, "Look. You have to keep an open mind. In the 1960s the Devil himself came to Mexicali. He actually killed a woman! Everybody knew it was the Devil. If you keep a closed mind, you can't believe it. But why not believe it?"

They live like cigarettes, said a Mexican journalist on a Sunday, cramming all his upright fingers together as if he'd shoved them into a box. He advised me to search for people who looked *like this* (pulling his eye corners upward), because only they could tell me everything. Although he'd never seen one, his sources inclined him to believe that there might be a tunnel under Condominios Montealbán, those ill-famed grimy concrete apartments beside the Río Nuevo, where tired women, some Chinese-looking, some not, complained about the illnesses of their children, and teenagers sat day after day in the shade of an old stone lion. It had been at Condominios Montealbán that a Mexican mother had compared her country and my country thus: "Here we're free. Over there they live like robots." We live like robots; Chinese lived like cigarettes. And they protected a vampire, and they *came out like ants.*

The people I met on the street didn't like the Chinese; nor, it seemed, did many of the intelligentsia, the journalists, or the archivists. A young boy I met, who had worked in a Chinese restaurant for five years, told me: "They come from far away from here, so their character is different from ours, and it's bad. They don't share." I asked him if he'd ever heard anything about tunnels? "Never," he said, "because these kinda people, they don't wanna talk to no one about their life." A white-haired, pleasant, round-faced lady named Lupita, who had once worked in the office of a semi company, had graduated to being a security guard in a prostitute discotheque, and now held afternoon duty as the moneytaker for a parking lot beside a shut-down supermarket, allowed that her favorite aspect of Mexicali was her friends, and her second favorite was the Chinese food. Would she consider marrying a Chinese? I inquired. "No! I'm not a racist, but no Chinese, no nigger!"

"Them Damned Nagurs"

Imperial, by which I mean not only the Imperial Valley but also that valley's continuation south of the border, is a boarded-up billiard arcade, white and tan; Imperial is Calexico's rows of palms, flat tan sand, oleanders, and squarish buildings, namely the Golden China Restaurant, Yum Yum Chinese Food, McDonald's, Mexican insurance; Imperial contains a photograph of a charred building and a heap of dirt: *Planta Despepitadora de Algodón "Chino-Mexicana."* Imperial is a map of the way to wealth, but the map has been sunbleached back to blankness. Leave an opened newspaper outside for a month and step on it; the way it crumbles, that's Imperial. Imperial is a Mexicali wall at twilight: tan, crudely smoothed, and hot to the touch. Imperial is a siltscape so featureless that every little dip made by last century's flood gets a christening, even if the name is only X Wash. In spite of its wide, flat streets and buildings, Imperial is actually a mountain, Gold Mountain to be precise.

By 1849 word of the California gold rush had reached China. Mr. Chung Ming got rich right away. Hearing the news, his friend Cheong Yum rushed to California and achieved equal success. In 1852 twenty thousand Chinese, mostly Cantonese,[1] made the journey to try their luck. A little more than a decade later, there were twelve thousand of them digging, blasting, mortaring, and shoveling on the transcontinental railroad. *Wherever we put them we found them good*, reported a white magnate who happily paid them less than he did his Irishmen. The Irishmen noticed. One of them lamented: *Begad if it wasn't for them damned nagurs we would get $50 and not do half the work.*

"Chinamen" and Indians received preference for employment in the vineyards around Los Angeles, and in 1860 a contingent of white laborers gave up and departed for Texas. In 1876 a chronicle of Los Angeles reports this news: *City still rapidly improving. During June anti-Chinese meetings were the order of the day.* Those words were written a mere five years after the infamous Chinese Massacre.[2] In spite of the anti-Asian movement's best efforts, *An Illustrated History of Los Angeles County*, published in 1889, estimates that between two and three thousand Chinese walked the streets: *The Chinese are a prominent factor in the population of Los Angeles. . . . The Chinaman, as a rule,*

---

[1] According to the owner of the Golden China Restaurant, in 2003 this was still the case, although a number of Mexicali's Chinese also came from Shanghai.

[2] The way one county history tells it, two rival Chinese mobs fighting over a woman "on either side of Negro alley" began shooting at each other on 23 October 1871. On the following day, a policeman and two citizens who were doing what they could to bring peace got wounded in the crossfire; one citizen died. "The news of his death spread like wild-fire, and brought together a large crowd, composed principally of the lower class of Mexicans and the scum of the foreigners." The predictable result: lynchings, shootings, arson, pillaging. Nineteen Chinese were murdered. (Another source gives the casualty figure of a probably inflated seventy-two.)

with occasional exceptions, is not desirable help in the household. On the ranch . . . he can be tolerated, when white men are not obtainable.

Meanwhile, in 1898, the Britannica Company contracted with Mr. Ma You Yong to bring a thousand Chinese to Mexico for railroad work. A tunnel cave-in killed seventy-seven. And they kept right on, from Oaxaca all the way to Salinas Cruz and Jesús Carranza. Onlookers no doubt remarked that they live together like cigarettes. In the sixth year of their labors, Jack London published a bitterly logical little essay entitled "The Scab." *When a striker kills with a brick the man who has taken his place, he has no sense of wrong-doing. . . . Behind every brick thrown by the striker is the selfish will "to live" of himself, and the slightly altruistic will "to live" of his family.*

Under capitalism, continues London, we are all scabs, and we all hate scabs. But not everyone takes his reasoning that far. The Chinese coolie, whom London mentions in the same breath as the Caucasian professor who scabs by being meeker than his predecessor, was to haters of *damned nagurs* a dangerously particular case. You see, in California the Chinese do more than we, in exchange for less. In that case, we'd better make it hot for the Chinese. Hence anti-Chinese riots; hence the Chinese Exclusion Act of 1882 and its many descendants.

"The Scab" saw print the same year as Mexicali's founding. The Chinese were already there.

They Came for the Work

A soft-spoken old Chinese shoe-store owner at Altamirano and Juárez (who became less open with me once I started badgering him about tunnels) told me that his grandfather came in 1906 to pick cotton. He worked for an American company, but he couldn't remember the name. I suspect it was the Colorado River Land Company, which had already hired Mariano Ma. In later years he'd be seen at the racetrack with the governor of Baja California, but in 1903 he spent his days with Chang Peio and the other *braceros*, leveling roads, digging canals, all for a wage of fifty centavos (twenty-five additional for food); whether this was paid daily or weekly is not recorded. Señor Ma remarks: *In that place there were a lot of mosquitoes. Many people died on account of the various sicknesses caused by insect bites, rattlesnakes, and the intense heat. Some people were buried underground by quicksand and whirlwinds.*

The old Chinese-Mexican mestiza Carmen Jaham told it this way: *Mex-*

icali began with about a hundred or a hundred and fifty Chinese. And between 1902 and 1921, forty or fifty thousand Chinese came to Mexico. In 1913 there were a thousand in Mexicali alone. And they kept coming.

Steve Leung, the owner of a shop on Calle Altamirano, a middle-aged third-generation Chinese, told me that most of the Chinese workers who came here had been farmers. They saw the desert wasteland standing fallow and they cultivated it. Later, when the Mexicans started moving in, the Chinese ran grocery stores and laundries. They were successful with the groceries, but then the Mexicans started taking over that business, so the Chinese pulled back to restaurants. "Mexican people have not been able to take that over, since Chinese work longer hours," Mr. Leung said. "They don't fight with the local people; they let them come in; they just pull back."

And in my mind's eye, as Mr. Leung said this, I could see them pulling back into the tunnels. Whether or not his version of events correctly explains the facts, it certainly fits in with them, for the photo albums in the Archivo Histórico del Municipio de Mexicali do show an awful lot of Chinese grocery stores.

"A High-Pitched Voice Was Screaming Chinese Orders"

The historian Hubert H. Bancroft, whose many-volumed work on California is a monument nearly as eminent as the border wall, expresses his epoch when he tells us: *These people were truly, in every sense, aliens. The color of their skins, the repulsiveness of their features, their under-size of figure, their incomprehensible language, strange customs, and heathen religion . . . conspired to set them apart.*

In around 1905 we find Mr. Hutchins, the Chinese inspector, carrying out his task at Jacumba, *which is to allow no unentitled Mongolian to cross from Mexico into the United States.* When he catches them, they're jailed and tried.

In one of Zane Grey's novels, published in 1913, a rancher on the Arizona side of Sonora explains to a cowboy that *of course, my job is to keep tab on Chinese and Japs trying to get into the U.S. from Magdalena Bay.* (That same year, the Colorado River Land Company imports another five hundred Chinese into Mexico from Hong Kong.)

In 2003 the man in the *casa de cambio* on First Street assured me in a gleeful murmur that of course there were tunnels *everywhere* in Calexico because if they started over *there* in Mexico then it stood to reason that they'd come up over *here*. He was Chinese. His building had three tunnel entrances, he said, but unfortunately he couldn't show them to me because they were closed. But he knew for a fact that the old building that now housed the Sam Ellis store had a tunnel. The kindly old proprietor of the latter establishment showed me photographs of the way the border used to be; he advised me to go to the Chamber of Commerce for an interpreter; as for the tunnels, every time I asked if I could just take a peek in his basement he didn't seem to hear me, but he did say: *You're never gonna find any of those tunnels.*

In 1925, Dashiell Hammett's crime story "Dead Yellow Women" envisions Chinese tunnels in San Francisco, all the while keeping faithful to the expectations of his public: *The passageway was solid and alive with stinking bodies. Hands and teeth began to take my clothes away from me. . . . A high-pitched voice was screaming Chinese orders. . . .* That was one passageway to alienness. In another, which the protagonist reached through a trap door, *the queen of something stood there! . . . A butterfly-shaped headdress decked with the loot of a dozen jewelry stores exaggerated her height.*

When Fu Manchu movies went out of fashion, new authentications of menacing alienness became available. Zulema Rashid, born in Calexico in 1945, remembers being scared every time she had to buy something in the Chinese store on Imperial Avenue *because the Chinese were Communists who tortured people.*

A fighting-cock breeder from near San Luis Río de Colorado, told me during a match in Islas Agrarias that *of course the Chinese are all into slavery.* That was why one never saw any Chinese beggars. He got even more animated in the course of telling me that seven years ago the authorities had rounded up many illegal Chinese in Mexicali and sequestered them in a stadium under heavy guard, but some had mysteriously escaped, an occurrence that he considered both uncanny and hateful; he turned bitter when he mentioned it. He supposed that they had disappeared into one of their tunnels.

"A Raw Smell"

They came out of the ground like ants. So why shouldn't there be tunnels? They exist, asserted Beatriz Limón, who was a reporter for *La Crónica*. She, however, had never seen one. One of her colleagues had entered a tunnel with Chinese guides, but the smell had been too terrible for her—a *raw* smell, said Beatriz with distaste, a smell like sewage.

Oscar Sanchez from the Archivo Histórico looked up at me from behind his desk and said: "They are there. But I can tell you nothing concrete. Originally they were there for shelter from the heat, but then they started to install the casinos. Oh, but it is difficult. These people are very closed!"

Men said that there once had been tunnels beneath the dance hall Thirteen Negro, which was whitewashed over its ancientness and cracked through its whitewash, doing business on and on at the center of the brick-fringed archways of arcades, lord of not quite closed sidewalk gratings, with blackness beneath. Why wouldn't there be tunnels under the Thirteen Negro? And if they *were* there, why wouldn't they still be there? But the waiter denied it. What did his denial mean? I asked him how often he got Chinese customers and he said every night. I asked him if he could introduce me to a Chinese regular; maybe I could buy the man a drink. But the waiter said he didn't want any trouble.

The Tale of the Air Ducts

My next tactic was to bang on Mexicali's nearest prominently ideogrammed metal gate, and that is how, ushered down a tree-shaded walkway and into a courtyard, I had the inestimable pleasure of meeting Professor Eduardo Auyón Gerardo of the Chinese Association Chung Shan.

This *world-renowned painter, known especially for his paintings of horses and nude women*, had a Chinese mother and a Mexican father. In 1960, when he was thirteen years old, his father brought him to Mexicali to join his grandmother.

Mr. Auyón was not especially pleased to see me. He told me that I really should have made an appointment. In fact I'd banged on the gate two days ago and made an appointment through his nephew. This did not mollify the *world-renowned painter*, who sat unsmiling amidst his *sumi* paintings and brass lions. Well, to business: First he tried to sell me a gold-plated commemorative medallion, which he had designed. It was pretty but expensive. Then he offered me a dusty copy of his book, *El Dragón en el Desierto: Los Pioneros Chinos en Mexicali*, for the special price of thirty dollars. Comprehending that if I didn't buy something from him my interview would be terminated, I paid for *El Dragón en el Desierto*, after which he brightened slightly and began to relate snippets of Chinese-Mexican history.

I asked him if I could please meet a Chinese family.

It's very difficult, he explained, because my countrymen are not very communicative. But *El Dragón en el Desierto* does have ten chapters. You can read all about the Chinese in there. That was perfect. My research was now at an end. We agreed that if and only if I read his book thoroughly and maybe memorized it, then came back in a month, it was possible that he might have found a Chinese family to tell me something innocuous.

That point having been settled, I asked him about the Chinese tunnels. They don't exist, the world-renowned painter of horses assured me. The people couldn't survive in them if they did. They could not sleep. It would be too hot down there.

Just in case there were tunnels after all, Mr. Auyón, where do you think they might be?

That heat, the body cannot withstand it, he replied. In the nighttime one has to sleep. One has to live down there—that's why the snakes live underground—but in the summer it's too hot.

So there are no tunnels?

Every locality has tunnels like a house has a cellar. There are businesses that have two or three branches. They have cellars and connections. On Juárez at Reforma, one man has seven businesses. Underneath, it looks like another city.

Could I see one of those cellars? He didn't think that that was possible. Then, looking into my face, and this was the one moment when I felt that he was actually being genuine with me, he said: Do you want to know the history of Mexicali? *Every ten acres, one Chinese died.*

I'm sorry, I said. He looked at his watch. The world-renowned medallionist had an important appointment.

I asked him if he could show me one of the cellars that he'd mentioned. He took me into the Hotel Chinesca next door and past the fancy lobby into the open-air courtyard giving onto tiny double-bedded rooms; and from a chambermaid he got the key to the cellar, which looked and smelled like a cellar. There he pointed to a "communication" passage in the corner of the wall. It was small and square and had a screen over it; it was, he said, an air duct. Inside it I could see light and stoneworked walls. A small child could have hidden there. Triumphantly, Mr. Auyón declared: This is what they call a tunnel.

Under the Volleyball Court

So it went. I could tell you about my interview with the taxi driver who knew for a fact that a tunnel had once led from the Chinesca right across the border, but they closed it; or the tale of Leonardo, the "tour guide" from Tijuana who was down on his luck, so he followed me down the street at around midnight, trying to interest me in young girls. Did I want fifteen-year-olds? I did not. Well, then, he could get me twelve-year-olds. He could deliver them right to me if I went to the Hotel Mexico. He had a hatchet-shaped, smooth little face, and he was little and vicious. Since he could do anything (he'd already told me the story of how he'd obtained excellent false papers for *pollos* in T.J.), I told him to take me into the Chinese tunnels, about which he'd never heard. So he did research. It took him a day. He found me an underground casino that would be possible to visit before opening time, but I had to promise not to talk to anyone, and he couldn't guarantee that I could take photographs. When he saw that I really wanted to take photographs, he said that he could work it out. Leonardo was the man, all right. Why shouldn't it be true? There'd been gaming houses in Mexicali since 1909. He described so well how it would be that I could almost see it. Soon a note was waiting for me at the Hotel Chinesca: the tour would cost me fifty dollars, and I had to pay in advance. Leonardo went first to give the password; he'd be back in two minutes. I waited for him in the pitch-dark alley on the edge of the Río Nuevo; the moon resembled an orange darkly pitted by cyanide fumigation injury, and I waited and waited for admission to that splendid underground world that Leonardo had promised me.

To my rescue came Professor Yolanda Sánchez Ogás, lifelong resident of Mexicali (born in 1940), historian, anthropologist, and author of *Bajo el Sol de Mexicali* and *A La Orilla del Rio Colorado: Los Cucapá*, both of which she sold me out of the closet of her house. The first time I asked her about Chinese tunnels, she said that she didn't know anything about them but would find out. The next time I saw her she calmly said: I went into the tunnels. That entire area under La Chinesca has a subterranean level. As for the casino, I know there *was* one, but right now I don't think so. But under the volleyball court many *Chinos* live.

Have you seen them living there?

No, but I have heard. And I met an old man who lived all his life under Restaurant Ocho.

Rats and Cockroaches

Next morning in Callejón Chinesca the proprietors of the watch stores and clothing stores were already rolling up their gratings. We were looking for the Restaurant Jing Tung. Nobody in the street had ever heard of it. But that didn't mean it wasn't there. Yolanda led us to the Hotel Cecil, which I'm told was the labor of love of a Chinese named Cecil Chin. We went upstairs. Yolanda said that there had once been a tunnel with bars, casinos, and a restaurant.

This is all new, said the manager, gesturing around him. When they constructed this hotel in 1947, the tunnel was already there. There used to be an entrance on the first floor.

Can we go into the tunnel? I asked.

The manager wearily spread his hands. It's closed, he said. He didn't care to nourish any myths.

Across the street from the Cecil, in another roofed passageway called Pasajes Prendes, there was an ancient barbershop whose owner's white hair resembled his ribbed and whitewashed concrete ceiling, and he said: No, you walked in from the street, and the restaurant was on the left by the bar, and it had really big chairs and a piano, and there was a man who played the piano. They took the piano away many years ago. In the tunnel there was a store, and right here in front there was a butcher shop aboveground. The hotel was finished in April of '47, and there was nothing here before, he said, beaming through his round glasses. Oh, he was happy, smiling, talking about the past.

So what's in the tunnels now? I asked.

Pure trash.

His single customer, who was tub-shaped, chimed in: And rats!

Yolanda said nothing. I knew that she hated rats.

I went down there, said the customer, and it's all trash. Rats, cockroaches, because of the humidity . . .

A woman over here had a store, said the barber. There is still an entrance over there, and it's full of water. There was a cantina below. Cecil Chin owned the cantina. The whole building, there's tunnels all over the place. Anyone could go in. It was public property.

Were there casinos below?

No, there were never any casinos.

I thought there was a casino under the Callejón.

There could have been, said the barber happily. There was a barbershop, a shoe store, a bowling alley, pool tables . . .

I think there are some places where people get together to play cards, said Yolanda.

The tubby man, who was a foreman, shrugged and said: There are tunnels all through here, and also on Juárez and Reforma. It's like a labyrinth.

As the fan slowly rotated along the edge of the mirror, they talked happily about the old days *when they were all killing each other.*

Around '46 a lot of this was burned, said the barber. Slowly he reached up to turn on the auxiliary ceiling fan. The first of these buildings caught on fire, in '45 or '46, a lot of Chinese died. The second fire, nobody was inside. That was in '91. That second fire was so big that they came from Calexico and El Centro to put it out. And by the way, it seems to me that there used to be a tunnel under the Hotel Imperial. There used to be a cantina . . .

There still is, but not underneath, said the fat man.

Were there ever any opium dens? I asked.

The barber said: I worked in the Hotel Cecil for six years. I started in '49 as a waiter. Then I became a manager of the laundry department. When I was up there washing clothes, I saw the Chinese people smoking opium. There was a basketball court, and under there were six or seven Chinese men with a big pipe, passing it around. The pipe was as long as my arm!

Another old man had come in to get his hair cut, and he said: Yeah, I was there then, too. They were up all night smoking and gambling. They were playing *baraja* for a lot of money. That happened in the tunnels. I am seventy-six, and I was born here.

Were there prostitutes in the tunnels?

No, that was above.

Did anyone live in the tunnels?

Over in this part, in the Chinesca, sure.

Can we see the place where the water is? I asked.

A woman named Inocencia has the key. I never had the key.

We thanked the barber and wished him good business. As he was saying good-bye to us, he remarked, very sadly: There really aren't any businesses here anymore. It's all boutiques. All the Americans come here to buy medicines.

And I knew that he would have loved to go back in time, even just for a day, to wander in the tunnels when they were crammed with life, glamour, commerce, and vice.

My First Tunnel

Near the Hotel Capri there was a certain clothing business owned by an elderly Mexican who knew Yolanda quite well. Behind the counter, next to the water closet, there was a metal door, which the man unlocked, inviting us into a concrete room, where clothes hung on a line. The man lifted up a trapdoor, and I saw stairs. Yolanda had her flashlight, and Terrie, my translator, was carrying the other flashlight, which we had bought an hour earlier for just this occasion. Smiling, the man stood aside.

Yolanda wanted me to go first, because she was afraid of the rats, so I did, and she came after me into that sweltering darkness, gamely half-smiling with her pale, sweat-drenched shirt unbuttoned almost to the breast and her head high and sweat shining on her cheekbones and sparkling in her short gray hair and her kind proud eyes alertly seeking just as the straight white beam of her flashlight did, cutting through the darkness like a knife. Terrie's flashlight was very steady. Where were we? The humidity was almost incredible. Dirt and darkness, flaring pillars composed my immediate impression. Lumber heaps leaped up as pale as bone piles under those twin beams of battery-powered light. I saw no rats. How stifling it was! Graffiti'd beams ran overhead, higher than I would have expected but still in arm's reach; and wire hangers with flaring underparts hung like the skeletal outlines of headless women. I glimpsed the folding X-frames of something, a table, and a metal wheel of protruding spokes. Beneath the heavy rectangular archways, the tunnel went on and on. Quite evidently it was much vaster than the store above it, even allowing for the fact that everything is always larger in darkness. Somewhere ahead of us, skeletal perspective lines approached one another palely within the ceiling darkness; the place where they lost themselves seemed to be a hundred feet away and was probably ten. I thought I could see a squarish passage. The floor was littered with trash, and broken chairs and empty cardboard boxes. Here gaped an open safe. I picked my way as carefully as I could; for all I knew, ahead of me there might be an uncovered well that would lead straight to death in cheesy black currents of the Río Nuevo, which, thank God, I couldn't smell at the moment. Yolanda and Terrie were out of sight; they were in other worlds; I could see only one or the other of their flashlight beams. I felt almost alone. Chamber after chamber went on, connected by squarish archways. A palish blotch on the black wall gazed at me; my mind was beginning its usual game of dreaming up faces. Drumming and music came down to me from somewhere up above. The old Mexican who owned the place had said that he thought there had been a casino down here, and when I heard that music I could almost imagine it.

It might well be that the quality of the tunnels that haunted so many of us was quite simply their *goneness*. When I imagine them, my ignorance allows them to be what they will. Before we knew how hot the surface of Venus is, we used to be able to write beautiful science-fiction stories of swamps and green-skinned Venusians. I could almost see myself descending the stairs into this place in the years when the electric lights still worked. Sometime between the first and second fires it might have been perfect down here. Having smoked opium in Thailand, I could imagine that one of these chambers might have had mats on the floor where I could have lain, watching the opium smoke rise sweetly from my pipe between inhalations. And from Thailand I also remembered Chinese men in black trousers, shiny black shoes, and white dress shirts; at an open-to-the-street restaurant in Chinatown, with stainless-steel tables and white tile walls, we were all drinking delicious sweet chrysanthemum juice the color of urine, and the handsomest man of all leaned on his elbow and gazed dreamily over his crossed fingers. Was this how the Chinese would have dressed when they went underground to drink, gamble, and womanize in Mexicali? Or would they have possessed nothing but the rough cotton clothes of the *braceros*?

There might have been a piano player here as there had been at Cecil Chin's, and when he paused to take a drink of Mexicali Beer, I would have heard all around me the lovely bone-clicks of mah-jongg. One hot summer day in the Chinese city of Nan-ning, I wandered through a park of lotus leaves and exotic flowers to a pagoda where ancient women sat, drowsily, happily playing mah-jongg amidst the scent of flowers, and that excellent sound of clicking tiles enchanted me; I was far from home, but that long slow summer afternoon with the mah-jongg sounds brought me back to my own continent, and specifically to Mexicali, whose summer tranquillity never ends.

I remember a lady who smiled when she was dancing naked, a sweet smile of black eyes and glowing white teeth; she seemed so hopeful, so enthusiastic, so "sincere," if that word makes any sense between two strangers, and she was smiling right at me! She held my hand; that's right, she held my hand all the way to the hotel; I kissed her plump red lips and sucked on them as much as I wanted; she kissed me back. *Caliente!* the men in the street said approvingly. Afterward we walked hand in hand back to the dance hall, and all the men applauded. She was Mexican, not Chinese, and the place where she'd rented me her illusion of love lay several blocks beyond the edge of the Chinesca; all the same, it was she whom I now thought of in that tunnel whose revelry had turned to lumber and broken chairs; those click-clacking mahjongg tiles in Nan-ning, the laughter and preposterously exaggerated moans of that prostitute, the sensations of opium intoxication in Thailand—these were the buried treasures that my flashlight beam sought in the Chinese tunnels of Mexicali, my memories, my happy dissipations, let's say my youth. No wonder I'd wanted to believe Leonardo the "tour guide"! Waiting for nothing in the hot thick night, with the ducklike quacking of a radio coming from one of the tin walls of that alley, that evil sand-paved alley overlooking Condominios Montealbán, I was already a citizen of this darkness; I was a spider luxuriously centered in the silk web of my own fantasies.

The Tunnel Letters

Next came the Restaurant Victoria, a tranquil paradise of coolness and reliably bland food (the Dong Cheng was better) where the waitresses were the only ones who hurried; the customers, who were mostly Mexican, lived out the hours with their sombreros or baseball caps on, lingering over their rice; here I had tried and failed on several prior occasions to find out if there might be any tunnels in the neighborhood. But it was just as my father always said, *it's not what you know, it's who you know*, and I knew Yolanda, who happened to be here, and who knew Miguel, the Chinese owner, a slender youngish man with jet-black hair who'd come here from Canton two decades before. He led us through the restaurant—white ceiling, white incandescent lights, white tables, at one of which a fat old lady and a young girl, both Chinese, sat slowly eating while the television emitted music that was sad and dramatic and patriotically Mexican. The white walls gave way to pinkish bathroomlike tiles as we passed beneath the rapidly whirling white fans and admired from afar the Chinese-captioned painting of the red sun floating on a turquoise sea—and through the swinging doors he led us, straight into the kitchen, where the Mexican cook and the Chinese dishwasher goggled at us; turning right, we came into a long narrow courtyard and entered a detached two-story building with what appeared to be an ancestral shrine just within the entrance. To the right, next to a shopping cart full of stale burned bread and a hand mill to grind the bread to flour for gravy, wide stairs descended.

This tunnel was less dark, uncluttered, and more self-contained. Indeed, it disappointed me at first; it appeared to be little more than a concrete cellar. Then I noticed that a five-socketed chandelier crouched on the ceiling like a potbellied spider, four of its sockets encased in ornate floral doughnuts, the fifth a bare metal bell. The ceiling itself was comprised of fancy-edged blocks like parquet flooring. But some blocks were stained or charred and some were moldy and some were entirely missing, leaving rectangles of darkness peering down from behind the rafters. It was a wide chamber that could have held many people, especially if they'd lived together like cigarettes. What had they done here? Had they gambled or simply banqueted? Had this place been an opium den? A tub held old Chinese porcelain bowls with floral designs. Then there were several dark and empty side chambers.

The Victoria was in Miguel's estimation sixty years old, maybe eighty. Since we were in the heart of the Chinesca, this tunnel would have possibly already been here but so what, and how could I possibly speculate anyhow? On my second visit to this tunnel I saw a few more traces of fire and I also found what might or might not have been a trapdoor in the concrete floor of the first chamber; it would not budge. In the dark room beneath some beds was a stack of bedframes. *Muchas prostitutas!* suggested one of my guides.

At the extreme end of the farthest room, another passageway had been bricked up. I asked Miguel how much it would cost me to have that obstruction broken down and then sealed up again when I had seen whatever there was to see. Smiling, he replied that there was no need for that; all I had to do was ask the pastor of the Sinai Christian Center down the street to let me into *his* tunnel.

When we turned back to the middle chamber we saw a desk, and we approached it without any great expectations since it was not so many steps away from the entrance to this place; all we had to do was turn around and we could see the supernaturally bright daylight of Mexicali burning down into the stairwell. I remember that a spiderweb as wide as a hammock hung on the wall; I remember how dismally humid it was in that place; I could almost believe Mr. Auyón, who'd claimed that of course the Chinese never lived underground, because that would have been too uncomfortable. In other words, I couldn't help but assume this desk to be a counterpart of the first tunnel's Sentry model 1230 safe, which sat upon the skeleton of a table that might once have had a glass top, lording it over broken beams and pipe lengths. Dust and filth speckled the top of the safe; behind rose a partly charred concrete wall. The door gaped open. Inside was nothing but dirt.

But as it turned out, under the Restaurant Victoria, in that rolltop desk with a writing surface of wood slats now beginning to warp away from one another just enough to let the darkness in between them, lay a hoard of letters, some of them rat-gnawed, all of them smelly, moldy, and spiderwebbed. Yolanda Ogás was standing against the wall whose pale sea waves of stains were as fanciful as the serpent plumes of painted Chinese dragons; Miguel bent over the desk, fingering the old letters that had been crammed into blackened drawers for who knows how long. The darkness was hot, wet, and slightly rotten. Then he rose and turned away with indifference.

Miguel was a nice man, and he gave me permission to borrow the letters. When I chatted with him upstairs, in the richly glowing shade of the Restaurant Victoria, looking out through the lingerie-translucent curtains and the double glass doors with the red ideograms on them, the white rectangles of the street walls, and dried-blood-colored gratings of other Chinese businesses, the world one-third occluded by angle-parked cars and trucks, I found that he didn't want to talk, because he'd only been here for twenty years, which, he reminded me, *wasn't long enough to voice an opinion.* He referred us to the Chinese Association. There were actually either twenty-six or twenty-eight of those, but he meant the Chinese Association whose head was a certain Mr. Auyón.

The tunnel letters brought to life the time when there was light in the partly stripped chandelier, when that ceiling whose fanciness has long since been gutted into occasional waffle pits of darkness was still whole, when the stacked tables were still laid out for reading, drinking, arguing, and gambling, a time before the walls were stained and the ceiling squares dangled down like laundry on the line. Here is one, an undated message from a wife in China to her husband in Mexico; perhaps he brought it downstairs to ask his Tong brothers what he could possibly do:

> *Everything goes well at home, except that my father-in-law cannot understand why there is no letter from you. Father-in-law questioned money sent via Hong*

Kong via Rong-Shi, and Rong-Shi denied receiving money. We borrowed money from neighbors. Father-in-law is not in good health. Please send money home. Also, when you send money home, do not send money via Rong-Shi, but addressed to . . .

Thinking of you. The way I miss you is heavy and long; however, the paper is too short to carry the feelings.

Days of Ivory

I've never really heard about the tunnels. The tunnels don't exist. Meanwhile, I kept going into tunnels. Half a dozen times I had the experience of descending below a Mexican-owned boutique or pharmacy, asking the owner where another tunnel might be, getting referred to this or that shop a door or three away, going to this or that shop's proprietor, and being told: There are no tunnels here. Sometimes they'd say: There is a tunnel but I don't have a key. The boss has the key. How long are you here until? Tuesday? Well, the boss will be in San Diego until Tuesday. One lady assured me that the tunnels were a myth; another said that her establishment's tunnel was being rented out as a storage space and she didn't have the key; a third, who'd operated her business in the Chinesca for twenty-two years, assured me that there had never been any tunnels in the Chinesca. Of course, with every passing year the tunnels did come that much closer to a state of nonexistence. Restaurant Nineteen, one of the oldest in Mexicali, was abandoned half a decade ago and in the early summer of 2003 had already been for three months reincarnated as a pool hall, with blue-felted billiard tables imported from Belgium. The Mexican owner, who wore blue to match his tables, was actually less interested in billiards than in carambola, which employs only three balls. He'd bought the building outright from the Chinese. He'd remodeled extensively and knew that there had never been any tunnels. I asked if I could visit his basement, but he didn't hear me. I asked again but he still didn't hear me. Yolanda Ogás, Beatriz Limón, and José Lopez from Jalisco were there; we each ordered a Clamato juice with real clams in it, and when he brought me the bill (I was the gringo; I always paid) it came to thirty-five dollars. He had one young Chinese customer who came to play; perhaps through him I could reach his father. The big fire? Yes, everyone still talked about that. He believed that it had happened in 1985; that had been when *those Chinese came running everywhere*; he didn't know where they'd run from. He couldn't care less about the past, except in one respect: he sighed for the days when cue balls were still made out of real ivory.

> *Dear Ging Gei. In response to your letter, we understand your situation. I asked Bak Gei to go to Wong Gei for the money Bak Gei had asked for to lend his friend for medical bills since Wong Gei owes your brother Bak Sei money. If you do not know who Wong Gei is, please go to Chung Wei for further clarification.—1924*

Creation Myths

Do you want to know how they started? Clare Ng told me how she and her daughter Ros went down to Condominios Montealbán as I had asked them to do, trying to find tunnels or at least to ask about tunnels, and she told it like this: *It was nighttime, and it was that big apartment down there, and we saw some Chinese woman who was fetching water for the vegetables down there, and in the beginning she was scared to talk. The husband has been there for ten years and she has been there only for three years. I asked how do you like it, and she said just since my husband is here I like it; that is the only reason. The daughter does not speak Spanish yet. So we were there, and they opened their hearts. They told us it was many many years ago, and too hot. These Chinese people cannot take the heat, so they decide to live underground in the tunnel. There was a big fire, and everything was burned. They don't live there anymore, but they still keep some things there. They say there's still a casino down there. Maybe it is kind of secret.*

That was one version. But since Chinese tunnels are involved, no version is definitive. When I asked Steve Leung where the tunnels had come from, he first advised me to meet a certain Professor Auyón, then, when I continued to question him, he said that "mainly they was made by the Mexicans, actually." The Mexicans had made the tunnels. Mr. Leung said the Mexicans had copied the Chinese, who dug tunnels to smuggle their people across the border, and made tunnels for smuggling drugs. Mr. Leung said that the Chinese at one time had casinos underground but that they were closed because of pressure from the Mexican government. *It is still a corrupt government, definitely, but it is more elegant now; it used to be you didn't need much connection as long as you got the money. Now you need the connection too.*

Women on Black Velvet

I remember tunnels that pretended to be cellars, and real cellars, and other tunnels of various sorts. I remember a plywood door partially ajar with two blood-dark ideograms painted on it, a hasp, a slender padlock. I remember cylindrical holes in the floor with locking hatch covers; these were the old Chinese safes. I remember how the palings of one tunnel wall resembled bamboo poles packed together, and around the top of them ran a stained metal collar. Then over a gap hung a torn ceiling, with strings and wires dangling down. The floor was a forest of paint buckets, toilets without tanks, cardboard, and upended chairs.

Late in the evening the sun caught the orangeness on the backward Restaurant Victoria lettering on the white window curtains, and the pleats of the curtains began sweating yellow and gold. A man on a crutch slowly hobbled out, and a boy held the door for him. For a long time I could see him creeping along outside, with backward Chinese lettering superimposed across his journey. The girls were already working across the street in the doorway of the Hotel Nuevo Pacifico; I counted six of them. Señor Daniel Avila, who'd worked at a certain supermarket for forty years and now owned a butcher shop, said that his son had once clerked at the Pacifico and that he had found tunnels but was never allowed to go inside them.

In your opinion, what is down there? I asked him.

He laughed and said: Secrets.

He took me down into his snow-white cellar tunnels, which had once been Chinese tunnels, and assured me that in a tunnel that had once connected with the tunnels under the supermarket and perhaps still did, there had been a cantina with paintings of naked women on black velvet; he knew for a fact that the paintings were still there, though he wasn't sure what condition they might be in. He was positive that the Chinese still lived underground just across the street. He couldn't say exactly where their tunnel was, because they entered at night *like rats*.

In that wonderfully Mexican way he had, he made everything seem possible; any time now I was going to descend through the floor of a pharmacy or watch-repair store and hear piano music; I'd smell opium; I'd hear laughter and the click of mah-jongg tiles.

He knew a woman who trusted him and who could help me, but the next time I saw him he was more doubtful, and the time after that he was in a hurry to go to the cemetery for the Day of the Dead.

A Chinese Lived and Died Here

To the supermarket that Daniel Avila had mentioned there sometimes came a Mexican caretaker who requested that I not use his name. He had worked long and faithfully for the Chinese owner, who had recently died and whose memory he adored. The children did not care to operate it anymore, and goods sat decaying on the shelves. Really it was no supermarket anymore but the shell of a supermarket. His job was to air the place out. He proudly said: This is one of the first stores that the Chinese opened in Mexicali.

After some persuasion the Mexican took me inside and through the double red curtains to the back, past an elevator cage (one of the first elevators in Mexicali, he announced loyally), and then we went downstairs into a white corridor. He said to me: This passageway originally went all the way to the cathedral on Reforma.

Aboveground it would have been a good fifteen-minute walk to that cathedral.

With his hand on his hip, thinking for a while amidst the humming electric whine of the lights, he finally said that the last time any Chinese had lived down here was in 1975.

Why did they stay in the tunnels?

They didn't have their papers, so they hid here. Around 1970 was the big fire. A lot of them came out, *with long beards*! I saw them. All old people! Many went back to China.

He pointed down into a cylindrical hole like many that I had seen in other tunnels, and he said: The Chinese didn't keep their money in the bank but in the wall. Here you would have had a safe, but it is full of water.

The tunnel went on and on, wide and humid, with salt-white stains on the walls. Huge beams spanned the ceiling. It was very well made.

Pointing to a square tunnel that went upward into darkness, he said: An emergency exit. This is how they came out during the fire.

I asked him why robbers and gangsters didn't live down here. He said it was because Mexicans are kind of timid. They think there are ghosts here. I have been working with the Chinese since I was twenty-seven. Now I am sixty. I myself believe in ghosts.

.   .   .

We reentered one of the middle chambers. The floor was stained white. The Mexican said the Chinese had slept in rows on small wooden beds. I asked if I could see one of the tunnels where they slept. All that has disappeared, he said. Then he took me upstairs to the boss's office.

The fire started with a man who sold tamales, the Mexican was saying. It burned right down to here, and he pointed off the edge of the roof. This whole street was cantinas back in 1955. There was a lot of conflict, delinquency, prostitution. It was like an old cowboy town, he said longingly.

I asked him again to show me the cantina where the velvet paintings are. And so he took me to the street behind the supermarket, in an alley I should say, a narrow dark place that smelled of the Río Nuevo and of birds, and on the far side of this there was a wall in which was set a white grating; when the Mexican unlocked this, the recess within was square, and within that stood another door. He had to go back to the supermarket to find the right key ring for that one. Laughingly he said: The Chinese have a lot of doors and a lot of keys.

This was all a cantina, he added with a sudden sadness. Pedro Infante sang here. Like Frank Sinatra.

He unlocked the inner door and pulled it open, a task that took most of his strength. Here at street level ran a very dark high-ceilinged space that seemed to have been gutted or perhaps was never finished; there were many wooden pallets, and he explained that illegal things had been stored here. What kind of illegal things? I wanted to know. Oh, butter and rice, he said hastily.

Dark stairs led down into black water; that was the cantina where the black-velvet paintings were. He said that it would take three weeks to pump it out, and he wasn't sure about the price. Three weeks later I was back, and he said that the pump had broken; he stood frowning with folded arms and said that the old Chino who would have shown me more had refused; I could tell that he wanted me to go away and never come back. But that was three weeks later; right now we still had an everlasting friendship ahead of us, and so after the flashlight finished glimmering on the stinking black tunnel in the cantina of the velvet paintings he took me up a crazy flight of wooden steps through the darkness to a concrete cell with three windows that looked down into that chamber of illegal butter and rice.

A Chinese lived and died here, he said.

There had been a stove, he told me, but the stove was gone. The dresser was still there. The bed was gone.

It was a ghastly, lonely place.

He was silent for a while. The place was so hot and humid that it was difficult to breathe. The Mexican said slowly: Our race is like Italians. We like to party. But they are very strange. Look down, and you can see that tunnel; it's full of water . . .

Where does it go?

They say that that one also goes to the cathedral, but I don't know.

We descended the stairs, happy to get out of that eerie place, and we went back out to the street, and he locked the inner door and the outer door. In the doorway of the abandoned supermarket he said: When I started working here, fifteen or twenty people lived below.

You mean, where you first took me?

Yes. They never left.

He pointed to another building and said: When the fire came, this is where the Chinese came out, the old ones with the beards . . .

Once Upon a Time in the Chinesca

Once upon a time in the Chinesca I peered in through the closed cracked window of the store that sold sombreros; there was supposed to be a tunnel underneath, but the owner had assured Yolanda and me that he'd never heard of anything like that. I looked in and everything was dim; how had I advanced my knowledge of tunnels? Now it was already six-thirty, and a few steps from me the fat lady was locking the white-painted, dirt-tinted gates of a roofed alley for the night. Sweet dreams to the store that sold communion dresses! A pleasant rest to the barbershop! There went the white number ninety-nine bus, crowded with standees; a man wheeled a dolly load of boxes down the gray sidewalk; a female radio voice was babbling cheerily from a store, and beneath that Mexican *carnicería*, which was very old, there presumably lay secrets dormant or active.

There was the old, low Restaurant Dong Cheng (Comida China Mexicana), where from time to time for half a dozen years now I've dropped in to get a beer or a half-order of fried rice, which was always as comfortingly large as a fat lady's breast. No matter how hungry I was, it was inexhaustible. Then a white fence stretched across a vacant lot, a palm tree behind; there was a parking lot, more Chinese restaurants, the Hotel Nuevo Pacifico, which is famed for its beautiful whores, many of whom are Chinese or half-Chinese; this was the Chinesca.

Once upon a time, in a certain street whose name I have already mentioned, not far from the sign where it said BILLARES and JAGUAR and unsurprisingly near to the ironwork letters that spelled out CHEE HOW OAK TIN, there was a gate, and a Mexican woman pointed to it and said to me: All the Chinese go there.

Do you think I can go inside?

They won't let you.

Why?

She shrugged. Who knows? A lot of Chinese come out of there to work. At night they come back here. Everybody says they live underground.

We were nearly at the basketball court, which was also the volleyball court that Yolanda had told me was the place beneath which the Chinese supposedly lived.

Every day that I passed by, I glanced at the CHEE HOW OAK TIN gate, but it was always closed until one morning in November when it wasn't; nakedly interpreter-less, I went in, and there was a Mexican standing in the courtyard. I gave him twenty dollars and said to him: *Por favor, señor, dónde está un subterráneo?* He laughed at me. He could speak English perfectly well. He told me not to tell anyone his name or where the tunnel was, but he could let me know that it was less than three doors from there. And it wasn't even a real *subterráneo*, only a *sótano*, a cellar, on whose floor a man in a blanket was sleeping; he was old and Chinese and might have been drunk; he did have a beard, though not as long as in the Mexicans' stories; a bag of clothes lay beside him; perhaps I should have photographed him, but it didn't seem very nice to steal a picture of a sleeping man. It all happened in a moment. Now I knew at least that people still slept in the tunnels; the myths were true; there remained secrets and subterranean passages, just as there used to be once upon a time in the Chinesca.

The Red Handprints

Smiling a little grimly or more probably just anxiously, the Mexican girl held the candle jar out before her. From an oval decal on the side of this light, the Virgin of Guadalupe protected her. Although her family had owned the boutique overhead for several years, she had never dared to go down here, because of her fear of ghosts. Behind her, the other girl struck a match; a whitish-yellow glob of light suddenly hurt my eyes. I looked up and glimpsed a faraway ceiling's parallel beams, which might have been wood or concrete. Then the match went out. I went down and down. Suddenly the flashlight picked out something shiny-black: water. I thought then that it might be impossible to explore that tunnel, that the water might be ten feet deep or more. When I was in high school in Indiana I'd once gone spelunking with some friends in a cave that required several hundred feet of belly-crawl with our noses almost in the mud and the backs of our heads grazing against rock; sometimes when it rained, fools like us were trapped and drowned. As I peered down into that Chinese tunnel, the feelings that I had had in that cave came back to me. And yet when I'd reached the bottom step and the flashlight split the darkness a trifle deeper, I could already see pale islands of dryness. Moreover, the floor appeared to be flat. So I stepped down into the wetness, and it came nowhere near the top of my shoe. Another step and another; that black water could have been a hundred miles deep the way it looked, but so far it wasn't. As always, my concern was that there might be a deep pit I couldn't see. I remembered helping a man from the Hudson's Bay Company drag a boat across weak sea ice, which broke under me without warning; that was how I took my first swim in the Arctic Ocean. This memory proved as inapplicable as the first. With pettish, trifling steps I made my way, and presently so did the others. Soon the flashlight picked out the end of the pool; aside from a snake of darkness that narrowed and dwindled like the Colorado River, the rest of that tunnel was dry.

We were under Avenida Reforma. The two dark-haired *mejicanas* said they believed that Chinese had lived in this wide, high-ceilinged chamber. Always that pair stayed close together, often forming a right angle as they gazed or tried to gaze at something, usually close to the wall, whose blocks rewarded their candle's nourishment with paleness. Behind the stairs were three more huge rooms. At the end of the farthest, diagonal bars blocked us from the darkness's continuation.

The two *mejicanas* said that they thought this tunnel went all the way to the Restaurant Victoria, which would have been several city blocks from here. Shuffling with my careful old man's steps, I came across a mysterious square well of black water that might have been one foot deep or a hundred. Had I been a drainage engineer I might have known what it was. Instead, I thought of Edgar Allan Poe.

The older girl, whose name was Karina, shyly said she'd heard that at one time people tried to kill the Chinese, so they came down here and hid. The other girl had already begun to feel nervous and declined to tell me her name.

Each concrete pillar in every niche had many shelves of dark spiderwebs. Receding rectangular arches of paleness made me feel as if I were inside some monster's rib cage. Perhaps everything was reinforced so well on account of earthquakes.

In the large chamber immediately under the stairs we discovered an odd cabinet that was really a thick hollow wooden beam subdivided into shelves and compartments, with empty darkness above and below its dust—no, it actually had three sides, which went from floor to ceiling; it was simply that some of the back's slats had been pried off; on the back, in a niche whose ceiling was pegboard, someone had taped three pictures of space shuttles beside an image of the Virgin of Guadalupe, who presided with clasped hands and almost-closed eyes over the two plastic flowers that her admirer had also taped to that wall; and then below the cabinet the Chinese tunnel went on to its barren bricked-up end.

The nameless woman had already gone almost to the top of the stairs, and my flashlight caught the impossibly white cylinders of her ankles almost out of sight, while Karina, holding the candle, stood sideways on two steps, gazing at me with her dark eyes. Her wet sandal prints on the stairs were almost as dark as her eyes. I remember her standing there and looking at me, looking at the darkness I remained in, and I will always wonder what she was thinking. Then she ascended the stairs and was gone.

I returned to that framework of bars from floor to ceiling; the tunnel kept going, but only rats and water could get through. Then I searched the niche behind the stairs.

On one whitewashed wall the flashlight suddenly picked out human handprints made in red; at first I thought it might be blood, but an experiment made with the rusty water on the floor proved that these handprints were part of a far less sinister game. Dashiell Hammett never wrote this.

The question of how vast the tunnels had been and still were preoccupied me. Old photographs seem to tell us how far they could have extended: In 1925, for instance, when Mexicali finally got its Chinese consulate, Avenida Reforma resembled a long, wide, well-plowed field of dirt, with little square wooden houses going up behind a rail fence; Avenida Madero was much the same.

How could there have been any subterranean passages here? But evidently these views must have been taken far from the heart of things, perhaps even as far as the future cathedral on Reforma; for here's a vista of the *edificio ubicado* on Reforma at Azueta *en zona "la chinesca," circa 1920*: a sign for the Mexicali Cabaret, pricked out in lightbulbs or wires, rises into the dirty-white sky above a two-story corner block of solid brick, fronted by squarish-arched arcades. Why *wouldn't* there have been Chinese tunnels there? Here's Chinese New Year, 1921: Two young boys, uniformed like soldiers or policemen, clasp hands atop a great float upon whose faded legend I can just barely make out the word CHINA; flowers, perhaps made of paper, bestrew the scene; behind them comes another float like a tall rectangular sail; an automobile's round blank eyes shine beneath it; a crowd of Chinese men and boys, their faces washed out by sun and time, gaze at us; everything is frozen, grainy, blurry, lost. Where are they? I don't know. And however many tunnels I ultimately entered, I would never be able to learn how many more remained. I tried to shine my feeble light as deep down into the past as I could, but I couldn't even see the bottom step of the tunnel's entrance.

October 2004

Part Five

The Arts

These days our arts are made largely like automobiles, in factories of sorts, where our films and our shows, our songs and our prose, are concocted in accordance with the finest Fordian precepts. Whether good or bad, culture today is undeniably *thought through*, subgenre by subgenre, with proven "best practices" agreed upon for each: the optimal release dates, page counts, chord progressions, plot points, effects budgets, guest stars, cross-promotional tie-ins, and subject "matter." Such dictates are hewed to and honed not only by those who superintend culture for a salary (executives, editors, producers, curators) but also by the sales-savvy artists themselves, who often imbibe the industry standards of the day by way of high-priced MFA programs. In such a milieu, journalism and judgment too often part ways, for the reporter covering the arts can hardly stand back to see them clear. He or she must become, in effect, a *trade* journalist, immersed in the argot, defining failure and triumph on the industry's own benighted terms.

One way to escape this fate—that is, to write about making culture today in a way that does justice to both process and product—is to sneak inside, as it were, winning the game while laying the rules (stated and unstated) bare. Such was the approach of the three authors in this chapter. Jake Silverstein, to answer the question posed in his title ("What Is Poetry?"), embeds inside the Famous Poets convention in Las Vegas, where he competes for a $25,000 prize. In "Devil's Work," Morgan Meis leads his minions through a three-month installation inside the Queens Museum of Art, giving that patron far more art than it ever expected. Finally, Bill Wasik, in "My Crowd," recounts his anonymous invention of the "flash mob" performance-art fad, and the media frenzy it engendered by design.

What Is Poetry?

And Does It Pay?

JAKE SILVERSTEIN

*In song oracles were given, and the way of life was shown; the favour of kings was
sought in Pierian strains, and mirth was found to close toil's long spell. So you
need not blush for the Muse skilled in the lyre, and for Apollo, god of song.*
—Horace, *Ars Poetica*

Summer in New Orleans is a long slow thing. Day and night, a heavy heat presides. Waiters stand idle at outdoor cafés, fanning themselves with menus. The tourists have disappeared, and the city's main industry has gone with them. Throughout town the pinch is on. It is time to close the shutters and tie streamers to your air conditioner; to lie around and plot ways of scraping by that do not involve standing outside for periods of any length.

I was so occupied one humid afternoon when I came across a small newspaper notice that announced in large letters, "$25,000 POETRY CONTEST." "Have you written a poem?" the notice began. I had written a poem. I had even considered submitting it to contests, but the prizes offered never amounted to much—a university might put up $100 in the name of a dead professor—and I hadn't sent it off. This was a different proposition. With $25,000 I could pay off my debts, quit my jobs, and run the air on HI COOL for a while. I submitted my poem that very day.

Two weeks later I had in my hands a letter from something calling itself the Famous Poets Society, based in Talent, Oregon. The Executive Committee of its distinguished Board of Directors, the letter informed me, had chosen my poem, from a multitude, to be entered in its seventh annual poetry convention, which would be held September 16–18 at John Ascuaga's Nugget hotel and casino in Reno, Nevada. "Poets from all over the world will be there to enjoy your renown," the letter boasted, "including film superstar Tony Curtis."

This was not exactly what I had imagined. The notice in the newspaper had said nothing about a convention in Reno, and I had expected simply to win, or not. I felt almost foolish. Poets, I suspect, make good marks. In his study of Dryden, Lord Macaulay observed that "poetry requires not an examining but a believing frame of mind." Evidently the same conclusion had been reached in a rented boardroom in Talent. I was about to throw the letter away when it dawned on me that there was still the matter of the $25,000.

The letter was from Mark Schramm, the executive director of the society. He informed me that should I choose to make the trip, I would be honored with the "Jacob Silverstein 2001 Poet of the Year Medallion" and the "Prometheus Muse of Fire Trophy," both of which I would find to be "unique." Schramm continued: "The fabulous Tab Hunter has asked that you personally walk with him in our Famous Poets Parade! As our Grand Marshal, he invites you to bring a poem of peace to release 'on the wings of Pegasus,' during our Famous Poets for Peace Balloonathon. Your poem is your message of love to the world. . . . I also look forward to seeing you win our poetry contest! Imagine yourself with a $25,000 check in hand and being crowned 'Famous Poet Laureate for 2001!' I can already hear the crowd cheering as the laureate crown is placed on your head! How beautiful you look!"

I knew that everyone who submitted a poem had been invited to Reno,[1] and I knew that Tab Hunter had never said anything to Schramm about my walking with him, but the fact remained that someone was going to win $25,000 and get to wear a crown. I wrote back to say that I would attend.

---

[1]Later on I was to learn that a few of the entrants are not invited to the convention. As Naythen Harrington, Schramm's assistant, explained it to me, "You can't put limits on poetry, but at the same time we're not going to offend a bunch of people if someone's like, 'I fuck goats five times a day and I'm gonna piss in my eye.'"

·   ·   ·

Five days before the convention was to begin, terrorists attacked the United States, but the Famous Poets Society decided to push ahead with its program as planned. It was felt that poetry was needed now more than ever. It was also felt that there would be no full refunds of the $495 registration fee, in the event of a canceled flight or a distraught flier. I flew to San Francisco, rented a car, and drove up into the Sierra Nevadas, over Donner Pass, to Reno.

I arrived at the Nugget and identified myself as a famous poet. The lackluster bellhop, who barely opened his heavy lids, directed me to the second floor for convention registration. There I was presented with my Prometheus Muse of Fire Trophy and Poet of the Year Medallion. My Muse of Fire Trophy was a cheap-looking wedge of plastic with an image of a man in a toga—Prometheus, I assumed—pressed into its back. A sticker personalized this gimcrack. My medallion seemed more valuable, since it was made from a metal into which my name had actually been punched. I also received a red T-shirt and a certificate honoring me as a recipient of both the medallion and the Muse of Fire. I stowed these laurels in my room and made for the Champagne Reception in the Rose Ballroom.

"First time here?" a man asked me. He was wearing a jeans jacket and jeans. He had a bristly brown beard and a long hawklike nose. His name tag identified him as Doc Smith.

"Yes," I told him. "Yours?"

"Nah," he said. "I been here before."

"So you like it?"

"It's all right." He scanned the crowd with a sour expression. "Thing that gets annoying is all these thirteen-year-old girls writing about broken hearts, lost love, suicide, that sort of thing. Try going to war."

Doc's voice was gruff, and his bearing suggested a long-standing annoyance with the world. He was a Vietnam veteran. Before the war he had been a singer in a band called People whose song "I Love You" had traveled up the charts to number fourteen in 1968. He sang a few bars for me. It sounded like a good song for dancing close with a girl. He gave me his card, which said "Vietnam Veterans of America, Chapter 290," in big letters; and in smaller letters, "John Doc Smith, *The Poet.*"

"This is an okay conference," he said. "But it's not as nice as the one the International Library of Poetry puts out. When they have a champagne reception, it's all the champagne you could want, plus punch and hors d'oeuvres, and top-flight entertainment. Classy."[2] He looked disparagingly at the tables. "This one's going downhill."

It was true that the scene lacked glamour. The Rose Ballroom did not feel much like a ballroom. The walls were carpeted in institutional gray, the floor in a tacky pattern of red and blue. The stage was empty save for an off-center podium. Fluorescent tubes lit the room unkindly. On folding tables covered in red paper, the champagne was lined up in plastic glasses. The supply was sorely insufficient. Mostly, the tables were covered with empty glasses, upside down and on their sides. "They don't put enough champagne," I heard an elderly Filipino man in a three-piece suit and snappy two-tone brogues complain.

Doc seemed to know his way around the convention, and I asked if he had any tricks for winning the cash prize.

"Nah," he said. "Just do your thing. Don't get nervous. Hardest competition is going to be from the black people. They tend to be more expressive, and that impresses the judges."

Before Doc could finish his counsel, the emcee of the convention, Alisha Rodrigues, called us to order. Doc had seen it all before and was going to try his luck on the slots. According to the General Schedule, we were to be introduced to the poets who would be our teachers for the next three days. There was Rigg Kennedy, who had a supporting role in the 1982 film *The Slumber Party Massacre*; Joel Weiss, who played an orderly in *The Meteor Man*; and Al

---

[2]Based in Maryland, the International Library of Poetry (ILP) is America's other amateur poetry society. The ILP is older and bigger than the Famous Poets Society (FPS), and stages its conventions in big venues like Disney World. There are, however, similarities between their two shows. Both feature a celebrity host; both dispense medallions. Both give away $20,000 or more to their top poet. Both publish anthologies of the year's best verse. Suspicion and acrimony characterize their interactions. During my own dealings with the FPS, I was mistaken for an undercover agent of the ILP.

The problems began when I sent Schramm a few questions about the history of the FPS. Several days later his reply arrived. "I have decided that I will not answer any of your questions," he wrote. "I think you are connected with the International Library of Poetry." Schramm went on to say that the ILP had attempted to infiltrate a prior FPS convention with a scout "posing as a poet." Schramm offered as proof of this assertion the fact that at the next ILP convention a bigger cash prize was awarded to the top poet. He assured me that the FPS was willing to let there be two societies but suspected that the ILP felt differently.

"To that extent," he wrote, "I think they recruited you, or you perhaps approached them."

D'Andrea, who appeared as Lieutenant Wilkins in the short-lived television drama *Brooklyn South*.

"Please help me welcome," Alisha said, "the acclaimed author of *Riggwords*, and a true famous poet: Rigg Kennedy!"

From the front row, a man in a white turtleneck and safari-style pants rose. As he mounted the stage, I noted a strange buoyancy to his bright white hair, as if each follicle housed a tightly coiled miniature spring. He grasped the podium with both hands, leaned into the microphone, and proclaimed, "As poets, each one of you, in your cellular structure, in your brain power, can change the universe." His hairs trembled. "I'm going to read 'Kozmic Alley.' It was first published in *Architectural Digest*."

Rigg shuffled his papers with a dignified air, took a sip of water, and cleared his throat. He then began to wail at the top of his lungs. Across the aisle a cowboy poet who had been napping sat up like a shot had gone off. The woman in front of me covered her baby's ears. Rigg modulated his wail up and down and then started breaking up the wails with some whistles. When he'd had enough of that, he intoned solemnly:

> space dust clouds spinning whirling
> gushing gases dancing throbbing divinely
> exploding indefinites definitely longer farer
> than i dare count to kingdom come

Rigg took a dramatic pause to let the first stanza sink in. The silence was partial. Like a shopping mall, a casino is full of hundreds of tiny speakers that play soothing background music in one genre or another. At that particular moment the Nugget's system was playing a punchy jazz tune, and the piano filled Rigg's caesura with unwanted gaiety. He did his best to ignore this, then opened his mouth extremely wide and began to croak. He took a drink of water and gargled into the microphone. He did some panting, then finished with more of the wailing and whistling that had gotten him started. Across the aisle, the cowboy poet tipped back his ten-gallon hat and frowned.

I could see that the cowboy's consternation was widespread. If this was the sort of poetry the judges were looking for, we might be in trouble. Our poems had no sound effects. Did they expect us to gargle?

These fears were allayed somewhat by the next poet, Joel Weiss, a younger man with a thick Bronx accent. When his name was announced, he bounded onstage and began an awkward striptease. "I'm not dressed right for this poetry," he said, swinging his jacket. Women hooted and rushed the stage with cameras. I recalled T. S. Eliot's complaint that "the poet aspires to the condition of the music-hall comedian." Underneath his shirt and slacks Joel sported New York Mets boxer shorts and a matching Mets jersey. "I'm a life-long baseball fan," he laughed. "That explains my poetry." Joel asked that the ladies return to their seats, then recited an original composition entitled "On My Way to Shea." The poem rhymed and had a metrical structure that he regularly defied. There was a clever twist at the end when the narrator, who you think is a fan, turns out to be a player, but because of the way Joel read the poem this effect was lost. His bungled recitation suggested either that this was the first time he had seen the poem in years, or that it had been composed in haste during Rigg's bag of tricks. Still, Joel's verses were warmly received, in large measure because they reassured us that we would be expected neither to gargle nor to pant.

There followed a confused interlude in which Alisha got up onstage, walked to the podium, started to speak, then stopped and went to the edge of the stage to confer. When the conferring was done she explained that Tony Curtis had lost friends in the tragedy in New York and would not be with us today. Alisha told us to hold hands and bow our heads together as we observed a moment of silent prayer for Mr. Curtis and his family. We did, and the theme song from *Bonanza* filled the ballroom.

After a short break, we reconvened for the Master Workshop, presented by Al D'Andrea. Al affected a professorial demeanor, repeatedly snatching off his reading glasses and gesturing philosophically with his hands. He ranged over a number of poets, from William Carlos Williams to Lucille Clifton, each one serving the overall point of his address, which was called "Saying Yes: Embracing the Life Force of Your Poem." He closed with a poem by James Scully entitled "What Is Poetry?" Having just witnessed the dramatic opposition of Rigg's experimental soundscape and Joel's corny baseball rhymes, and with $25,000 hanging somewhere in the balance, I found the question pertinent. Unfortunately, Scully offered no definitive answers. He posed instead a series of odd counter-questions, such as "if it were a crib/would you trust your baby to sleep in it?" Al added to the weight of these quandaries by chewing on his glasses.

As we filed out of the Rose Ballroom, I thought about Scully's poem.

Samuel Johnson had struggled with the very question before conceding that "it is much easier to say what it is not. We all *know* what light is, but it is not so easy to *tell* what it is." I had little hope that Joel Weiss would be able to top that. To prepare our poems for the judged readings, we had been divided into ten "classes" and assigned "homeroom monitors." Joel was mine.

"Just to give a brief introduction to myself," Joel began, as we found seats in a gigantic room we only half-filled. "I'm an actor. I've got a movie coming out in October with Wesley Snipes. I've been in forty-two films, and in most of them I get beat up or killed. I started writing poetry on trains and stuff. I never really call myself a poet. I just try to get out my frustrations. Who's got a question?"

"Do I need to cut my poem to twenty-one lines?" This came from Bertha Venson, a small black woman with a lisp from Euclid, Ohio.

"That's important," Joel said, dropping his voice an octave to indicate that he was leveling with us. "If your poem's going over, cut the extra lines. You have one solid minute when you're up there. I know you care about your poem, but once you're up there, you're trying to win the moolah."

This was true. Whatever Dr. Johnson might think, in Reno a poem was a lottery ticket, and none of us shied from this important fact. Poetry might be "the spontaneous overflow of powerful feelings," as Wordsworth said, but what good would it do you if it flowed over the time limit? Joel's caveat sparked an anxious discussion, in which it came out that many of the poets were in violation of the time limits and at a loss for how to prune their verses. Realizing he had caused a minor crisis, Joel hurriedly offered up the best panacea he could muster. "You know what I always say?" he said, leveling with us even more. "If it ain't broke, don't fix it." This settled things down somewhat. A blonde woman with heavy eye makeup and a German accent stood up. "I have a glittery dress," she said. "Do I wear my glittery dress before the judges?"

"What about a peach dress?" another poet cried. "Is peach a good color for the camera?"

Joel relaxed a little, sensing that he was out of the woods with having to edit all our poems and back in familiar territory. "Peach, glitters, or whatever you're gonna wear," he said. "Figure it out tonight and lay it out on your bed so you won't have to think about it tomorrow morning."

We took a dinner break after the first round of readings, and I considered the field. About half of the Class Six poems suggested that poetry was an instructive art, a pleasant way of passing along an uplifting lesson. In this they fit the neoclassical mode outlined by Sir Philip Sidney in his 1580–81 *Defence of Poesie*, which defined poetry as "a speaking *Picture*, with this end to teach and delight." There was "An Imperfect World," by Anita Jones of Cincinnati, which put forth, in list fashion, all of the things that were wrong with the world, that we might learn to accept them; "Taking Time," by Lydia Heiges of Kempner, Texas (she of the glittery dress), which reminded the reader to slow down and enjoy life; "At a Time Like This," by Myra Ann Richardson of Kernersville, North Carolina, a patriotic verse that aimed to rally our spirits; and "I Want to Know Please," by Lou Howard of Azle, Texas, which used the device of an inquisitive child to illustrate how "it takes both sunshine and rain to make rainbows." These poems relied on poetic tropes—flowers that stood for hope, sunsets that led to contemplation—and standard formats—the list, the apostrophe, the regular metrical line—to convey certain messages to the audience. They would have pleased Sir Philip, who felt that poetry's purpose was to appeal to those "hard hearted evill men who thinke vertue a schoole name, and know no other good but *indulgere genio*, and therefore despise the austere admonitions of the *Philosopher*." Sir Philip figured these men would swallow the uplifting message of a poem, "ere themselves be aware, as if they tooke a medicine of Cheries."

Around 1800, Sir Philip's utilitarian idea gave way to that of the Romantics, from whom the remaining Class Six poets seemed to take their cue. These poems were meant to convey the rawest inner emotions, most of which turned out to be gloomy. Reena Louis's poem, "The Lost Letter," matched up against the most melancholy that Keats had to offer, and Wes Dodrill's "The Last Race," an elegy for stock-car driver Dale Earnhardt, was every bit as mournful and sad as Shelley's "Adonais" or Wordsworth's "Extempore Effusion upon the Death of James Hogg." For these classmates, poetry was, as Lord Byron had seen it, "the lava of the imagination whose eruption prevents an earthquake."

My own poem was neither a medicine of Cheries nor a blowhole of the soul. It was called "New York, so often recorded in photographs." I suppose you would call it modernist.

After dinner I took a stroll around the casino floor. There were famous poets everywhere, easily identifiable by their gold medallions and red T-shirts with the proclamation I'M THEIR MOST FAMOUS POET! printed in black across the back. They stuffed coins into nickel and quarter games with such names as "Quartermania," "Betty Boop," "Blazing 7s," and "I Dream of Jeannie." At their sides, cigarettes burned untouched in ashtrays. Every once in a while, a machine shouted, "Wheel! Of! Fortune!"

I made my way over to the Aquarium Bar, where in a pale blue light, surrounded by wooden tiki lanterns, plastic banana trees, and red totem poles, I ran into Doc. He was peeved.

"They don't have the alumni jacket," he said, shaking his head.

"The what?" I asked.

"The alumni jacket. If you go to one one year you're supposed to get an alumni jacket the next year. They don't have them. You know, you get your people who swear by the Famous Poets Society, but to me it's just amateur compared to the International Library."[3]

It was hard to believe this business with the jacket alone had set him off, so I asked him if he had been losing money too.

"Nah," he said, gazing out at the casino. "I'm up eight hundred bucks. Been at 'Blazing 7s' all day."

---

[3]The headquarters of the ILP are located at 1 Poetry Plaza, in Owings Mill. I telephoned their main switchboard and laid out my cards. Right away I could tell theirs was the bigger outfit. From the background noise on my FPS calls, I'd gotten the impression that Schramm's entire operation was crammed into two rooms. At the ILP, I was transferred around and around. They put me on the line with Steve Michaels, the convention coordinator. Michaels painted me the big picture. He planned his conventions to accommodate more than 2,000 poets; the FPS had, what, a few hundred? He then gave me a detailed account of why the ILP was better than the FPS.

"Where they give out their trophy we give out a real silver-plated bowl," Michaels argued. "We also give out tote bags and mugs and a medallion. There's just more to do for our poets. We have two banquet dinners as opposed to their one. We have Florence Henderson, the Coasters, and the Shangri-las, and our celebrities stay the entire weekend. I don't think Tony Curtis stayed more than the afternoon this year at theirs. Our contests are completely fair. We don't even judge them ourselves, we outsource the judging to college professors. This year we have a Pulitzer Prize winner, W. D. Snodgrass, as our keynote speaker. So we're not really too concerned if the FPS has a small convention once a year. To be honest, we don't really recognize the FPS at all."

I gave it to him straight. Accusations had been made. Schramm thought I was just one in a line of ILP spies.

"They've said similar things about people that went to their convention in the past," he told me. "I think they're very worried. You know, I went to their convention years ago when I was still in college. There wasn't really that much to do, to be honest. You read your poem, sometimes as late as midnight, and you went to one banquet."

It turned out that what was really eating at Doc was some teenage poet who had won a prize for the last three years running. The kid was back again, looking for a four-peat.

"Kid doesn't even change the poem," Doc complained. "Just keeps bringing the same one back and winning the prize."

"Well, it must be pretty good," I said.

"Nah, it's nothing special. But he does a whole Ricky Martin routine on it. Goes down on his knees for the sad parts. The judges like that crap."

The Aquarium Bar's evening entertainment—Darcy on vocals, January on keys—started in on a cover of "Captain of Her Heart." Through the banana trees I saw a woman run out of coins on a "Quartermania" machine and jokingly try to stuff her Poet of the Year medallion down the slot.

"The main problem I have with poetry is this," Doc said. "It's totally subjective."

On Monday morning I woke in a tangle of sheets and lay there turning things over in my head. I thought I should be dramatizing my poem if I was serious about winning the $25,000. Maybe this kid with the Ricky Martin routine had the right idea. I ran over my poem a few times, looking for places where I might go down on a knee. My poem did not seem to lend itself to that kind of theater.

Joel was scheduled to deliver the morning lecture, "How to Be a Poet on Your Feet." The session was under way when I arrived. "As actors we always deal with being in the moment," Joel explained in his Bronx accent. "As famous poets, we do the same thing. When we read it, we want to make the feelings and everything happen just like when we wrote it. Just to go back to the acting thing for a minute, we do a play like ninety times, and every night we eat the same doughnut, and even if you like doughnuts it becomes repetitious. But that audience that comes in shouldn't know that you've been eating that doughnut every day, and that, you know, the doughnut's *terrible*, because you're still eating it like it's the first time you're ever biting into that doughnut and *boy*, that is so *good*, that doughnut! Or apple or whatever."

Joel referred to this as "In the Moment," the second of the poet's four basic tools. The others were Focus, Emotions, and Life Experiences. In the Moment, however, was the most important of the four, and to get us there Joel had devised a game he called "How to Be a Poet on Your Feet." The idea was for each famous poet to take three random words from the audience and just rattle off a poem, employing the words like verbal stepping-stones. No one volunteered, and Joel had to jump-start us with a few demonstrations. By the time he'd banged out his fifth poem-on-his-feet, the Ponderosa Room was boiling with volunteers. In a matter of minutes the whole thing had devolved into a rancorous competition between Classes Five and Six over who had the best poets. As each poet took the stage and announced his allegiance, the audience responded with cheers and taunts.

"Class Six! Class Six!"

"Class Five represent!"

"You're the best, Class Six!"

When Bertha Venson of Class Six took the words "Strawberry," "Pancake," and "Nugget," and turned them into, "In the morning I love to eat pancakes/And with them, I love to eat nuggets./But the best of all is when I eat strawberries," the crowd went wild.

"That is Class Six!" the German woman screamed.

A woman from Class Five stood up, shaking her head, and said, "Class Five is 'bout to take home the cash money, though." Pandemonium ensued. Joel was pressed for a verdict. "Enjoy your next class!" he shouted. "You're all winners!"

We headed across the hall for Rigg's talk, "The Importance of Being a Poet for Life." Today he had on a blue turtleneck, with the same safari pants as before. I recalled that he had been photographed wearing a black turtleneck for Schramm's color brochure. This run of turtlenecks seemed in keeping with the whole Rigg Kennedy persona. Perched atop a stool at the head of the Bonanza Room, he looked like some sort of eccentric zoologist, on tour to promote his unorthodox theories about natural selection. As we filed in, he stared thoughtfully at the ceiling, nodding periodically as a familiar face drifted by. The program was as different from "How to Be a Poet on Your Feet" as "Kozmic Alley" was from "On My Way to Shea." Whereas Joel's style as a lecturer had been to challenge us with fun games, Rigg's was to confound us with weird philosophical questions.

"How do you spell a sound like this?" he asked, crumpling his lecture notes into the microphone.

Silence fell.

"Crumple?" offered a woman.

"Crinkle! Crinkle!" shouted a man.

Rigg stroked his goatee meaningfully. "Crinkle, crumple. Okay. But what is the *sound*? The *sound* is not saying, 'Crinkle, crinkle, crinkle.' It's saying . . ."

"Rumble!" someone yelled from the back.

It was hard to know what Rigg was driving at. He nodded his head as if we had hit a familiar wall. "I don't know if we'll get an answer today, but I want you to think about it. You, as poets, have the godlike privilege of inventing words. I find that pretty amazing. Can you imagine the person who created the word 'peace'? Or the person who created the word 'war'?"

There followed another baffled silence. It occurred to me that baffled silence might be Rigg's primary goal as a poet. He told us about the numerous Eskimo words for snow; the possibility of using extrasensory perception to compose poetic verses; the parallels between writing poetry, acting, and doing cancer research; and aliens. "What do you think?" he asked us. "Do extraterrestrials enjoy the power and pleasure of poetry?"

The whole lecture seemed to be built around questions that caused the mind to go slack. They had the opposite effect on Rigg, however. He had worked himself up into a lather with all his nutty ideas.

"Adventure awaits!" he exclaimed. "Once I let a blind person lead me to a poetry class in West Hollywood. I drove several elderly poets there, but when I parked the car the rest was up to her. She used her cane and her superior instincts, and I held her arm, with my eyes closed, trusting her to navigate the busy boulevard." Here, eyes closed, he fumbled about, dramatically enacting the scene. "Tires were screeching, horns were honking. The blind leading the blind to a poetry class. It was a beautiful afternoon. And when, my colleagues, you let go and trust that a spontaneous creation is about to happen, then you will have become twenty-four-hour-a-day poets for the rest of your lives."

The lecture came to an abrupt close. It mystified me on many fronts, and I hoped he would take questions. What had he meant by "Many poets have been proven to have six senses"? And had he been speaking literally when he encouraged us to "listen to the conversations of the spirits that live in tree trunks"? But Rigg was curious to hear our poems and opened the floor of the Bonanza Room to all. A bottleneck formed instantly.

The judged readings had been going on since 8:00 A.M. in the Celebrity Showroom, an old dinner theater with heavy tables and plush cocktail booths. This was the Nugget's swankiest venue. The railings were dark polished mahogany. Red velvet covered the walls. A gold lamé curtain bordered the stage, bunched in dazzling symmetrical folds around the proscenium. Tiny Tivoli lights outlined the aisles and the steps and the ample round lip of the stage, making it safe to maneuver the room's darkness. Gordon Lightfoot had played this room.

I arrived in the midst of Class Five's performances. A pretty young woman with heavy eye makeup and a tight black T-shirt was reading a poem called "Aloha Blue" that made the case for Hawaiian sovereignty. Emblazoned across her shirt in rhinestones was the title of her poem. In the center of the stage, behind the poet, hung a giant movie screen, on which was projected her enormous image, as if she played to a crowd of thousands.

The three judges sat in three cocktail booths, rapidly shuffling through mountains of paper as the readings proceeded. Despite the importance our lecturers had placed on dramatization, the three barely lifted their heads to watch the action on the boards. The top judge, Mary Rudge, wore massive spectacles and a red velvet dress. She was pear-shaped, with curly white hair and big round cheeks, and reminded me a little of Mrs. Claus.

The poets of Class Five finished their readings, and Class Six formed into a line that snaked through the darkness to a door that led to the wings of the stage. I was the final poet in this line, with the best view of the readings. It was not a show I was particularly looking forward to. In the past twenty-four hours, I had witnessed most of the performances four times. When Emma Tutson Thompson of Clinton, Louisiana, began with her poem "Our Love," I was able to recite the opening couplet along with her: "Our love is like a dream that comes true./Really because, I love you."

I soon found that I had involuntarily committed much of Class Six's verse to memory. Kevin Banks read his poem "You're Not Alone," which told the story of a supernatural visit from his dead grandmother. The last line was "Grandmother's rocking chair is rocking." One of Doc's teenage girl poets, Nicole Noël Miller, stepped up to read her poem "The Encounter," a melodramatic account of a suicide attempt averted at the crucial moment through Jesus' intervention. Extensive choreography accompanied her verse. Initially I had found the gestures rigidly theatrical, but seeing them repeated so many times in exactly the same way gave them an almost ritualistic appeal.

As the next poet's head filled the screen, it occurred to me that such gestures were what the Class Six poems had in common. They might be flamboyant, like Nicole's; or they might be as subtle as Flora Dozier's odd way of ending every line with a spondee, or Audrey Soto's practiced shrug in the midst of her final couplet. Every poet had a certain action she repeated in exactly the same manner every time she read. It had taken a few viewings for me to catch on to this. The poems were spells against time. They put the poet in a trance, within which the much debated time limits were rendered irrelevant.

The earliest poems in English were lamentations on the theme of time. To the anonymous poets of the thirteenth century, time was organic and indifferent.

> Nou goth sonne under wode—
> Me reweth, Marie, thi faire rode.
>
> ("Now goes the sun under the wood—
> I pity, Mary, thy fair face.")

To Shakespeare it was brutal.

> O! how shall summer's honey breath hold out
> Against the wrackful siege of battering days,
> When rocks impregnable are not so stout,
> Nor gates of steel so strong, but Time decays?

In Reno, it was incomprehensible and cruel. Most of the famous poets had begun to write their verses in the aftermath of a great pain. Some were widows. Many had lost children, parents, and friends. Yet in the chanting of their poems, time and loss were forgotten for a minute. Grandmothers endured.

Some of the first poets to have read began leaving. As they swung open the glass doors I heard that machine cry, "Wheel! Of! Fortune!" It was my turn to read:

> New York, so often recorded in photographs,
> Must have trouble believing its crows can fly,
> Or that when snow, in clouds
> Of misdirection, is falling, it falls.
>
> The weight in the withstanding snubs
> The whitened flakes of logic, flees
> Wet streets that are streets, scoffs
> At routine measurements of what is there.

New York, so often recorded in photographs,
Must have trouble believing its heart can stop,
Or that as doves, in nests along the river, forever
Swept and sweeping, are hatching, they have hatched.

That night at the Shakespeare banquet we hashed out the odds on the twenty-five grand. From the open field a few favorites had emerged. At my table a dental hygienist from Dallas advised that the smart money liked a man from her class.

"His name is James Stelly," she said, "and he's given his whole life to going around and telling what drugs did to him. He can bring tears to anyone's eye that hears him."

My tablemates chewed on that one for a minute. A Brownsville poet wanted to know what Mr. Stelly's poem was about. The hygienist explained, "It's about how if every time zone in the world would pray for one hour we could have a week of solid prayer. Or two weeks. I can't remember, but he had it all worked out with a chart. Some people were crying just from the chart."

A silence fell over the table as we readjusted our own hopes in light of this new information. How were we to contend with this man and his chart? Charlotte Partridge, a fellow Class Sixer from Trinity, Texas, said, "I have a poem called 'You Are My Everything' that is awesome, but it was too long."

Irregularly enforced time limits had become the convention's dominant controversy. I myself had been well within the minute.

After dinner I ran into Doc outside the ballroom, and we stood off to the side for a while, watching the poets promenade. Many had seen the banquet as a chance to air their finest soup-and-fish. There were red tuxedos, pink tuxedos, green tuxedos, and black tuxedos; satin ball gowns and ruby slippers, strapless evening dresses and short skirts with red spike heels. Some poets wore Elizabethan-era costumes with bodices and billowy sleeves; some wore great African robes with matching turbans. They paraded back and forth in the hallway in front of the ballroom, admiring one another's drapes and reciting their verses aloud.

Doc was still in his jeans. He had some complaints about the banquet.

"First of all, at the International Library they bring you into the dinner with trumpets," he said. "Then they have a real fucking meal. None of this boiled chicken."

"People get pretty dressed up though," I said.

"Nah, this is nothing. The International Library is much classier. It's got real class."[4]

Across the hall Rigg Kennedy stood at the center of a small crowd. Copies of his book *Riggwords* were for sale. I told Doc I was going to go see what Rigg's lyrics looked like on the page.

"Yeah," he said. "I'm gonna check out the slots." He had lost about half of the $800 he won the night before.

The crowd around Rigg was mainly older women pestering him to reveal his age. Although we had never met, Rigg seemed overjoyed to see me. I asked for a copy of his book. On the front cover, there was a psychedelic drawing of a tricycle floating over a moonscape under a lunar eclipse. The back cover was entirely filled with a photograph from Rigg's second wedding, which took place on the set of *Jesus Christ Superstar*.

"She was a dentist," Rigg explained. "I didn't stick around too long. But that front cover, that is art. It's done by R. Cobb, who did the cantina scene in *Star Wars* and the national ecology logo. George here remembered it all these years and just came over here, didn't you George?" He turned to a large oafish man with a video camera standing outside the inner circle of women. Many

---

[4]For all its class, the ILP turned out to have a rap sheet as long as *The Faerie Queene*. In 1994, Dave Barry had slammed the ILP in his nationally syndicated column. In 1996, the *Guardian* had exposed the ILP's U.K. branch. ABC's *20/20* aired a segment two years later. All three reports had arrived at the same conclusion: in order to increase the number of paying poets registered at its conventions, the ILP sets its poetic standards unfathomably low; possibly, it dispenses with them entirely.

Each report resorted to a secret test of the ILP's discernment, featuring A-Poem-Worse-Than-Which-Cannot-Be-Imagined, which when entered in the ILP contest automatically won placement in the $49.95 anthology of the year's best verse. The compositional techniques employed in the production of these poems turned out to be far more interesting than the reports themselves. The *Guardian*'s report featured "Acclaim," a dadaist poem composed by juxtaposing lines from advertisements in the Portsmouth Yellow Pages. In the *20/20* piece, reporter Arnold Diaz visited a classroom of second-graders, persuaded them to write poems about their pets, then submitted these. Barry's poem, "Love," was an original work, in which he took great pains to write something silly and unpolished.

I had intended to gather information from these reports and lay it out for Schramm, in the hopes that denouncing the ILP would prove my allegiance to the FPS. Unfortunately, the conclusion these reports came to regarding the ILP could just as easily have been the result of a study of Schramm's outfit. The main reason the FPS had not attracted the gumshoes was probably the much smaller threat it posed.

years ago George had been a ship's librarian in the Navy, and one of the books on his shelves was *Riggwords*.

"A couple of my shipmates came in," George said, "and they copied love poems out of this book and sent them on home to their girlfriends. Then later they got married."

Rigg's expression was beatific. "It transcends time and space," he said, turning to his tiny audience. "You all know how I believe that poets can change the world, and here George tells me that these people got married. I only hope they're still together."

"You can't be expected to control *that*," I pointed out.

"No," he said, a faraway look on his face. "But I can control time and space."

By Tuesday morning the Famous Poets staff had managed to fill the Rose Ballroom with hundreds of colorful balloons bearing the words FAMOUS POETS PARADE AND BALLOONATHON. Under these words was a caricature of Shakespeare looking like an Italian. A misstep in balloon layout put the words TAB HUNTER GRAND MARSHAL directly underneath the caricature, as if it depicted Hunter. Each chair in the ballroom had one of these balloons tied to its back with a long shiny ribbon. Now and then a balloon would slip loose and float up to the ceiling.

I found balloonless Doc standing off to the side with his arms crossed, staring critically at the stage, where Annette Ackerman, one of the assistant judges, was singing "The Rose" but with her own words, which tackled the war issue. Next, Judge Rudge climbed onto the stage in her Mrs. Claus suit (some said she had been up all night deciding the winners) and launched into a wild sermon that ranged over the Big Bang and "eternal sound vibrations" and eventually got to: "Oh, you day beyond dawn mist, beyond comets and night-falling creatures, and those who even by rubbing their legs make rhythm sounds. Oh, you brilliant, rose-surrounded day of fingers and lips, of hearts, of flutes."

"She's gone," Doc muttered.

There was some truth to that, but spending ten hours watching more than 300 poets recite their verses, and then staying up all night long trying to pick the best of these while around you a casino rings and dings, would likely have devastated even Doc. Frankly, it surprised me to see Judge Rudge holding it together at all. Gesticulating with her right arm, she went into a jag about "my Super Bowl" and "5 billion souls." Just as she was winding up to the meat of her idea, however, a balloon popped loudly, causing a ripple of nervous laughter. She stopped to acknowledge the interruption and then continued but had not completed more than two sentences before another balloon went off. This time she pretended not to notice. The crowd was buzzing now, and Judge Rudge had to raise her voice to be heard: "I'm gonna shine like the stars, the moon, the sun," she yelled, "which are the microphones of the gods, through which they recite their—" Two balloons burst at the same time, and we did not hear any more about the gods.

I looked up at the ceiling. The balloons up there had been heated by the light fixtures and were going off like popcorn kernels in a skillet. A quick count of the unpopped balloons informed me that there would be no respite for the Judge. Because the balloons had flown up at varying times, they were all on different schedules, ensuring pops for at least the rest of her speech. "In universal mind you can really be anything you truly want!" she hollered, as three balloons exploded above. "You are like a golden child!"

Doc shook his head. "The balloons always cause problems," he said. "Last year the hotel was right next to the airport, and when they let them go in the balloonathon a big gust of wind came and blew them straight into the flight path. Runway was full of balloons."

Judge Rudge finished to kind applause. Everyone felt bad about how her speech had gone. During the clapping, I asked Doc what his poem of peace would be.

"I'm not sending one up," he said. "That's just for the people who haven't been here before."

The program continued illogically. Alisha, decked out in a purple velveteen Renaissance gown and matching coronet, introduced the Famous Poets Society Dixieland Band. Tab Hunter appeared and gave a short forgettable speech. The band struck up and began to lead the Famous Poets Parade through the casino. Not all of the bleary-eyed gamblers glanced up from their games. Outside the Reno sky was clear. It was a warm day. Judge Rudge formed us into a huge circle and said a prayer. Her voice was hoarse; it was hard to make her out. Then we let go of our balloons.

"There's mine! There's mine!" people shouted. A few of the balloons got trapped under the Nugget's eaves, but most of them made it, and for a quarter of a minute or so they filled the sky. It was something. The Dixielanders played. Tab Hunter signed autographs. High above it all our poems of peace fluttered and waved. They floated so deep into the blue that people put down their cameras and just stared, trying to keep their eyes focused on what they thought was theirs. Each balloon became a minuscule dot, then disappeared entirely.

Some of the poets were denied this pleasure. Their poems outdid their balloons. Off to the side they congregated and swapped ideas about how to get airborne. Class Six's Anita Jones emerged as the leader of this band. It was she who hit on the idea of tying all the drooping poems together. She laid into the task and presently had a craft comprising twenty-one balloons.

"We gonna make this sucker go!" Anita shouted. You could tell by the lazy way the balloons were hanging that those poems were going nowhere. Anita pushed and another girl blew, but that only served to move the poems around on the ground. Anita called for more balloons.

The Famous Poets Society had impressed upon us throughout the convention that we were all winners: that as far back as the first night when we had put pen to paper we had ceased to lose. But some would leave Reno with less than others. This fact was underscored by the $6,000 in door prizes that greeted our return to the Rose Ballroom.

After this preamble, Alisha made ready to announce the names of the winning poets. Behind her, the stage was set with a winners' circle of chairs— seventeen for the $1,000 third prizes, and one each for the second, first, and grand prizes, worth $3,000, $5,000, and $25,000. We all stared hungrily at the $25,000 seat, on which lay a red fur robe with a leopard-print fringe and a twelve-foot train; a matching crown in red, leopard, and gold, inlaid with red and green jewels; and a golden scepter.

Things were tense. Nails were chewed. I saw at least one lucky charm brought out. "Extry Sarff for 'Wild and Free'!" Alisha cried, and the first winner, an old fellow from Ketchikan, Alaska, with a giant white beard, mounted the stage. He read his poem, which was about orca whales, and we gave him a short hand. There was no time to dwell on the relative merits of the poem. Fortuna's wheel was spinning.

"Saundra Young Obendorf for 'Celestial Butterflies'!" A woman seated several tables to my left let out a small scream and ran through the crowd, throwing her arms in the air and leaping. When she read the title of her poem she imitated the flight of a butterfly with her hands. "Vanessa O. Sullivan for 'Born Black'!" A white woman in a cowboy shirt rushed the stage. "This is the second time I've been here, first time I won. So to all of you: Keep trying!" Her poem was about being an oddball in a conventional family. "Robert Nielson for 'Dance'!" Over to my right, a man in a dark suit with a thin tie popped up and pumped his fists in the air, screaming, "Yes! Yes! Yes!"

Some of the winners let out huge sighs of relief and gazed graciously to heaven. Some were catapulted into frenzies of hugging and crying and clutching of the cheeks. One girl, whose winning poem was entitled "My Elusive Heart," immediately began to fan herself, as if she were worried she might overheat. She fanned herself all the way up to the stage and then stood speechlessly at the podium for a quarter of a minute. Finally she shrieked, "World peace!" and burst into tears.

The number of empty chairs onstage was thinning when Alisha grasped the edges of the podium and yelled a name so familiar I didn't recognize it at first. My legs, however, took her meaning immediately and propelled me into a standing position, where I believe I then exhibited all the celebratory tropes that the others had. Blushing and grinning and waving my arms in the air, I stumbled through the crowd while a trumpeter blasted out a here-comes-the-king sort of tune. Along the way I ran into various friends from Class Six, who gave me the thumbs-up sign or snapped a picture. When I got to the stage I met Alisha, who seemed much bigger up close and more freckled. She shook my hand, slipped me a check for $1,000, and led me to the podium, where I turned and looked out at the sea of famous poets.

On Sunday, I had fallen into conversation with an old man who had accompanied his poet wife to the convention. When I asked him if he thought his wife would get nervous if she had to read in front of the crowd, he said, "She will most likely have to refer to her notes because she may forget who she is." This is precisely what happened to me when I looked out at the crowd. I seemed to slip out of my body entirely. It was a very strange sensation, and I could see how it might lead a person to break down and shout, "World peace!" I held myself together as best I could, referred to my notes, and read my poem.

My chair in the winners' circle afforded me an entirely new perspective on the convention. Who really gave a damn about what poetry was or wasn't? Poetry was the check in my hand. Poetry was the golden scepter, only five chairs away. Alisha cried out, "Gladys Ogor-Edem for 'I'm a King's Kid—Jehovah's

Princess'!" A black woman in a long black dress got up and gave a stirring performance in which she sobbed, screamed, waved her hands, stamped her feet, lost her voice, and then collapsed in her chair completely spent, clutching a $3,000 check. "Calvin G. Benito for 'Apache'!" A bald Oklahoman read an elegy to the great tribe's warriors with their "long black hair," and sat down with $5,000. The moment was upon us. Twenty-five thousand dollars.

"Cathy L. Kaiser for 'I Choose to Dance'!"

Here was our queen. We looked around excitedly, but no one stood up. Was she gone? The initial applause began to peter out. All at once a buzz swept through the crowd, fingers pointed, and our eyes swung to an unused corridor of the ballroom, behind a series of pillars, where with a look of grim determination Cathy L. Kaiser of Phoenix, Arizona, was slowly advancing toward the stage in a motorized wheelchair.

The applause erupted. Poets on the opposite side of the ballroom hopped up on their chairs to get a better look at the handicapped laureate. Some held their cameras above their heads and snapped photos. A wave of energetic disbelief passed from table to table. Short people asked their taller companions what was going on. Kaiser motored silently along, her chin pressed to her chest. It was not yet time for her to celebrate. There was still the matter of what she would do when she got to the stage, which had no ramp.

Try to imagine the most melodramatic scene you have ever witnessed. Add to this as many soaring eagles as your imagination can muster. Color it in pinks and purples. Do all of this and more and still you would have no hope of touching Cathy Kaiser's performance that day in the Rose Ballroom. As she rolled up to the foot of the stage, the trumpeter belted out his last hurrah and fell silent. Grasping Tab Hunter's suntanned arm, Kaiser took a deep breath and heaved herself up onto her feet. She was standing! Gritting her teeth, she began to struggle up the stairs, one excruciating step at a time. She was walking! Once on the stage, she shook loose of Tab's support and stood free under her own power. The crowd lost its mind. Alisha's husband, Bob, rigged out in a jewel-encrusted doublet with a white frilly collar, placed the laureate's crown upon Kaiser's head. Tab hung the robe from her shoulders and presented her with the scepter. Her coronation complete, Kaiser began to wobble across the stage toward the podium. Alisha crept along behind her, bearing aloft the leopard train.

Her poem did not disappoint. "A song leaps from my heart at the beginning of each new day," Kaiser began. "A song with a melody that never plays a sad song." At several points she appeared near collapse, but clenched her fists behind the podium and pushed on. "If I have the choice of sitting this one out, I will choose to dance!" she chanted. "If you have a choice dance, dance, dance!" As far as raking up the judges' coals was concerned, you had to admit this was hard to top.

Kaiser gave the crowd a royal nod and fell into her throne. Alisha thanked us all for coming. "See you next year!" she shouted. Poets began to file out surprisingly fast. There were planes to catch. Cathy Kaiser sat in silence, a dazed look in her eyes. Her crown was tilted. Sweat ran down her cheeks. Poets rushed forward to congratulate the prizewinners they knew from their classes, but it did not look like Kaiser had any intention of moving, perhaps for days. While the other prizewinners—her court, I suppose—bustled around the stage taking pictures and shaking hands and even signing autographs, Kaiser, whether with exultation or exhaustion, remained seated on her throne. Hers was a quiet reign.

Within twenty minutes it was over. All in all, the glory was, as the man on the balloons put it, "too like the lightning, which doth cease to be/Ere one can say, It lightens." Out in the hallway, I ran into Doc. I asked what he thought of the winners.

"Dunno," he said. "I left. As soon as I heard that crap about dolphins and butterflies I left. I could see where the judging was going."

"We feel," another man said, "furthermore, that the time limits were unfairly imposed. There were some on the stage who should not have been there."

"She could walk!" said a wiry little guy with a Hawaiian shirt and tattooed forearms. "We all saw her walking across the stage. I been to L.A. I seen how the panhandlers do it in their wheelchairs and with their crutches."

"Gentlemen," said a man with luxurious dreadlocks, "we have been duped."

The man with the dreadlocks proceeded to make an allegation that I had some trouble swallowing. He claimed that Cathy Kaiser was an employee of the Famous Poets Society, the idea being that by awarding her the prize money they could fold it back into their revenue, with maybe a little coming off the top for Cathy's show.

"Following the tragedy in New York," he explained, "a man whose acquaintance I have made here in Reno called in to the office. Today when Ms.

Kaiser read her poem, he recognized her voice as the same one he talked to on the phone that day. We've been had."[5]

The tattooed man let out a long low whistle. "I knew something was up," he said. "I could tell the fix was in from the way the judges were acting. They weren't even paying attention. Why not? Because they knew who was gonna get the prize. I went *down* for my group, just trying to wake them up. When my turn came, I says to the guy behind me, I says, 'This is for you, buddy,' and I went out and took a nosedive, yelling at them, doing my best Pee-Wee Herman routine, jumping around on the stage like a retard, you know, just to get them to open their *eyes*. Well, it worked, one of the guys in my group won a prize. I got the shaft, and I got the shaft from this other society too. I came out here with just my shirt on my back, all the way from Jersey without a penny, and now I'm gonna have to ride the train cars back, which I don't mind because a freight car is a fuck of a place to write some poetry."

My plane did not leave until the following morning. I spent Tuesday night in the casino. The Nugget is not actually that big, and most of my time was passed at the Aquarium Bar. The musical entertainment came in the form of a well-oiled duo known as Bobby and Ricky, whose engagement is listed in Nugget literature as "indefinite." Bobby was a sax player with a genial smile; Ricky, a guitarist in a leisure suit with curly gray hair. When I arrived Bobby was tying up the last few bars of "Secret Agent Man." When the song was through he grabbed the microphone and shouted, "Have some more tequila!" pronouncing the last word with a lascivious Mexican accent. The mostly geriatric crowd responded with a lusty cheer. I noticed a table of famous poets, all wearing their medallions and drinking heavily. Bobby and Ricky started into "Unchained Melody." Dancers crowded the floor. An elderly couple stood in the center, barely swaying, locked in a tender embrace. A man wearing a cowboy hat and a shirt patterned with the American flag asked one of the poets to dance. I knew her. She had bent my ear the night before, telling me all about

---

[5]I could be relatively sure that these allegations were baseless. If the judging was rigged, why had I, a suspected agent of the ILP, walked away with $1,000? The FPS was honest, I knew that much. It may not have had a Pulitzer Prize winner for its keynote speaker, but the FPS ran a straight show. As for the ILP, with its silver-plated bowl, I could not say. Had Dave Barry's poem proven the ILP to be criminally unexclusive, or just democratic? Or was Barry simply a bad poet? After all, he could have played to win. It is easy to say what poetry is not, but why not at least try to say what it is?

her unhappy marriage that fell apart a few years back and the poetry that had helped her through it. She smiled up at the cowboy and laid her hand on his outstretched forearm. Some of us began to sing along with Bobby. The din of the slots died away. Out of the fake thatched roof descended Apollo, god of song. The waitress stood and watched, her tray full of tequila shots, limes, salt. The muse of the lyre visited Ricky, and he strummed a lovely chord. Time and loss for us seemed distant, made-up things. At the center of the world were Bobby's lips, singing the immortal verses, and in these verses we took our solace and our hearts were gladdened. This was poetry.

August 2002

Devil's Work

Secret Doings at the Queens Museum of Art

MORGAN MEIS

Day One

We're doing absolutely nothing. I sit on the floor in an orange jumpsuit designed for this occasion, with twenty-four other people also wearing orange jumpsuits. I catch Stefany's eye for a moment and then Jean's, and we smile at one another because it feels nice, exciting even, to be in the midst of our first day. We will spend seven hours a day in this room for the next three months. "What are we trying to do today?" Jason "Funky" Brown asks me as a few museumgoers wander in with some trepidation and then scurry out. "Not much," I reply. "Not much all this week and maybe into next week too." "That's good," he says, looking jolly and overstuffed in his jumpsuit. "You have to let it take its time." He wanders off to another corner of the room and I continue to sit there, cross-legged, my hands folded in my lap.

We're at the Queens Museum of Art. People generally come to this museum, if they come at all, for the Panorama. The Queens Museum is in Flushing, in the middle of Flushing Meadows/Corona Park near the Tennis Center, where the U.S. Open is played, and down the way from Shea Stadium. It's a long walk from the 7 train and separated from the rest of Flushing by the network of highways that Robert Moses cooked up when he was beating New York City into something new. At the center of the museum squats the Panorama, a giant 9,335-square-foot scale model of the entirety of New York City, all five boroughs, commissioned by Robert Moses himself. The Panorama includes hundreds of thousands of tiny buildings, the buildings of New York City. Out in the Flushing section of the model there is even a model of the Queens Museum itself, and as your gaze sweeps across the whole of the city it can pause at the museum and watch itself in a moment of solipsism. The Panorama is, in a sense, the soul of the museum. I imagine those who work here must dream about the Panorama sometimes. There isn't much you can do with it; it just sits there, decade after decade. That's what produces the glimmer of melancholy about the museum, and the moldering remnants of past World's Fairs scattered around the park produce more of the same. It isn't a sad place, but it's quiet and filled with memories as well as the sense that some things have simply been forgotten.

We spend the last forty-five minutes of the day having a group nap in one of the corners of the room, a mass of orange limbs, and then go home.

Day Nine

We, the members of Flux Factory, have been coming in every day for more than a week. We have a room just past the entrance of the museum where we are expected to do something every day and keep doing it until the International Show is over in three months. We've been invited to participate in the show because we're an art collective and we live in Queens. The idea we pitched was that we would create a living artwork that would grow and change and build over the course of the show. We would call it a "Fluxture."

We exercise this morning because we have decided to exercise every morning. The guards and the old ladies at the gift shop were suspicious at first, but now they expect it to happen. Maybe they even like that it happens. Lisa, one of the guards, asks us what kind of exercises we'll do today. "We do strong ones," Aya, Jean's girlfriend, says, and proceeds to lead us through a series of vigorous jerkings like the ones Japanese autoworkers do every morning. She scrunches up her girlish, Hello Kitty face and proceeds to scream out commands to us in Japanese for fifteen minutes until we fall to the floor, gasping and sweaty. I am fattish, and Funky is fatter still. Jean Barberis is young and sprightly, and Stefany Anne Golberg has the delicacy of another age. A couple visiting the museum stand at the open end of our room and watch us trying to live up to the rigors of being Japanese. After the exercise we go back to setting up video cameras and video projectors and still cameras and recording and documenting and displaying the footage of past days on the walls. The footage being displayed generally consists of footage of ourselves taking footage of ourselves. Thus arises the inevitable problem of what it all really means and where it might go. Being forced to ask that question is part of the whole point of the project, but we all disagree about the answer and secretly doubt our own conclusions.

Dana Gramp lies on the floor of the room taking pinhole camera pictures of me sitting in the corner with a typewriter. I am writing about the fact that she is taking pictures of me with her camera. Stefany is standing on a stool trying to get one of the video cameras to work properly, a camera that is pointed down at Dana and me capturing moments with each other. Sally Herships has come in for a few hours to record some of our thoughts and collect bits of our hair and fingerprints. Even she, a part of the project, wonders aloud to me, "But what, really, is this thing?" "It's just all of this, and it's just getting started anyway," I reply. She smiles down at me, being tall and kind, and the day proceeds.

At around two o'clock Hitomi Iwasaki, the museum's associate curator, comes down from the offices upstairs and blasts into the room, her usual mode of entrance. It had become clear to us from early on that Hitomi is one of those rare people in whom trust and exasperation can exist simultaneously. She sits down next to Jean and me in such a way that we are both convinced she will never stand up again. And then she stands up again. You ought to take a person like that pretty seriously. She seems to have lost patience with the relationship we've been cultivating with nothing. She says, "Are you actually going to do something?" It isn't a question really, though it is grammatically framed as one. "Things take time to develop," I say. "That's the point!" I say excitedly. She doesn't look entirely convinced, and Jean looks sad and small on the floor next to me. I wonder later if some part of her would have preferred that we answered, "No, we're not doing anything. We're going to sit in this room for two more months and then go home." It has long been a theme of myth and tragedy that the object of desire is sometimes also the punishment. But then, to put it in terms of tragedy is certainly overwrought. Yet it's moments like this, in the empty room with Hitomi, that start things, and once they get started they end up in places that hadn't been anticipated.

A few minutes after she leaves we begin to build. Timothy Don, who manages to look strong and handsome in his jumpsuit, Stefany, and I start to carry in metal beams from storage and fit them together with nuts and bolts. It's like a modernist barn raising, with the industrial building materials and the weird bronze glowing against the stark white walls. We now have an open metal box in the room. It's slightly taller than a person and large enough for four. To this we add more cameras and more VCRs and more pictures of ourselves and more pictures of it. We're filling the room up with itself, as it were. And we're making the thing have a history, a history consciously presented. Now you can walk into the room and see that something was going on and had been going on for some time. It's a start, but it's a tense one because there simply isn't a clear idea as to what will be created in the room or what the structure will be for.

At the day's end, Jean and Stefany and I stand around in the World's Fair section of the museum and commiserate while Funky does a "nap performance" in artist Emily Jacir's Palestinian tent, which sits in the room next to ours and commemorates villages destroyed in 1948. "I love the room, but I hate the room," Jean says. "We have to extend the room," Stefany says. Jean and I agree, but none of us is sure what that really means.

Day Twenty

We cut the ribbon this morning to vaguely ceremonious music composed by Stefany. We'll mend it tonight to more music and then do the same thing the next day and every day from now on. We chat with Andre, another of the guards, who's fond of strolling into the room and saying, "You know, I actually like this. I'm not sure what it is, but it's different." We have Andre cut the ribbon this morning. It's our goal to have someone different cut and mend the ribbon every morning and evening, but there are so few visitors that our videotapes show basically the same five or six security guards performing our ceremonies day after day. We take daily tea at 1:30 on the museum lawn and serve it to anyone who happens to be around, after Hitomi suggested it might be a good way for us to interact with the public. Most of the time there's not much "around" around, but every once in a while we convince some person passing by the museum to have tea with us. We've taken hours of footage of the guard's desk with a surveillance camera, and today we project the footage out from our room onto a wall of the museum, and the guards stand around and laugh at themselves doing the things that they do every day. Laura from the education department brings a group of special-needs adults into our room and tells them that they can touch everything and that the whole thing is art, including us. Several of her students seem pleased by this idea, and one simply begins to cry.

In the afternoon, Jean covers himself in double-sided tape, and Stefany and I collect a number of random objects and blow up a hundred or so balloons. We do this to benefit another group, a children's group this time, being brought by the education department. Stefany dubs our educational art project "Sticky Friend." Soon, a gaggle begins to filter into the room. "Just stick these things right on him," Stefany tells them. "He's your Sticky Friend." At first they are somewhat trepidatious, but soon it becomes a rampage as they crazily affix balloons and stuffed animals to Jean's face. Children collide and bounce off one another in their glee to stick more things on Jean. Their laughter becomes indistinguishable from shrieking; they can't really control themselves. A crowd of guards and museum employees gathers round watching the spectacle. Richie, the head of all miscellaneous things at the museum, trudges past with a can of paint, as amused at the sight as he is anxious to get away from it.

The end of the day is quiet. Dana takes a long exposure of the room with her homemade camera, and Stefany and I try to capture something of it all in a daily log, I on my old mechanical typewriter that beats out a soundtrack to those hours and she with a pen. There is something sweet and calm in the room, and the few museumgoers who come by merely peek their heads in for a moment, seemingly in respect for something that ought not be disturbed. The room is cluttered now with images and texts and objects and a metal structure that has grown from a simple box to a series of open rooms and wires and strings hanging everywhere. It is even a little dangerous, and Stefany walks around the room taping up sharp corners and beams in order to give them a little padding.

For the last half hour of the day we fight. Not about anything in particular but just because of the tensions always lingering under the surface from being in this room hour after hour, day after day. "Don't put that tape there," I say to Stefany, who looks back at me slowly and continues to wrap the beam in tape. Stefany is mad at Jean and me because we disagree with her about the next part of the structure to be built, and I am mad at Stefany and Jean because they don't do things the way I want them to. Jean looks like an idiot because we had to cut half his hair off in order to get the tape out from Sticky Friend. We do the closing ceremony and leave, separately.

Day Thirty-three

Today we're going to tunnel into the walls of the museum. We had thought about extending the room, and we had joked about different ways of doing it. But suddenly today feels like the day to do it. There is enough in the room already, and we have been here for many, many days. Maybe it is simply an escape act. More than that, the Fluxture is simply growing of its own accord. It might also be because the walls of the museum are so thick you have to wonder what's inside them. Perhaps there's no way to fully explain it, and that is what makes the idea exciting and somewhat frightening. I say to Jean, "Let's create a false tunnel in the room and then use it to cut into the real wall." He says, "Of course." Stefany says, "I wonder how far we could tunnel into the museum?" All three of us wonder about that. "We can't tell anyone else about it," Stefany says, "not even the other Fluxers." Jean and I agree. "We'll leave hints though," Jean says. "Okay," I say, "we'll leave hints." And that is the end of the discussion. It had simply become obvious that we must tunnel into the walls of the Queens Museum of Art in Flushing Meadows/Corona Park, home of the great Panorama.

First we build a small chamber against the wall and within the metal box that was the first structure we made. The room is so built up that it isn't even noticeable. Jean and Stefany take extra care to bang around in the room a good deal, and I crawl inside the chamber and saw a hole through the south wall. I do it slowly with a crappy little knife that Jean loans me, and it takes forever. I stop every time someone comes into the room or I hear the rush of Hitomi on one of her rounds. After an hour or so there is a person-sized hole in the wall. I pull the last piece of drywall away and crawl into a new world. The walls of the Queens Museum of Art are so wide that they hide what is essentially a series of smaller, skinnier rooms that house the infrastructure. No one realizes what we are doing and no one is bothered by the noise. Jean and Stefany and I take turns crawling into the tunnel and just sitting in there. We try to tunnel through an internal wall within the tunnel that might lead farther into the museum innards, but it lands us at a concrete wall. We have tunneled into a secret room barely wider than a person, lined with the studs that hold up the walls and topped by the ductwork for the central-air system. The question now is what to do with it. I create a small peephole into our main room, and we cover it with a picture of Seb—an absent Fluxer—with a hole in his right eye that we can peek out. "We just secretly tunneled into the walls of the Queens Museum of Art," Stefany says as we leave.

Day Thirty-four

We gather some nice fabric, a clarinet, a balalaika, a toy phonograph, a mounted deer's head, a chandelier, glasses, and some aged tequila for the new tunnel room. It is agreed that the secret room should contrast in decadence with the stark environs of the room outside and the rest of the museum. We agree that the room should be kept secret from everyone else in the group. It will be part of the evolving complexity of everything happening at the museum, but we start taking pictures of ourselves in the room and leaving various hints and clues of what we have done in full public view. We start a scrapbook called "Devil's Work" about these secret doings and leave it out in the room among the other scrapbooks we have for people to look at. We have pictures of ourselves in the secret room posted up on the walls outside, but there are so many pictures now that no one ever bothers to figure out what the pictures depict. We have little notes that, if properly discovered and followed by other Fluxers, would lead them to the tunnel, but if and when a note is found, it's generally ignored. Jean sits for hours at a time in the secret room, which he has now dubbed the Kissing Booth, playing old 45s on the toy phonograph, sipping tequila, and doodling in his notebook. Other Fluxers show up to work in the outside room, and I feel that some faculty of their mind is trying to let them know that they are hearing faint music coming from nowhere. But the mind has a liking for coherence, and we find that it is very difficult to get anyone to notice our new activities. Funky is working on a computer in the room, and I can hear him humming softly to a Johnny Cash tune coming from the Kissing Booth. "What are you humming?" I ask him, feeling simultaneously nervous and brazen. He thinks for a moment. "I don't know."

In a sense, we have switched around the relations in the room. For weeks we had been completely exposed, objects at the mercy of whatever public might filter through. Now, with the Kissing Booth and its spy holes and the layers of secrecy, everything has doubled over on itself, and we can just step into the tunnel and morph from an object into a subject and back again. Jean and Stefany and I scurry in and out of that tunnel all day long just to experience the transformation.

We spend the last part of the day standing at the top of the ramp that loops around the Panorama, just watching it and reflecting. The lights go off every fifteen minutes or so for a minute or two in order to simulate night falling on New York City. The whole museum is starting to feel like an occasion for the extension of our room now, with the Panorama smack in the center.

Day Thirty-seven

One of the problems with the world, and one of the interesting things about the world, is the way limits and possibilities interact. Breaking through the South Wall had been a possibility and it had crossed a limit, and it had suggested other possibilities and other limits. It's nice to sit in the Kissing Booth, in what is, by simple fact, a secret hideout. Maybe it is the fulfillment of that childhood impulse that seeks out those kinds of spaces. But the restlessness of everything, of the whole project and our being there every day, makes the Kissing Booth feel incomplete and increasingly empty as the day goes on.

In the afternoon I rig up a piece of our metal building material as a ramp from one part of the structure to another so that a ball can roll down it and onto the floor. A simple act of motion. But it makes me realize that if the ball can be released from within the room it can also be released with a string from within the Kissing Booth. The implications are exciting. It means that Stefany and Jean and I can sit in the Kissing Booth and, using a system of pulleys and gadgets, make all kinds of things happen in the room. We begin to contemplate the possibility of Art as Booby Trap.

Over the next few hours the room becomes a network of rolling and dropping objects, of released balloons and secret messages and squirting water bottles and fans. All this we control from the Kissing Booth, where we've installed a video monitor that is hooked up to every camera in the room. The Kissing Booth has become a control chamber for kinetic chaos. On the one hand, it is exhilarating to sit in the Booth and know that you are in complete control of a secret Art Toy that has totally transformed the room, and by extension the museum, but on the other hand infuriating that you can't tell anyone about it. The problem, we quickly realize, is that it is a machine all revved up with nowhere to go. Our most consistent audience has been museum employees, and we can't unleash the trap on any of them since it might lead to the discovery of our tunneling. The booby traps lead to waiting and the waiting leads rather ignominiously to boredom, a tense boredom but boredom nonetheless. There are high moments. We amuse several people who don't stay in the room long enough for us to activate much but who smile at the dropping ball or the sliding disks. A man walks into the room while the three of us are in the Kissing Booth and slowly makes his way around. I manically grab a few wires and send metal disks sliding around on a track and then dropping to the floor. He stops and watches. Stefany clicks different monitors off and on in the room, letting him know that he's being tracked by our cameras. She pulls a wire that shifts some cans tied together and Jean releases a few balloons. Now the man is truly alarmed. Jean flips a switch that turns a fan on and blows a whole ream of paper down from a higher level. The man watches this happen for a few more moments and then abruptly turns and runs from the room and leaves the museum. We have frightened him. This was not the intent of course, but we've achieved something more delightful than we had ever initially imagined.

Except that it has already become boring and empty. The only way to go farther in this direction would be to actually hurt someone, and we are generally peaceful artists. The only thing left to do is penetrate farther into the museum. One way to do this is simply to go farther, to extend the tunnel or to tunnel elsewhere. But another way is to think about different senses of the term "penetrate." We now know every back stairway and passageway and entrance and exit to the entire museum. We've been everywhere, and that familiarity has given us, essentially, complete access. The only way to give an honest portrayal of the situation is to say that we have taken advantage of our situation, which is to say that we have taken advantage of the trust and the genuine friendship we have built with all the people at the museum. But at the same time we're attuned to the impishness of the museum director, Tom Finkelpearl, and to the intensity of Hitomi. We've spent days with museum employees like Carolyn and Debra at Bryant Park helping promote the museum for CultureFest and taping one another to trees and tables and each other. And we have always felt that Tony and Richie and Lisa speak for something of the guards' feelings when they simply sit at the desk and chuckle to themselves at our machinations within the room and without. A certain extension of our license isn't merely immanent to our project; it is immanent to the general mood of the place, a collection of mostly likable people working together in a

half-forgotten corner of Queens surrounded by good but not terribly important or sought-after art.

At the end of the day it is raining, and I always feel that the place becomes
most what it is on rainy days. I walk around the museum with Stefany, and we
can hear every footstep, and the white walls seem like they're a little wet from
all the dampness in the air. This is when the isolation and melancholy are
most obvious, but there is also something good and human about the place
that you don't get at every institution, to be sure. We come back and sit on the
floor of our room again, and I'm clacking at the typewriter while Stefany talks
to Dorothy, one of the guards, about her life, and Jean sits in the Kissing Booth
letting off a balloon or turning on the fan every now and again, though no
one notices.

Day Forty-nine

This morning we grab a few cans of orange paint, some paint rollers, and a
number of cinder blocks from a back room and put them on a dolly. Stefany
and I roll them across the museum to the back stairway that leads to the roof.
It seems like a long way from the back room across from the guard's desk to
the other side of the museum where the access to the roof is. We bump into
Richie along the way, and we exchange a glance and a word or two that says,
"I know that you're doing something stupid, but you know what you're doing,
and we're all far beyond the place where anyone is going to police you." And
that is pretty much the truth. We carry the stuff up to the roof using a pulley
mechanism Jean rigged up for the cinder blocks, and we stand on the vast roof
of the museum looking out all the way to Manhattan. It is a spectacular
vista. And it is directly in the flight path of planes coming into and out of
LaGuardia airport. We have managed to transport a number of museum materials, which are certainly not ours to transport, to a location that is without
question not to be accessed, and also we have brought a tent.

We paint a huge message on the roof for the planes taking off from
LaGuardia. It reads, PERSONS IN PLANES PLEASE CALL 718-707-3362, which is the
Flux Factory business line. Then we put up the tent using the cinder blocks as
supports. It is a miniature colonization and a gesture at communication. We
put a message on our answering machine later that asks persons calling from
planes to leave an address so we can send them an art prize. We sit up in our

tent for a while and watch the jetliners come down across the park and disappear into the trees as they land. The people in the planes flying by are looking down at us and the landscape that stretches out from the park in the same way that we stand around the Panorama in the evenings watching the whole city in miniature. Later, I go downstairs and make a video describing to people how to get up on the roof and visit our little tent, and leave it among a number of tapes we have out at a viewing station. We resolve to sleep in the tent one night and to leave it up there until the day someone finds it and takes it away.

Day Fifty-seven

This afternoon we embark on the time-capsule project. The idea is to extend our stay at the museum. It comes out of something Jean says about our various incursions. "This is our permanent exhibition," he says, and there is a wonderful sound to that idea. Stefany picks up on that immediately, that we are also stretching the temporal boundaries of our stay at the museum. She and I start stuffing things into little boxes and tubes and balls of fabric. We date things and explain them. We make video- and audiotapes for people who might be at the museum years from now. "People of the future," I say on one of the tapes, "you have discovered a secret project of Flux Factory, who once lived in this museum in the fall of 2002." Stefany sings sweetly into a cassette. I can't hear what the lyrics are, and I don't know where she goes to hide it. Over the weeks we had noticed how many nooks and crannies there are to the museum, how many empty spaces. We decide to fill them up. We climb up into trap doors and down into shafts, behind stairwells and into ductwork. Everywhere we leave these little packages for the future. We decide to keep making more and more of these capsules. When we walk around the museum now Stefany will nudge me or Jean will nudge me or vice versa and just point at a crevice or a door or a ledge, and then later one of us will walk by as nonchalantly as possible and stuff a capsule there when no one is looking. I'm absolutely certain that people will be finding them years from now, maybe decades. In some of the places we leave mini-installations, small representations of the Fluxture, stashed into the farthest, deepest reaches of the museum. I imagine some of those things will never be found. I don't even remember where half the things are anymore.

Day Sixty-eight

Our gaze is greedy. The entire museum has become our Fluxture.

The room next to ours is full of drawings by the artist Gilberto Triplitt. There are roughly thirty of these sketches, all of varying sizes and composed of tight, obsessive circles. Jean sits down on the floor and makes a smallish replica of one of these drawings. It's a passable work. We decide to hang it on the wall next to the real drawings. There is, of course, the distinct possibility that someone will notice the addition, perhaps the artist himself. But by this point the logic of "augmentation" has become its own justification. Jean and I simply walk over to the wall and nail it on. Its real purpose, however, is slightly more subtle: to cover a small hole in the wall that we are going to make.

Later, Jean and Stefany begin a new tunnel. The tunnel starts near an emergency exit in the direction of the bathrooms, and we think it will lead into a between-the-walls room similar to the Kissing Booth but within the wall on which Mr. Triplitt's drawings hang. Alas, no two tunnels are the same, and this one is fitted with an internal wall of wood and Sheetrock that prevents our accessing the back side of Mr. Triplitt's wall. We realize that we'll need to cut through the wood and Sheetrock in order to get farther into the tunnel and behind the wall of drawings. Once inside that wall, it will be possible to cut a spy hole under the fake drawing Jean put up. We must extend the tunnels and we must create more spy holes, lines of sight from the infrastructure of the museum out to all the public spaces.

Day Seventy-three

Jean and Stefany are alone in the Fluxture today. It is a quiet day, but then again most days are quiet. The plan is this: After a perfunctory opening ceremony, Stefany is to make a great deal of noise in our room, to turn on every noisemaking item and type noisily and continuously. This noise is to cover up the sound of Jean gutting a hole in the wall with an electric sawing tool, a Sawzall. The Sawzall is a bit of a monster and has been brought to the museum surreptitiously for precisely this purpose. It is designed to cut through walls. The plan has the distinct disadvantage that the sound of the Sawzall is the loudest sound that has ever existed anywhere. Jean is supposed to wait for a signal before he starts, but there really is no proper moment to begin sawing away at the internal walls of a museum. Also, the toy walkie-talkies Jean and

Stefany use to communicate are not of the highest quality. Stefany's desperate cry of "Wait, not yet" is met with some inchoate static and then the loudest sound in the world. So she just keeps typing, politely trying to pretend not to hear the loudest sound in the world as Jean saws through the museum walls and she keeps glancing up, expecting to see museum staff rushing in to find out what is going on. But you don't investigate what you don't even recognize as a possibility, and many things are often happening in an institution without everyone knowing where or why. So the staff continue to go about their own business, and the saw screams and moans and rattles for a few more minutes. Unable to hear the "Stop, stop, it's too loud," Jean just keeps on chopping and Stefany keeps on typing, and within a few minutes there is a new hole and a new tunnel.

A bit later, Jean goes back into the tunnel and works his way to the spot where he makes the new peephole behind the fake drawing. We decide to tell Seb about some of the secrets. The pressure to tell someone is just too great, and the fact that his own picture was the "cover" for our first peephole is too delicious. In fact, Jean has come dangerously close to letting Seb in on the secrets over the past few weeks, but it seemed almost impossible to do. "How do you subtly suggest to someone that we may have tunneled into the walls of the museum, created a secret spy hole, and covered it with a picture of his face?" I asked Jean. He didn't have an answer. Stefany tells Seb to stand in front of the wall of drawings, and as he does, Jean, who is in the new secret room, slides the fake drawing aside and Seb can see Jean's eyeball peeking through the wall. Seb turns back to Stefany and me with a look on his face that is difficult to describe, a mix of shock, terror, and admiration.

Day Eighty-two

Today we decide to enter ourselves retroactively into history. We've devised an alteration to a model of the 1964 World's Fair that sits on a circular table just outside the entrance to the Panorama. Corona Park was, in fact, expressly built for the purpose of hosting the 1939 World's Fair. The model, which is protected by a Plexiglas dome, shows all the pavilions around the fairground from 1964. One thing it does not show is the Flux Factory pavilion. A screwdriver, a small box, and a tiny flag are the means to remedy that. Afterward I make a clue trail leading to the model. I take a picture of the model with our new pavilion and tape it under another exhibit about the World's Fair close to the model. Then I take a picture of the picture under that exhibit and tape it under a bench in the next room of the museum. Then I take another picture of that picture and so forth. I tack the last picture up on the Fluxture so that, conceivably, one could follow the picture clues from our room all the way around the museum to the model alteration. Stefany and Jean and I agree that altering the model was preparation, as it were, for the Panorama.

Day Eighty-eight

We've discovered how to get under and onto the Panorama. This is, of course, a transgression of the highest order. If there is one thing at the museum that verges on the sacred it is the Panorama. And that is what makes it irresistible. This evening just before closing Jean takes his shoes off and goes out onto the Panorama with a small model of a building given to us by John Norwood. John is the only other artist showing in the international exhibit who ever comes to the museum regularly. He has a wall full of architectural models made from the detritus of the material he used as a model builder for I. M. Pei. John's exhibit consists of an infinity of tiny impossible buildings of which no engineer would ever approve, with even tinier Playboy bunnies sitting nonchalantly atop them. It's like a strange Utopia inhabited by the cast of *Benny Hill*. We are always very happy to see John, tugging at his cigarette and showing us the peculiar graphs and tables he made about his trips to Europe decades earlier. He likes to say, "I'm very lucky, I have a good life." It isn't a very profound statement, but I've never heard anyone say it like he does and in the way that you know it to be true. Jean takes the Norwood Building and places it roughly on the spot in College Point, Queens, where John has his studio. If such a building did exist in College Point, Queens, it would be a marvel; it's larger than the model of the Statue of Liberty. Then, in an unplanned moment of inspiration on his way back, he grabs a boat from the Hudson River and scurries off the Panorama. We drive from the museum out to the far West Side of upper Manhattan. Jean holds the boat out of the window of the car and shoots a video of it traversing the streets and bridges from Queens to Manhattan. It is Stefany's thinking that the boat should be returned to the actual Hudson River at about the spot where Jean removed it from the model. We park and walk out onto the rocks. Jean writes, IF FOUND, PLEASE RETURN TO THE QUEENS MUSEUM OF ART on the side of the boat. We attach it to a piece of Styrofoam and toss it out onto the water. The sun is extremely bright as it sets. At first the boat just bobs along. Then it catches a current and disappears north along the Hudson. Maybe one day it will be found.

Day Eighty-nine

It is time to leave. But it is difficult to leave for two reasons. One of the reasons is emotional: We've grown accustomed to the place and the people in it. We created the room and the Fluxture, and it has become a remarkable thing to us, even a beautiful thing. We're fond of the Queens Museum of Art. The second reason is practical: We have a room filled with stuff part of the purpose of which is to hide giant holes in the walls. And so we begin a rather tender process of trying to repair them. I find Jean lying on his back in the Kissing Booth, listening to a Kenny Rogers song on the 45 player, looking weepy. We decide to leave the minibar, the red velvet drapery, the pillows Stefany stuffed with parts of the Fluxture, and some other clandestine bits to future visitors. The 45 player and the giant deer head were to go back to our space in Queens with the rest of the Fluxture, and live out their days as a permanent installation in the Flux executive bathroom. I grab a can of Spackle and half a sheet of drywall from the back and bring them into the room. Jean and Stefany are moving things around and positioning themselves in the room so that I can huddle in various areas and do my patchwork. It is quick work and it is sloppy work. Really, it is a disaster. It looks like the work of a small child. When we finally pull some of the things from the room and take a glance around, it is clear that we will have no way to explain it. Richie walks into the room a few minutes after I've finished and looks at me quizzically. We just stare at each other for a few seconds, and then he says, "What the hell happened in here?" I look at him for a few more seconds without responding. "We had to . . . anchor some things in the walls . . . and then rip them out . . . and we wanted to help you out by fixing things up again," I say. It is an absurd explanation for the mangled walls. Richie looks at me again with pity; it is a terrible explanation, though he can provide no better one. But perhaps the best of several possibilities has occurred. He has decided that we are simply idiots. The cost of being viewed as morons confers one important benefit: the secrets will be preserved for a little while at least.

We walk out of the museum for the last time with armfuls of junk slowly carried in over the past months and emerge into the cool fall of Corona Park. We have entombed the Kissing Booth, sealed it up until some future date when they reconfigure the walls inside the museum and unearth our secret oasis. There are riches in their walls and ceilings and forgotten places. The whole museum had become our sepulchre, but one in which every visitor had the potential for becoming an archaeologist, discovering a whole world beyond what was expected in a visit to the Panorama, revealed in tiny bits of debris and dated beans, pictures and notes. All one had to do was get a little off the beaten path. The anonymity of treasure is always personalized by the finder, and this would be how we continued to communicate with visitors long after our exeunt—to tell them a little about ourselves, about becoming a part of the museum, about our Fluxture. We have left behind all of our time capsules and alterations to their own fates and to the ways that they happen to reenter the history of the Queens Museum of Art in the future. And so we're leaving it all to the past and to the future simultaneously, not exactly what we anticipated on that first day but something we won't soon forget. Neither, we imagine, will the Queens Museum of Art.

April 2004

My Crowd

Or, Phase 5: A Report from the Inventor of the Flash Mob

BILL WASIK

[T]hey have a goal which is there before they can find words for it.
This goal is the blackest spot where most people are gathered.
—Elias Canetti

Introduction

Before we break down our present cultural situation, it will be worthwhile to
revisit the concept of *deindividuation*, which psychologists put forward in the
mid-twentieth century to address the question of evil more generally. As first
defined by Festinger, Pepitone, and Newcomb (1952), deindividuation is "a
state of affairs in a group where members do not pay attention to other individuals *qua* individuals"; when in a crowd or pack, the theory ran, each man
sees he doesn't stand out and so his inhibitions melt away. Indeed, the writers
observed, even "the delegates to an American Legion convention, all dressed in
the same uniform manner, will sometimes exhibit an almost alarming lack of
restraint." Zimbardo (1969) broke down the causation into ten input variables,
enumerated A through J, ranging from anonymity (A) and arousal (E) to sen-
sory input overload (F) and altered states of consciousness (J). Experimental
heft was soon supplied by Diener, Fraser, Beaman, and Kelem (1976) in their

paper "Effects of Deindividuation Variables on Stealing Among Halloween Trick-or-Treaters," which put hard numbers to the theory (see Figure 1).

FIGURE I — PERCENTAGE OF CHILDREN TRANSGRESSING

	Total number of children	Percent transgressing
Nonanonymous		
Alone	40	7.5
Group	384	20.8
Anonymous		
Alone	42	21.4
Group	297	57.2

In recent decades, the concept of deindividuation has fallen into scientific neglect, and yet I believe that it possesses great theoretical usefulness today. Consider the generational cohort that has come to be called the *hipsters*—i.e., those hundreds of thousands of educated young urbanites with strikingly similar tastes. Have so many self-alleged aesthetes ever been more (in the formulation of Festinger et al.) "submerged in the group"? The hipsters make no pretense to divisions on principle, to forming intellectual or artistic camps; at any given moment, it is the same books, records, films that are judged au courant by all, leading to the curious spectacle of an "alternative" culture more unanimous than the mainstream it ostensibly opposes. What critical impulse does exist among their number merely causes a favorite to be more readily abandoned, as abandoned—whether Friendster.com, Franz Ferdinand, or Jonathan Safran Foer—it inevitably will be. Once abandoned, it is never taken up again.

Over those who would *sell* to the hipsters, then, hangs the promise of instant adoption but also the specter of wholesale and irrevocable desertion. One thinks of Volkswagen, which for years has produced lavish network spots with plots that play to hipster preoccupations, all artfully shot on grainy stock, layered over with the latest in ethereal priss-pop, and for what? Fleeting ubiquity and then ruin; today the company is in disastrous straits, its target U.S. demographic once again favoring Toyotas, Hondas, and even the upstart Koreans. With a rising generation so mercurial, one wonders whether even the notion of "branding," i.e., the building of long-term reputations, which has remained the watchword among our corporations for more than a decade, will itself come to lose its luster; whether the triumph of Internet commerce, the widening readership of online news and blogs (with the concomitant narrowing of the news cycle, such that stories are often considered stale by the time a newspaper can print them), and the proliferation of cable television channels (many of which are devoted either explicitly to shopping or effectively to product placement) will swing tastes so faddishly that rather than courting consumers for life, the corporation will be content merely to hitch itself to a succession of their whims.

Perhaps this is the explanation for Fusion Flash Concerts, an otherwise inexplicable marketing program this past summer in which Ford, attempting to sell a new sedan to the under-thirty-five market, partnered with Sony to appropriate what may be the most forgettable hipster fad of the past five years. That fad is the "flash mob," which, according to a definition hastily added in 2004 to the *Oxford English Dictionary*, is "a public gathering of complete strangers, organized via the Internet or mobile phone, who perform a pointless act and then disperse again." In fact the flash mob, which dates back only to June 2003, had almost entirely died out by that same winter, despite its having spread during those few months to all the world's continents save Antarctica. Not only was the flash mob a vacuous fad; it was, in its very form (pointless aggregation and then dispersal), intended as a metaphor for the hollow hipster culture that spawned it.

I know this because I happen to have been the flash mob's inventor. My association with the fad has heretofore remained semi-anonymous, on a first-name-only basis to all but friends and acquaintances. For more than two years, I concealed my identity for scientific purposes, but now that my experiment is essentially complete, corporate America having fulfilled (albeit a year later than expected) its final phase, I finally feel compelled to offer a report: on the flash mob, its life and times, and its consummation this summer in the clutches of the Ford Motor Company.

Phase 1: Initial Experiment

On May 27, 2003, bored and therefore disposed toward acts of social-scientific inquiry, I sent an email to sixty-some friends and acquaintances. The message began:

You are invited to take part in MOB, the project that creates an inexplicable mob of people in New York City for ten minutes or less. Please forward this to other people you know who might like to join.

More precisely, I *forwarded* them this message, which, in order to conceal my identity as its original author, I had sent myself earlier that day from an anonymous webmail account. As further explanation, the email offered a "frequently asked questions" section, which consisted of only one question:

Q. Why would I want to join an inexplicable mob?
A. Tons of other people are doing it.

Watches were to be synchronized against the U.S. government's atomic clocks, and the email gave instructions for doing so. In order that the mob not form until the appointed time, participants were asked to approach the site from all four cardinal directions, based on birth month: January or July, up Broadway from the south; February or August, down Broadway from the north; etc. At 7:24 P.M. the following Tuesday, June 3, the mob was to converge upon Claire's Accessories, a small chain store near Astor Place that sells barrettes, scrunchies, and such. The gathering was to last for precisely seven minutes, until 7:31, at which time all would disperse. "NO ONE," the email cautioned, "SHOULD REMAIN AT THE SITE AFTER 7:33."

My subjects were grad students, publishing functionaries, cultured technologists, comedy writers, aspiring poets, musicians, actors, novelists, their ages ranging from the early twenties to the middle thirties. They were, that is to say, a fairly representative cross section of hipsters, and these were people who did not easily let themselves get left out. I rated the project's chances as fair to good.

As it happened, MOB #1 would fail, but on a technicality—apparently the NYPD had been alerted beforehand, and so we arrived to find six officers and a police truck barring entrance to the store.[1] Yet the underlying science seemed sound, and for MOB #2, two weeks later, only minor adjustments were required. I found four ill-frequented bars near the intended site and had

---

[1]This would prove to be the project's only run-in with the law, though the legality of the project remains a murky question to this day. As the sender of the email, I suspect that I might have been found guilty of holding a demonstration without a permit, and could also have been held liable for any damages done by the mob. For the Nuclear Option—a follow-up to the Mob Project that remains unimplemented—these sorts of legal issues are to be skirted through an automation of

the participants gather at those beforehand, again split by the month of their birth. Ten minutes before the appointed time, slips of paper bearing the final destination were distributed at the bars. The site was the Macy's rug department, where, all at once, two hundred people wandered over to the carpet in the back left corner and, as instructed, informed clerks that they all lived together in a Long Island City commune and were looking for a "love rug."

E-MAIL MOB TAKES MANHATTAN, read the headline two days later on *Wired News*. The successful result was also hailed in blogs, and soon I received emails from San Francisco, Minneapolis, Boston, Austin, announcing their own local chapters. Some asked for advice, which I very gladly gave. ("[B]efore you send out the instructions, visit the spot at the same time and on the same day of the week, and figure out how long it will take people to get to the mob spot," I told Minneapolis.) One blog proprietor[2] gave the concept a name— "flash mobs"—after a 1973 science-fiction short story, "Flash Crowd," which deals with the unexpected downside of cheap teleportation technology: packs of thrillseekers who beam themselves in whenever a good time is going down. The story's protagonist, Jerryberry Jensen, is a TV journalist who inadvertently touches off a multiday riot in a shopping mall, but eventually he clears his name by showing how *technology* was to blame. Similar claims, as it happens, were soon made about flash mobs, but I myself believe that the technology played only a minor role. The emails went out a week before each event, after all; one could have passed around flyers on the street, I think, to roughly similar effect. What the project harnessed was the *joining urge*, a drive toward deindividuation easily discernible in the New York hipster population.

The basic hypothesis behind the Mob Project was as follows: seeing how all culture in New York was demonstrably commingled with *scenesterism*, the appeal of concerts and plays and readings and gallery shows deriving less from the work itself than from the social opportunities the work might engender, it should theoretically be possible to create an art project consisting of *pure scene*—meaning the scene would be the entire point of the work, and indeed would itself constitute the work.

the entire process. In Nuclear, a network of computer servers, located offshore, will serve as sign-up points for a worldwide email list. When the total number of addresses on the list reaches some threshold—10 million, perhaps—the servers "detonate," and all on their lists receive an email in the morning instructing them to converge in the center of their city that same afternoon.

[2] Sean Savage, of Cheesebikini.com.

At its best, the Mob Project brought to this task a sort of formal unity, as can be illustrated in MOB #3, which took place fifteen days after #2 and was set in the Grand Hyatt, a hotel fronting on Forty-second Street adjacent to Grand Central Station. Picture a lobby a whole block long sporting well-maintained fixtures in the high eighties style, gold-chrome railings and sepia-mirror walls and a fountain in marblish stone, with a mezzanine ringed overhead. The time was set for 7:07 P.M., the tail end of the evening rush hour; the train station next door was thick with commuters, as was (visible through the hotel's tinted-glass facade) the sidewalk outside, but the lobby was nearly empty: only a few besuited types, guests presumably, sunk here and there into armchairs. Starting five minutes beforehand the mob members slipped in, in twos and threes and tens, milling around in the lobby and making stylish small talk.

Then all at once, we rode the elevators and escalators up to the mezzanine and wordlessly lined the banister, as depicted in Figure 2. The handful of hotel guests were still there, alone again, except now they were confronted with a hundreds-strong armada of hipsters overhead, arrayed shoulder to shoulder, staring silently down. But intimidation was not the point; we were staring down at *where we had just been,* and also across at one another, two hundred artist-spectators commandeering an atrium on Forty-second Street

FIGURE 2 — SCHEMATIC, MOB #3 IN GRAND HYATT HOTEL

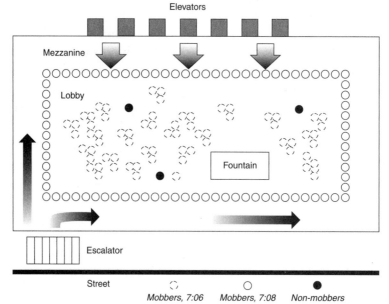

as a coliseum-style theater of self-regard. After five minutes of staring, the ring erupted into precisely fifteen seconds of tumultuous applause—for itself—after which it scattered back downstairs and out the door, just as the police cruisers were rolling up, flashers on.

Phases 2 & 3: Propagation and Backlash

I endeavored to devise a *media strategy* on the project's own terms. The mob was all about the herd instinct, I reasoned, about the desire not to be left out of the latest fad; logically, then, it should grow as quickly as possible and then—this seemed obvious—buckle under the weight of its own popularity. I developed a single maxim for myself, as custodian of the mob: "Anything that grows the mob is pro-mob." And in accordance with this principle, I gave interviews to all reporters who asked. In the six weeks following MOB #3, I did perhaps thirty different interviews, not only with local newspapers (the *Post* and the *Daily News*, though not yet the *Times*—more on that later) but also with *Time*, *Time Out New York*, the *Christian Science Monitor*, the *San Francisco Chronicle*, the *Chicago Tribune*, the Associated Press, Reuters, Agence France-Presse, and countless websites.

There was also the matter of how I would be identified. My original preference had been to remain entirely anonymous, but I had only half succeeded; at the first, aborted mob, a radio reporter had discovered my first name and broadcast it, and so I was forced to be Bill—or, more often, "Bill"—in my dealings with the media thereafter. "[L]ike Cher and Madonna, prefers to use only his first name," wrote the *Chicago Daily Herald*. To those who asked my occupation I replied simply that I worked in the "culture industry." (I was, and still am, an editor at this magazine.)

Usually a flash-mob story would invoke me roughly three quarters of the way down, as the "shadowy figure" at the center of the project. There were dark questions as to my intentions.[3] "Bill, who denies he is on a power-trip, declined to be identified," intoned Britain's *Daily Mirror*. Here is an exchange from Fox News's *On the Record with Greta Van Susteren*:

---

[3]It became evident that the "shadowy" nature of the project was helping to spread it in the media. In the Nuclear Option, the project is designed to seem even more dangerous—not only anonymous and automated, but threatening to inflict "benevolent catastrophes" (as the Nuclear manifesto would describe them) on all major world cities—so as to spread even more widely.

ANCHOR: Now the guy who came up with the Mob Project is a mystery man
  named Bill. Do either of you know who he is?

MOBBER ONE: Nope.

MOBBER TWO: Well, I've—I've emailed him. That's about it.

MOBBER ONE: Oh, you have? . . .

ANCHOR: What—what—who is this Bill? Do you know anything about him?

MOBBER TWO: Well, from what I've read, he's a—he works in the culture industry, and that's—that's about as specific as we've gotten with him.

By MOB #6—in which, on the first Thursday evening in August, five
hundred mobbers suddenly fell to their knees in the Times Square Toys "R" Us
and cowered before the store's animatronic, to-scale Tyrannosaurus rex—
flash mobs had been either scheduled or executed not only in scores of U.S.
cities but also in Toronto, Zurich, Vienna, Berlin, Rome. The following week,
the interview request from the *New York Times* finally arrived. On the phone
the reporter, Amy Harmon, made it clear to me that the *Times* knew it was behind on the story. They would be remedying this, she told me, by running a
prominent piece on flash mobs in their Sunday "Week in Review" section.

What the *Times* did, in fascinating fashion, was not just to run the backlash story (which I had been expecting in three to five more weeks) but to do
so *preemptively*—i.e., before the backlash actually had materialized. Harmon's
piece bore the headline GUESS SOME PEOPLE DON'T HAVE ANYTHING BETTER
TO DO, and its nut sentence ran: "[T]he flash mob juggernaut has now run
into a flash mob backlash that may be spreading faster than the fad itself." As
evidence, she mustered the following:

> E-mail lists like "antimob" and "slashmob" have sprung up, as did a Web
> site warning that "flashmuggers" are bound to show up "wherever there's
> groups of young, naive, wealthy, bored fashionistas to be found." And a
> new definition was circulated last week on several Web sites: "flash mob,
> noun: An impromptu gathering, organized by means of electronic com-
> munication, of the unemployed."

Two email lists, a website, and a forwarded definition hardly constituted a
"backlash" against this still-growing, intercontinental fad, but what I think Harmon and the *Times* rightly understood was that a backlash was the only avenue
by which they could advance the story. The competition had soundly beaten the

Times already on what, using my taxonomy, one might call the Phases 1 and 2 stories (the experiment and its rapid propagation), and so their thinking progressed naturally to the subsequent phase—i.e., the backlash. It followed inexorably from the subconscious logic of contemporary journalism: just as a popular president requires momentous-looking photo spreads in newsweeklies, or as the rise of a new technology requires think-pieces about its threat to the very fabric of civil society, so a fad like the flash mob requires a backlash.[4] Whether through direct causation or mere journalistic intuition, the *Times* timed its backlash story (8/17/03) with remarkable accuracy (see Figure 3).

FIGURE 3 — MEDIA REFERENCES TO FLASH MOBS, BY WEEK

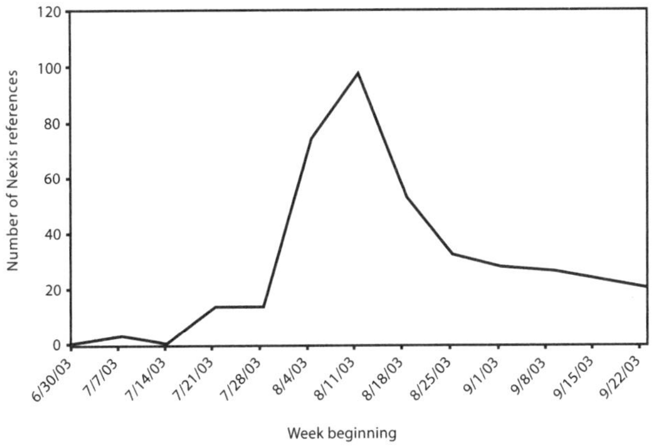

Week beginning

I announced that MOB #8, in early September, would be the last. The site was a concrete alcove right on Forty-second Street, just across from the Condé Nast building. Participants had been told to follow the instructions blaring from a cheap boom box I had set up beforehand atop a brick ledge. The cheering of the hundreds grew so great that it drowned out the speakers. The mob had become unmoored. All of a sudden a man in a toque, apparently some sort of opportunistic art shaman, opened his briefcase to reveal a glowing

[4]To my further surprise, Harmon wrote a second article on flash mobs on August 31, in which she attended MOB #7 and wrote with noticeable excitement about the same trend she had peremptorily dismissed just two weeks earlier. Here, I think, it was not journalistic logic but rather her own professional logic that held sway; this piece was for the City section, in which *Times* reporters are sometimes allowed to "write." E.g., "I tore myself away from observing the bizarre ballet and hurried to the back. A muted euphoria kicked in. The mob was proud of itself. It was almost impossible to detect ironic detachment. People smiled. I smiled."

neon sign, and the crowd bent to his will. He held up two fingers and the mob began chanting "Peace!"

The project had been hijacked by a figure more charismatic than myself. The stage had been set for Phase 4.

FIGURE 4 — STANLEY MILGRAM'S CROWD EXPERIMENT

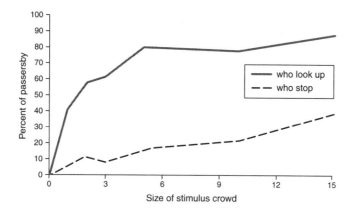

Prior Research

When a British art magazine asked me who, among artists past or present, had most influenced the flash-mob project, I named Stanley Milgram—the social psychologist best known for his authority experiments, in which he induced average Americans to give seemingly fatal shocks to strangers. As it happens, I later discovered that Milgram himself did a project much like a flash mob, in which a "stimulus crowd" of his confederates, varying in number from one to fifteen, stopped on a busy Manhattan sidewalk and all at once looked up to the same sixth-floor window. The results can be seen in Figure 4, a chart from his paper "Note on the Drawing Power of Crowds of Different Size."

Stanley Milgram deserves recognition, I believe, as one of the crucial artists of the preceding century. Consider his crowd experiment, which, it must be admitted, is fairly thin gruel as science: everyone knows that such an effect would be observed, and what value is there in quantifying it? No, the value of this experiment is entirely in its performance, the unadorned audacity of it, a small crowd in simple unison bucking the city's flow—a Fluxus-style "happening" but without the blinkered optimism, and in that respect closer, perhaps, to a Ray Johnson "nothing." Milgram's crowd study was far less explanatory than it was *expressive*, serving as an elegant metaphor for conformism while adding little to our scientific understanding of who conforms or why.

Other of Milgram's creations seem more akin to collaborative art. He had Parisians draw "mental maps" of their city that he then himself collated into a consensus work—prefiguring, for example, the contemporary artists Komar and Melamid's brilliant "favorite painting" projects of the 1990s. In yet another premonition of Ray Johnson, Milgram also fixated on the mail as a medium; this was chiefly through his famous "lost letter" technique, in which dozens of sealed, stamped letters addressed to controversial-sounding organizations (e.g., Equal Rights for Negroes, Friends of the Nazi Party) were left such that they would be found by passersby and mailed (or not) to their destinations. In this manner he even attempted to predict the outcome of the 1964 presidential election, leading to a remarkable *coup de théâter* in which hundreds of letters in support of each candidate were dropped onto Worcester from a prop plane.

The Milgramite tradition in art would be defined, I think, by the following premise: that man, whom we now know to respond predictably to social forces, is therefore himself the ultimate artistic medium. This is certainly the primary force of Milgram's authority experiments: others had done research on conformism and authority, but what set Milgram's apart was the vertiginousness of the narrative he made out of men. On the faux shock machine itself, with its manufacturer's label (SHOCK GENERATOR, TYPE ZLB) from the fictitious "Dyson Instrument Company" in Waltham, Mass., was a series of thirty labeled switches, beginning with SLIGHT SHOCK and ending with EXTREME INTENSITY SHOCK, DANGER: SEVERE SHOCK, and, simply, X X X. This final switch, so ominously marked, was nevertheless quite willingly employed, even after the subject's screams had subsided into silence. This was what stirred the public—the sheer barbarity of what Milgram had made men do, and how easily he made them do it.

There is also a virulent counterstrain of this tradition, one that Milgram himself characteristically foresaw: reality television, which seeks to entertain through simple documentary voyeurism. In one of his last published papers before his death, he co-authored an essay on the subject of *Candid Camera*, which could fairly be called the ur-reality-TV show. His essay was largely and justifiably laudatory—the show "gives us a new vision through the disruption of the habitual," he wrote, in a neat summation of the Milgramite aesthetic. And yet: "Above all, *Candid Camera* is a commercial activity. The overriding goal of the producer is to create materials that can be sold to a network or a sponsor. . . . The scientific"—and here we may as well substitute *artistic*—"deficiencies of the *Candid Camera* material stem from its origin as commercial entertainment."

His most telling example of such deficiencies is in the way the show is managed down to a simple, digestible narrative message—in *Candid Camera*'s case, for laughs, but the point could have been as easily applied to the cheap drama of *The Apprentice* or the luridity of *Trading Spouses*. "[T]he viewer is instructed by the narrator about exactly what to look for; his comments reinforce the notion that what we are about to see will be funny," Milgram wrote. "Studio laughter accompanies each episode as a way of continually defining the actions as funny, prompting the home viewer to experience the scene as amusing, rather than feeling sympathy or compassion for the victim's plight, or searching to understand it." It is precisely here that we who would make Milgramite art must keep vigilant: in resisting simple story lines and embracing, instead, the ambiguities in our data.

Phase 4: Co-optation

To the many demerits of City Hall Plaza in Boston I can add this: it is a singularly poor spot to hold a flash mob. It is as if the space were calibrated to render futile any gathering, large or small, attempted anywhere on its arid expanse. All the nearby buildings seem to be facing away, making the plaza's eleven acres of concrete and brick feel like the world's largest back alley. There is no nearby community to speak of, the historic neighborhood there—the old Scully Square, a convivial knot of tightly packed apartment houses and popular burlesque theaters—having been entirely razed in the early 1960s. In its stead was laid down a plaza so devoid of benches, greenery, and other signposts of human hospitality that even on the loveliest fall weekend, when the Common and Esplanade and other public spaces teem with Bostonians at leisure, the plaza stands utterly empty save for the occasional skateboarder grinding a lonely path across its long, shallow steps to nowhere. The Hall itself, hailed at its construction as a paragon of what then was approvingly called the "New Brutalist" movement, approximates both the shape and the charm of an offshore oil platform; its concrete facade is now pocked with spalls and dulled by weeping dark patches of smut.

I had traveled to Boston last summer to observe a "Fusion Flash

Concert"—a marketing campaign I had first learned of two weeks earlier, through a *Financial Times* column emailed to me by a friend. A "series of flash mobbing events," the *FT* had reported, was "being staged by Ford Motor with Sony Pictures Digital to promote the launch of the new Ford Fusion car." *Weren't you always concerned about this?* my friend had written in the subject heading. I had never been concerned about it but rather had expected and even welcomed it, since co-optation of the flash mob by the nation's large conglomerates would, I reasoned, be its final (and fatal) phase. Up to this point, the only sign of co-optation so far had been a 2004 episode of *CSI: Miami*, one of the five top-rated television shows in the nation, that centered around a flash mob. Entitled "Murder in a Flash," the episode begins with a flash mob that leaves a dead body in its aftermath, but by the end—and here is where the writers really earn their residuals—we learn that the stiff *had been there already*, the mob sent later by an honest teen to clue police in to the deed.

That had been a mere reference to flash mobs, whereas Fusion Flash Concerts was a true co-optation: Ford was itself *appropriating* the trend, and was doing so in order to make a product seem cool.[5] By presenting myself as an interested member of the news media, I was able to confirm this latter point with Ford directly. Ford was, a spokesman told me by phone, "looking for cool ways to connect with their target audience," at both a "price point" and what he called a "cool point." The flash concerts idea, he said, had "a spontaneity and a cool factor that was attached to it."

He invited me to come and see a flash concert for myself, and of course I agreed. The featured act would be a band called Staind, whose upcoming album *Rolling Stone* had described as "a unique combo of AA-meeting ballads and fetal-position metal." Most concertgoers would have to register at the site and wait to receive the details just beforehand, but to a reporter in good standing he was willing to reveal the secret show date. It was a week and a half away, in early August—the same date, as a matter of fact, that Staind's new album was to be released.

---

[5]I have been alerted to an even more ambitious co-optation of the idea by Swatch, the watch company. This winter and spring it is running a competition in which contestants stage flash mobs and send videos of them to the company; the winner will be awarded a free trip to Switzerland. A Swatch press release explains: "By using 'Flash mobbing'—spontaneous gatherings that act out humorous and fun exercises—a simple yet strong synergy with the Swatch brand was unearthed and an opportunity to become the 'Flash Mobber's watch of choice' was there for the taking."

Wandering the site two hours before showtime, I was struck by how every vestige of "flash" had already been stripped from the evening's event. The "last-minute" emails had in fact gone out six days beforehand. Two radio stations had been tapped to promote the show with ads ("just to pump everything up," another Ford rep had told me). Newspapers had listed the concert in their daily arts calendars. Here at City Hall Plaza a tremendous soundstage had already been erected, its prodigious backdrop displaying the cover art from Staind's new album. Phalanxes of motorbike cops rumbled around, eyeing the hundred-strong klatch of diehard Stainders lumped directly before the empty stage. Ford had already set up a hospitality tent, had cordoned off a VIP area, and, atop yard-high stands in the near distance, had perched two new Ford Fusions, the eponymous guests of honor, tilted widthwise as if banking gnarly turns.

While we waited for the sound check, Barry Grant, a Ford rep, offered to show me around the product. Barry was a sunny fellow whose face had a pleasingly Mephistophelian aspect, with a neat goatee and a shaved head atop which unnecessary sunglasses were perched. I knew that recent years had not been kind to Ford; its auto operations were losing nearly a billion dollars a quarter, and in May its bonds were reclassified as junk. Its stock price was down by a third since the beginning of the year, and soon (during the course of the Fusion Flash Concerts series) it would drop by even more.

As Barry and I cut through the crowd toward the Fusions, I asked him in very general terms who Ford thought the car's ideal customer was likely to be. As it turns out, he said, the company had done a great deal of "psychographic profiling" on just this question.

"What we're looking at here is someone who's moving ahead in their lives, they're moving forward in their career," he said. "It's a person who's entrepreneurial, thinking outside the box. They're generally young, they're either in a relationship now or are getting married sometime soon, and they're into activities like music, technology, exercise."

Really, I reflected, he was describing no one so much as myself, whose own marriage was then only six weeks away and who was, at least at that moment, in possession of a gym membership.[6]

"See the contrast stitching, and the nice chrome accents and details, the piano-black finish—all for less than twenty and a half." Barry gestured through the window at the dash. "It's all about how this vehicle looks, how it feels, how

---

[6]Since canceled.

it moves, you know?" He delivered his final judgment with genuine awe: "I think we've hit on all the senses with this one."

As we talked, a roadie onstage had begun to test the drums individually. With each stroke a deafening clap shot out across the plaza, caromed off a Brutalist wall, and rebounded past us again, barely diminished. I looked around at the crowd, the average age of which was perhaps nineteen, a motley collection of wan goth girls, leathery semidrifters, wiry North Shore bullies in wifebeaters. A bleach blonde wandered by in a tight T-shirt reading NO BAR'S TOO FAR. I remarked to Barry that, psychographically speaking, the crowd did not seem to be what he and Ford had in mind.

It was true, Barry acknowledged, that the Fusion was "really going for people who are mid-twenties to, say, late thirties," but he added, "We know the vehicle has youth appeal. . . . This vehicle, it kind of shakes things up a little bit. I mean, look at the black one—I think it looks a little bit different from an Accord or Camry." His tone implied severe understatement.

I looked at the black one. In point of fact, the vehicle shook nothing up. Its design was supremely generic, as if an Accord, a Camry, and every other sedan on the market had been meticulously averaged together. I could safely say that no one present at this concert hoped ever to have to buy this car. A word began to hover in my mind with respect to the Fusion Flash Concerts program, and that word was *desperation*.

Subject Population

Boston's first flash mob, in July of 2003, had been entitled "Ode to Bill." In it, hundreds had packed the greeting-card aisles of a Harvard Square department store, telling bystanders who inquired that they were looking for a card for their friend Bill in New York. Although the gesture was rendered somewhat hollow by the fact that I failed to receive a single card, I nevertheless approved of Boston's mob on strictly artistic grounds. Nothing is more defining of hipsterism than semi-ironic coronation of its own *celebrities*, and by making a halfhearted, jesting attempt to elevate me to celebrity status, Boston had given its mob an appropriately sly turn.

Although the field of hipster celebrities is constantly changing, I have attempted a partial version of the current schema in Figure 5. This phenomenon is, I think, a simple corollary of the *drive toward deindividuation* as postulated above. I made explicit reference to this in MOB #7, where partici-

FIGURE 5 — SELECTED HIPSTER CELEBRITIES, CIRCA WINTER 2005-6

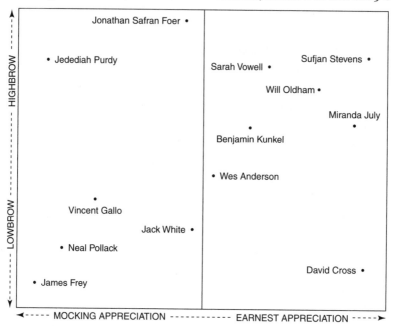

pants were instructed to materialize suddenly as an immense single-file line leading from a disused door on the side of St. Patrick's Cathedral. The line, which would eventually stretch a quarter mile around the entire block-sized church, was to be unaccountably present for precisely five minutes; and if, during this time, a bypasser asked the mobbers what they were lining up for, they were to respond that they "heard they're selling Strokes tickets." The Strokes were a then-popular rock band among the hipsters.

Almost all of the mobs I organized had been, in some sense, jokes on the subject of conformity. MOB #4 pretended to be a tour group from Maryland (my home state) so excited to be in a New York shoe store that they had to pull out their cell phones and tell their friends about it. There was #6, with the genuflecting in the corporate toy store, and then #8, of course, where in essence the mob followed orders made by speakers on a pole—nothing more straightforward than that, I thought. In #7, though, my point was sharpened somewhat, in that the mob was enacting obedience not just in some generic sense but in specific reference to hipster culture, so that the self-ridicule was made explicit. I was pointing out that hipsters, our supposed cultural avant-garde, are in fact a transcontinental society of cultural *receptors*, straining to perceive which shifts to follow. I must hasten to add that this is not entirely their fault: the Internet can propagate any flashy notion, whether it be a style of eyewear or a presidential candidacy, with such instantaneity that a convergence on the "hip" tends now to happen unself-consciously, as a simple matter of course.

But hipsters, after becoming aware of this very dynamic, have responded in a curious and counterintuitive way. Even as they might decry this drive toward unanimity, they continually embrace it and reembrace it in an enthusiastic, almost ecstatic fashion. No phenomenon of recent years illustrated this point as clearly as the aforementioned Strokes, who for most of 2002 held the top-band spot in hipsterdom. This was a band that, albeit enjoyable and skilled, had been clearly manufactured precisely for hipster delectation. Moreover, the hipsters were well aware of this fact, and they complained about it incessantly even as they cued up the record at parties and danced with special abandon. Indeed, one could perceive something palpably different, something animal, in the hipster species when the Strokes came over the speakers; and it was, I think, the reckless, self-abnegating joy of this simple unanimity, of oneness for its own sake. The Strokes made a natural object of this unanimity because their sound—derivative candy, 1970s punk simplicity dressed up with some 1990s indie-rock aloofness—was an easy common denominator. They were no Pixies, no Fugazi, no Joy Division, no band to which pledging allegiance implied the endorsement of a principle. They were, moreover, easily discarded, and the top-band mantle has been passed many times since then, in rapid succession—to equally derivative groups possessing the required sheen of sophistication, such as Franz Ferdinand, Interpol, Bloc Party, and, as of this writing, an outfit called Clap Your Hands Say Yeah.

Popular music, perhaps, has always been a fickle thing. So let us turn to literature. The most significant literary movement the hipsters have produced is *McSweeney's*, which itself had essentially the characteristics of a pop-music fad. Soon after Dave Eggers started the journal/website/publishing house in Brooklyn, its writers became not just sought-after publishing prospects but also minor celebrities whose readings across the country soon overflowed with devotees. The style of these readings, which blended attempts at semiserious prose with comedic flourishes and live music, was itself widely mimicked. (If you have ever been forced at a reading to watch Rick Moody play guitar, you have *McSweeney's* to blame.) Its minimalist graphic design, sometimes down even to its Garamond typeface, was fast borrowed by publications ranging from webzines to major book houses. And its elliptical prose stylings were duly parroted by what seemed at times to be an entire generation of writers.[7]

Like the Strokes, *McSweeney's* promised a cultural watershed for hipsters while making no demands on them. Readers accustomed to a choice between low entertainment and serious literature did not, with this journal, have to make such a choice at all. And for would-be writers, buckling under the weight of the literary task, *McSweeney's* mapped out an easier and far more pleasurable route. In its pages literature appeared as a sort of pot-luck barbecue where the young litterateur, merely by whipping up some absurdist trifle or other, could throw the Frisbee with established authors who were publishing their castoffs there. Almost none of the young writers could deploy *McSweeney's* style to anywhere near the effect that Eggers, a genuinely affecting writer, could; one suspects that most would have been better (if less well known) writers today if the journal had never existed.

Inevitably, even as *McSweeney's* has matured and gained more seriousness of purpose, it has receded in hipster esteem, just as did trucker hats, Hush Puppies, the mullet. Like starlings on a trash-strewn field the hipsters alight together, peck intently for a time, and at some indiscernible signal take wing again at once. If they are the American avant-garde it is true, I think, in only this aspect—the unending churn of their tastes, this adult faddishness in the adolescent style.

Propagation Tool: The Blog

While waiting for the sound check, I was given the opportunity to chat with Howie Cockrill, who wrote the official weblog on the Fusion Flash Concerts website. I had very much hoped to meet Howie and had familiarized myself with his work beforehand, because I hoped to make further study of the blog's utility as a propagation device. The role that blogs had played in the spread of flash mobs came very much as a surprise to me; at the time, I had thought word of the mobs would spread through forwarded emails alone, so that the mobs themselves would be cross sections of an unbroken network of

---

[7]I should mention here that I myself made a few minor contributions to *McSweeney's* and its website. Also, with regard to the preceding paragraph, I own records by all the bands mentioned and have seen some of them live in concert.

acquaintanceship—i.e., any mob attendee would sit at the end of an email chain that stretched back directly, if distantly, to myself. I refused to put up a website for the project, or to reveal the project's email address to reporters who had not yet learned it, in order that the mob would be made only by this sort of direct person-to-person contact, extended out exponentially. Each person who forwarded the email was, in my view, taking on the project as their own; in enlisting his or her own social network each was as responsible for the mob, earned as much praise or blame for it, as I.

Yet when people had begun to ask if they might post the mob emails on their blogs, I concluded that the answer should be yes. It is true that blogs, like all websites, are inherently undirected, in that anyone can navigate to them as he or she pleases, and this was definitely a concern: I did not want anyone to learn the mob details without making human contact with another mob member. But blogs are by their nature such intimate endeavors that even the most widely read among them seem to foster a sense of close connectedness among their readers. This stems, perhaps, from their inherently arcane content—i.e., the blogger's ceaseless mental minutiae, of which any avid reader will be a truly compatible soul. A mob spread partly by blogs was still, as I had intended, a virtual community made physical.

Howie's Fusion Flash Concerts blog, though, was a somewhat more complicated case. He normally wrote on a group blog called "Crazy Talk," where he offered such comments as the following:

> [W]hen bands start to get noticed, all sorts of people come out of the woodwork with contracts & pens, looking to "help their career"—record labels, managers, publicists, publishers, producers, distributors, accounting firms and let's not forget lawyers. . . . [M]ost artists live completely in the dark about the terms of the contracts they sign, the money coming in and going out, their obligations to the different parties they sign on with and vice versa. . . . [M]usicians are so fucked its not even funny.

But on the Fusion Flash Concerts blog, one encountered a different Howie:

> I'm out of breath from typing so much, but there's just so much to say! So here's the details for the next flash concert: JERMAINE DUPRI will hit the stage @ 8 PM @ CENTENNIAL PARK in Downtown Atlanta! (Doors open at 6:30 PM). You think its hot in Atlanta now . . . just wait 'til tomorrow night!

Or:

The Jermaine Dupri show in Atlanta was just plain nuts! His So So Def
crew stirred it up good, and the crowd got down so hard that it rained.
           Now its time to pass the torch for the next flash concert!

When I met Howie, I brought up this issue of *tone* and found him ad-
mirably self-aware on the subject. He called his posts "experiential reviews,"
by which he meant "not, this is what I think of the band, or this is what I think
of how the show went, but this is what the audience thought of the show." He
made his point a little more explicit: "I try to infuse a little bit of hyperbole
into it. Make it a little bit of a short story, you know what I mean?" In order to
chat, he and I had retreated from the din of the crowd into the Plaza's modernist tundra. Howie is an affable Arkansan with half-tinted glasses and a full
but well-maintained blond beard; when not blogging he was a law student at
the University of San Francisco, and had been set up with the gig, which he
called "the most sweet summer job of all time," by a friend who worked at
Sony. On the subject of Staind, Howie was noncommittal, but he added: "It's
popular for a reason, I guess—you know? And that's sort of what I have to tap
into when I write the reviews. These people obviously love Staind, and there's
a reason that they love Staind."

The sound check finally went on at nearly 6:30, and afterward I returned
to the media desk to wait for the show. A giant Ford rep with a graying goatee
asked me about my story. I was writing about what happened to flash mobs, I
told him.

He looked at me intensely. "They're dead," I thought I heard him say.

I stared back at him. Here, finally, was a Ford rep willing to throw
down.

"The Dead," he said again. "They'd do concerts like this. And raves. Flash
concerts are pretty much like raves." I could barely hide my disappointment at
this turn. We looked out at the restless crowd of "flash mobbers" packing up
against the stage, their boredom having prompted them to throw a hailstorm
of increasingly dangerous material into the air: balloons, then empty water
bottles, then full water bottles, then aluminum cans. Sporadic fistfights had
begun to break out.

The Ford rep shook his head at the scene and smiled. "Everybody wants
to feel like an insider," he said.

Social Ramifications: Howard Dean and "The Perfect Storm"

In the media coverage of flash mobs, the most curious undercurrent was the no-tion, almost a wish, that they would someday become something serious. A very smart person named Howard Rheingold happened a year before the fad to have published a book called *Smart Mobs*, about the phenomenal social ramifications of mobile-phone and other miniaturized computing technologies—ideas that the "flash mob" frankly seemed a nihilistic perversion of, but Rheingold let him-self be drawn into the media scrum nevertheless. Without fail it became his role to supply a quote alleging that this completely puerile fad was in fact a harbinger of something important. "[A] symptom of a phenomenon that has a long-term and large-scale effect," said Rheingold tactfully in the *Dallas Morning News*, which also referred to him as a "futurist"; "early signs of something that's going to grow much bigger," he said in the *Christian Science Monitor*.

Bloggers tended to share this vision, and as the Mob Project persisted in its absurdism they began to chafe. Even those who did not want the mobs to espouse explicit politics nevertheless hoped they might begin to *demonstrate* in some way to the surrounding spectators. For example, MOB #6, in the Times Square Toys "R" Us, was the largest and arguably most successful of all the mobs, but almost unanimously the bloggers panned it. "Another Mob Botched," was the verdict on the blog Fancy Robot: "[I]nstead of setting the Flash Mob out in public on Times Square itself, as everyone had hoped, The Flash Master decided to set it in Toys 'R' Us, with apparently dismal results." SatansLaundromat.com (a photo-blog that contains the most complete visual record of the New York project) concurred—"not public enough," the blogger wrote, without enough "spectators to bewilder." Chris from the CCE Blog wrote: "I think the common feeling among these blogger reviews is: where does the idea go from here? . . . After seeing hundreds of people show up for no good reason, it's obvious that there's some kind of potential for artistic or political expression here."

The idea seemed to be that flash mobs could be made to convey a mes-sage, but for a number of reasons this dream was destined to run aground. First, as outlined above, flash mobs were gatherings of *insiders*, and as such could hardly communicate to those who did not already belong. They were intramural play; they drew their energies not from impressing outsiders or freaking them out but from showing them utter disregard, from using the outside world as merely a terrain for private games. Second, flash mobs were by definition *transitory*, ten minutes or less, and thereby not exactly suited to standing their ground and testifying. Third, in terms of physical space, flash mobs relied on *constraints* to create an illusion of superior strength. I never held mobs in the open, the bloggers complained, in view of enough onlookers, but this was entirely purposeful on my part, for like Colin Powell I hewed to the doctrine of *overwhelming force*. Only in enclosed spaces could the mob generate the necessary self-awe; to allow the mob to feel small would have been to destroy it.[8]

Four months after the final New York flash mob, there was a series of gatherings in Iowa whose dismal outcome supported my theory on these points. Those gatherings were the "Perfect Storm," four weekend-long pushes by the Howard Dean campaign in Iowa in advance of that state's January 19 caucus. In keeping with their name (which, like "flash mob," employed a properly meteorological metaphor), the Perfect Storm weekends brought in 3,500 out-of-state Dean supporters to walk door to door and stump for their man. The volunteer headquarters occupied an entire city block; the out-of-town storm troopers all wore matching orange stocking caps, precisely to accentuate their number, to flaunt their ubiquity. They were, like a flash mob, a virtual community made physical, in that the great preponderance of the members had developed their relationship with the campaign online.[9] Indeed, Dean's klatch of cybergurus had come to envision the entire campaign as a form of "social software," in which supporters dwelled in a virtual locale called "Dean-Space." When *Wired* magazine asked one of these gurus (a tech entrepreneur named Joi Ito) how these online masses would be led, he replied, "You're not a leader, you're a place. You're like a park or garden. If it's comfortable and cool, people are attracted. Deanspace is not really about Dean. It's about us."

That is: just like flash mobs, the Dean campaign was also *pure scene*, the appeal having become less about the candidate than about his chat rooms, and

---

[8]This also is why the plan for the Nuclear Option is so grand: huge numbers (hundreds of thousands) of attendees will be required to make a mob-style gathering feel large enough out in the open.

[9]Unsurprisingly, those who believed flash mobs should become political often thought that the beneficiary of this advocacy should be Howard Dean. In a particularly surreal development, after the comic strip *Doonesbury* featured a character planning a "flash mob for Dean" at Seattle's Space Needle, the mob actually took place as a result.

FIGURE 6 — DEAN

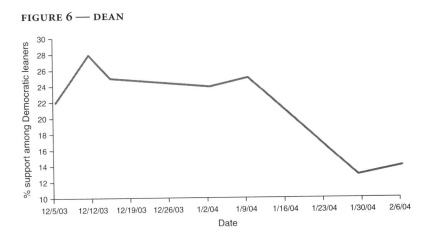

about how connected one felt inside his youthful and seemingly numberless throng. To allow the Dean campaign to feel small—outnumbered, embattled— was to destroy it; and during those four weeks in Iowa, as the orange-hatted 3,500 dissipated out into the frozen plains, spilling out their passion to the po- litically benumbed, the candidate's chances collapsed (see Figure 6).

Experimental Effect on Subjects

There was, however, one successful element of politics in the flash mob—a vague and dark thing, a purely chaotic impulse that (surprisingly enough, for a fad born of the Internet) was tinged almost with Luddism. It could best be seen at the very moment that a mob came together: a sort of fundamental joy at seeing society overtaken, order stymied; at silently infiltrating this pseudo- public space, this corporate space, these chain stores and shopping malls, and then rising at once to overrun them.

The acme of this feeling was (ironically, given its subsequent panning on just these grounds) MOB #6, which for a few beautiful minutes stifled what has to be the most ostentatious chain store in the entire city: the Times Square Toys "R" Us, whose excesses are too many to catalogue here but include, in the store's foyer, an actual operational Ferris wheel some sixty feet in diameter. Up until the appointed time of 7:18 P.M. the mobbers loitered on the upper level, among the GI Joes and the Nintendos and up inside the glittering pink of the two-floor Barbie palace. But then all at once the mob, five hundred strong, crowded around the floor's centerpiece, a life-size animatronic Tyrannosaurus rex that growls and feints with a Hollywood-class lifelikeness. "Fill in all around it," the mob slip had instructed. "It is like a terrible god to you."

Two minutes later, the mob dropped to its knees, moaning and cowering at the beast behind outstretched hands; in doing so we repaid this spectacle, which clearly was the product of not only untold expenditure but many man-months of *imagineering*, with an en masse enactment of the very emotions—visceral fright and infantile fealty—that it obviously had been designed to evoke. MOB #6 was, as many bloggers pointed out pejoratively, "cute," but the cuteness had been massed, refracted, and focused to such a bright point that it became a physical menace. For six minutes the upper level was paralyzed; the cash registers were cocooned behind the moaning, kneeling bodies pressed together; customers were trapped; business could not be done. The terror-stricken store personnel tried in vain to force the crowd out. "Is anyone making a purchase?" one was heard to call out, weakly. As the mob dispersed down the escalators and out into the street, the police arrived downstairs, telling us to leave, but we had already accomplished the task, had delivered what was in effect a warning.

Did these dark impulses remain with the participants, I wondered, or did they dissipate with the mob? This question, as it happens, also troubled Stanley Milgram long after his authority experiments were complete; he was bedeviled his entire life by critics who claimed he had permanently changed his subjects, had in fact victimized them. One such critic, the Welsh poet Dannie Abse, wrote a play entitled *The Dogs of Pavlov* that was loosely based on Milgram's authority experiments. Before its publication as a book, he sent his introduction, which was directly critical of Milgram, to the professor himself for comment.

In the subsequent exchange, Milgram relates the story of a young man who had been through the study in 1964 and six years later sent a letter to Milgram telling him that, as a result, he was seeking CO status to avoid fighting in Vietnam.

> He was going to be sent by our government to Southeast Asia to drop napalm on innocent villagers, to despoil the land, to massacre. He informs me, as many others have done, that the experiment has deepened his understanding of the moral problems of submitting to malevolent authority. He has learned something. He takes a stand. He becomes a conscientious objector. Has he been victimized by the experiment, or has he been liberated by it?

In the same letter, Milgram offers Abse a rationale for the experiments that is stunning in its utter lack of scientific disinterest:

> The obedience experiment is not a study in which the subject is treated as a passive object, acted upon without any possibility of controlling his own experience. Indeed the entire experimental situation has been created to allow the subject to exercise a human choice, and thus express his nature as a person.

Was this not what flash mobs could have done, in some purer and more ideal form? I had meant them as an authority experiment, in the Milgramite style, but was not their promise instead to have been the mirror image—an anti-authority experiment,[10] a play at revolution, an acting-out of the human choice to thwart order?

Conclusion

I myself left the "flash concert" ten minutes after it began: the maximum length of a flash mob. I remained, to my own surprise, a flash-mob purist, even though the day's event had abandoned every precept of the original idea. For the subway ride back to my car I had bought the day's *Globe*, and prominent in the Arts section I found a story about the evening's show.

It began: *The "flash mob" concept where people gather on short notice after contacting each other through e-mails and text messages has come to rock 'n' roll. This summer's Fusion Flash Concert series . . .*

And this, I realized, was the extent of the co-optation, and perhaps its only point. Ford and Sony did not care to steal the concept, or even to sap its essence.

---

[10]This is precisely what the Nuclear Option is intended to be. When first hearing about the project, each person is presented with a private choice: to join the list and thereby become an insider, privy to the details in advance, or else to face being left out. Even strident opponents, I expect, would reason their way toward joining the list—to monitor its activities, for example, or to wage a counterdemonstration on the appointed day—and thus contribute to its growth. Similarly, once the numerical threshold is crossed and the world awakens to find the Nuclear communiqué in its inbox, each of us will again be faced with a choice: to stay inside, stick to the day's agenda items as laid out in the planner, or watch as civic order is cut off at the knees. Could a society of spectators resist bearing witness to its own undoing?

To place stories like this, they needed only to take the term, even if in so doing they stripped it entirely of its meaning. Ford and Sony had managed to take my fad, an empty meditation on emptiness, and to render it even more vacuous. They had become, that is, the new and undisputed masters of the genre.

March 2006

Part Six

Confessions of War

Iraq is the emblematic debacle of this decade, and the hubris of that war's conception—a blinkered faith in the unassailability of one's own wealth, the ineluctability of one's influence, the virtuousness of one's hegemony—is the fundamental attitude of the era. Are not the denial of global warming, the burden of unsustainable consumer debt, the dot-com and housing bubbles all species in the same phylum of magical thinking that produced the prediction of a Baghdad proffering hugs and sweets? We look to the press to puncture such nonsense, but journalists themselves are hardly immune to self-serving fantasies. They spin out new world-historical arguments daily, based on scraps of data. They look at war and strife and suffering and see raises, prizes, promotions, book deals, the mission accomplished as soon as the check has been deposited, no matter the subject's eventual factual fate.

Our anthology closes with two confessions from the field in Iraq, and both can be profitably read as allegories not only of that war but of overreach within the journalistic act itself. "Misinformation Intern" is a memoir by Willem Marx, a young would-be foreign correspondent from England who finds himself employed planting American propaganda in Iraqi newspapers. In "Out of Iraq," Adam Davidson recounts his days as the landlord of a former Baathist house full of journalists and explores how his own foolhardy decisions ultimately led to the house's dissolution and abandonment. Both men refrain from self-justification, opting instead to tell us their stories straight and unadorned, as if for the judgment of history. The arrogance of the men who planned this war may one day receive a full and honest reckoning, but for now these two tales of journalistic folly in the desert will have to suffice.

Misinformation Intern

My Summer as a Military Propagandist in Iraq

WILLEM MARX

Last spring, during my final semester at Oxford, a cousin wrote to tell me that she was planning to work for an American company in Iraq over the summer. She suggested I join her. The company was called Iraqex, and it claimed on its website to have "expertise in collecting and exploiting information; structuring transactions; and mitigating risks through due diligence, legal strategies and security." Iraqex was also looking for summer media interns, my cousin pointed out, who would "interact with the local media" in Baghdad and "pitch story ideas." This was almost too good to be true.

I have wanted to be a reporter, and particularly a foreign correspondent, ever since I was given a copy of John Simpson's *Strange Places, Questionable People* as a teenager. In this memoir, Simpson recounts his many adventures as a BBC reporter: lying in a gutter at Tiananmen Square in 1989, his camera rolling as bullets zipped by; being arrested during the revolution in Romania; and broadcasting from Baghdad in 1991, with U.S. bombs exploding around him. Inspired, I began writing for my high school paper, eventually becoming its editor, and at Oxford, where I majored in Classics, I joined the staff of a campus weekly. (Simpson had edited a quarterly at Cambridge.) By the time I heard from my cousin, I was already slated to begin journalism school in the fall, but I was yearning for some John Simpson–type real-world experience. In fact, Simpson had actually spent years toiling in the BBC's London office before being sent overseas. And here I might be able to get a break right out of college.

I submitted my internship application within days. (Yet by then my cousin's parents had decided she couldn't go to Baghdad and Iraqex had changed its name to Lincoln Group.) After an anxious wait, I was called by one of the company's employees. He was young, himself just out of school, and he ended our short interview by asking whether I would be able to stay focused on work "with mortar fire at the end of the street." I was honest about my credentials. I had been to the Middle East, having vacationed in Egypt and Syria a couple of years before. During a spring break, friends and I had cycled some two thousand miles from Geneva to Damascus. And at university I had handled the pressures of translating Cicero and Polybius. But, I admitted, I couldn't say for sure about the mortar fire. He seemed to think this would be fine.

I soon received phone calls from both of Lincoln Group's founders, Paige Craig and Christian Bailey. Craig, a former Marine, told me that he had spent a great deal of time in Iraq and spoke very generally about the company's important work there. When I asked about security, he assured me that for them this was not a problem. Other foreign companies drove around the country in massive 4 x 4 armored vehicles, basically advertising themselves as targets. But Lincoln Group, he said, operated "under the radar," with employees dressed as locals and Iraqis manning the front offices.

Christian Bailey, like me, was an Oxford man. Yet whereas I had whiled away my time in pubs, he had set up an expensive Bloomberg computer terminal in his dorm room and successfully played the stock market. Although Bailey initially described the media internship as the perfect launch pad for my journalism career, he later offered me a position working on private equity projects in Washington. It was not my dream to become a financial analyst, I had to tell him. I wanted to spend the summer in Baghdad working with real Iraqi reporters. Bailey said he understood but would have to get back to me. A month later, in June, I was told the media internship was mine.

I was flown across the Atlantic to meet my new employers. In downtown Washington, I was surprised by the ubiquity of fresh-faced young men, their blue short-sleeved buttondowns tucked neatly into khakis. Lincoln Group had its headquarters above an Indian grocery on K Street; a small placard in the building's foyer read: VISITORS TO LINCOLN GROUP/IRAQEX, 10TH FLOOR,

SHOULD BE ANNOUNCED IN ADVANCE. On the tenth floor, electricians wired lights in some rooms while in others suited men conferenced behind glass walls. The company's head of human resources, who had only just been hired herself, told me with a weary smile that things had been crazy lately.

Paige Craig popped in to see me as I filled out work papers in a tiny waiting room. Shaking my hand with a mighty grip, he uttered something to the effect of "welcome aboard." He was very well built, with short, tidy hair and the tight khaki trousers and shirt of a military man. As he strode away, he seemed purposeful. Bailey, by contrast, was baby-faced and slight, his sandy-brown hair cut in a Bill Gates bob. In his corner office, we chatted about Oxford. He had studied economics and management at Lincoln College. When I asked whether his college had inspired the company's new name, he shrugged. "Partly," he said cryptically. He did say that Lincoln Group was rapidly expanding and that it offered incredible opportunities for bright young people like me: stock options were available to employees after just three months, and I might consider staying on after the summer. Christian Bailey hadn't yet been to Iraq himself. Although he had planned numerous trips, he said, something always came up that kept him in D.C.

There was still one remaining formality before I was set to go. I had to travel to Fort Belvoir, Virginia, to pick up a Common Access Card, a kind of *passepartout* for military facilities all over the world. The women running the office where I was given immunizations and completed more paperwork said they had a young friend back in the District who would love my British accent. They were going to call her this very instant, they teased, and then I'd have a companion for the evening. They also talked in more solemn tones about all the brave men and women who came through the base and then shipped off to Iraq. In another room a chatty African-American nurse, contracted by the Halliburton subsidiary Kellogg, Brown & Root (KBR), took my vitals and drew blood. She joked as well about the way I spoke and wanted to know about England. Yet when I asked why she needed to make copies of my dental X rays, she suddenly was speechless. "It's for our files," she finally said, shooting me a quick glance and then turning away. In the long silence that followed, I understood. With a body charred beyond recognition or exploded into irretrievable parts, a dental match might be all that remained to identify me.

Only then did I really consider that I would be risking my life for men I had just met and for a company I knew very little about. My pay, I had recently learned, would be a measly $1,000 a month, meaning I would likely lose money over the summer. When I had begged out of eight days of Stateside military training so I could get to Baghdad sooner, the company was only too willing to oblige. "It makes more financial sense for us," I was told. "We'll get more work out of you."

I might have aborted the venture then had I not been envisioning my burgeoning career. I had come to see myself braving the dangers of Iraq for the sake of the good news story, and I liked it when others saw me this way as well. Shortly before flying to America, I had visited my younger brother in Scotland, and he had said he was proud that I was willing to take real risks to pursue a profession. (He also was relieved that I was not becoming another investment banker, like so many other Oxford grads.) When a group of us went to an Edinburgh restaurant one evening, I was seated next to a raven-haired beauty, a half-Italian who had just graduated from university as well. After one of the courses, she asked perfunctorily about my plans for the summer holiday, and I began to talk excitedly about my impending trip. I needed to know whether I could survive in an environment like Iraq, which was now the center of the universe for the kind of reporting I wanted to do. Although dangerous, such work was essential, I said, since people back home needed to understand the painful realities at the other ends of the earth. She now leaned toward me, her dark eyes wide with interest. When I finally finished, she whispered, "That's very sexy."

I arrived at the Baghdad airport on July 7, after waiting for my luggage in Amman for nearly a week. People at the baggage claim shouted like tour guides for KBR employees to gather in one spot, while others, holding aloft signs with the names of various security firms, urged bulky, tattooed men to congregate in groups. But I saw no one there to greet me. As the hall emptied, I noticed a man and woman loitering indifferently near the exit. I eventually made my way over and asked if they were here to meet Willem Marx. They were. Each shook my hand, and then they led me in silence out of the airport and to the back seat of a battered sedan.

On the short drive to the U.S. Army's Camp Victory, a sprawling complex of prefabricated buildings in what was one of Saddam Hussein's many estates, I caught sight of my first bomb-wrecked palace. Its dome had collapsed, and exposed girders poked violently skyward. I asked my new colleagues about their work and what they had done before joining the company. Gina, a fair-skinned woman in her late twenties, said she had a military background in Iraq, and Ryan, who seemed not much older than me, had been a soldier as well. Their answers were so curt that I decided not to delve further.

Once inside Camp Victory, Ryan sent me to buy a transparent neck pouch for my military-contractor identification. I queued behind a group of soldiers, all of whom carried their rifles with them inside the base's PX. Then I was deposited in a dusty trailer, where I sat alone for the rest of the day watching *Lara Croft* and other action films on a giant flat-screen TV.

To get to the villa where I would be living for the summer, I was awakened before dawn and loaded onto what was essentially a Greyhound bus with armored plating and shatterproof windows. The road to Baghdad's Green Zone, where the Lincoln Group villa was located, is known as the Highway of Death, for the number of convoys that have been attacked along its route. And so we trundled along the dangerous road in complete darkness, flanked by a quartet of Humvees and watched over by helicopters with nightscopes.

There were four bedrooms on the villa's ground floor, and I was to share one of these with an Iraqi named Ahmed.[1] Ahmed, who had attended American University in Washington, always wore immaculately pressed shirts and remained clean-shaven. Because he often shared his bed with one of several Baghdadi girlfriends, I moved down the hall after only a few nights. My new roommate, Steve, a recent Brown graduate, had signed on with Lincoln Group for a full year and seemed to be pacing himself accordingly. Most nights he would drink beers bought from a nearby market, and the next day he would sleep well into the afternoon.

The villa's other inhabitants had been sent to Iraq as part of a contract Lincoln Group had with USAID to build training centers for Iraqi businesses.[2] None of them had much experience in the region nor had worked very long for the company. A tall San Franciscan, who passed whole days in the tarpaulin-covered courtyard smoking cigarettes with a former air-conditioning-systems executive from Arizona, had spent a year or so on an archaeological mission in Egypt. When they weren't in the courtyard, these two trawled the Internet, pretending

---

[1]To protect the Iraqis I worked with during my internship, I have changed their names for this article.

[2]This contract was first delayed and then finally canceled, and by mid-August many of these Lincoln Group employees had returned home. Most were outraged by the vast disparity between the vital work that had been promised them by the company back in Washington and the pointlessness of their actual time in Iraq.

to work. They often speculated about the company, suspecting that it might secretly be owned by the Carlyle Group or that some of its employees were really CIA. I asked them whom I should speak to about getting going on my media internship, but they only shrugged. They had no idea. The Arizonan declared the whole organization a mess but couldn't say specifically what he meant by this.

Because I had just two short months in Iraq, I emailed Bailey and Craig back in Washington after several days of inaction. What projects could I begin working on? I wanted to know. Who was in charge here? What could I do to contribute? A day later I received a rather brusque response from Paige Craig. They didn't have time to deal with my little problems. I needed only to take my lead from Jim Sutton, the country manager, whom I had seen just once during my first week.

But my badgering did seem to pay off. I was soon contacted by a Lincoln Group employee named Jon, who formerly had run political campaigns in Chicago and now worked on the company's I.O., or Information Operations. Over lunch at the recently bombed and rebuilt Green Zone Café—an air-conditioned tent with plastic chairs and a TV airing Lebanese music videos—Jon explained that he was returning home for several weeks of R & R and that Jim Sutton had chosen me to be his replacement. Jon quickly sketched out my new I.O. responsibilities. An Army team inside the Al Faw palace, another of Saddam's former residences, would send me news articles they had cobbled together from wire stories and their own reports from the field. It was my job to select the ones that seemed most like Iraqis had written them. I was then to pass these articles along to our Iraqi employees, who would translate the pieces into Arabic and place them in local newspapers. Jon told me that the U.S. Army could hardly carry out this work in their military uniforms, so they hired Lincoln Group, which could operate with far fewer restrictions. It was a bread-and-butter contract, he said, that paid the company about $5 million annually. I asked if the newspapers knew that Lincoln Group or the U.S. military were behind these articles. They did and they didn't, Jon said. The Iraqis working for us posed as freelance journalists, but they also paid editors at the papers to publish the stories—part of the cost Lincoln Group billed back to the military. "Look," Jon assured me, "it's very straightforward. You just have to keep the military happy."

Despite some misgivings, I returned to the villa feeling like my career was starting. I would contribute to the news-making process during war and be embroiled in the politics that this entailed. The experience of doing any work in Baghdad, in and of itself, would help instill in me the skills necessary for survival in other perilous environments. Perhaps I could even change how the company operated and, if at all possible, maybe improve the situation in Iraq through my efforts.

I began my media work on July 14, waking up early to shave in the bathroom's cracked sink and brew some coffee in the sandy kitchen. I chose a spot on the large red sofa in the villa's living room, which also doubled as its office space, and waited for an email to arrive from the military. For several hours I checked the BBC website for news on Iraq, brewed more coffee, and sent emails home, telling friends and family that I was beginning to do real work here. In the afternoon I finally received an email from a First Lieutenant Christopher Denatale that was also copied to a long list of American military personnel with @iraq.centcom.mil address suffixes. The communiqué was labeled "Unclassified/For Official Use Only" and stated simply, "Here are the Corps IO storyboards for 14 JUL 05."

I carefully read the five articles that were attached as PowerPoint slides. The first reported on a speech by then prime minister Ibrahim al-Jaafari, in which he announced that Iraqi troops would soon be able to replace foreign forces. It was accompanied by a photo of Jaafari at a lectern and ended with this bit of uplift: "Combined with the recurring successes of the ISF, Prime Minister Jaafari's remarks inspire a greater degree of hope for the peaceful and progressive future of Iraq."[3] In the second article, also on the progress of the Iraqi Security Forces, the U.S. Army writers at the Al Faw palace put an even more positive spin on the country's prospects. "Unlike the terrorists, who offer nothing but pain and fear, the ISF bring the promise of a better Iraq. No foreign al-Qa'ida mercenary would ever consider bringing gifts to Iraqi children. The Iraqi Army, however, fights for a noble cause. . . . Together with the Iraqi people, they will bring peace and prosperity to the nation."

The remaining stories continued in this vein. The American soldier writing one of them took on the persona of an Iraqi to denounce the terrorist Abu

---

[3]Because I knew so little about Iraq at this point in my internship, I had to spend a good part of that first day looking up acronyms on Google—somewhat more obscure ones such as ISF (Iraqi Security Forces), MCNI (Multi-National Corps Iraq), and PAO (Public Affairs Office) but even, embarrassingly, such things as Centcom and PSYOP. I also realized very quickly that I needed to learn much more about this country, so I ordered a small library of books on Iraqi history and politics from Amazon.

Musab al-Zarqawi, another argued that insurgents were attacking Iraqis solely to instigate a civil war, and the final one concluded with an apparent public-service announcement: "Continue to report suspicious activities and make Iraq safe again." These were far from exemplars of objective journalism, but Jon had said that I should think of the storyboards not so much as news but as messages Iraqis needed to hear. I supposed they were that.

I was to publish at least five stories each week, so I now had to decide which of these, if any, made the cut. After some deliberation, I chose the piece on the insurgency inciting Iraqi-on-Iraqi violence. Its rhetoric was powerful, even Ciceronian, I thought, with the grand sweep of its opening line: "Great triumphs and great tragedies can redirect the course of a people's destiny." And I agreed with its overall message that one destructive act should not beget others. I was to pass along the article to a man named Muhammad, who would see that it was translated from the English. It also fell to me to tell Muhammad where to place the translated piece. Jon had left me a spreadsheet listing Iraqi newspapers and the amounts they charged to run our stories. Yet I knew nothing at all about the media in Iraq, and certainly didn't know the difference between the newspaper *Al Sabah* and the similar sounding *Al Sabah Al Jadeed*. Jon didn't believe this would be a problem, however, having himself started with no regional expertise, and he made it very clear that I should under no circumstances ask the military team for guidance. He warned me that the two majors in charge, Scott Rosen and John Muirhead, would hound me for information on exactly how Lincoln Group placed the stories, and that I should remain cagey about the process, allowing secrecy to swell the perceived value of the company's work. I was to send them only the results of what had been published, detailed in a spreadsheet. The military, Jon said, loves statistics.

From the dozen publications on the list, I picked out *Al Mutamar*, or *The Congress*, because it was one of the least expensive (around $50 per story) and I could see we hadn't used it in a while. (I thought it would be good to mix things up a bit.) Later that day, Steve came into the living room with a story Jon had asked him to put together. Written from the perspective of a frustrated Iraqi citizen, it condemned a recent insurgent attack that had left twenty-three children dead. Steve's information came directly from news sources on the Internet, with no actual reporting of his own, but he had authored what I considered to be a very decent opinion piece. I emailed this to Muhammad as well, asking that it be published in another of the newspapers, *Al Sabah* (*The Morning*), which I selected because it was the most expensive on the spreadsheet, charging over $1,500 to run one of our pieces. Steve's writing, I felt, deserved the best.

I received an email back from Muhammad the following day, acknowledging my instructions and including two Word files. They separately contained the two stories in English and in what I assumed were their Arabic versions, and I saved the files onto my laptop, as Jon had instructed me to do. Two days later I felt a little thrill when Muhammad sent me scanned versions of the "articles" as they appeared in the Iraqi newspapers. Despite the subject matter of Steve's piece, he and I both laughed at the thought that he was now published in a major Iraqi newspaper.

I forwarded the scanned articles to Rosen and Muirhead and received emails thanking me for my work. Then I sat back on the red sofa, proud that I had successfully completed my initial run through this process. I had even made what I believed were sound journalistic decisions.

Over the next weeks, my U.S. military liaisons at the Al Faw palace continued to send me around five storyboards each day. I soon had a better sense of how Lincoln Group was positioned between the Army team and our Iraqi staff, who were themselves the company's sole link to the local press. Lincoln Group had originally signed its media contract with the military's Public Affairs Office, which supplies "real" information to reporters wishing to know about troop casualties or reconstruction projects. But Paige Craig had later convinced the military that his company was better suited to the more covert Information Operations sphere.[4] I was still struggling to get a grip on all this information myself but recognized that there was some power in selecting which storyboards to publish. Although not exactly intoxicating, this power was certainly more significant in the grander scheme of things than anything I had experienced at university.

I also learned that whatever power I possessed was not absolute. When senior commanders labeled storyboards a priority, this trumped my particular journalistic proclivities. One storyboard, with the alliterative headline

---

[4]Although Lincoln Group claims that aspects of this article are inaccurate or exaggerated, it declined to offer specific corrections. "Because the policies of some clients are regarded as controversial and newsworthy by a few members of the media," Suzanne McKoy, the company's director of human resources, wrote, "there has been interest in covering some of our activities. Lincoln Group's commitment to client confidentiality has constrained its ability to correct errors in coverage of the firm."

"Badr Corps Not Baited into Fight," was given a special "emphasis" by General George Casey, the most senior U.S. officer in Iraq at the time, and as such was made a top priority by Majors Rosen and Muirhead. The story took a new tack, it seemed, praising Shiite militias for refraining from retaliatory attacks against Al Qaeda. "The restraint of the Badr Corps and their faith in all Iraqis to stand up to terrorist violence bring great credit to themselves and great honor to all of Iraq," the article opined. "History does not fondly remember murderers and destroyers. History reveres the people who stand up against pain and risk of death to say 'No' to the murderers and destroyers. This is why it is such treacherous blasphemy when the al-Qa'ida gang claims the honored title of 'martyr' for their murderers."

I had by then developed what I considered a rapport with Muhammad and his staff, who had been remarkably forgiving of my naiveté. Although I had assumed that all of the newspapers on the list Jon had left me were daily publications, Muhammad told me that, in fact, many were weekly, triweekly, or just unreliably issued. When I requested that an article appear in a specific paper, he would sometimes go against my request if he knew that the paper wouldn't publish for several days, and would place it instead in a daily. As he explained to me in an email, if he didn't do this, "Some of those articles will delay in time for couple or three days, and in this case their importance will reduce and attenuate and other newspapers will deal with them before us. This is one of the most important points which leads the newspapers' editors to know about the connection of those articles with the American, because who would pay money to publish an article which got old news!!!"

I passed Muhammad the Badr Corps story, explaining that it was of the utmost importance and feeling a bit excited to be carrying out the orders of such a senior officer. Days later, however, the story still had not been published. Muhammad told me that an editor at the newspaper I had chosen, *Addustour*, had rung the evening before it should have run, claiming that his managers had objected to its politics. By Muhammad's account, the same editor had then relented after some discussion, agreeing to publish the piece. (I assumed this meant that Muhammad had swayed him with an offer of more Lincoln Group money.) But when the newspaper came out the following morning, there was still no "Badr Corps Not Baited into Fight." I sent an apologetic email to the two majors, explaining why such a high-priority story had not been published. I hadn't taken up this issue with the newspaper's management, I wrote, because I didn't want to sour my relationship with the paper's editors. Rosen accepted this reasoning and was even somewhat pleased by the insight he thought it pro-vided. "It is good feedback actually that the piece rubbed up against political/philosophical boundaries," he replied. "Is this something we should use to shape future pieces for that paper, for all papers, etc.? It is good to keep us on our toes and it shows that they are not our lapdogs."

Indeed, because Rosen and his team assumed I interacted regularly with the Iraqi press, they believed I was someone to take seriously. And Rosen's en-couraging words actually emboldened me to offer additional suggestions on ways to improve our "pro-democracy" pieces. I told him that an article on the military's discovery of a cache of bulletproof vests was too outdated to run in a daily newspaper and read like a catalogue of munitions, with none of the "hu-man appeal" that grabs readers. "This is not criticism," I wrote Rosen, "merely my honest opinion as a media analyst." (Jim Sutton had bestowed this title upon me, and it was by then printed on my Lincoln Group business cards.) For other articles, I pointed out that the military had failed to properly mask its own voice and intel, such as in one piece when the Army writers directly responded to an Abu Musab al-Zarqawi claim: "It is true that during one security operation a woman was detained by Coalition Forces." I told them that their entire ap-proach to Zarqawi was wrong, as they were giving him far too much expo-sure—bad press being better than none at all. Rosen thanked me for all my "efforts to steer us toward better products." Although they, too, were reconsid-ering how to write about Zarqawi, the team had been "given some fairly rigid guidelines from our boss." Rosen added that they also were "synchronizing mes-sages with PSYOP and PAO," and were thus limited in what they could do. But attached below Rosen's comments was a forwarded email to him from a con-fused subordinate: "Should we continue to write the same way?"

In one correspondence with me, Rosen confided that his biggest frustra-tion was when his colleagues—"a bunch of white guys"—nitpicked over this or that word for a piece that would eventually be translated into Arabic. "Not ONCE have they consulted one Arab on the best way to write the THOUGHT in Arabic. They forget that it is the message that we are trying to get across not the word."

One morning toward the end of July, Jim Sutton decided that I needed to check up on Muhammad and his team in their downtown offices. He picked me up outside the villa in a black BMW and drove us to the concrete blast bar-riers and razor wire at the outer limits of the Green Zone. A sign instructed drivers and passengers to "Lock and Load," and Jim gave me a Glock 9mm pistol to hold out of sight in my lap.[5] Then we drove on, into the vast portion of Baghdad every American I had met called the Red Zone. At six two, with a shock of blond hair, I had little chance of blending in there, and my striped polo shirt and Ray-Bans hardly put me "under the radar."

Along a narrow street of ramshackle stores beside the Tigris River, Jim slowed the car to a crawl, waving to some kids on a nearby doorstep who returned the gesture. Then, without warning, another vehicle speeding toward us from behind slammed on its brakes and came to a halt directly in front of our BMW. Jim jumped out, and I frantically looked from him to the strange car, out of which large swarthy men were now emerging. One of these men ran past Jim toward our car. Before I could react, he was in the driver's seat beside me. He quickly introduced himself in rudimentary English as part of Lincoln Group's security detail. Able to breathe again, I saw Jim get into the second car, a silver-gray BMW, along with a couple of armed guards, and we were joined by a man wielding an AK-47 who sidled in behind me. My driver was Kurdish, from the area around Fallujah, and as he steered us into the downtown center he barked orders to the car in front through a two-way radio.

I was twenty-two years old, and here I was holding a loaded gun while being ushered through Baghdad's dangerous, detritus-laden streets by two total strangers. Maybe this was the real Iraq. Maybe this was what it was like to be John Simpson.

By this time, I was winning plaudits for my work. Jim Sutton liked my easy manner with the Iraqis and attempts at basic Arabic. He praised me, too, for my cool-headedness in unfamiliar situations—such as the automobile switch beside the Tigris, which seemed to have been at least in part a test. Even Gina, who had been so cold when I had first arrived in Iraq, became far less frosty

---

[5]Jon, who was known to spend hours in the villa's courtyard drinking beer and attempting to land bullets ejected from a pistol into a paper cup, taught me how to handle the company's various firearms before he left for Chicago. With practice, I was able to put together and load the Glock but had much more trouble with the larger MP5 submachine gun. Its dirty-bronze-colored bullets would lodge in the chamber whenever I tried cocking the gun, and it repeatedly jammed as I tried to fire rounds into the ground. Jon told me not to take it personally, as this MP5 was a cheap Iranian knockoff.

toward me. Because of the Oxford background I shared with Christian Bailey, she initially thought I might be his spy, here to report back to him on company problems and employee activities. But when Gina learned I was risking my life in Baghdad for just $1,000 a month, as opposed to her $70,000 annual salary, she mostly felt sorry for me.

Jim Sutton sat me down one afternoon at the villa to talk about what he said was "the next step" in the company's operations. In line with Lincoln Group's longer-term aims, he and the established team (the half dozen or so who had been in Iraq longer than two months) were intent on carrying out a much larger military contract. "Western Mission" would be a hugely expanded version of the current media efforts. It would be an all-out "media blitz," Jim said, and the largest contract ever of its kind. During the months of August and September alone, we were proposing to place sixteen different pro-government/anti-insurgent spots on Iraqi television stations for a fee of $16.5 million. There would be twenty radio broadcasts as well, with the military paying us around $20,000 for each. We would publish eighty half-page color advertisements and thirty-two op-ed articles, for which we would charge nearly $400,000. Blanketing Baghdad with 140,000 posters would earn us another $400,000, and we would design nine Internet news sites, at a cost of $2,500 each, and produce five DVDs, for just over $580,000. Lincoln Group's overall haul for the two months: $19 million.

We were also to create something called a Rapid Response Cell. Lincoln Group would hire Iraqi journalists and send them to the Anbar province west of Baghdad, which Jim called the "insurgency's center of gravity." Working in the violent cities of Ramadi and Fallujah, the journalists would be paid by Lincoln Group to report news that bolstered the U.S. military message. They would be on hand as well to capture breaking stories, about which they alone would be conveniently forewarned by Coalition forces, and would thus be able to "positively" portray events before the insurgency could put out its own account. Ahmed and I were told to recruit cameramen, reporters, and television stations to do this work. We were also to line up op-ed writers, so that once Western Mission was formally approved our team would be ready on August 1 to "execute." Finally, in order to show the military officers at the Al Faw palace that we were giving them more bang for their buck, I was now to pass ten stories along to Muhammad each week.

Ahmed had worked in the press office of the Coalition Provisional Authority, where he issued professional accreditations to Iraqi reporters, and also as a fixer for ABC News. (He often reverentially recounted a brief meeting he had with Peter Jennings a couple of years before the broadcaster's death.) So to find willing op-ed writers, we began by visiting Ahmed's past associates. Two of them I met several times at the Baghdad Press Center—an office that the U.S. State Department funded to provide Iraqi reporters with equipment and to train them in journalistic ethics and professional conduct. And yet we were hiring these same Iraqi reporters to work indirectly for the U.S. military. When State Department officials at the press center asked me about my work in Iraq, I would tiptoe around an answer, saying I ran advertising campaigns in local newspapers on behalf of multinationals. (Which was effectively true.) A director in the office explained their belief that an independent media would help buttress the country's nascent democracy, and she thought it was great that my efforts were allowing local newspapers to gain commercial independence.

It was easy to find Iraqi reporters who would write U.S. military–friendly op-ed pieces for a little extra cash. But hiring those who would go to the dangerous Anbar province was altogether a different matter. The reporters, cameramen, and sound operators we spoke with all said the same thing: they would work in Ramadi and Fallujah as part of a Rapid Response Cell only if they were embedded with U.S. troops. But because the whole point was that they were to report news that at least appeared to be independent of the military, this was impossible. We even explored whether we could embed our reporters with Iraqi troops there. But this also proved to be untenable.

Gina then had the idea of placing a Lincoln Group team permanently in a U.S. base near Ramadi or Fallujah, where they would operate one half of a satellite uplink system that would send footage or sound recordings to Baghdad. At the other end, Iraqis working in the company's Green Zone villa would receive the footage and splice it into whatever form was required. Breaking news, the thinking went, could then be rushed to a TV station and aired immediately.

To explore this option, Ahmed and I visited a number of upstart production companies in their heavily guarded compounds. We found one company that would produce one of our half-minute TV spots for as little as $10,000. At Iraq's national station, Al Iraqiya, located within Baghdad's old Jewish ghetto, an English-speaking commercial director said he could air the spot during the station's nightly news, the most expensive time, for only $2,000. Production and distribution together, then, would cost us around

$12,000. The amount Lincoln Group was charging the military for develop-
ing, producing, and airing each commercial had already been determined:
just over $1 million.[6]

At Al Iraqiya, Ahmed and I were then escorted to another part of the de-
crepit compound and introduced to the station's news director. We were left
alone with him, and Ahmed began to explain that we were part of a recently
formed independent news-gathering service that sought to cover the Anbar
province. I followed the Arabic with difficulty but heard Ahmed launch into
an account of his work with ABC. Then he said I was a former BBC reporter,
which was an outright lie. I kept quiet, and Ahmed proposed that Al Iraqiya
consider airing the footage from our Iraqi reporters. Ideally we would get paid
for this, Ahmed said, but at this stage we wanted to make a reputation for ourselves and would in certain circumstances be willing to pay to have our footage
shown on the news programs. The news director nodded repeatedly and then
vigorously shook our hands. He seemed thrilled by our proposal.

The chubby head of the Lebanese Broadcasting Corporation's Baghdad
bureau, yet another of Ahmed's old friends, was less enthusiastic about doing
business with us. Over small glasses of sweetened tea, Ahmed again portrayed
us as a start-up news service but revealed to his past associate that the U.S.
military was bankrolling our operation. The station director listened in silence, finally speaking to warn us that we were embarking on an extremely
perilous campaign. All would inevitably be uncovered, he said, and we, our
employees, and our partners would be placed in grave danger.

With all I was doing on Western Mission, I had begun to pay far less attention
to the military's daily storyboards. Although I was passing along more than
ten articles to be published each week, thrilling the stats-obsessed military
team, I had stopped reading all the items the military sent me, and I'm sure I
forwarded on to Muhammad stories I would previously have held back. Every
week I was required to confirm the details of the military's spreadsheet, which
listed the stories written by the I.O. team, the stories published, and which

---

[6]Jim, Gina, and other senior Lincoln Group employees who worked on Western Mission all
eventually left the company, after large bonuses they were promised failed to materialize. Although Bailey and Craig had initially offered them 10 percent of the profit on the entire Western Mission contract, after arbitration this summer the employees were able to recoup only a
fraction of this amount.

newspapers had published them. But it wasn't until early August that I really looked closely at the figures for the previous three weeks. When I examined Muhammad's records, I saw that the amounts some newspapers had charged us for placing articles had shot up dramatically. During July, pieces published in the newspaper *Addustour* had gone from $84, to $423, to $1,345, and finally to $2,156. For another newspaper, *Al Adala*, what we were charged had climbed from $82 at the start of July to $1,088 by month's end. I checked the word counts of the articles, since we paid more for additional column inches, but all the stories were roughly the same length. On closer inspection, I also noticed that articles had been published in newspapers I had not specified. One particular paper, *Al Sabah Al Jadeed* (*The New Morning*), had been paid around $12,000 over a ten-day period from late July to early August, although I had never told Muhammad to place stories there.

I traveled the Highway of Death to discuss all this with Jim Sutton at Camp Victory. We spoke on a fourth-floor balcony, the clicks of military boots echoing on the palace's red marble atrium. Jim said it was up to me to ferret out the thief or thieves: it could be Muhammad, members of his staff, or the entire office. I told Jim that I now believed I had naively misread the Iraqis at our downtown office, mistaking their effusive "Yes, Mr. Willem" and "Soon, Mr. Willem" for real fealty. I had allowed them to exploit my ignorance: because I didn't know exactly how they published the military-written storyboards or whom they dealt with at the papers, they were able to inflate prices and take advantage of Lincoln Group. Jim said there was some important Western Mission work to take care of the next morning, but after that I needed to make my way downtown to get to the bottom of this matter.

Western Mission, after an initial delay, was finally beginning in earnest. Lincoln Group, as usual, had promised more than it could deliver, so in order to purchase airtime up front, it was forced to request an unusually large advance payment from the military. In fact, as Gina and I drove with Jim to the Green Zone villa that next day, the advance sat a few feet behind us, in the trunk of Jim's car: $3 million in cash, separated into thirty plastic-wrapped $100,000 blocks.

Just beyond the concrete blast barriers at the camp's exit, where we waited for our Kurdish guards, Jim told me to turn off my cell phone so that our location couldn't be traced. I held one of the Iranian submachine guns at the ready, and Gina, who rode shotgun, hid behind gold-rimmed sunglasses and a black kaffiyeh head scarf. The guards were late, and as cars slowly passed and our wait lengthened, an ambush began to seem imminent. My fears were somewhat allayed when the Kurds finally pulled into the parking area, apologetic and prepared to escort us and our secret cargo to the villa. The seven-mile ride turned out to be uneventful, and the $3 million was locked up in a safe inside my bedroom.

A few hours later, after lunch, I drove into Baghdad to speak to Muhammad and his staff. Jim, who said he was a former FBI field agent, had instructed me on the best ways to question my suspects. During each interview a staff member was to be seated in a single empty chair in the center of Muhammad's office—without a wall nearby, Jim explained, the man would feel vulnerable and lose his nerve. It was very important as well that I remain calm yet forceful at all times, and Jim said that I should test various hypotheses by accusing each man of carrying out the crime in a different manner. According to Sutton, I would be able to hear guilt in their denials. To further unsettle the staff, Lincoln Group had also arranged for two Sunnis to be there while I conducted the examination. These men had worked for Saddam's notorious Mukhabarat, the intelligence arm of the Iraqi Baath party. And I had asked an Iraqi I had come to know quite well to accompany me, essentially to serve as my personal bodyguard and translator. Hamza worked for another American firm based in the same compound as our villa and was responsible for delivering our soft drinks. I offered him $100 for his time.

I began by interviewing Muhammad, and we all squeezed into his cramped office, with its gaudy ashtrays and low leather chairs. I took Muhammad's seat at his desk, and Hamza, in baseball cap and Oakley sunglasses, sat to my left. The Sunnis positioned themselves on a couch along one of the walls while Muhammad remained standing by the solitary chair. Muhammad was surprised as well by the discrepancies in the ledger, and his suspicions fell on two Christians in his office, Farooq and Majid—those on his staff who physically transported the translated articles to the newspapers. Farooq, he thought, was our man. I, too, found Farooq to be dodgy. His hands were clammy whenever he greeted me, and he seemed always to have an elaborate excuse ready for Mr. Willem. On several occasions when I had phoned to question him about late work, our connection had suddenly gone dead. He would later blame this on the country's notoriously bad telecommunications network, but I believed he had simply hung up on me.

So we brought in Farooq, pointing him to the empty seat in the middle of the room. His protestations of innocence began even before he sat down, his face quickly turning a deep shade of red and the lip beneath his bushy mustache quivering in indignation. As I tried to follow Hamza's rapid-fire translations, I was distracted by the loaded Glock that I had tucked into the belt of my trousers and that now jabbed into my groin. We generally were armed whenever we traveled outside the Green Zone, and on this occasion I had to consider that the entire office of Iraqis could be in collusion and willing to act against their young British accuser. I shifted to try to alleviate the discomfort but soon found the weapon's position unbearable. Removing it from my pants, I placed the gun on the polished surface of Muhammad's desk. Farooq looked from the weapon to me and then back again, and I realized too late just how threatening my action seemed. Yet I couldn't simply apologize and remove the pistol—this would seem a sign of weakness. Now panicking, Farooq begged frantically that I consider his livelihood, that I think of the well-being of his young family.

Along with adrenaline and fear, a profound feeling of disgust welled up inside me. I had become a kind of stock character in a movie, someone I categorically despised. I hated violence and guns, was against the American presence in Iraq, and was sympathetic to almost every Iraqi I had met during the summer. The Glock's barrel even pointed directly at Farooq, for Christ's sake! John Simpson may have been on the receiving end of interrogations, but he certainly never carried one out. And I was doing all this to recover a few thousand misappropriated dollars, for a company that was set to make millions from the American war effort.

With Farooq gone, the Mukhabarat heavies said there was no doubt about the Christian's guilt. They encouraged me to threaten him with a CIA criminal investigation. "Those three letters scare every Iraqi," the taller patrician-looking one said.[7] As we went through the motions with Majid, his calm denials sounding the very timbre of innocence, we learned that Farooq had fled the building. Since it was also beginning to get dark, I decided I had had enough. It was time that Hamza and I returned to the Green Zone.

Back at the villa, Hamza waited in the living room while I went to get his money. Before he left, he said he didn't understand how I could drive around

---

[7] Less than two months later, gunmen entered this Sunni's house and shot and killed him and a number of his male relatives. The killings could have been retribution for his activities under the former regime. They also could have been reprisals for his involvement with our American company.

Baghdad without real protection and enter an Iraqi office where I had no idea what was going on. He liked me and appreciated the extra money but said he would never do this again.

The day had been extremely long, and I was exhausted and more than a little shaken. The blocks of cash that we had locked up in my room had been picked up and moved to a bank in central Baghdad. In my email inbox, there were messages from both my parents, asking me when I would leave Iraq and saying they hoped that it would be very soon. Lincoln Group had also sent me a newly drawn contract; they were offering me up to $70,000 to postpone journalism school and to work another ten months in Baghdad. But I couldn't fathom doing the work any longer. I had become what I had to admit was the antithesis of a journalist. And if I continued to suborn Iraqi reporters with U.S. military money, this would surely mean I would never be able to work as one.[8]

That night I rang Christian Bailey and Paige Craig at the company's D.C. headquarters and told them I wanted to go home. On August 20, I boarded a plane out of Baghdad, and my summer internship was over.

September 2006

[8]When U.S. newspapers broke the story late last year of Lincoln Group's secret propaganda work, it seemed a small victory had been won for journalistic ethics. Editorial writers condemned the business of paying Iraqi editors to run U.S.-military stories, and even the White House and the Joint Chiefs of Staff declared the practice a matter of serious concern. But such clarity was quickly obscured. A Pentagon investigation in March actually cleared Lincoln Group of any wrongdoing, with Secretary of Defense Donald Rumsfeld extolling such "non-traditional" means of fighting terror in Iraq. In a companywide email sent around that time, Paige Craig assured his employees that their work had been honorable. "We've taken the fight to the enemy," he wrote, "and every member of the Lincoln team can be proud that their sacrifice and hard work has advanced the cause of the free world."

Out of Iraq

The Rise and Fall of One Man's Occupation

ADAM DAVIDSON

We were living in the Flowers Land Hotel when I decided I wanted a house. This was partly pragmatic. The hotel, like most of the good ones in Baghdad, cost around $100 a night, and that was more than I could afford if I was going to stay for many months. But there was something else—something emotional or psychological. I can't describe it precisely. I wanted permanence there. I wanted to feel that I was closer to Iraq than all those other, itinerant journalists. When I went home to New York on vacation, I wanted to say: well, yes, my home in Baghdad is quite lovely.

I had a very specific vision of my house. It would be not just the perfect home in a war zone, or a home as good as could be made in postwar Baghdad. But the perfect home. A home that would be ideal if it were anywhere in the world. I intended to become a great war correspondent, and this would be more easily done, I thought, if my home were a refuge from the chaos outside. The house would be quiet, spacious, full of light. There would be enough bedrooms to house my favorite visiting reporters. There would be an agreeable mix of Iraqis and Americans, so we would not feel cut off, as others did, from the local population. There would be high-speed wireless Internet and satellite TV.

I knew the house would be in Jadiriyah, one of Baghdad's two wealthiest neighborhoods. The other, Mansour, is much larger, with busy commercial streets—nice for shopping but far too chaotic to live in. Also, Mansour was home to many American contractors and their massive security details, and so it felt like a possible target. Jadiriyah, by contrast, was quiet and safe. Adjacent to the largely Christian Karada district, it was friendly to foreigners: home to the Hamra Hotel complex, where most of our journalist friends were staying, and a short drive to the Green Zone, the protected U.S. enclave where we interviewed American officials.

One afternoon in September 2003, I went out with my girlfriend, Jen, my translator, Muhamed, and my driver, Ahmed, and we drove around Jadiriyah looking for TO LET signs. They were everywhere. The first house we toured— a wide, two-story mansion on the main road, Karada Outside Street, across from Baghdad University—was like many we would see in the coming weeks. The outside was boxy and plain: concrete walls, a large metal gate, dark and heavily curtained windows. Inside there was a kind of gaudiness that a friend of mine had once dubbed "the Louis Saddam style." The walls and floors were a rich, black marble, and the furniture tried desperately to signify wealth—red velour couches with thick gold braiding, glass cabinets filled with ceramic sculptures of birds in flight and horses galloping through surf. The house smelled of sweat and dust. We were guided around by the owner's teenage son, who gestured wordlessly at each room as we passed. Upstairs, in the master bedroom, his entire family sat on two beds, surrounded by packed suitcases. They said they were ready to leave as soon as someone took the house.

On our way out the door, I asked how much they wanted. The young man, who had been joined by a slightly older cousin, said $200,000 a year. I nodded and continued to walk. The cousin said: how about 150,000? . . . 100,000? . . . Would you rent it for 90,000?

That day and for the following week, we saw homes that were similar: gaudy, gone to seed, the owners desperate but overcharging. One house was right out of the Hollywood Hills, all horizontal lines and huge walls of glass. Another imitated a giant sandcastle; yet another was a faux Greek temple, with a dozen life-sized statues of rearing horses. The homes were just as bizarre inside. One was a spiral, with curved walls and round rooms. Another was built in a star pattern, with hallways jutting off at extreme angles. Most of the homes had two kitchens—one for show and the other for actual work. Most also had several living rooms, each with a specific purpose: one for family, another for regular guests, the gaudiest for important visitors.

At first, we approached only homes with TO LET signs, but we soon discovered that any home owner would eagerly invite us in and offer to rent us his home. Although most of Jadiriyah's residents had once been wealthy, because of sanctions they had spent the last fifteen years or so living off of their savings, selling their furniture and carpets, or finding other ways to survive. One proud old man told us that he owned Iraq's largest candy factory, but it had gone to ruin under sanctions and was destroyed by looters just after the war. Renting out his house would allow him to make enough money to care for his children and grandchildren, all of whom lived with him. Another day, in the smallest and most broken down of the houses we saw, we sat in the living room as the husband told us how his home had once been among Baghdad's finest. In the 1970s he had rented the place to a major German firm and, he implied, had made a great amount of money. He seemed to believe that just maybe, despite the horrible smell and the dirt and the peeling paint, he could rent it out again and have some money and comfort in his final days. I wished I could rent the place and take away his troubles, but I knew I never would. I did take the obligatory tour, during which I accidentally opened the bathroom door on his wife.

One day soon after, Jen came back to the hotel and told me they had found a realtor. She, Ahmed, and Muhamed had come across his office on Arasat Street, one of the ritziest addresses in Baghdad. The realtor, Abu Hannah, was extremely eager to help, and soon we were visiting him daily. He told us that he had been a general in the Iraqi Army in charge of antiaircraft defense. He had retired in 1998 but was ordered back to service just before the war. He was shocked by how badly the military had declined in five years. The antiaircraft guns were ruined by neglect. But it didn't matter, since the soldiers had no idea how to use them. "We knew we'd lose," he said. "But what can you do? You have to defend your country." He had become a realtor just after the war, and I got the idea that we were his first clients.

Eventually, Abu Hannah mentioned that his next-door neighbor was looking for tenants. We went to the place, and it was simply perfect. It was almost exactly what I had pictured. Behind a tall concrete wall and metal gate, lovely flowers and thick bushes bordered a large green lawn. At the end of the garden, an umbrella of water sprang from a circular fountain, lit up by a ring of lights around the base. The house itself, though a bit grand by American standards, was among the more understated and elegant we had seen in

Jadiriyah. The floors were a beige-and-white marble that made the space feel open. There were two kitchens—again, very common, one for show and the other for work—and a small settee just inside the entrance for the drivers and translators. To the right of the show kitchen was a long hallway with a beat-up upright piano and a small rock garden, leading to an indoor fountain set high in the wall and cascading down an abstract fresco of colored tiles. The living room was so large that we would later subdivide it into three: a dining room, a work area, and a smaller living room. Across the hallway, on the other side of the fountain, was a traditional Arabic sitting room, with thick cushions all along the walls—perfect for relaxing with drinks and cigarettes.

The house had six bedrooms, two on the first floor and four upstairs. The master-bedroom suite, where Jen and I would live, was particularly inviting. Twice as large as the other bedrooms, it had a master bath with Jacuzzi and had, above the bed, a hand-painted scene out of the Kamasutra, in which two Indians—she flesh-colored, he painted blue—sit on a swing and stare at each other longingly.

We told Abu Hannah that we wanted the house. He said it would cost $80,000 a year. This touched off an elaborate series of negotiations. The process was made more difficult by the fact that the owner had fled to Jordan. We never found out exactly what he did—"I am in the perfume and other businesses," he said once—but we were suspicious of anyone who had to flee so soon after the fall of the old regime. Eventually we realized that Abu Hannah's chief concern was his own commission, which normally would be a percentage of the rental price. One day we told him that we would pay the same large commission—$1,000 per month—no matter what the house rented for. That did it. Soon we worked out a deal: $14,000 (including Abu Hannah's commission) for three months, renewable every quarter for the rest of that year.

We filled out a long contract in Arabic, which I signed. That night we celebrated in the cushioned sitting room. Abu Hannah came over from next door with beer. He is a Christian from Mosul, he explained, so he could drink. For the first time, we chatted with him about matters other than real estate. He told us how much he admired Saddam Hussein. During the first Gulf War, he said, he had been in the north, and his unit had shot down an American plane. Saddam had called and promoted everyone in the unit on the spot. Abu Hannah said that if Saddam came to his house, he would welcome him and protect him. This was when Saddam was still in hiding and there were rumors about him staying in the homes of regular Iraqis. I told Abu Hannah that if

Saddam did come to stay, he should make sure to invite us over for an exclusive interview.

At first, the house was home only to Jen and me and to one other couple: Jack Fairweather, the Baghdad correspondent for Britain's *Daily Telegraph*, and Christina Asquith, a freelancer for the *Christian Science Monitor*, among other newspapers. (Jen, whose last name is Banbury, was covering the war for Salon.com.) Jack said that they would pay $2,000 per month. That meant I had to come up with a little more than $2,000 per month for the rest of the rent, $750 per month for a DSL line, and a few hundred each month for food and water, as well as something for the staff. I was shocked to learn that we would be getting phone and electricity bills from the appropriate Iraqi ministries—it was hard to believe they were functioning well enough to meter lines and bill customers. Luckily, they were still using the Saddam-era heavily subsidized tariffs, so those costs would be around a dollar per month.

Our first staff members, of course, were Muhamed and Ahmed, with whom Jen and I had become quite close.[1] Ahmed, stoop-shouldered and wiry, was constantly amused at the absurdities of Iraqi life; Muhamed more often brooded, sometimes angrily, about the future of a post-Saddam Iraq. I asked them how I could put together a security staff, and right away they told me that they knew the perfect people. Muhamed proposed his uncle, Abu Ali. Ahmed proposed his brother-in-law, also named Abu Ali, and his father-in-law, Abu Faris. These men, they assured me, were well-trained former army soldiers who had fought in various wars and were vicious. We would also need a housekeeper; and since neither Ahmed nor Muhamed wanted any of the women in their families working for us, Muhamed approached Um Qais, one of the women who cleaned our room at the Flowers Land. He reported that she had agreed to come in a few times a week.

Ahmed and Muhamed felt that the reasonable rate to pay the guards was $500 per month for full-time work. Since the two night guards would each work half-time, this somehow worked out to $350 per month for each. Um Qais was to receive another $350. This brought my monthly expenses up to more than $3,200 per month—more than I was paying at the hotel and considerably more than the $1,000 per month my employers had offered to reim-

---

[1] In this account I have changed the names of the Iraqis, who today might be threatened or worse if it were known that they had once worked with Americans.

burse. But, I hoped, enough other journalists would rent the spare rooms that I could make up the difference, and perhaps even make a little bit of profit.

Soon we had our first tenants: Rory McCarthy, the *Guardian*'s Baghdad correspondent; Patrick Graham, a Canadian freelancer who was covering the war for various newspapers and magazines; and Samantha Appleton, a photographer who worked mostly for *The New Yorker* and *Time*. I made up a rate for each person based on how much his or her company could reimburse. I charged freelancers a fraction of what I charged staffers, because the staffers could expense a lot more. So someone on full-time staff might pay $600 per week, while a freelance photographer might pay $1,000 per month or even $500 a month if he or she would sleep in the Arabic sitting room, which was less private. Anyone who pleaded poverty would inevitably get a sizable discount.

The tenants each came with drivers and translators of their own. The Iraqi staffers would all sit together in the alcove at the entrance or around the dining table in the front kitchen. They chatted and laughed with one another and prayed together right there at the entrance of the house. Jen and I often would have lunch with the drivers and guards; I would practice my Arabic and ask them to clarify things about Iraq that confused me. Daytime Abu Ali (we called him this to distinguish him from the other Abu Ali, the night guard) was, I discovered, the sheikh of his small tribe, and I was particularly interested in talking to him about this role. I had known some Arabic before I arrived, but with the help of a tutor and of the always encouraging Abu Alis, I was becoming conversational in the particularly difficult Iraqi dialect. I had fun shocking Iraqis with my decent command of Baghdad street slang—something no other Westerner I met could do. I even bought a *dishdasha*, the full-length robe worn by Iraqi men, and took to wearing it around the house.

My entire staff was Shi'a, but Jack's—for no particular reason—was Sunni. Ghassan, his translator, and Abu Ghassan, his driver, had never been friends with a Shi'a before, and I was a bit afraid that there would be tensions. But within days, they all got along so well that I would have to remind myself they had only just met. Samantha's driver/translator, Abu Emir, became a particularly large presence in the house. Tall, rotund, and jolly, he greeted everyone who passed the alcove with a hug and handshake and elaborate kissing of cheeks. He and Jen became fast friends, and Abu Emir made a point of telling me that Jen was now in his tribe. If I did anything wrong, he said, a few hundred tribesmen from Sadr City would come to set me right.

Most of our tenant-guests—Jen called them "frenants," because they tended also to be friends of ours—came for two or three weeks, while some stayed for a few months. They were mostly print reporters: a few from major American magazines, some from smaller newspapers. We had several photographers, a couple of documentary filmmakers, and at least one other public-radio reporter besides myself. I tried to be selective, inviting only those people I thought would fit in well. I didn't want any reporters who were too competitive. When a lot of reporters get together—especially newspaper reporters—there can sometimes be an unpleasant one-upmanship that affects every conversation. I tried to pick housemates the same way I might pick guests for a cocktail party. As time went on, we had more and more photographers, because, it turns out, photographers are generally more fun than writers. We tended to have more women than the other houses and hotels, which usually were exceedingly male.

Pretty much every night became a dinner party. Jen or Christina would cook. There were a couple of decent supermarkets where we could buy canned goods, pasta, juices, milk, and coffee. All over Baghdad were great vegetable stands with fresh in-season green beans and lettuce and cucumbers and okra. There were plenty of butchers selling lamb and beef. Since we were right next to the Christian neighborhood, Karada, we had several liquor stores nearby. There was usually some Johnnie Walker whiskey or Absolut vodka available, and it was easy to get beer: Heineken, Amstel (not light, just Amstel), and Efes, a Turkish brand.

I made a point of inviting outsiders often—particularly U.S. officials from the Coalition Provisional Authority, who were always thrilled to escape their gilded prison with its heavy cafeteria food from Kellogg Brown & Root. Because they were not allowed to leave the Green Zone, we had to sneak them out across the bridge to our neighborhood. I promised them that the dinners would be entirely off the record. My general aim was to get them drunk enough to actually say something truthful. And often they did. One night we hosted a friend of a friend who had flown out just a week before to start a six-month tour as a CPA bureaucrat. By the time he came to dinner, he had already decided to abandon Iraq. The CPA's horrible bureaucracy, he said, prevented any improvement in the country. We soon learned, over the course of our dinners, about the warring camps into which the CPA was divided. Career civil servants despised Republican political appointees, and vice versa. The military hated the civilians. We heard story after story of months spent on a project—trying to rewrite Iraq's traffic laws, or to fix a power station, or to fashion a new constitution—that was ultimately stymied by bureaucratic interference. The CPA public affairs office had been quite good at preventing us from learning anything substantive. Only at our dinner table did we learn how low morale was, and how little was getting done.

Most nights we would hear gunfire, maybe an explosion or two. We learned to differentiate. Car bombs made the floors shake; rocket-propelled grenades popped; mortars made a distinctive whoosh. But we felt extremely safe. Our colleagues in the Green Zone or the big hotels might be at risk, but no one would waste a bomb on our little house.

Problems with the staff began almost immediately. When Abu Faris, one of the two nighttime guards, arrived at dusk before his first shift, his first question was, "Where do I sleep?" Obviously I thought that he shouldn't sleep at all. A few weeks later, when I had been napping at a time I normally was out, I came downstairs to find daytime Abu Ali sacked out on the couch in our living room, watching the satellite TV. Seeing me, he jumped up and went to patrol the street in front of the house. I recounted this to some of my guests, and they told me that this happened all the time. Abu Ali, I learned, spent much of the day either watching TV or sitting in the back yard making shish kebabs.

Nevertheless, there soon was a series of raises. Muhamed and Ahmed had both argued that the pay scale was unfair. Ahmed was furious that Muhamed's uncle made more than his relatives. Muhamed complained that Ahmed's family made more on a per-day basis. Um Qais, the cleaning lady, wanted more money, too. I liked them all, and they were older than me and made only a few hundred dollars per month risking their lives for me. I gave them all whatever raise they asked.

There were other, unexpected costs. One of our two refrigerators broke, so I bought another for $400. In addition to the DSL modem and Internet hub and cords, which together cost more than $500, I had to hire Muhamed's brother to install everything—another several hundred. We needed desks and chairs and lights and heaters and towels and pillows. When the generator broke—at 5:00 P.M. on the night of the start of the weeklong feast of Eid Al Fitr, meaning we would need a new one that night or else live in darkness for a week—I drove out and bought a refurbished Indian model from a store owner who, sensing my desperation, charged me $5,000 rather than the $3,000 it was worth. When our guests complained that there weren't enough showers or hot water, I bought a new water heater and paid for a plumber to install a shower downstairs.

In short, I was hemorrhaging money and desperately needed the tenants to pay some of it back. I didn't keep very good accounting records and just hoped that the money coming in would somehow equal the money going out. It never did. Compounding the problem was that I was very casual about reserving rooms. A friend would email that he or she wanted to come stay, and I'd agree. Then the friend's trip would be delayed and a room would be unused—and uncharged—for a couple of weeks or so.

Meanwhile, our housekeeper was becoming increasingly erratic. Um Qais told us that she had worked in the household of Saddam's sister, and had given manicures and haircuts to many of Saddam's female relatives. She brought in photos of these relatives, in elaborate hairdos and nail extensions. She offered to make up all the women in the house in this fashion. She would show her affection to some of our female guests in another, more disturbing way: on occasion, Um Qais would come into their rooms in the middle of the night—at three, four in the morning—to wake them up, hug them, and kiss them on the cheek.

Soon Um Qais began to insist that we hire her husband as a guard. She said that daytime Abu Ali was a thief and a very bad man. Every day she reported to me that Abu Ali had stolen a bottle of apple juice, or a few frozen chickens, or some ground beef. Indeed, I did notice that our food seemed to be disappearing a bit too rapidly, but I couldn't tell for sure. When I brought it up with Muhamed, he replied that his uncle would never do such a thing; it must be one of the other guards, one of Ahmed's relatives. Eventually, I told Abu Ali that someone was stealing things from our fridge and that he, as the guard, would be held responsible.

Thus began a not-at-all subtle war among the staff. On one side were the pro–Abu Ali staffers—Abu Ali himself, Muhamed, and Muhamed's brother Kasem, whom we had hired to install and monitor our computer network. On the other side was the anti–Abu Ali team, captained by Um Qais but joined by Ahmed and his relatives: nighttime Abu Ali, Abu Faris, and Abu Mahmud, who was an occasional driver. Both sides agreed that I needed to make a decision. I had to fire either Abu Ali or Um Qais.

Um Qais grew more and more frenzied, to the point that she was unable to do her job well. The residents' clothes soon became interchanged—I would find other people's underwear in my drawer and see them wearing my shirts.

Eventually, she began simply to pile all of our wet clothes together on the couches. In the end, she was the one to go. Daytime Abu Ali could barely hide his triumph.

Although the full-time staff held steady at four—we had a new housekeeper, Um Dumya, a Christian woman who never bothered anyone—dozens of other Iraqis were drawn into the house's orbit. The kitchen and vestibule were filled with our drivers and translators, as well as those of previous guests; when a reporter left Iraq, often his or her driver would continue to come by the house, hoping to pick up work from the next resident. Some of these men soon became fixated on our female guests. The women who stayed in our house understood that they needed to dress reasonably modestly when out on the street, but at home they sometimes wore tank tops. For the Iraqi men this was difficult to deal with. It was simply more female flesh than they had ever seen in their lives. As a few of the single women began to date other reporters, Muhamed told me that all the men could do was talk about this woman or that one who had let a man sleep in her room. One night, Muhamed told me, all the drivers and translators heard one of our houseguests loudly making love to her new boyfriend. Daytime Abu Ali became quite serious about one of the single women, even offering to make her his second wife. Another woman, a photographer, became the subject of obsession because of her frequent male guests. Muhamed told me that he heard she might sleep with an Iraqi man.

An even more serious source of tension among the Iraqis was Abu Emir. Although he first came to the house as Samantha's driver, Abu Emir had since become a sort of transportation mogul in the postwar journalism scene. From his nephews and neighbors and friends he had built a network of drivers, whom he would pay $10 per day from the $70 to $100 per day he charged each journalist. Now Abu Emir had decided that he wanted to control all the driving for my house. One day he had asked me if he could leave his large, black SUV parked in our driveway, and I had agreed. A few weeks later, though, I learned that this was causing profound distress to the other drivers. Muhamed explained that Abu Emir's car in our driveway was a symbol to all other drivers that he, and he alone, controlled access to the house. After this, I tried to be fair in parceling out the newly arriving guests between Abu Emir and the others, but it made little difference: they continued to detest him.

By January our dinners, which at first had been pleasant, adult affairs, had as often as not become drunken blowouts. It had become clear that the situation in Iraq was getting worse every day, and dozens of Westerners from other houses and hotels would show up unannounced to drink away their tension. I would tell people—sometimes yell at them—not to park all their cars in front of the house, because I didn't want to attract attention. But they rarely listened. Things got particularly rowdy after we befriended Jeff and Ray, two Boston natives who had hitchhiked to Baghdad—just to "check the shit out," they said—and had somehow become volunteers for the CPA. Several nights a week they would walk a few miles from the Green Zone to our house and invariably get very drunk, as we all would. One particularly hard-drinking night, I was up quite late talking to a special-forces soldier when I excused myself, walked out of the living room, and vomited all over the marble hallway.

Managing the house had become a full-time job. When I was in my bedroom trying to write or rest, the tenants and staff would knock on the door every few minutes. A guest would complain that the Internet connection was down for the fifth time that day, or Muhamed would tell me that two drivers were fighting and needed me to resolve the dispute. Frequently I would have to rush out and replace whatever had broken: a microwave, a new modem, countless lightbulbs. Some days I could do no reporting at all.

At first, I had been so eager to make sure that everyone liked me—the Iraqis, our guests—that I had agreed to almost anything. But the constant staff mutinies and guest laxities convinced me that just as Iraqis say their country needs a strong leader, our house would need one as well. I began to charge a flat and firm $100 a night and became furious when people asked to pay less. I became deliberately icy to the staff and screamed at them in Arabic when they acted poorly. I would still joke with them often, and they began to call me "*Saddam al-Beyt*"—the Saddam of the House.

In March 2004, my ex-girlfriend Nancy came to town, and she asked me for help in finding a driver. I arranged for her to work with Abu Walid—a sweet man in his fifties who had worked for Abu Emir long enough to buy his own station wagon. Abu Emir was furious to hear that Abu Walid had begun working on his own. He went to Nancy's hotel and told her that he, Abu Emir, would be serving as her driver instead.

When I learned this, I was livid. I had long known that Abu Emir was manipulating journalists and his drivers to make money for himself. But I felt that he recognized my position as head of an important house. He had always treated me with special respect. Now Abu Emir had disrespected me, and I could no longer trust him. I told every driver I saw that I was furious with Abu Emir, and that he was to come see me immediately.

Later that night, Jen and I were in the master bedroom when Abu Emir knocked on the door. He was shaken and sweaty. He had only just gotten back to Baghdad from a trip out of town, he said, and had been told that I was angry. He had taken the long trip from his house, despite the dangers of driving late at night.

I told him that he should not treat me like just another journalist. That I gave him a great deal of work and considered him a good friend. That he had betrayed my trust.

He began to talk very fast, as he often did. He said that of course he respected me tremendously. Of course he wanted me to remain his friend—no, more than a friend; a brother. He did not think of money when he thought of me, he said. He would happily give me all his money and work for free. He would do anything, anything, to prove that our friendship was real.

I reassured Abu Emir that all was fine; that we were friends, yes, even brothers. But he would have to move his car from our driveway. He could not park there anymore.

By the next morning, every driver in Baghdad knew that Abu Emir had been humiliated. To save his pride, I soon found out, Abu Emir had begun spreading a different story. He did not move his car because I had demanded it, he told everyone; he moved it because my house was under surveillance by the insurgency and might be attacked at any moment. He told some people that he had warned me to move out immediately.

Soon this rumor had traveled throughout the entire community of Iraqi staff and, in the process, had become grander and less specific. A driver for a major U.S. newspaper told me that he heard my house would soon be blown up. Was this still Abu Emir's rumor, I wondered, or something real? Either way, I worried that my guests would hear the rumors and start moving out. I had yet to break even on the house, but I had calculated that if I could keep it at full occupancy for another two months, I would make all of my investment back.

Around a week later, on March 17, the Mount Lebanon Hotel was destroyed by a car bomb. First reports had the death toll at twenty-seven (though we later learned that only seven died). Everyone who covered the

event agreed that something had changed that day. The crowds of onlookers
were not just curious; they were angry. And they were angry not just at the
U.S. soldiers but at the U.S. reporters. Before this, Iraqis had always seemed to
differentiate American citizens, whom they generally liked, from the American military they despised. But no longer. A few days later, when I went to an
Iraqi home, a man told me, "I don't like America." Not the customary "I hate
your president, I love your people" but "I don't like America."

The next night I had an experience that was, in a way, even more terrifying. I was staying late at a party at a nearby hotel and took a cab home. The
driver was not a regular driver of journalists, and he and I had never met. As
I was explaining how to get to my house, he said, "Oh, you mean *Beyt Said
Adam*"—"Mr. Adam's house." Later, I told this story to some friends and they
said that, yes: whenever they got in a cab, they would simply say, "Mr. Adam's
house," and the driver would know exactly where to go. I was, I realized, one
of the best-known Americans in Baghdad.

For the following few days, I became severe with the staff. I screamed at
them to actually start guarding our house. They needed to realize that we were
in danger and would likely die. Should even one guest be killed, I reminded
them, the others would leave immediately, and all the money the staff was
making would disappear. Ahmed frequently assured me that we were safe and
had nothing to worry about. I finally screamed at him that we were not safe.
We had everything to worry about, and if he refused to take that seriously, he
should leave. I feared for him and Muhamed as much as I did for myself. Although no Western journalists had yet been kidnapped or killed by the insurgency, some Iraqi staff of foreign press outlets had been attacked, and at least
one had been killed. Muhamed wasn't worried, he told me, because he never
told anyone that he works with Americans. Ahmed joked that Muhamed
should worry but that *he* was safe; the insurgents had targeted only translators, not drivers. The lives of our tenants and staff were in my hands, and I had
no idea how to protect them.

We consulted some friends who were more experienced war correspondents than we. They told us that our house offered no protection from anything. Even if our guards were vigilant, they were too inexperienced, old, and
out of shape. Our house was so well known by now that surely we were on the
list of every insurgent in Iraq. And since we so frequently had large parties
with women and alcohol, we had given mortal offense to the Muslim sensibil-

ity. Indeed, the fact that we had hosted so many CPA guests for dinner meant
that our house had become an extension of the occupation, and thus was, in
one friend's exact words, "a legitimate military target."

Up until just a few days before, I had considered the security excesses of
wealthier newspapers and TV networks to be utterly absurd. Even when
Baghdad had been relatively calm, one TV producer I knew had not been allowed to leave his hotel without the permission of his network's British security company, and then only with an armed escort, who would study the route
and plan various escape paths beforehand. The house of one newspaper I visited had enough armed guards to constitute a small militia; I've heard that
their head security contractor, also British, once proposed they bury land
mines in front of the house to stop suicide drivers. I was convinced that these
contractors did little more than make their customers paranoid enough to
keep paying their exorbitant fees.

But now I could see that these private security companies were the only
hope for saving my home. I ordered Ahmed to drive me to Mansour, to the
network of small streets that had been commandeered by the companies, each
with its own checkpoints and team of armed guards. Perhaps two dozen of
them were operating in Baghdad then, most hailing from the United States,
Britain, or South Africa. As we drove, Ahmed made it clear that he was angry
and insulted that I would trust foreigners more than my own Iraqi staff.

We settled on two, and paid visits to their fortified offices. The first was
ISI, which made its headquarters in a large and pleasant mansion well within
its own, large security zone. There, the security director—a calm and confi-
dent American—listened to us and drew out a sketch of our home. The other
we approached was Erinys, which had recently been founded by people with
connections to Ahmad Chalabi. It had quickly procured contracts to guard
Iraq's oil pipelines and had grown to a staff of more than 14,000 in a matter of
months. The Erinys offices were in several interconnected houses, at the center of which we saw a command center worthy of a James Bond film. Rows of
muscled Afrikaners, formerly of South Africa's special forces, manned high-
tech communications consoles under detailed tactical maps of Iraq. Both
companies offered to send a man by.

The ISI security director visited a day or two later. He showed up at our
house alone, in a regular old car. He was tall, quite thin, and balding, and he

wore a pistol on a belt holster. I think he said he had been a cop in the United States. He moved slowly, with great measure, pacing around the house; he went up to the roof and scrutinized every angle. His conclusions were relatively modest. We might want to hire some more guards, he said. Also, we might erect some barriers—staggered, like a slalom—at the end of our street. These would slow down car bombers. Mortars were not an issue, because Iraqis did not know how to aim them. The only way we would be hit, he said, was if they were aiming for someone else. In his opinion, our most pressing danger was a kidnapping or drive-by shooting.

Shortly after he left, an Afrikaner from Erinys arrived in a hulking SUV. He had with him several armed Iraqi guards, who immediately took up positions along our street. Short and stocky, but with quite a lot of muscle, he cut a very professional figure. He carried a briefcase and made his notes on pre-printed security analysis forms. His recommendations were a bit more drastic and in line with my own, growing terror. We needed to take control of the entire neighborhood, he said, by putting up a series of manned checkpoints at every intersection. We should inspect all cars and forbid entrance to anyone who seemed suspicious. Also, he said, we should put sandbags around the interior of our outer wall; Iraqi cement is so weak that it would do little to stop damage from a car bomb. Finally, he advised that we station a sniper on the roof.

I gathered the Iraqi staff together. I told them I had come up with a plan—a melding of the two consultants' advice, scaled down for our budget. All guards would have walkie-talkies, and one guard would always be stationed at the corner where our road met the main street. No one would be allowed to leave the house until the guards had checked the street first. To further confuse would-be abductors, our drivers would have to vary their routes to and from the house, and the guests would have to vary their daily schedules. I asked Muhamed to hire a few friends to make sandbags and pile them inside the outer walls.

We hired more guards—another uncle of Muhamed's, some relative of Ahmed's—and for a day or two the guards made a show of following my new directions. But soon it was clear that they saw this as yet another of my momentary whims. I stopped reporting almost entirely and spent my days supervising the guards. I bought wireless cameras and installed monitors in the kitchen so we could constantly watch the street. The chatter about me, meanwhile, had not abated. A friend told me that a tribal sheikh I knew was telling people I was a CIA agent.

The next day, Jen and I were sitting in Ahmed's car while he bought sandwiches at a shish kebab stand. A black BMW passed us, then circled the block and passed again. It might have passed a third time. Insurgents were known for driving black BMWs. We screamed at Muhamed, who was in the passenger seat, to drive. He thought we were joking, and it took some doing to convince him. As we sped off we saw a black car behind, but so far behind that we couldn't tell—was it a black BMW? Muhamed weaved through side streets. Eventually, we stopped and looked: there was no car behind us.

That evening, Abu Emir again knocked on our bedroom door. I let him in, and he sat down. He looked at the floor and then looked at me and said, seriously, "It is time for you to leave." He spoke softly. As if he knew that it would be difficult for me to hear but that, as a friend, he had no choice but to tell me. Jen asked him why. He just repeated himself: "It is time for you to leave. It's time. Take a break from this place." He would not tell us anything more.

We could not leave fast enough. Every extra day seemed an invitation to death. I told Muhamed and Ahmed that they could fight over everything I owned and take it all. Four large closets were completely filled with our belongings. We had amassed dozens of books and hundreds of DVDs and some Iraqi art. Jen and I threw a few of our most valuable things into boxes and hired a driver to cart them to Amman. We ourselves would fly. At the Royal Jordanian office in the Green Zone, we bought tickets for the next day's only flight out of Iraq.

On Sunday, March 28, Ahmed drove us to the airport. A checkpoint had the airport highway stopped nearly dead. A quarter mile from the entrance, Jen and I finally got out of the car and walked. At airport security, an American contractor told me that my ticket was void. I would have to leave the airport. I screamed at her, telling her she had no idea how to read a ticket. I pointed out that it was a one-way ticket, so only the return was void. At the airline check-in counter, a Royal Jordanian attendant told us we were not on the manifest and therefore couldn't fly. Again I began to scream. I told him that people were trying to kill me. That if I stepped outside the airport I would die. I needed to be in Amman that night. He told me there was nothing he could do. I grabbed the manifest and read it. Many of the names on it were repeated multiple times. There are plenty of seats, I told him, if he would only look. Finally, he relented. That night we checked into the Grand Hyatt Amman and slept for most of the next few days.

Within two weeks, the rest of the occupants of our house fled to secured hotels. My few friends who remain in Baghdad tell me that these days Westerners there no longer live in private houses, unless those houses are well within secured safe zones. One friend told me that he drove by the old house recently, and it was empty. Nobody lives there now.

February 2005

Contributors

Charles Bowden is a contributing editor of *GQ* and *Mother Jones,* and the author of *A Shadow in the City: Confessions of an Undercover Drug Warrior,* among other books.

Adam Davidson is a business and economics correspondent for National Public Radio.

Barbara Ehrenreich is a contributing editor of *Harper's Magazine.* Her most recent book is *Dancing in the Streets: A History of Collective Joy.*

Steve Featherstone is a freelance writer and photographer in Syracuse, New York.

Kristoffer A. Garin is the author of *Devils on the Deep Blue Sea: The Dreams, Schemes and Showdowns that Built America's Cruise-Ship Empires.*

Gary Greenberg is a psychotherapist and a freelance writer.

Roger D. Hodge is the editor of *Harper's Magazine.*

Jay Kirk teaches in the Creative Writing Program at the University of Pennsylvania, and is currently writing a book about the taxidermist Carl Akeley.

Willem Marx is a freelance writer and television producer in New York.

Morgan Meis is a founding member of Flux Factory, an arts collective in New York, and the author of a novel, *Angelus Novus.*

Jeff Sharlet is a contributing editor of *Harper's Magazine* and *Rolling Stone,* and is the author of *The Family: The Secret Fundamentalism at the Heart of American Power.*

Jake Silverstein is a senior editor of *Texas Monthly* and a contributing editor of *Harper's Magazine.*

Ken Silverstein is the Washington editor of *Harper's Magazine.* His most recent book is *Turkmeniscam: How Washington Lobbyists Fought to Flack for a Stalinist Dictatorship.*

Wells Tower is a journalist and fiction writer in North Carolina. His short-story collection *Everything Ravaged, Everything Burned* will be published in 2009.

William T. Vollmann is the author of many books, including *Europe Central,* which won the National Book Award in 2005.

Bill Wasik is a senior editor of *Harper's Magazine.* His book about new-media culture will be published in 2009.